Commentaries on Eric Voegelin's Late Essays and Meditations

Other Books of Interest from St. Augustine's Press

Barry Cooper, *Consciousness and Politics: From Analysis to Meditation in the Late Work of Eric Voegelin*

Montgomery Erfourth, *A Guide to Eric Voegelin's Political Reality*

Klaus Vondung, *The Pursuit of Unity and Perfection in History*

Jeremy Black, *In Fielding's Wake*

David. N. Whitney, *Maladies of Modernity: Scientism and the Deformation of Political Order*

Michael Davis, *Electras: Aeschylus, Sophocles, and Euripides*

David Ramsay Steele, *The Conquistador with His Pants Down: David Ramsay Steele's Legendary Lost Lectures*

Rémi Brague, *Moderately Modern*

Thomas F. Powers, *American Multiculturalism and the Anti-Discrimination Regime: The Challenge to Liberal Pluralism*

John von Heyking, *Comprehensive Judgment and Absolute Selflessness: Winston Churchill on Politics as Friendship*

Peter Fraser, *Twelve Films about Love and Heaven*

Gene Fendt, *Camus' Plague: Myth for Our World*

Jean-Luc Marion, *Descartes's Grey Ontology: Cartesian Science and Aristotelian Thought in the Regulae*

Frederic Raphael and Joseph Epstein: *Where Were We?: The Conversation Continues*

Roger Scruton, *The Politics of Culture and Other Essays*

Roger Scruton, *The Meaning of Conservatism: Revised 3rd Edition*

Roger Scruton, *On Hunting*

Gabriel Marcel, *The Invisible Threshold: Two Plays by Gabriel Marcel*

Stanley Rosen, *The Language of Love: An Interpretation of Plato's Phaedrus*

Winston Churchill, *Savrola*

Winston Churchill, *The River War*

Commentaries on Eric Voegelin's Late Essays and Meditations

Michael Franz, editor

St. Augustine's Press

South Bend, Indiana

Manufactured in the United States of America.

1 2 3 4 5 6 28 27 26 25 24 23

Library of Congress Control Number: 2023947775

Paperback ISBN: 978-1-58731-236-6
Ebook ISBN: 978-1-58731-237-3

∞ The paper used in this publication meets the minimum requirements of the American National Standard for Information Sciences – Permanence of Paper for Printed Materials, ANSI Z39.48-1984.

St. Augustine's Press
www.staugustine.net

Table of Contents

Introduction:
Michael Franz 1

Chapter 1
Voegelin's "The German University and the Order
of German Society: A Reconsideration of the Nazi Era"
Barry Cooper 10

Chapter 2
Voegelin's "On Debate and Existence"
Steven F. McGuire 27

Chapter 3
Voegelin's "Immortality: Experience and Symbol"
Henrik Syse 49

Chapter 4
Voegelin's "Configurations of History"
Paul Kidder 64

Chapter 5
Voegelin's "Equivalences of Experience and Symbolization in History"
Glenn Hughes 79

Chapter 6
Voegelin's "On Henry James's *Turn of the Screw*"
Charles R. Embry 106

Chapter 7
Voegelin's "The Gospel and Culture"
Thomas Heilke 130

Chapter 8
Voegelin's "On Hegel: A Study in Sorcery"
David Walsh 165

Chapter 9
Voegelin's "On Classical Studies"
Julianne M. Romanello 190

Chapter 10
Voegelin's "Reason: The Classic Experience"
William Petropulos 228

Chapter 11
Voegelin's "Response to Professor Altizer"
Paulette Kidder 244

Chapter 12
Voegelin's "Remembrance of Things Past"
Paul Kidder 260

Chapter 13
Voegelin's "Wisdom and the Magic of the Extreme: A Meditation"
Michael Franz 284

Chapter 14
Voegelin's "Quod Deus Dicitur"
Thomas Heilke with Paul Caringella 334

Introduction

Michael Franz

Eric Voegelin (1901-1985) is widely regarded as one of the greatest political philosophers of the 20th century, yet adequate understanding of his writings is not a standing accomplishment but rather a challenge for current and future generations. Voegelin's thought continued to develop at a rapid pace during the last two decades of his life, and as Ellis Sandoz has written, his work found "not only its final but its most profound expression" during this period. Voegelin's standing as a philosopher was based mostly on his many books and the laudatory review articles published in response to them, but he was "preeminently an essayist," as Sandoz observed. The meditative analyses and essays written in the culminating phase of Voegelin's career not only expand and deepen his work as a whole, but also revise central components of it in ways that compel reconsideration of even his most widely read texts.

Voegelin's books gave rise to a vast secondary literature that continues to grow, yet the exceptionally impactful late essays and meditative works have never received the scholarly commentaries they deserve. These writings were published originally as journal articles or chapters in edited collections, and unlike books, such publications are almost never reviewed in scholarly journals, regardless of their quality or importance. This volume remedies that shortcoming in the secondary literature with 14 critical analyses that elucidate the late essays while also addressing their implications for the entirety of Voegelin's thought. We believe these commentaries will prove quite valuable to students and scholars in political science, philosophy, history, theology, and other disciplines, serving as a companion piece to the singularly important Vol. 12 of Voegelin's *Collected Works, Published Essays 1966-1985.*[1]

1 Eric Voegelin, *Published Essays 1966-1985*, Vol. 12 of *The Collected Works of Eric Voegelin* (Baton Rouge and London: Louisiana State University Press, Ellis Sandoz, ed., 1990). Hereafter cited as *CWEV* Vol. 12.

That volume was edited by Ellis Sandoz, a friend to many contributors to this book, who passed away just as this manuscript was going to the printer. In addition to editing Vol. 12, Sandoz also wrote a concise but profound "Editor's Introduction" summarizing Voegelin's thought during this final phase of his work. Because our collaborative volume is a companion piece to that volume of the *Collected Works*, I shall simply direct readers to Sandoz's "Introduction" without undertaking a second summary of Voegelin's late work here, though I will address several questions prompted by points raised by Sandoz below. He chose not to address the Voegelin essays included in Vol. 12 in any detail, which is precisely our objective in the chapters that follow, so the complementary nature of the two books should be evident.

An account in this Introduction that might be helpful to readers of this book as well as Voegelin's *Published Essays 1966-1985* is one addressing the ongoing challenges posed by his writings as a whole. This will help illuminate why the late essays and meditations are so important, and why critical commentaries on them can prove essential for understanding the entirety of Voegelin's work.

A first challenge of obvious importance is the sheer breadth of Voegelin's oeuvre. The *Collected Works of Eric Voegelin* (hereafter, *CWEV*)—consisting of 34 volumes—have already been published in their entirety. Some books in the collection are rather compact, whereas others run to nearly 1,000 pages. Similarly, some of the writings are admirably accessible, but many require painstaking study even by readers who are accustomed to working with demanding philosophical texts and who have already familiarized themselves with a sizeable portion of Voegelin's writing. Much of the material in the *Collected Works* required translation from the original German, and much of it was not published before appearing in the collection, including some writings of lofty importance that Voegelin simply left in his wake as he pressed ahead to new writings employing developing approaches or new source materials. Completion of the *Collected Works* publication project was an achievement that is invaluable for anyone wishing to access Voegelin's philosophizing, yet accessing the writings is hardly the same as understanding them adequately.

A related challenge is that the scope of Voegelin's work cannot be grasped by simply counting published pages or volumes. He read and worked in nine languages across many different disciplines while addressing historical and philosophical materials ranging from the Neolithic period to the late 20th century. His erudition was astonishing—even to his few true peers—and it is hardly surprising that specialists of all sorts have strained to cope with the sheer scope of his work and the multiplicity of its well-springs.

A third source of difficulty is that Voegelin's books and articles are filled with neologisms, as he experimented constantly with different concepts and terms drawn from his sources or simply invented outright. This peculiarity poses great difficulties for newcomers, and the caliber of the problem can be appreciated when one learns that the editors of Voegelin's *Collected Works* elected to provide a glossary in the final volume—one that runs for 37 pages.

A final factor of great importance is that Voegelin's body of writings is highly variegated internally, with at least two major transformations in his thinking producing "breaks" in his publishing program. Exactly how "major" these breaks should be considered is a matter for dispute between reasonable and well-informed observers,[2] but the fact of the first break is clear, and Voegelin's characterizations of the second one are quite striking.

Between 1939 and 1954, he wrote a massive *History of Political Ideas,* but then abandoned the manuscript (published posthumously in 8 volumes) due to shifts in his thinking and advances in his methodology. Voegelin's new approach informed the first three volumes of his magnum

2 For example, Sandoz wrote in his "Editor's Introduction" that "It is worth stressing that no dislocating break in Voegelin's thought occurred after publication of *The New Science of Politics* in 1952; that work signaled the watershed in the philosopher's thinking....Voegelin was a very steady character, one can say" ("Editor's Introduction," *CWEV* Vol. 12, xi-xxii, xiv). I do not share this view. Of course, I understand that what constitutes a full "dislocation" in a philosopher's work is a matter of interpretation rather than a demonstrable fact, as when an orthopedic radiologist points to an x-ray showing bones disconnected from a joint socket. However, in my assessment, the change in Voegelin's thinking in the wake of his immersion in the philosophy of consciousness and set forth in *Anamnesis*, manifested in *The Ecumenic Age*, and pursued in various ways in the late essays and meditations does indeed stand as a major shift from the foundation underlying *The New Science of Politics*. I will pursue this point more fully below.

opus, *Order and History*, published in 1956 and 1957, with an *Introduction* promising three more volumes to come.

However, Voegelin elected not to publish Volume IV, *The Ecumenic Age*, until 1974, and the first sentence of the book announced that it, "breaks with the program I have developed for *Order and History*" (*CWEV*, Vol. 17, p. 45). Both transformations in Voegelin's work are quite tricky in the sense that, on one hand, much of the content and many of the principles underlying earlier writings remain valid in light of later works. Yet, on the other hand, Voegelin had very good reasons for "abandoning" (his term) his earlier approaches. The most important consequence of the two breaks for readers today is this: it is impossible for a reader to distinguish what remains valid in early works from what has been discarded without mastering all Voegelin's writings, and this is true above all for writings from the last two decades (which, as we've seen, Sandoz characterized as the period when Voegelin's work attained "not only its final but its most profound expression").

The books that Voegelin published during his last twenty years were widely reviewed, but as noted above, this was not the case for book chapters or journal articles. Our lack of a secondary literature on Voegelin's late essays and meditative writings would not stand as a major problem if they were mere side-projects of minor importance by comparison to the books. But that is not the case at all. Indeed, as Sandoz wrote in his "Editor's Introduction" to Vol. 12, Voegelin was, "Preeminently an essayist…".[3] Similarly, Paul Caringella and Thomas Hollweck observe that, "It can be argued whether Voegelin was a book author in the commonly used sense. His method consisted rather in working out problems in the form of reflective and meditative essays; only when the problems could be arranged in meaningful clusters would he organize them into a book."[4]

Sandoz, Caringella, and Hollweck are three of the four members of the Editorial Board to which Voegelin assigned his literary estate, so their authority seems well established. The passages just quoted not only emphasize

3 Ibid., xiii.

4 "Editors' Introduction," Thomas A. Hollweck and Paul Caringella, in What is History? And other Late Unpublished Writings, *CWEV* Vol. 28 (Baton Rouge and London: Louisiana State University Press, 1990), xi–xxxvi, here at xv.

the importance of essays as Voegelin's primary mode of theoretical expression but also counsel against granting privileged status to his last books, which can be thought of as collections of essays regarding discrete problems that were published together only because they "could be arranged in meaningful clusters."

By extension, this suggests that essays that didn't "fit" with other writings were best published as freestanding journal articles or as chapters in edited collections. These writings from the final decades of Voegelin's work are not categorically less important than the studies that were clustered into Voegelin's last books, and indeed, some of them clearly hold greater salience regarding central problems or new directions in Voegelin's evolving work than chapters in the last of the books he saw through to publication.

For example, with regard to Voegelin's mature understanding of Christianity, the late essays, "The Gospel and Culture," and, "Immortality: Experience and Symbol" are both arguably more illuminating than "The Pauline Vision of the Resurrected," Chapter 5 from Voegelin's *The Ecumenic Age*. This is not to disparage the chapter on "The Pauline Vision," which "fits" with the other studies in *The Ecumenic Age* because it focuses on St. Paul and contributes to the "meaningful cluster" of essays in a book addressing a specific historical period. Nevertheless, the fact remains that the broader scope of "The Gospel and Culture," and, "Immortality: Experience and Symbol" make them seem more important for those seeking a general understanding of the status of Christianity within Voegelin's philosophy.

A second example is in order. My commentary for this volume analyzes Voegelin's essay, "Wisdom and the Magic of the Extreme: A Meditation." This extended piece (60 pages in the *Collected Works* edition) is by far the most important diagnostic analysis of ideology and spiritual disorder published by Voegelin after *The New Science of Politics*. Its importance springs principally from how clearly it shows Voegelin breaking from the analysis and conceptual framework employed in *The New Science*, Voegelin's single most famous book (to which *Time* magazine devoted a cover story on March 9, 1953).[5]

In the late "Wisdom and Magic" essay, Voegelin dispenses entirely with the general concept of "Gnosticism" that was central to his diagnosis of

5 "Journalism and Joachim's Children," *Time*, March 9, 1953, 57–61.

modern ideological violence and spiritual disorder in *The New Science*. Moreover, he discards the argument of *The New Science* that later "gnostics" arose by means of literary influence from earlier "gnostic" writers or the historical Gnostics themselves. He replaces this in the "Wisdom and Magic" essay with a much more sophisticated and compelling explanation of instances of spiritual disorder as largely independent outbursts of rebellion against perennial experiences and challenges posed by the human condition.

This "Introduction" is not the place to explain advances such as this one fully, as that challenge is taken up in the pages that follow, including my Chapter 13 on the "Wisdom and Magic" meditation. However, it is simple enough to indicate the importance of the advances pointed to in the preceding paragraphs. For example, writings about "Voegelin's theory of Gnosticism" continue to be published under the sway of *The New Science* as though that book remains "the last word" in Voegelin's analysis of personal and political disorders and ideologies (and their relation to modes of revolt against the political limitations of human existence from earlier eras). Yet the reality I seek to demonstrate in my commentary is that *The New Science* is not only *not* the "last word" from Voegelin on this complex of problems, but also an outmoded approach that is conceptually, methodologically, and theoretically inferior to the analysis in the "Wisdom and Magic" meditation.

This observation highlights another theoretical benefit provided by the commentaries assembled in this new collection, which is that they are mutually reinforcing. Voegelin's late advances in epistemology and the theory of consciousness are vital underpinnings for the breakthroughs to be found in his "Wisdom and Magic" meditation, but these advances are mostly implicit in "Wisdom and Magic," whereas they are powerfully illuminated by Voegelin's, "Equivalences of Experience and Symbolization in History," as Glenn Hughes shows in his commentary. Similarly, the developmental process that led to Voegelin's work in the theory of consciousness is clarified greatly by the autobiographical account in Voegelin's, "Remembrance of Things Past," as Paul Kidder indicates by reference to Husserl and phenomenology in ways that contribute very importantly to his commentary while also bolstering my analysis of "Wisdom and Magic." As a final example, "Reason: The Classic Experience" offers Voegelin's clearest expression of the core of his thought in its most fully developed phase, and William Petropulos's commentary on it can illuminate all the other chapters in this book while also enabling readers who are new to Voegelin's work to advance quickly toward a substantial understanding of one of the 20th century's most penetrating but notoriously challenging political philosophers.

To ward off any suspicions that I'm making extravagant claims for the commentaries in this volume, I'll utilize a term already employed, hastening to emphasize that they are not intended to be "the last word" on the essays they analyze. I have already indicated my reservations about Sandoz's assertion that there is "…no dislocating break in Voegelin's thought…after publication of *The New Science of Politics* in 1952…," but rather than considering that issue resolved in my favor, my intention is to aid readers in exploring the issue for themselves. I believe this relatively modest intention is shared by all my colleagues in their contributions to this collection, even though some chapters include some rather bold assertions forwarded either by argument or implication. To place my own chapter in the crosshairs as a potential target once again, it offers a sustained and multi-faceted case that Sandoz was essentially mistaken when maintaining that "…Voegelin refined but never abandoned the theory of gnosticism's role in philosophy and history that he so powerfully advanced…."[6] My case is forcefully stated and so too is Sandoz's argument, but neither is forceful enough to simply blow down the other. Nor should such matters be determined by which view is stated most emphatically, as I'm confident Sandoz would have agreed, based on my many years of friendship with him. The point is to encourage readers to mine the riches contained in Voegelin's late writings with critical perspectives and hypotheses in their tool kits, and if there are multiple and contending perspectives available to readers, so much the better.

To extend this notion one last time while relying on my friendship with Sandoz when addressing an issue on which we differ, I understand but still depart from his observation that, "Voegelin was a very steady character, one can say." Sandoz was surely correct that one can find "a continuity of intention" across the last three decades of Voegelin's life.[7] However, when

6 Sandoz, "Editor's Introduction," *CWEV* Vol. 12, xi.

7 Ibid., xiv.

considering Voegelin's particularities as a philosopher by comparison to other thinkers, I'm far less inclined to emphasize his "steadiness" than his relentlessness as a theoretical searcher and his remorselessness in being willing to change course when his searches revealed new approaches that were superior to past ones—even when his fame rested on the earlier approaches he "abandoned." Above all else, it is this remarkable characteristic of Eric Voegelin as a philosopher that makes meticulous and critical consideration of his last writings an essential undertaking for anyone who wishes to do justice to him as a reader.

* * *

When offering thanks to those who made this book possible, clearly my fellow contributors come immediately to mind, yet none of our chapters would have seen the light of day without the steadfast support of Benjamin Fingerhut of St. Augustine's Press and his late father, Bruce Fingerhut. This project has taken far longer to complete than I anticipated when I first conceived of it, recruited collaborators for it, and proposed it to Bruce Fingerhut. His reply to my detailed proposal began with the exceedingly kind and relieving sentence, "Of course, we will publish this work." Benjamin has been as resolute and enthusiastic about the project as his father, and all of us are gratefully indebted to both of them.

The book benefitted greatly from the assistance of Paulette Kidder, author of Chapter 11, who generously devoted much of a sabbatical to editorial work on the manuscript that involved much more than simply correcting typographical errors and moving commas around. Producing a reasonably consistent manuscript from chapter drafts submitted by contributors from multiple nations and academic disciplines who write in quite different styles is no small feat. Paulette commented on many matters of substance in her work with me, also fighting through the tedium of checking hundreds of quotations for accuracy. Any errors that remain are entirely my responsibility, but I might well have nothing for which to take responsibility if not for all her graciously contributed help. The total of her efforts is surely equal to what would have been required for her to write another entire chapter.

Thomas Heilke and Paul Kidder both stepped up to take on very sizeable writing assignments—after completing their initial chapters—when that became necessary because other authors encountered difficulties preventing them from completing their work. It may seem odd to liken them to defibrillators, but I'm certain that anyone who has had something they care deeply about jump-started by others will recognize this for the high compliment that it is. Amy Wolfson of Loyola University Maryland helped me with an unusually generous sabbatical that enabled me to tackle the most difficult phase of the project, and David Walsh slated panels at two meetings of the Eric Voegelin Society to permit contributors to work together and build momentum for this enterprise.

Over the years I have been helped by so many people—and learned so much from so many scholars—that I cannot thank all of them here. Hopefully I've managed to express my appreciation along the way, but a few individuals deserve mention in any case. Reading this Introduction could lead one to believe that Ellis Sandoz and I were at odds regarding Voegelin's work when almost nothing could be further from the truth. This will become apparent (even regarding matters such as continuity in Voegelin's thought disputed here) to anyone who reads my "Editor's Introduction" to Voegelin's *The Ecumenic Age*, Vol. III of *Order and History*, which shows we agreed about most issues of prodigious importance (aside from but including our agreement that Hermitage from the Rhône Valley is the world's finest wine for pairing with roasted goose). To his great credit and the benefit of all who contributed to this volume, Sandoz advanced and broadened appreciation of Voegelin's thought in the English-speaking world more than anyone else. Special thanks are also owed to Sally Swift, James L. Wiser, Cathy Bruckbauer, Eugene Webb, Richard Boothby, Paul Caringella, Manfred Henningsen, Carsten Vala, Stephen A. McKnight, Barry Cooper, Klaus Vondung, and the late John A. Gueguen.

–1–

Voegelin's "The German University and the Order of German Society: A Reconsideration of the Nazi Era"

Barry Cooper

On two occasions, in the summer semester, 1964 and then two years later, Eric Voegelin delivered formal lectures to a German audience regarding Hitler. This paper deals chiefly with the second of these, "The German University and the Order of German Society: A Reconsideration of the Nazi Era."[1] The contents of Voegelin's lecture, however, presuppose a familiarity with the argument of the earlier series of talks, now published as *Hitler and the Germans.*[2] Accordingly, reference must be made to the 1964 series as well.

"The central German experiential problem of our time," Voegelin said in 1964, was "Hitler's rise to power. How was it possible? What consequences does it have today?"[3] The theoretical approach was indicated by a term used in *The New Science of Politics.* Voegelin would apply Plato's "anthropological principle" to the German problems in order to analyze what sort of persons the Germans were to have chosen an individual such as Hitler to represent them.[4] Voegelin initially formulated the problem in

1 Eric Voegelin, "The German University and the Order of German Society: A Reconsideration of the Nazi Era," (1966) in *Published Essays 1966-1985*, ed. Ellis Sandoz, *CWEV* Vol. 12, 1990. Hereafter cited as Voegelin, "The German University."

2 Eric Voegelin, *Hitler and the Germans* (1964), ed. Detlev Clemens and Brendan Purcell, *CWEV* Vol. 31, 1999. Hereafter cited as Voegelin, *Hitler.*

3 Voegelin, *Hitler*, 52.

4 Eric Voegelin, The New Science of Politics (1952) in Modernity without Re-

terms of "stupidity," or to use the more sonorous German term, *Dummheit*, with which, Schiller reminds us, "even the gods struggle in vain."[5]

Voegelin began his analysis by considering the response to a discussion by Albert Wucher in the *Süddeutsche Zeitung* of the attempt by Percy E. Schramm, a celebrated professor of medieval history, to present an account of Hitler in the pages of *Der Spiegel*.[6] Wucher summarized Schramm's effort as one of systematically excluding relevant facts and interpretations that would allow readers to understand Hitler's personality. The journalist wondered why Professor Schramm proceeded in this fashion, which provoked a number of responses as letters to the editor of the *Süddeutsche*. Wucher was right, wrote Hilde Seitz, and Schramm was naïve: the real problem was that Hitler was elected and that he was popular. Voegelin agreed. That *was* the real problem. Wilfred Wiegand wrote that he did not consider millions of Germans to be stupid (*Dummköpfen*) but that is just what Wucher implied. Voegelin remarked: "If Hitler was stupid or a criminal, and the people voted for him in droves, then they too must have been stupid and criminal. But that is not possible, so Hitler was not stupid and no criminal."[7] Some

straint: The Political Religions; The New Science of Politics; and Science, Politics and Gnosticism, ed. Manfred Henningsen, *CWEV* Vol. 5, 2000, 136–38.

5 Friedrich Schiller, *The Maid of Orleans*, Act III, Scene vi.

6 The series of articles bore the title "Anatomy of a Dictator" and was later reprinted as the introduction to the German edition of Henry Picker's edition of *Hitler's Tabletalk*. An English version is available in Schramm's *Hitler: The Man and the Military Leader*, ed. Donald S. Detwiler (Chicago: Quadrangle Books, 1964). During the war, Schramm was the official historian of the Operational Staff of the Wehrmacht High Command. He testified on behalf of General Alfred Jodl at the Nuremberg Trials of major war criminals (Jodl was hanged in 1946 and posthumously acquitted in 1953). The aforementioned book on Hitler as a military leader was published in German in 1962. In it Schramm argued that, unlike the patriotic and professional soldiers in the High Command, such as Jodl, Hitler was a fanatic, which was hardly a revolutionary insight. Schramm also indicated that he had experienced a good deal of personal contact with Hitler during the war. These basic facts of Schramm's biography were well known to Voegelin. For Voegelin's appraisal of Jodl, for example, see Voegelin, *Hitler*, 115, 119, and 235.

7 Voegelin, *Hitler*, 56.

other explanation therefore had to be found for Hitler's success. Wiegand refused to consider seriously the possibility that Wucher was correct and that a very great number of Germans were in fact extraordinarily stupid and/or criminal. Voegelin called this resistance to considering such a question, let alone answering it properly, the "Buttermelcher Syndrome" named after a Munich street, Buttermelcherstrasse, where another letter-writer, Gerhard Hess, who made the same point, lived.

A few weeks later Wucher reported on a panel discussion, which included Schramm, on the theme "Hitler as Alibi," sponsored by the Congress for Cultural Freedom. Here the learned participants discussed several alternative explanations for Hitler's success. Perhaps Hitler was just an "accident," or perhaps he had a "demonic personality." Perhaps a lot of other things, but one way or another, it seemed, the Germans had to be absolved from responsibility. One of the panelists, Wlademar Besson, a political scientist from the University of Erlangen, raised the possibility that Hitler was not so much a demonic personality as an "idiot." To this possibility Schramm replied that it would be a "frightening" realization for 70 million Germans to learn they followed an idiot. Such resistance by Schramm, Voegelin observed, was a further manifestation of the Buttermelcher Syndrome. Moreover, there was "something" to Besson's characterization, "[f]or this problem of the idiot ultimately is related to the problem of the *stultus*, of the fool in the technical sense."[8] The problem that caught Voegelin's attention was how Hitler could be a *stultus* and a successful, even a brilliant, politician.

The Buttermelcher Syndrome shared by letter-writers Gerhard Hess and Wilfred Wiegand, and the distinguished historian, Percy Schramm, was said to be a particular example of the alleged "unmastered past" of the Germans. Voegelin then argued that this familiar term was a cliché designed precisely to avoid serious analysis. If one asks, "for whom is the past unmastered?" the problem is clarified in the sense that the past, specifically the Nazi past, "was mastered by very many persons while it was still the present, since by no means did all those who experienced the period of National Socialism cheerfully cooperate with it."[9] Some persons, Voegelin

8 Ibid., 60.
9 Ibid., 70.

included, "knew precisely what was going on" so that the past "was a completely masterable present for the people who lived at that time."[10] Percy Schramm, employed by the Wehrmacht High Command and before that the incumbent of an important chair at the University of Göttingen and later chancellor of the order *Pour le Mérite*, was apparently unable to know what was going on. For Voegelin, however, there was a continuity between the cheerful cooperation of Schramm in the past with the National Socialist regime and his present position as an esteemed historian. Accordingly, "we live in an unmastered *present*," the symptoms of which are the Buttermelcher Syndrome and other kinds of *Dummheit*.[11]

In order to understand clichés such as the unmastered past or the concept of the Buttermelcher syndrome or the realities of an unmastered present and the political success of a *stultus*, these things must be examined in light of philosophical anthropology, or an "idea of man," the most adequate accounts of which, Voegelin said, were discovered in Hellenic and Israelite societies. The reality of an unmastered present, for example, has to be considered in the light of its transcendent dimension, which Voegelin called the "presence under God," and referred to the myths of judgment in the *Gorgias* and the *Republic* as adequate expressions of what he had in mind.[12] Voegelin then summarized the first three volumes of *Order and History*: "In the Hellenic society, man was experienced by the philosophers of the classical period as a being who is constituted by the *nous*, by reason. In the Israelite society man is experienced as the being to whom God speaks his

10 Ibid.

11 Voegelin then provided analysis of ancillary clichés such as "collective guilt" and "contemporary history" the purpose of which was to create alibis in order to ensure there was no effort to master the present. Ibid., 75ff. To simplify somewhat, in this context mastering the present would mean "that all among the German elites were involved in the criminality and stupidity of the National Socialist regime and are burdened with this involvement up to today; for those people are indeed still alive and do not want to admit that what happened was criminal and mad because then they too would have to admit that they themselves are criminals and madmen." Ibid., 81.

12 See also Jürgen Gebhardt, "On the Critical Understanding of Politics: Voegelin on Austria, Hitler and the Germans," *Review of Politics*, Vol. 65 (2003), 270-71.

word, that is, as a pneumatic [spiritual] being who is open to God's word." Methodologically, then, reason and spirit were the two modes in which human being was constituted. "That seems to be the definitive discovery."[13] Whether symbolized as reason or as spirit, human being experienced itself as a being that participated in the divine, whether zetetically or by an encounter with the Word. Such experiences, Voegelin said, constitute the basis of human dignity.

It followed that the loss of human dignity arose from the denial of human participation in the divine. And because such participation was essential to the constitution of human being, "dedivinizing is always followed by dehumanizing," much as the speculative Gnostic murder of God has been followed by the activist Gnostic murder of human beings, as Voegelin argued on many occasions. Once a person had closed himself off from the noetically or pneumatically symbolized experience of the divine, and refused to participate, "there occurs a loss of reality, insofar as this divine being, this ground of being, is indeed reality too."[14] The typical manifestation of the loss of reality has been, historically, to substitute a diminished or shrunken human reality for the Divine Ground of Being.[15]

A number of consequences followed. First, because of a loss of reality, a human being becomes unable properly to orient his or her action in the world. Accordingly, he acts stupidly. In the language of Psalm 14, "the fool (*nabal* = *stultus*) hath said in his heart, There is no God." In the language of Plato, the stupid person was *amathes* (*Rep.*, 350c; 409d; 467c). Because the fool acted on the basis of his defective image of reality, he caused disorder. Second, once having lost the experience of certain sectors of reality, such a person also has lost the language to characterize and evoke reality. "That means that parallel to the loss of reality and to stupidity there is always the phenomenon of illiteracy."[16] There followed Voegelin's witty demonstration of the illiteracy of Schramm that relied on the literacy of their contemporary, Karl Kraus.

13 Voegelin, *Hitler*, 86.

14 Ibid., 87.

15 Voegelin discussed this problem extensively in his 1969 essay on "The Eclipse of Reality," in *What is History? And Other Late Unpublished Writings*, ed. Thomas A. Hollweck and Paul Caringella, *CWEV* Vol. 28, 1990, 111ff.

16 Voegelin, *Hitler*, 90.

Voegelin warned his audience that terms such as stupidity and illiteracy (along with ignorance, rabble, and several others) were not terms of abuse but of concrete description. He then turned to Musil's 1937 essay, "On Stupidity," which began with a commonsensical understanding of stupidity as an incapacity to perform a task that would, by normal expectations and conventions, be resolvable in a particular social and historical context. Thus, "[w]hat in one society and one historical situation has to be considered as stupid, in another situation may perhaps be described as clever."[17] Musil further distinguished between the simple, straightforward, or honorable stupidity of one who "has what one calls a 'dim wit'" and a higher or intelligent stupidity. Here the problem was "not so much lack of intelligence as failure of intelligence" for the reason that it "presumes to accomplishments to which is has no right."[18] With intelligent stupidity therefore one found a kind of "spiritual arrogance" or a "disturbance in the equilibrium of the spirit" of which the intelligently stupid one was never unaware.[19] That is, intelligent stupidity was a pneumopathological condition.[20] This was why Voegelin several times insisted: there is no right to be stupid.

We need not consider the details of Voegelin's delightful demolition of Schramm nor his account of how the German academics, church-personnel, and lawyers descended into a spiritual abyss by embracing the pneumopathological second reality embodied in Hitler.[21] Rather, let us consider Voegelin's remarks in Part II, "Toward a Restoration of Order." Here his focus was on the more "agreeable" sectors of society, those "very interesting

17 Ibid., 98.

18 Musil, "On Stupidity," in Burton Pike and David S. Luft, ed. and tr. *Precision and the Soul: Essays and Addresses* (Chicago: University of Chicago Press, 1990), 282–83.

19 Voegelin, *Hitler*, 101.

20 Voegelin also discussed the "secondary virtues" such as "propriety" (*Anstand*), which was the subject matter of a book by Carl Amery, and "criminal stupidity," whereby a stupid person finds himself in a position to issue criminal orders. See Amery, *Capitulation: The Lesson of German Catholicism*, tr. Edward Quinn (New York: Herder and Herder, 1967) and Voegelin, *Hitler*, 102–6.

21 I can say, however, that having taught *Hitler and the Germans* several times to undergraduates, they were both amazed and indignant at the results, which showed they retained considerable common sense.

Germans" who did not cheerfully participate in crimes. The analytical tool for discussing this problem was the distinction between first and second reality, which he also borrowed from Musil. In commonsense language, Voegelin distinguished between the "frame of human existence," as he put it in a letter to Robert Heilman, and ideology.[22] Second realities may have been differentiated and identified by contemporary German-speaking thinkers, but the reality so indicated was both older and more general.[23]

Voegelin began his analysis not with Musil and Doderer but with an earlier example of an author responding to social disorder and disruption by evoking a fictional or at least a non-existent second reality. His first examples were from the early sixteenth to the seventeenth century, often referred to as the "waning of the middle ages," to use the title of Huizinga's great book. Voegelin identified Thomas More's *Utopia* as an instance that contrasted the existing evil social conditions of England with the "true moral order" sketched in More's book.[24] Rabelais' *Gargantua and Pantagruel* belongs to this same period of transition and loss of reality, but Voegelin's main discussion centered on Cervantes' *Don Quixote*.

The overarching problem Cervantes addressed in his satire was the decay or obsolescence of chivalry under the new conditions created by the nation-state. He structured his "novel" in terms of Don Quixote's three expeditions. In the first expedition the Don was a knight errant who in the spirit of chivalry sought, outside legal conventions, to assist the humble and humble the proud. He was alone and he retained more than a sense of justice: he wanted to rid the world of injustice. Moreover, he was indulged

22 *Robert B. Heilman and Eric Voegelin: A Friendship in Letters,* ed. Charles R. Embry (Columbia: University of Missouri Press, 2004), 168–9. Voegelin began reading Musil's *Man without Qualities* and Heimito von Doderer's *The Demons,* both of which used the term "second" or "other" reality, while convalescing from a bad case of the flu in early 1957.

23 Voegelin, *Hitler*, 239.

24 Ibid., 240; see also Voegelin, *History of Political Ideas, Volume IV: Renaissance and Reformation*, ed. David L. Morse and William M. Thompson, *CWEV* Vol. 22, 1998, 109–30 and Voegelin, *Science, Politics, and Gnosticism* (1968) in *Modernity without Restraint: The Political Religions; The New Science of Politics; and Science, Politics and Gnosticism*, ed. Manfred Henningsen, *CWEV* Vol. 5, 20005: 305–7.

in his buffoonery as was illustrated by the tolerance of the innkeeper and his patrons. No one started a quarrel with the Don by challenging his fantasies of the basis of commonsense reality.[25] The Don's world, as Voegelin's friend Alfred Schütz said, contained "all the elements of Greek theology at the time of Homer: the envy of the gods, their intervention in favor of their protégés, their struggle for power, the subjection under inevitable fate."[26]

The second expedition, where the Don was joined by his squire, Sancho Panza, was more complicated because Sancho lived in first reality, commonsensical reality, or "paramount reality" as Schütz, following William James, called it. Accordingly, Sancho warned the Don that he was about to tilt at windmills, not giants, as the Don maintained. In order to communicate at all—because windmills were not in fact giants—Cervantes introduced a third party, the "enchanters" or "transformers" who could change windmills into giants for Don Quixote. And, of course, if they later turned out only to be windmills, this meant the magicians had been at work turning giants back into windmills. For Voegelin, the interesting aspect of this new situation explored by Cervantes was that commonsensical Sancho was willing to make concessions at least to the extent that, perhaps, magicians were involved after all. As the novel continued, Sancho lived increasingly in the second reality of the Don and thereby became increasingly imbecilic or stupid (*blöd*) as well as a "fellow-traveler and collaborator" in the Don's enterprise.

By the time of the third expedition, detailed in the second volume of the novel, Cervantes' audience had become familiar with his characters. Readers had come to expect a certain type of behavior from Sancho and the Don. This changed circumstance allowed Cervantes to introduce another ring of subscribers to the second reality. Sancho was persuaded to

25 Cervantes, *Don Quixote*, tr. Edith Grossman (New York: Collins, 2003), ch. 3. 29ff.

26 Schütz, "Don Quixote and the Problem of Reality," in his *Collected Papers*, vol. II, *Studies in Social Theory*, ed. Arvid Brodersen (The Hague: Nijhoff, 1964), 141. Voegelin did not refer to Schütz's paper but it is clear that he used it in his own interpretation. See also the commentary of Miguel Unamuno, *Our Lord, Don Quixote: The Life of Don Quixote and Sancho with Related Essays*, tr. Anthony Kerrigan, Princeton Bollingen Series, LXXXV: 3 (Princeton: Princeton University Press, 1967).

abandon his common sense because of the exalted social status of Don Quixote. On the third expedition, the two of them encountered a duke and a duchess who, as fictional readers of Cervantes' fiction, knew all about these two characters. The two presumptively real readers of Cervantes' real novel then entered into the second reality of the Don and made fun of him. By Voegelin's interpretation, Cervantes was indicating that the bored, unemployed, and useless Spanish nobility made of his story a *divertissement* to entertain themselves. Voegelin used the Pascalian term to indicate how a real social class, the Spanish aristocracy, was prepared to enter the second reality because it was "fun" and was an alternative to the experiences of boredom and ennui that otherwise useless aristocrats would have to endure. Under later circumstances, Voegelin said, revolutionaries would likewise engage in intellectual stupidity because it constituted a *divertissement* from their otherwise boring lives.[27]

The implications were clear enough. First, second realities, whether that of the Don or of a contemporary ideologue (think of the importance of "environmentalism" today) can become socially dominant. Then, as did the Don in his conversation with the canon (Part I, Ch. 50), one might introduce the argument from authority. After all, if what the Don said was repeated in books published under the king's license, who would dare challenge that? Here Voegelin again referred to the Buttermelcher Syndrome. And then, in Part I, chapter 25 (p. 201), the Don declared: "I imagine that everything I say is true, no more and no less." Thus does the second reality displace the first, which is followed necessarily by friction between the imaginary and the paramount.

The great challenge in the treatment of second reality from Cervantes to Musil and Doderer is the change from satire to farce (*Burleske*). The difference, for Voegelin, was that satire is still connected to reality whereas there is no connection to reality with the "murderous imbecility" (*Mordsblödsinn*) of latter corruption exemplified by National Socialism. By Voegelin's interpretation, Karl Kraus certainly saw the problem of describing

27 Voegelin, *Hitler*, 242–3. Hannah Arendt discussed this later phenomenon in terms of the "temporary alliance between the mob and the elite" in *The Origins of Totalitarianism,* new edition (New York: Harcourt Brace and World, 1996), 326–40. Hereafter, Arendt, *The Origins of Totalitarianism*.

properly what social and spiritual corruption entailed, whereas "Doderer and Musil go deeper, insofar as they represent the problem as farce." Politically speaking there existed a formal community who sought to live within the second reality. "But such a society perpetuates the highest betrayal of humanity. And in this kind of society anyone who is not alienated from the first reality can only commit high treason."[28] Accordingly, the literary form best suited to "imbecility," *Blödsinn*, which Voegelin later discussed in terms of a "loss of reality," was farce, not satire.[29]

The significance of these German-language novelists (and occasionally Voegelin added Broch, Gütersloh, Mann, and Canetti) is that they were perfectly capable of mastering the present by taking its measure either at the time or, in the case of Doderer, after the war. In this respect they were much more in touch with reality symbolized as reason and spirit than were the official guardians of Western culture in the churches and the legal and academic professions. Notwithstanding his achievements as a medievalist, Percy Schramm proved himself to be an ignoramus as well as the embodiment of Musil's higher stupidity when it came to making sense of Hitler.[30]

Two years after delivering the Hitler lectures, Voegelin was asked by the rector of Ludwig-Maximilian University, Ludwig Kotter, to participate in a lecture series on the German university and the Third Reich.[31] He was reluctant to revisit "this most disagreeable of topics" but agreed to do so on the grounds that it was an opportunity to attempt to dispell a certain "uneasiness" or "restlessness" among young persons when it came to discussing events associated with the Third Reich. The source of the uneasiness of the younger generation was obvious: they were entangled, by virtue of their membership in the historical community of Germans, in consequences of events for which they were in no way responsible and often unaware. Voegelin's criticism therefore was again directed not at the uneasiness of students and other young

28 Voegelin, *Hitler*, 256.

29 Voegelin, *Anamnesis: On the Theory of History and Politics* (German edition 1966), ed. David Walsh, *CWEV* Vol. 6, 2002, 360–1.

30 Voegelin also discussed Schramm's bad literary German, his incorrect translations from Latin, his evasiveness and "spiritual illiteracy," and above all his apparent ignorance of such commonsensical analyses of Hitler as Alan Bullock's classic biography. See Voegelin, *Hitler*, 61, 125, 147.

31 Voegelin, "The German University," 1–35.

persons (one is reminded perhaps of the appeal of Glaukon and Adeimantos to Socrates) but at the older generation (exemplified by Percy Schramm) and their "alibi" that younger persons must not judge because they did not experience National Socialism directly or at first hand (*miterleben*). He began by stating the obvious: just because one witnessed an event or suffered through it was no guarantee that one had the understanding, intellectual capability, character, and spiritual insight to grasp what had been going on.

More specifically still (and with reference to Nietzsche's *Uses and Abuses of History for Life* and Thomas Mann's *Doctor Faustus*), Voegelin said that the history of a "spiritually forsaken" era can be written only from a perspective of spiritual integrity that permitted a spiritual judgment. In this context, by "spirit" Voegelin referred to the "openness of man to the divine ground of his existence: by estrangement from the spirit, the closure and the revolt against the ground."[32] Openness can be symbolized by the already familiar terms, *imago Dei* or Nous, and closure or estrangement by *stultus*, *idiotes*, and so on. The political significance of the typology lies in the fact that the person estranged from the reality of the spirit can become socially and politically dominant and impress his or her estrangement on public life. Through the life of the spirit, common to all persons, the existence of individuals can become existence in community. Similarly estrangement from the life of the spirit can result in the destruction of community and its replacement with a collection of *idiotes*.

Voegelin then illustrated his argument by examining three socially dominant figures. The first was Heidegger, who had great "linguistic-philosophic ambitions" but so little spiritual or noetic sensitivity "that he was taken in by the author of *Mein Kampf*.[33] The second was Martin Niemöller, who, although a sometime opponent of Hitler, found it a "very painful and vexing state of affairs" that God "revealed himself in the Jew, Jesus of Nazareth."[34] The third was Schramm.

In contrast to these socially dominant individuals Voegelin referred to German literary achievements over the previous half-century, which he characterized as "equal in spiritual rank to that of any other Western literature,

32 Ibid., 7.
33 Ibid., 8.
34 Ibid., 12.

though it is distinguished from these other literatures by virtue of the fact that it is not socially dominant." Here Voegelin again mentioned Musil, Doderer, Gütersloh, Canetti, and Mann but added that they had "no recognizable influence."[35] And that too helped constitute the problem of the spiritually forsaken character of the German public scene, the evasiveness of the older generation, and the restlessness of the younger one.

Voegelin then reformulated the problem as a question. There was a substantive or spiritually literate public as represented by German literature, but "Why can't the substantial public, which clearly exists, be more effective in molding society in setting the pattern by which Germans act towards their fellow human beings?" Where did the transmission between private and public culture break down?[36] Voegelin answered by pointing to the "Iron Curtain" that separated the two publics, namely the existence of the university and of university culture, not simply during the period of the Third Reich, but starting in the eighteenth century with Wilhelm von Humboldt and his tenure, early in the nineteenth century, as Prussian education minister. Voegelin's pointing to Humboldt must have surprised his audience because Humboldt was widely admired for the educational reforms that created the still-existing dual high-school track of technical schools and "Gymnasien" and for establishing the University of Berlin (later Fredrick William University and later still Humboldt University).

Voegelin's criticism, however, was directed at the substance of Humboldt's achievement, not the extent of his success. Specifically, Humboldt's notions of *Bildung*, development or even cultivation, and his historicist assumption that there existed substantive progress from antiquity to the present, were the foci of Voegelin's criticism. He then summarized Humboldt's 1792 essay, *Ideas to Determine the Limits of the Effectiveness of the State* and Humboldt's conclusion: "As long as the subject obeys the laws, and keeps himself and his dependents well provided for in an occupation that is not harmful to others, the state is not concerned about the exact manner of his existence."[37] Voegelin did not discuss Humboldt's liberalism but considered

35 Ibid., 16–18.

36 Ibid., 18.

37 Ibid., 20. For a wider perspective on German liberalism see John H. Hallowell, *The Decline of Liberalism as an Ideology with Particular Reference to German*

rather the language he used to express his opinions. Humboldt's discussion of individuality, of development, of the perfection of one's inner being, and so on, was expressed from the start in a language of estrangement from, not openness to, reality. Such language, Voegelin argued, was evidence of Humboldt's existential closure against the Divine Ground, which Voegelin also characterized psychologically as being narcissistic.

Voegelin had often argued that existential tension toward the Divine Ground did not disappear when human beings refused to recognize it as the reality of experience. "Its problems continue to exist and in order to express them the language of philosophy must be replaced by a new idiom of estrangement."[38] For example, instead of the philosophical *zetesis* one finds "moral perfection," instead of the Ground (*arche*) the "idea of perfection," in place of faith, "religious ideas," in place of God, an "ideal," and so on. In sum, in place of the genuine education expressed in Plato's art of "turning around," the *periagoge* of *Republic* 518d, one gets romantic and narcissistic *Bildung*.[39] In place of the substantive subject one finds the obedient subject providing for his dependents and who leaves to the monarch and the state the conduct of public affairs as the state leaves to the subject the liberty of living his life in an obedient search for the idea of perfection.

For such an individual, whom Voegelin characterized as "the man of antispirit, antiphilosophy, and antipublic," Humboldt drew up his 1810 memorandum on "the inner and outer organization of the institutions of scientific learning." During the early nineteenth century Humboldt's reforms of Prussian education was an act of genuine liberation from the heavy hand of the state and of religious orthodoxy. By the last third of the nineteenth century, the narcissistic and romantic Humboldtian language of estrangement from reality had succeeded both in obscuring reality and destroying the sciences of human being. Accordingly, philosophy degenerated into epistemology, philology into linguistics, and historiography into

Politico-Legal Thought (Berkeley and Los Angeles: University of California Press, 1943). See also Voegelin, *Selected Book Reviews,* ed. Jodi Cockerill and Barry Cooper, *CWEV* Vol. 13, 2001, 124–5.

38 Voegelin, The German University, 21.

39 Ibid., 22. Cf. *Order and History, Vol. III: Plato and Aristotle* (1966), ed. Dante Germino, *CWEV* Vol. 16, 169ff.

historicism. This was "the phase of decline against which Nietzsche revolted," Voegelin said, and was followed by a "second estrangement idiom" that attempted to recover the sciences of human being.[40] Here the great example was Max Weber.[41] The problem, however, was that, according to Weber's science, there was no questioning possible of whether "values" actually referred to reality. So long as the national German state retained a degree of stability, the consequences were not politically catastrophic. From the end of the First World War, however, "the insight has grown that the Western ideological movements, as well as the non-Western political orders, require a specific analysis which cannot be dispensed with merely by declaring the various experiences of order to be 'value positions' and then not bothering further about their structure."[42]

After a century of education understood as *Bildung*, and notwithstanding the spiritual sensitivity of a person such as Weber, the consequences could not easily be managed, let alone reversed. The education transmitted through German universities, which was expressed in the language of estrangement and closure against the reality of the spirit, had the result of producing an "educated" elite incapable of having any public effect. They had become private persons, *idiotes*, incapable of understanding what happened around them, even if they experienced it "firsthand." A generation later, which is to say, the generation of uneasy and restless students, universities were still staffed by individuals who remained incapable of understanding what had happened and who remained committed to transmitting narcissistic existence as if it were an education.

That is, to the extent that Humboldtian education has remained effective it continued to seal off socially relevant numbers of persons from the life of the spirit. As a consequence, since the nineteenth century public authorities have been able to maintain public estrangement from reality under the category of national conservatism, whereas the life of the spirit has been confined to the opposition of intellectuals who have no serious political

40 Voegelin, "The German University," 25.

41 For details of Voegelin's complex relationship to Weber, see Peter J. Opitz, "Max Weber und Eric Voegelin," in *Politisches Denken: Jahrbuch 1992*, ed. Volker Gerhardt, *et.al.* (Stuttgart: Mezler, 1992), 29–52.

42 Voegelin, "The German University," 25.

alternatives to suggest. The opposition of national conservatives to left-wing intellectuals, however, does not constitute a genuine politics. This "nonpolitical politics," carefully nurtured by the Humboldtian university, constituted the context for the understanding of National Socialism and its successful rise to power. This did not mean that National Socialism was a nationalist movement for the simple reason that no political nation existed in Germany. Rather, as Hannah Arendt argued in great detail, there were "masses" whom Hitler organized.[43] Many of them, of course, happened to have "national-conservative mentalities" and then embraced with more than cheerful cooperation, with genuine enthusiasm, the new but "humanly so grotesque authority."[44]

The great works of literature expressed this confrontation and suffering of estrangement even as "they work through the problem meditatively in order to penetrate to the freedom of the spirit. But they are not yet created out of freedom."[45] On the contrary, resistance to estrangement had simply emphasized the ambivalence of literature along with its ineffectiveness.

Summing up, Voegelin said that the problem of pneumopathology lay at the heart of the German university. It started with Humboldt's harmonization of the non-political subject with romantic and narcissistic individuality. A Humboldtian subject was not concerned with public affairs and so the university need not transmit knowledge of how to discuss public affairs rationally. Such a non-political narcissist was considered a virtuous person. This was possible only because of the initial non-recognition of reality and closure to the reality of the spirit. Henceforth "ideas" could provide psychological comfort to the spiritually weak. Rejection of the existential tension toward the Divine Ground entailed a destruction of the ordering center of a human being who then could no longer make a rational analysis of, or a rational appeal against, the phenomena of disorder. By denying the realities of the spirit because human beings must live within at least the appearance of reality, "there appears in place of the neglected reality the ersatz reality of the ideologies up to and including National Socialism."[46]

43 See Arendt, *The Origins of Totalitarianism*, 347–58, 380ff.
44 Voegelin, "The German University," 27.
45 Ibid., 28.
46 Ibid., 32.

And with the destruction of the reality of the spirit came the destruction of a public language relating to the reality of the tension towards the Ground and its replacement with various ideological symbolizations of estrangement.

As a result, when using one or another idiom of estrangement, there was nothing that could "really" be intended or wanted. It all took place within an imaginary second reality. This did not, however, make the language of estrangement or of second realty a "harmless illusion" because second realties could nevertheless form the basis for human action.[47] That is, even though the delusions of a paranoid person correspond to no reality, yet the paranoid can still act on them and the consequences of that action reverberate in commonsense reality; so too the second reality of a Humboldt has had its effect in the real world. The reason is obvious enough: universities, as other social institutions, are not structures established once and for all time "but a process in time whose course of development under certain circumstances can deviate considerably from the intention of its founders."[48]

What, Voegelin asked, in conclusion, could be done about the current state of the destruction of the commonality of the spirit characteristic of the German (or of any other) university? Because the heart of the malady resided in the pneumopathological consciousness inspiring university life, "the first step to recovery would involve making people aware of the evil and opening the situation up to public discussion." That was the intent of Voegelin's lecture. As for the individual, Voegelin pointed to God's words to Ezekiel (Ezek., 33: 7–9):

> So you, son of man, I have made a watchman for the house of Israel; whenever you hear a word from my mouth, you shall give them warning from me.

47 Ibid., 33.

48 Ibid., 30. For similar observations concerning the condition of universities in North America, see: Benjamin Ginsberg, *The Fall of the Faculty: The Rise of the All-Administrative University and Why It Matters* (New York: Oxford University Press, 2011); Mark Edmundson, *Why Teach? In Defense of a Real Education* (New York: Bloomsbury, 2013); William Deresiewicz, *Excellent Sheep: The Miseducation of the American Elite and the Way to a Meaningful Life* (New York: Free Press, 2014).

> If I say to the wicked, O wicked man, you shall surely die; and you do not speak to warn the wicked to turn from his way, that wicked man shall die in his iniquity, but his blood I will require at your hand.
>
> But if you warn the wicked to turn from his way, and he does not turn from his way, he shall die in his iniquity, but you will have saved your soul.[49]

49 Ibid., 35. Voegelin quoted this same passage in *Hitler and the Germans* in order to teach German clerics and theologians the "elements of Christianity" that they seemed to have forgotten. See Voegelin, *Hitler,* 200.

–2–

Voegelin's "On Debate and Existence"

Steven F. McGuire

In "On Debate and Existence," Eric Voegelin addresses the "breakdown of rational discourse" caused by the prevalence of ideological thinking in the modern age.[1] The breakdown to which he refers is not an impasse owing to disagreement between two positions within the parameters of what might plausibly be true, but, rather, a conflict between "two modes of existence, of existence in truth and existence in untruth."[2] This sort of conflict occurs when one or more of the parties to a debate refuses to recognize and live within reality as it is commonly experienced, opting instead to operate in a "Second Reality," a term Voegelin uses to "denote the imaginative constructs of ideological thinkers who want to eclipse the reality of existential consciousness."[3] Motivated by existential anxiety and a desire for greater certainty concerning their place and purpose in reality, ideologues refuse to accept the human condition as it is and construct alternate realities that are more to their liking. Ideology is thus rooted in revolt rather than error—it is a state of spiritual alienation or, as Voegelin calls it, pneumopathology.[4]

1 Eric Voegelin, "On Debate and Existence" (1967), in *Published Essays 1966-1985*, ed. Ellis Sandoz, *CWEV* Vol. 12, 1990, 37. Hereafter cited as Voegelin, "On Debate."

2 Ibid., 36.

3 Eric Voegelin, *Order and History, Volume V: In Search of Order* (1987), ed. Ellis Sandoz, *CWEV* Vol. 18, 2000, 61. As he notes, Voegelin borrows the term from Robert Musil and Heimito von Doderer. Hereafter cited as Voegelin, *In Search of Order*.

4 See, for example: Eric Voegelin, *Science, Politics, and Gnosticism,* (1952) in *Modernity without Restraint: The Political Religions; The New Science of Politics; and Science, Politics and Gnosticism*, ed. Manfred Henningsen, *CWEV* Vol. 5, 2000, 306. Hereafter cited as Voegelin, *SPG*.

As a result, rational discussion with ideologues is unlikely to succeed, since their mode of existence is willfully untrue insofar as they ignore or deform one or more constitutive elements of reality. Nevertheless, Voegelin's purpose in the essay is to show how we might try to address and overcome the problem of ideology.

He turns to Aquinas and Aristotle in order to make his argument, a procedure which seems random until we consider the audience for whom he wrote the essay. His explanation in the text is that the ideologies we must confront—the second realities—are peculiarly modern phenomena, and that we can best grasp the nature of the problem we face by going back "to a period in which the universe of rational discourse was still intact because the first reality of existence was yet unquestioned."[5] For this reason, he begins with Aquinas' *Summa Contra Gentiles* because "rational debate with the opponent was still possible—or we should say more cautiously—seemed still possible to Aquinas."[6] If this explanation is insufficient to fully explain the choice of Aquinas (at the very least, there might be other thinkers to whom he could have turned), Voegelin indicates another motive for his choice in a letter he wrote to his friend, Robert Heilman. Therein he reports delivering at Notre Dame a "...lecture on debate and existence showing why Aristotelian and Thomist metaphysics are antiquated and useless as far as the doctrinal formulations are concerned, and that one has to recover their truth by going back to the underlying philosophy of existence."[7] In addition to explaining why he decided to focus on Aquinas and Aristotle, these circumstances illuminate the opening line of the essay, in which Voegelin remarks that "we all have had occasion at one time or another to engage in debate with ideologists—whether communists or *intellectuals of a persuasion closer to home*."[8] Voegelin's audience is not the communists and other usual suspects, but the Aristotelian-Thomists with whom he was working at the time as a visiting professor at the University

5 Voegelin, "On Debate," 37.
6 Ibid., 38.
7 Eric Voegelin, "Letter to Robert Heilman," dated January 14, 1961, in *Selected Correspondence, 1950-1984*, ed. Thomas Hollweck, *CWEV* Vol. 30, 2007, 429. Hereafter cited as Letter to Heilman, 1/14/61.
8 Voegelin, "On Debate," 36 (emphasis added).

of Notre Dame.[9] His purpose in the essay is to show these fellow travelers that they cannot simply rely on the language of Aristotle and Aquinas to combat the ideologies that threaten moral and political order in the modern world. Instead, they must recover for themselves and others the fundamental experiences that animate that language; otherwise, they are in no position to argue with others about the truth of existence, and they risk becoming ideologues themselves.

The present essay places Voegelin's argument in "On Debate and Existence" in the context of his mature philosophies of consciousness and history and indicates two ways in which it might need to be modified in order to become consistent with his later thought. The first and most significant point is that Voegelin's later reflections on the "paradox of consciousness" suggest that we cannot draw a strict dichotomy between those who live in truth and those who do not. Voegelin's observation that the very structure of consciousness entices us to reify luminous experiences of transcendent order raises the question of whether any human being could be insightful or vigilant enough to escape fully the lull of ideology. Second, and relatedly, Voegelin's later philosophy of history suggests a need to refine his claims that the problem he is addressing is a strictly modern one. On the one hand, it is true that the modern ideological mass movements as distinct phenomena that arise in modernity, and surely specific movements such as national socialism and the varieties of Marxism, can only be dated back to their founders. On the other hand, he notes in other works that ancient thinkers seemed well aware of the possibility of rejecting reality. Indeed, in his analyses of ideology, he often refers to ancient thinkers, including Aeschylus, Plato, Cicero, Augustine, and others, thus suggesting that existence in untruth is a perennial human possibility. Most importantly, in light of Voegelin's account of the paradox of consciousness and his insight reported in the *Ecumenic Age* that history is non-linear, it seems unlikely that, for

9 It should also be noted that Voegelin published the essay in the *Intercollegiate Review*, which means that most of his readers would have been "conservatives" of one type or another. Voegelin also says in the letter to Heilman that, while in South Bend, "...I got to know a bit more about 'conservatives,' with the resulting insight that if anything is more of a drip than a liberal it's a conservative." "Letter to Heilman," 1/14/61, 429.

Aristotle and Aquinas, "the truth of existence, of the first reality as we called it, in their time was not yet questioned; hence there was no need to distinguish it from an untrue existence; and consequently no concepts were developed for a problem that had not yet become topical."[10] Far from undermining Voegelin's argument in the essay, these updates reinforce Voegelin's arguments that we need to attend to the ways in which even non-ideologues might exhibit elements of ideological thought patterns and that we must constantly seek to recover and attend to the experiential sources of our symbolizations of order.

Recovering the Truth of Existence

Voegelin's reflections on the necessary conditions for rational debate begin with an analysis of Aquinas' *Summa Contra Gentiles*, a text in which Aquinas recognizes the need to find a common framework for discourse with one's interlocutors. This is illustrated in the introduction, in which he explains that one can use the New Testament to argue with Christians, the Old Testament to argue with Jews, and reason to argue with gentiles (and, in particular, Muslims). Aquinas thus recognizes, as Voegelin writes, that "every debate concerning the truth of specific propositions presupposes a background of unquestioned *topoi* held in common by the partners to the debate."[11] With regard to Islamic scholars, Aquinas assumes that rational debate will be possible with them because they share a common exposure to Aristotle's texts and the account of noetic reason contained therein. As Voegelin writes, this is "a quite justified assumption in view of the fact that the Mohammedan thinkers were the very transmitters of Aristotle to the Westerners."[12] Of course, even ideologues share a common framework for debate with those who share their ideology. Jewish, Christian, and Greek thought are further distinguished by the fact that they are ordered toward the truth of existence. The work of the philosopher—to articulate truth

10 Voegelin, "On Debate," 39.

11 Ibid., 50. This procedure places the nature of our present difficulties in relief by taking us back to "to a period in which the universe of rational discourse was still intact because the first reality of existence was yet unquestioned."

12 Ibid.

and defend it against error—includes finding or developing such common frameworks, so that genuine debate can take place within them.

The situation today requires a prior step, however. As Voegelin observes, we cannot assume, as Aquinas did, that our interlocutors operate within a shared tradition of reason and are interested in the fundamental questions of existence.[13] Modern ideologues reject the experiential foundations of Aristotle's and Aquinas's arguments, which means that it is not sufficient in our time to recapitulate the thought of Aristotle and Aquinas: "The speculations of classic and scholastic metaphysics are edifices of reason erected on the experiential basis of existence in truth; they are useless in a meeting with edifices of reason erected on a different experiential basis."[14] This, in turn, means that we cannot assume the possibility of rational debate "because rational argument presupposes the community of true existence; we are forced one step further down to cope with the opponent (even the word *debate* is difficult to apply) on the level of existential truth."[15] Communists and Aristotelian-Thomists lack a shared framework for debate and a common commitment to the pursuit of truth. For this reason, Voegelin argues that something more fundamental is required, namely, the recovery of the "truth of existence."[16]

The "truth of existence" is a neologism, which Voegelin defines "as the awareness of the fundamental structure of existence together with the willingness to accept it as the *condicio humana*." In contrast, he also speaks of untrue existence, which is "a revolt against the *condicio humana* and the attempt to overlay its reality by the construction of a Second Reality."[17] Voegelin's invention of these terms is consistent with his proposed method. He notes that "by using this language I have terminologically modernized the problem that lies at the core of St. Thomas' endeavor"[18] and argues that "[t]he modernization is legitimate…because it does not modify the problem but only its symbolic expression." He adds that it is also "necessary, because

13 Ibid., 51.
14 Ibid.
15 Ibid.
16 Ibid., 39.
17 Ibid., 49.
18 Ibid., 39.

without it we cannot understand that the scholastic and classic problem is indeed identical with our own."[19] It is evident from these claims that Voegelin is neither rejecting nor historicizing Aristotle's and Aquinas's insights into the order of reality; rather, he is indicating that we must recover those insights for ourselves and develop our own language for talking about them.

In order to understand why Voegelin thinks this updated language is necessary, it will be helpful to present his own philosophy in more detail before proceeding with the argument. His analysis is grounded in the observation that human existence takes place within the "metaxy," by which he means that we exist in the midst of tensions between poles of existence symbolized as transcendence and immanence, good and evil, immortality and mortality, and so forth.[20] He further observes that our existence within the metaxy is participatory: we are actors within reality rather than observers of it from afar. This means that we cannot obtain a God's-eye view on reality—we do not have access to complete knowledge of the whole of reality. It also means that we cannot pretend to be disinterested in the structure of reality and our place within it. We are participants in reality whether we like it or not; we sense that there are better and worse ways to live, and it is up to us (individually and collectively) to find our way toward the good life.[21] To not take up this task is to choose to fail in it. Thus, he says we live in the truth of existence: truth is not just a question of knowledge, but a question of the stance we take toward reality: do we seek the true, the good, and the beautiful, or do we turn away from them?

Within this context, Voegelin develops his philosophy of consciousness, which is not yet in its fully mature phase by the time he writes "On Debate and Existence." The important distinction for present purposes is the one he draws between symbols and experiences. Voegelin argues that we are conscious of various experiences of the nature of reality, and we attempt to

19 Ibid.

20 He borrows the term "metaxy" from Plato's *Symposium*, but develops it as his own technical term beyond Plato's usage.

21 Voegelin, *In Search of Order*, 49. See also Eric Voegelin, *Order and History, Volume I: Israel and Revelation* (1956), ed. Maurice P. Hogan, *CWEV* Vol. 14, 2001.

recognize and articulate those experiences through symbols that can then be communicated to others and become socially effective means of building community around shared experiences of the order of reality. In this dynamic process of experience and symbolization, experience takes priority because it is the source of the symbols. Recovering the truth of existence means recovering the fundamental experiences that are the sources of the symbols we use to articulate it. This is why Voegelin thinks we can and ought to recognize the insights of Aristotle and Aquinas while also dispensing with some of their language and arguments. He maintains that their experiences of order are in principle universally recognizable, even if their symbolizations have become opaque.

Recognizing the universal significance of fundamental experiences and their symbolization, Voegelin is attentive to the historical character of human existence without becoming a historicist in the sense of a modern relativist.[22] The human search for moral and spiritual order is oriented toward transcendent truth but it takes place in historical time. Failing to take this into account can have devastating consequences (as seen, for instance, when foreign political or spiritual systems are inorganically imposed on other peoples). Moreover, as Voegelin notes, if we use outmoded symbols, this can have the unintended effect of furthering ideological consciousness: "the sensed, if not clearly known, invalidity of the symbol at a later point in history will be extended by the critics of the symbol to the truth nevertheless contained in it. An obsolete symbol may have the effect of destroying the order of existence it was created to protect."[23] It must be stressed again, however, that this does not mean abandoning the essential insights of the great thinkers of the past, since it is the "motivating experiences" rather than their symbolizations that serve as the foundation of metaphysics.

Thus, when Voegelin turns to Aquinas's metaphysics his key point is that we can and should look beyond the formulations in order to recover the

22 As Leo Strauss explains in *Natural Right and History* (Chicago: University of Chicago Press, 1974), "historicism asserts that all human thoughts or beliefs are historical, and hence deservedly destined to perish." This historical relativism contrasts with classical natural right, which claims at least the possibility of universal knowledge. Voegelin acknowledges that various symbolizations are historical, but maintains that they emerge from universal experiences.

23 Voegelin, "On Debate," 44.

underlying experiential motivations for them. In some cases, we should even reject the formulations because they are outmoded. For example, the idea of the prime mover is affected by the fact that "we do no longer live, as did Aristotle and even Aquinas, at the center of a cosmos"; their understanding "has been superseded by the universe of modern physics and astronomy."[24] But even in such instances we should look for the motivating experience underlying the symbolic representation. In this case, Voegelin finds "the argument that a universe which contains intelligent beings cannot originate with a *prima causa* that is less than intelligent"[25] and notes that this "argument itself draws specifically on an experience of human existence."[26] He then turns to Aristotle, on whom Aquinas relied, to find the experiential source of this idea.

Voegelin's analysis of Aristotle, which he develops in more detail elsewhere,[27] serves as the true basis for his argument. He observes evidence of a variety of underlying experiences in Aristotle's texts that lead to his metaphysical constructions. These include: "the experience of finiteness and creatureliness in our existence...of being born and bound to die, of dissatisfaction with a state experienced as imperfect, of apprehension of a perfection that is not of this world but is the privilege of the gods, of possible fulfillment in a state beyond this world."[28] He also notes that Plato, who he thought "had a sharper sensitiveness for the problems of existence than either Aristotle or Thomas,"[29] characterizes philosophy in a variety of ways that reference the fundamental experiences that motivate the philosopher. Well-known examples include: "the practice of dying," "the eros of the transcendent Agathon," and "the love of the Wisdom that in its fullness is only God's."[30] According to Voegelin, these formulations show "philosophy

24 Ibid., 40.
25 Ibid., 40–41.
26 Ibid., 41.
27 See Eric Voegelin, *Order and History, Vol. III: Plato and Aristotle* (1966), ed. Dante Germino, *CWEV* Vol. 16, 2000; *Anamnesis: On the Theory of History and Politics* (German edition 1966), ed. David Walsh, *CWEV* Vol. 6, 2002 (hereafter cited as Voegelin, *Anamnesis*); "Reason: The Classic Experience," (1974) in *Published Essays 1966-1985*, ed. Ellis Sandoz, *CWEV* Vol. 12, 1990.
28 Voegelin, "On Debate," 41.
29 Ibid., 42.
30 Ibid. .

emerging from the immediate experiences as an attempt to illuminate existence."[31]

Voegelin proceeds to unfold the "exegesis of existence that is implied, though not explicitly given, in classic and scholastic metaphysics."[32] The central discovery of the Greeks, as Voegelin explains in "Reason: The Classic Experience," is the discovery of reason understood as *nous* (to which "intellect" in Aquinas corresponds). Noetic reason symbolizes both the structure of existence and the human capacity to recognize that structure. Existence is intelligible to us because our minds participate in its rational structure. Moreover, noetic reason is not static, but "reaches out beyond itself in various directions in search of knowledge"—an experience captured by the opening line of Aristotle's *Metaphysics*, which states that "All men by nature desire to know."[33]

Voegelin divides his account of Aristotle's quest for knowledge into two categories: "(1) things of the external world and (2) human actions."[34] With regard to the first category, he notes that Aristotle searches for the origin of things with regard to both their existence and their essence, in both cases arriving at the idea of a first cause. He then suggests that the experience at the source of Aristotle's speculations is similar to the one expressed by Leibniz with the following questions: "(1) Why is there something, why not nothing? and (2) Why is something as it is, and not different?" In his view, these questions are "the core of true experience which motivates metaphysical constructions of the Aristotelian and Thomist type."[35] These are representative questions, that is, they are ones with which every human being is familiar, or at least capable of being familiar if they attend to them. In keeping with his prioritization of experience to symbolization, Voegelin maintains that the questions are more important than the answers, "since obviously no answer to these questions will be capable of verification or falsification," whereas the "questions arise authentically when reason is applied to the experiential confrontation of man with existent things in this

31 Ibid.

32 Ibid.

33 Aristotle, *The Basic Works of Aristotle*, ed. Richard McKeon (New York: The Modern Library, 2001), 689 (980a22). Voegelin, "On Debate," 42–43.

34 Ibid., 43.

35 Ibid.

world."[36] Even if the questions cannot be answered, preserving them as legitimate human experiences of the order of the things is essential to living in the truth of existence. An ideologue, by contrast, "disregards this fundamental structure of existence and pretends that the questions are illegitimate or illusionary."[37] One of Voegelin's favorite examples of this phenomenon is Karl Marx's insistence that socialist man will not need to ask about God.[38]

In the case of the second category of inquiry, human action, Voegelin looks under the edifice of Aristotle's account to find underneath it the experience that "human action is rational, but that rationality hinges on the condition of an ultimate end."[39] The claim here is that each of us recognizes, when we think about it, that our actions depend on believing that there is some ultimate reason for those actions. Without such an end, "there would be pragmatic rationality…but there would be no substantive rationality."[40] In other words, our actions could have extrinsic but not intrinsic purpose, in which case they would seem meaningless in the final analysis. We might even find ourselves paralyzed into inaction, if there is no ultimate reason for what we do with our lives. Voegelin finds this experience in another quote from the *Metaphysics*:

> The *final cause* is an end, and that sort of end which is not for the sake of something else, but for whose sake everything else is; so that if there is to be a last term of this sort, the process will not be infinite; but if there is no such term, there will be no final cause, but those who maintain the infinite series eliminate the Good without knowing it (yet no one would try to do anything if he were not going to come to a limit); nor would there be reason in the world; the reasonable man, at least, always acts for a purpose, and this is a limit; for the end is a limit.[41]

36 Ibid.
37 Ibid.
38 Voegelin, *SPG*, 261–65.
39 Voegelin, "On Debate," 45.
40 Ibid.
41 Aristotle, *The Basic Works of Aristotle*, ed. Richard McKeon (New York: The Modern Library, 2001), 714 (994b9 ff.). Cf. Eric Voegelin, "What is Nature?" in Voegelin, *Anamnesis*, 170.

As Voegelin observes, without the limits of a final end, then a rational account of reality and human action within it cannot be sustained. Either the world is intelligible and meaningful, or it is not.

This fundamental experience, derived from reflection on reason applied to human action, is the basis for Aristotle's metaphysical thought as a whole, including his analysis of the source of the existence and essence of things. As Voegelin writes, "The limit seems to be something inherent in reason; and this qualification appears in the context of the analysis of action, betraying that here we have reached the experiential origin from which derives the argument concerning a limit also in the demonstrations concerning the knowledge of things."[42] Moreover, Voegelin notes that the objection to an infinite regress is not an abstract theoretical one; it is not that it leads to contradictions. Rather, the argument against an infinite regress is grounded in "an experience that reason is indeed embedded in the order of being and it is the property of reason to have a limit." In other words, it is based on the experience of the purposefulness of existence through which "intellect discovers itself as part of human existence."[43] Voegelin thus demonstrates the priority of existence in Aristotle's thought. As he writes:

> The analysis has tried to show that the problems of transcendence, the questions of origin and end, and the postulate of the limit, are inherent to the noetic structure of existence; they are not doctrines or propositions of this or that metaphysical speculation, but precede all metaphysics; and these problems of existence cannot be abolished by discarding this or that speculation as unsatisfactory or obsolete.[44]

Having demonstrated the questions or experiences that sit at the foundation of Aristotle's metaphysics, Voegelin halts his analysis. His purpose has been to show his Aristotelian-Thomistic colleagues what they must do if they hope to engage with ideologues productively. They must recapture for themselves the fundamental experiences of existence and then point those

42 Voegelin, "On Debate," 45.
43 Ibid.
44 Ibid., 49.

out to others and insist that any account of human existence must attend to them. Further reflection will indicate just how difficult this is, however.

The Paradox of Consciousness

Although every human being has experiences of order, it is difficult to recognize and remain attentive to them. According to Voegelin, even the best thinkers in human history have struggled in this regard. For example, we saw above that he held Plato to be more sensitive to experiences of order than Aristotle. He argues this point in more detail in *Plato and Aristotle*, the third volume of *Order and History*, wherein he notes several examples of Aristotle missing the transcendent significance of Plato's works and applying immanent categories to his analysis of the human being.

The essential difficulty, according to Voegelin, is that human consciousness is paradoxical. We have a permanent tendency to objectify experiences of order, which are by their nature non-objective. In "Immortality: Experience and Symbol," an essay written around the same time as "On Debate and Existence," Voegelin explains how the human mind is permanently susceptible to deformed experiences and understandings of reality. Rather than remain perpetually attentive to the participatory character of experiences and symbolizations of order, we have a tendency to rest with the symbols and eventually to dogmatize them and forget their experiential origins. This is problematic because the symbols only point to (rather than contain) the experiences of truth they symbolize. If the symbols fail to lead us to re-experience the truth they symbolize, then they become dead dogmas. As Voegelin writes, "The symbols in the sense of a spoken or written word, it is true, are left as traces in the world of sense perception, but their meaning can be understood only if they evoke, and through evocation reconstitute, the engendering reality in the listener or reader."[45] He notes that it is perfectly understandable that symbolizations of order "will assume the form of doctrine or dogma, of a truth at second remove."[46] Given the variations

45 Eric Voegelin, "Immortality: Experience and Symbol," (1967) in *Published Essays 1966-1985*, ed. Ellis Sandoz, *CWEV* Vol. 12, 1990, 5--53. Hereafter cited as Voegelin, "Immortality."

46 Ibid, 53.

in human spiritual attunement, the need to order societies according to truths experienced, and even the need to get on with the business of living, symbols are dogmatized as socially-effective shorthand that can order and animate individuals and communities. This is all a necessary process given the metaxic and participatory nature of the human condition. The problem is that doctrines and dogmas can become separated from their engendering experiences by too wide a gap, and, as a result, they "are liable to condition corresponding types of experience, such as fideistic acceptance or even more deficient modes of understanding."[47] Believers will dogmatically cling to their doctrines without recognizing them as inadequate representations of the profounder experiential truth from which they originally derive. Finally, the experiential nature of the experiences is completely forgotten and the symbols are treated as propositional claims that can be debated as such. Thus:

> When doctrinal truth becomes socially dominant, even the knowledge of the processes by which doctrine derives from the original account, and the original account from the engendering experience, may get lost. The symbols may altogether cease to be translucent for reality. They will, then, be misunderstood as propositions referring to things in the manner of propositions concerning objects of sense perception; and since the case does not fit the model, they will provoke the reaction of skepticism...[48]

Once the engendering experience that gave rise to a particular symbol is forgotten (or when there is a failure to recover it), doctrines give rise to ridiculous debates between believers and non-believers over the propositional truth of symbols meant to refer to non-propositional reality. For example, Christians and atheists will argue about whether the soul is immortal or God "exists," when immortality and God refer to experiences of participation in a reality that transcends the category of mundane existence.

As Voegelin develops his mature philosophy of consciousness, he continues to develop his insight into the "paradox of consciousness" and the

47 Ibid.
48 Ibid., 54.

perennial difficulty of recognizing the distinction between experience and symbolization and living in the truth of existence by attending to fundamental experiences. He introduces a distinction between two structures of consciousness, which he refers to as "intentionality" and "luminosity." Intentionality refers to our experience of consciousness as "a something located in human beings in their bodily existence. In relation to this concretely embodied consciousness, reality assumes the position of an object intended."[49] At the same time, consciousness is itself part of the reality treated as an object within the intentional structure of consciousness. From this perspective, "reality is not an object of consciousness but the something in which consciousness occurs as an event of participation between partners in the community of being."[50] As Voegelin further explains, in this second structure, i.e., luminosity, "reality moves from the position of an intended object to that of a subject, while the consciousness of the human subject intending objects moves to the position of predicative event in the subject 'reality' as it becomes luminous for its truth."[51] He notes that consciousness thus has a "between-status," for which he borrows the word metaxy from Plato, as mentioned above. As he explains with reference to the language of luminosity, "if the spatial metaphor be still permitted, the luminosity of consciousness is located somewhere 'between' human consciousness in bodily existence and reality intended in its mode of thingness."[52]

With these two structures of consciousness in mind, Voegelin then refers to "the paradoxical structure of consciousness and its relation to reality."[53] Human beings find themselves constantly caught between these two structures of consciousness and must struggle to articulate their experiences of order with symbols from within this perspective. The problem is that we are always tempted to objectify luminous experiences by reducing them to intentional objects. Thus, Voegelin notes "the inherent temptation that is every questioner's burden, the temptation to deform the Beyond and its formative Parousia, as they are experienced and symbolized in the respective quest, by transforming

49 Voegelin, *In Search of Order*, 29.
50 Ibid.
51 Ibid., 29–30.
52 Ibid., 30.
53 Ibid., 29.

the Beyond into a thing and its Parousia into the imposition of a definite form on reality."[54] Insisting that "the paradox [be] taken seriously as the something that constitutes the complex as a whole," Voegelin observes that the paradox also includes language and truth: "There is no autonomous, nonparadoxic language, ready to be used by man as a system of signs when he wants to refer to the paradoxic structures of reality and consciousness. Words and their meanings are just as much a part of the reality to which they refer as the being things are partners in the comprehending reality."[55] This leads to a situation in which seemingly contradictory statements and theories can both contain truth. The source of the problem is that we have no choice but to speak of non-propositional reality in propositional terms. As Voegelin writes:

> The paradox of the true contradictions has its roots in the paradox of a language that speaks in the mode of thing-reality of things that are not things in the sense of external objects; and the paradox of language is part of the paradox of an It-reality becoming luminous for its truth through a consciousness that is located physically in the body of man while it is existentially located in the comprehending metaxy.[56]

Thus, even when we are aware of the distinction between symbols and concepts, we must recognize that "the symbols expressing the poles of tensional experiences do not only radiate their luminosity, but also carry the intentionalist mode of reference and can, therefore, induce the misconception of the poles as 'being things,' a misconception that causes their later deformation into 'metaphysical' entities."[57] Thus, in Voegelin's account, both our experience of reality and our account of it through language are inherently paradoxical, as we are constantly tempted into the error of treating nonobjective reality in objective terms.

Moreover, we cannot escape the paradox of consciousness because it is constitutive of our existence. We can, however, maintain our awareness of

54 Ibid., 47.
55 Ibid., 31.
56 Ibid., 42.
57 Ibid., 110.

it. Thus, the articulation of experiential truth must always be accompanied by efforts to remember the inadequate nature of the language used. Here Voegelin introduces a third dimension of consciousness, "reflective distance." This refers to our awareness of our own consciousness and its paradoxical structure. Human beings participate in "a consciousness that is structured not only by the paradox of intentionality and luminosity, but also by an awareness of the paradox, by a dimension to be characterized as a reflectively distancing remembrance."[58] Therefore, part of the task of the philosopher is to maintain the balance of consciousness by gaining reflective distance on its paradoxical structure. Nevertheless, the paradoxical nature of consciousness makes it likely that human beings will constantly attempt to objectify non-objective reality.

The paradoxical nature of consciousness explains why it is so difficult to attend to the fundamental experiences and live within the truth of existence. While it is true that "the analysis of existence can do no more than make explicit what everyman knows without it,"[59] as Voegelin writes, it is also the case that we are constantly in danger of losing our grasp on that knowledge. Moreover, consciousness can be corrupted, as it often is, by patterns of dogmatism, skepticism, and ideology that pervade a culture. Aquinas, for example, recognizes this possibility when he considers "whether the law of nature can be abolished from the heart of man" and answers that secondary precepts "can be blotted out from the human heart, either by evil persuasions…or by vicious customs and corrupt habits."[60] Thus, we need to undertake philosophical analysis of experiences of order so that we might recognize, communicate, and defend them. On the one hand, Voegelin's analysis suggests the difficulty of analyzing existence. On the other hand, he observes that the "motivating" or "immediate experiences" that ground "existence in truth" "come as an anticlimax because of their apparent simplicity."[61] Recovering our awareness of these fundamental

58 Ibid., 55.

59 Voegelin, "On Debate," 48.

60 Thomas Aquinas, *Summa Theologica*, translated by Fathers of the English Dominican Province (New York: Benzinger Bros., 1947) https://www.ccel.org/a/aquinas/summa/FS/FS094.html#FSQ94A6THEP1 (accessed 8/23/2023), I-II, Q. 94, A. 6.

61 Voegelin, "On Debate," 41.

experiences can be akin to the experience of realizing that one has been searching for something that he was already holding in his own hand.

These reflections on the paradoxical nature of consciousness raise important questions about the nature of ideology and its history. Just as movements of order and disorder are present at any moment in history, so it would seem are there movements of openness and closure in every human soul. This calls into question the viability of maintaining a strict dichotomy between ideologues and non-ideologues. Instead, it seems more accurate to suggest that all human beings live on a continuum between openness and closure toward truth, never reaching either end. This is not to say that all thought is ideological or that we are incapable of distinguishing between ideological and non-ideological existence, but only to say that the metaxic character of human existence prevents us from living fully within the light of non-ideological truth on a permanent basis. Through our participation in transcendent truth, we are capable of recognizing ideological thought as ideological (although we do not always do so), but since we do not possess transcendent truth, we are also perennially subject to the possibility of sliding into ideological thought. This would mean that even the most spiritually sensitive among us have moments when they fail to maintain attunement to the luminosity of truth. The paradigmatic lives of men such as Socrates and Jesus of Nazareth present standards that few, if any of us, can achieve, even if we recognize that we ought to.

At the same time, it is clear that Voegelin would want to maintain a clear distinction between ideologues and non-ideologues. For example, while Voegelin is concerned about the philosophical approach of his Aristotelian-Thomistic colleagues, it is certain that he did not think they belonged in the same category as communists or national socialists. Their dogmatic approach to philosophy is perhaps a step on the path to ideology—it is one component of ideological thinking—but they are not yet ideologues in the complete sense. One crucial difference has to do with the phenomenon of revolt.[62] Adhering to the luminous nature of truth is thus an ongoing struggle, and, therefore, everyone suffers "the temptation to fall from uncertain truth into certain untruth."[63] We all want to find a solid

62 I am grateful to David Walsh and John von Heyking for discussions on this point, although they bear no responsibility for the positions I take in this essay.

63 Voegelin, *SPG*, 310.

foundation on which to build our lives, but the participatory and metaxic character of existence means that a perfectly solid and objective foundation is unavailable to us. The ideologue distinguishes himself by revolting against the tensional truth of existence and seeking a more secure account—a second reality that he or she knows is at odds with the common or first reality in which we all exist. Thus, there is a fundamental difference between the person who strives to live in the luminosity of truth and the ideologue who revolts against it.

Even taking this distinction into account, however, it seems difficult to maintain a strict dichotomy according to which some people are ideologues and others are not. Is there not a hint of ideological revolt in the scholar who adheres dogmatically to a doctrinal account of reality as if it were true and complete? Does not this indicate an unwillingness to embrace fully the participatory or experiential nature of truth and existence? And while Voegelin's thought allows for a distinction between failures of intellect and failures of will, are these not more likely to be concretely related in the life of particular persons? In other words, is it not the case that intellectual errors result in part from revolt and vice versa? In sum, while we can draw a distinction between truth and ideology in principle, it would seem that every concrete human being lives somewhere in between the two. It is thus imperative to avoid the assumption, which is suggested by the opening line of the essay (in perhaps a kind of playful misdirection), that the reader is not subject to the problem of ideological thinking—a point which Voegelin seems to have in mind.

These reflections also lead to questions regarding the linear account of history suggested in "On Debate and Existence." It fits with the narrative recounted in "Immortality," wherein Voegelin notes that we can observe patterns of experience and symbolization followed by dogmatization and skepticism in history. He claims that in Western civilization "the sequence has run its course twice: once in antiquity, and once in medieval and modern times."[64] The ancient sequence runs from the noetic discovery of Greek philosophy to the dogmatism of the philosophical schools and then the skeptical reaction to those schools that succeeded them. The second sequence begins with the insights of philosophy and

64 Voegelin, "Immortality," 54.

Christian revelation and then runs through the resulting cycle dogmatism, skepticism, and, ultimately, violent ideological revolt. Voegelin wrote "On Debate and Existence" and "Immortality" before he developed his mature philosophy of history as it appears in various late essays and the final two volumes of *Order and History* (*The Ecumenic Age* and *In Search of Order*). Voegelin came to argue that meaning could not be traced in straight temporal lines, but, rather, that a philosopher of history must be prepared to "move backward and forward and sideways, in order to follow empirically the patterns of meaning as they revealed themselves in the self-interpretation of persons and societies in history."[65] When he wrote "On Debate and Existence," however, he still adhered to a linear account of history. At the same time, the "Immortality" essay shows that Voegelin already recognized that a simple historical pattern does not hold, as he notes that the "second cycle is more complicated than the first one."[66] We see there is a fourth component, the introduction of ideological dogmas, that he does not mention in his brief account of the first sequence (although he uses madness in "the Aeschylean sense of *nosos*" to describe the ideological revolt of modernity, thereby indicating his awareness of the ancient provenance of the phenomenon). Certainly, in the later writings just mentioned Voegelin moves away from the position, exemplified in "On Debate and Existence," that the problem of second realities is an exclusively modern one. The modern mass ideological movements are distinct phenomena in some respects, but, as movements of individual and collective disorder, they are variations on a theme that is already evident in pre-modern history. Just as every human being lives between truth and ideology, so do all moments in history exhibit simultaneous movements of disorder and movements toward order. The shift in Voegelin's view derives from the empirical evidence of the historical materials he studied.[67] Whether as cause or effect, it is also tied to developments in his philosophy of consciousness, specifically his insight into the "paradox of consciousness" and

65 Eric Voegelin, *Order and History, Vol. IV: The Ecumenic Age* (1974), ed. Michael Franz, *CWEV* Vol. 17, 2000, 106. Hereafter cited as Voegelin, *Ecumenic Age*.

66 Voegelin, "Immortality," 55.

67 Voegelin, *Ecumenic Age*, 46, 106–7.

the perpetual nature of the human struggle to live in the truth of existence.[68]

In sum, while the struggle for order is a perennial challenge that must be faced by every individual and society, the components or stages of deformation are distinguishable. First, there is the process of doctrinalization and dogmatization; second, there is the skeptical response; and, third, there is the phenomenon of revolt. These stages occur due to two kinds of obstacles to existence in truth. The first is the perennial obscurity of the truth of existence. Although we all live in the midst of it, we struggle to grasp and maintain our hold on it. The second is the ongoing possibility of the temptation to revolt. We can succumb to the existential desire for a more secure footing and willfully distort reality by forcing it to fit into an ideological system. In the face of these difficulties, the recovery of existence in truth requires a constant effort to attend to the experiential source of our symbolization of order that is itself true to the participatory nature of human existence. Thus, in his conclusion, Voegelin notes the diagnostic and therapeutic work that must be conducted in order to resuscitate our awareness of the experiential nature of truth and existence. We must undertake, first, "a careful analysis of the noetic structure of existence," and, second, "an analysis of Second Realities, with regard to both their constructs and the motivating structure of existence in untruth."[69]

Before concluding, it should be noted that, as Voegelin knows, even these tasks will not be sufficient to turn the tide. Since the problem of ideology is not due to intellectual error alone, pointing to the fundamental experiences of order cannot guarantee that others will embrace them. In fact, what is required is a conversion from existence in untruth to existence in truth. It is interesting to note in this connection Voegelin's observation that "the fundamentals of existence" in question concern those "areas central to the person." As such, we cannot provide an objective (or intentional) account that would solve the problem, since personal existence is participatory and luminous. In our efforts to recover the truth of existence, we must recognize the personal nature of the task. In addition to recognizing that logical arguments will only be part of the effort, this also means recognizing

68 Voegelin, *In Search of Order*, 81.
69 Voegelin, "On Debate," 51.

that any movement toward order will involve the whole person, including the spirit, intellect, emotions, appetites, social existence, and so forth. This means that we cannot compel the conversion from ideology to truth in our interlocutors through rational argument or any other means. As Voegelin says elsewhere, "one cannot prove reality by a syllogism; one can only point to it and invite the doubter to look."[70]

Conclusion

"On Debate and Existence" offers a succinct account of the necessary existential basis for rational discussion and the impossibility of genuine debate with ideologues. Lest we assume too confidently that we are on the correct side of the debate, however, it is important to keep in mind that it was crafted for a particular purpose and with a particular audience in mind. It is not an essay written for ideologues, but, rather, those who would join Voegelin in the struggle against ideology. The central message of the text is that even those who strive to overcome the ideological threats to order in modernity might inadvertently contribute to disorder, if they do not recognize and operate within the historical context of the human search for order. While human experiences of order are perennial, the symbolizations are not. There have been and will continue to be a variety of symbolic expressions across time and space. True debate involves discussion of which of those symbols best and most completely point to the nature of reality. Before such debate can occur, however, we must attend to our own fundamental experiences of reality and recognize their priority to the symbols we use to express them. And then, when necessary, we must attempt to bring those who have forgotten or reject those experiences back into contact with them. At the same time, we must recall that forgetfulness and revolt are possibilities for each of us and that the struggle between ideologues and non-ideologues mirrors a "debate" that takes place within each individual.

With these considerations in mind we can understand just how difficult it is to reconstitute the conditions for genuine debate—and how fortuitous it is when we succeed. The paradoxical nature of consciousness and concomitant metaxic character of human existence means that even people of

70 Voegelin, "Quod Deus Dicitur" in *CWEV* Vol. 12, 388.

good will struggle to recognize and articulate the truth that lies right in front of them. It is that much more difficult to move someone resistant to truth into a position where he or she sees and accepts the structure of reality as we experience it, especially when we consider the various forces beyond reason that might pressure such a person not to change. The struggle for order is truly a struggle, one that is rooted in the very nature of human consciousness itself. In light of that, it seems reasonable to view it as miraculous that we manage to establish personal and social order at all.

–3–
Voegelin's "Immortality: Experience and Symbol"

Henrik Syse

Introduction

It is a well-worn cliché but also the most sobering existential fact: we are all going to die. No human being escapes the clutches of physical reality: life in this world is marked not by birth and life alone, but also by the inevitable physical decay of the body and by death—sometimes later rather than sooner, sometimes with peace and sometimes painfully, but always with a certitude that only an empiricist philosopher at his or her most stubborn moment could ever question. (Indeed, as the consistent empiricist would point out, since we have not yet experienced our own death, we cannot know for certain that it will happen. But there is an overwhelming likelihood bordering on certitude that it will.)

In nearly every human civilization we also find the sometimes comforting, sometimes sobering or even chilling idea that life does not end with death—that there is a life or a reality beyond death, which means that the physical death that we experience is not absolute or final. Normally, this is put in terms of "immortality": not just a longer life, but a life that does not end, a life without death.

In one of Eric Voegelin's most penetrating philosophical essays, it is exactly this idea of immortality that lies at the heart of his trenchant analysis. As anyone familiar with Voegelin's later work will know, he does not, however, speak in terms of an *idea*. He wants to get to the heart of the *experience* that has engendered the symbol of immortality (which in turn has become an "idea" or even a "dogma"). Hence, the essay carries the telling title

"Immortality: Experience and Symbol." In this writer's view, it stands as one of Voegelin's most penetrating analyses of the complex relationships between experience, symbol, dogma, ideology, and reality, and maybe one of his most important philosophical essays overall.

The Scope of the Essay

The "Immortality" essay is arguably less about immortality *per se* and more about the interplay between experience, symbol, and reality. It is almost as if immortality is used merely as an example—one of several that could be imagined of the species of symbols that immortality represents, namely, symbols of religious or spiritual experiences. If one goes to this essay to find an analysis of actual experiences of or theories about immortality—such as near-death experiences or discussions of whether life after death is conceivable and, if so, how it might be conceived, physically, mentally, or spiritually—one will come away disappointed. The essay also does not delineate or categorize different understandings of immortality. Reincarnation, for instance, is not analyzed, and the Christian terminology of "resurrection" rather than "immortality" is commented on only in passing.

More indirectly, however, the essay contains a rich philosophical analysis of the sorts of symbols we must analyze, as well as the engendering experiences underlying them, if we are to make sense of immortality. And in that sense, the essay *is* surely about immortality and takes immortality very seriously as part of the structure of human existence.

Two key concepts arguably structure the movement and direction of the essay: "nonexistent reality"[1] and "the fallacy of misplaced concreteness."[2] The first denotes the referent of what Voegelin, with a nod to William James, calls "the varieties of religious experience."[3] The second, borrowed from Alfred North Whitehead, denotes what ensues when one in essence employs "hypostatized symbols,"[4] as, for instance, when the symbols of

1 Eric Voegelin, "Immortality: Experience and Symbol," in *Published Essays, 1966-1985*, ed. Ellis Sandoz, *CWEV* Vol. 12, 52–94, hereafter cited as "Immortality," 52.

2 Ibid., 65.

3 Ibid., 52.

4 Ibid., 65.

God or immortality are no longer seen as representing experiences of nonexistent reality, but rather are understood to be referring to things, entities, or ideas that can be analyzed, critiqued, and dissected in the same way as any concrete, immanent thing, entity, or idea can be. The latter is nothing short of a serious category mistake, according to Voegelin, and it is to address this grave mistake and explain how it can be properly addressed that Voegelin writes this essay.

What, then, is nonexistent reality? Immortality and the divine belong to this category. It is that which is experienced as part of the total reality within which human beings exist, but which does not belong to the subset of phenomena which exist as concrete things or manifestations, or ideas thereof, in our life-world. Such experiences structure the way in which human beings experience and think about reality; indeed, they are part of what Voegelin calls the "structure of existence."[5] Human existence is existence in tension "between time and the timeless,"[6] as Voegelin puts it, and the variety of symbols that point toward the timeless, immortality among them, are ways in which we as human beings attempt to understand and make sense of that larger reality and the structure of existence.

From Experience to Dogma to Skepticism

Voegelin's analysis in the essay points to three stages that experiences of nonexistent reality typically go through when they become articulate and enter society as an ordering force. These are the phenomena of "original account, dogmatic exposition, and skeptical argument."[7]

This happened in Antiquity, when the noetic experience of classic philosophy emerged from the culture of the myth. This philosophy, which Voegelin calls exegetic[8]—that is, it formulates and interprets the meaning of myth and thereby creates a more differentiated expression of human existence and its tensions than the myth itself could do—in turn became dogmatized in schools, and this dogmatism led in the end to a skeptical

5 Ibid., 83ff.
6 Ibid., 84.
7 Ibid., 54.
8 Ibid., 55.

reaction. Thus, one has ended up with what Voegelin calls an "ominous bifurcation"[9] between faith on the one hand and dogmatic fideism on the other; between true mysticism on the one hand and an empty nominalism on the other. A Christianity that had become doctrinaire clashed with skeptical counter-assertions, the latter being fueled and strengthened by the violence and devastations of the religious wars of the period around the Reformation.

The same sequence takes place within modernity, with its spectacle of ideology-fueled wars and revolutions. According to Voegelin, this modern, explosive and bifurcated world—or one should probably say "multi-furcated" world—leaves little room for rational discussion and creates all the more danger of both sectarian and skeptical intransigence and quarrel, as dogma, skepticism, and ideological movements clash in incessant and sometimes violent conflict. In this world, the experience of God, the soul, or immortality has degenerated into merely an "idea" or a dogma—one among many, and one which the skeptic can easily dismiss and destroy.

The deeply existential and dramatic core of Voegelin's argument is arguably his claim that this dynamic is deeply linked to the nature of humanity and existence in the world and not to any particular historical circumstance, never to be repeated again. Developments in history, with its different regimes and political contexts, may indeed contribute to unique manifestations of the relationship between experience, symbol, dogmatization, and skepticism. But the underlying dynamic is inherent to the human condition. This is illustrated movingly by Voegelin in his recounting of an ancient Egyptian text,[10] dating back to the Middle Kingdom (approx. 2000 BC), containing a dialogue between a man and his *ba* (soul) about whether one should keep living if life is actually and truly filled with disorder and chaos.

The man in the dialogue is intensely disturbed by the disorder of his time. He argues that his life may not be worth living at all. He is gainsaid by his soul, *ba*, who recites what seems to be a conventional piety of Egyptian mythology, namely, that life is a gift, and it is not for man to decide on its fate. The man replies by pointing to the extreme situation of disorder

9 Ibid.
10 Ibid., 58–64.

that he lives under, and, furthermore, he assures the soul that through proper provisions for burial and sacrifice, the passage to the afterlife will be pleasant. This is where immortality makes its more explicit entrance into Voegelin's re-telling of the dialogue. The soul again appears to recite commonly held opinions in reminding the man that no one has returned from the realm of the dead—in other words: we have no assurance of an afterlife. The man is not swayed, because he takes the disorder of his time so seriously that he simply *has to* address it, and by crossing over into the afterlife and thus—at least potentially—taking his side as a companion of *Re*, the sun-god, he can address and confront this disorder much more directly than he can in this life. The soul replies that the man should not take life and its failings so seriously: live while you can—and try to ignore the experience of disorder.

It is against this background and debate that the protagonist ("man") of the dialogue must make his decision about whether to live or not. While there is a dispute among scholars about the extent to which suicide is actually and concretely contemplated in the dialogue (a debate not addressed by Voegelin), there is no doubt, from the text available to us, that this is indeed a dialogue concerned with the value of living, the meaning of life, the disorder of society, the tension within (or with) one's soul, and the possibility of immortality.[11]

Voegelin explains why he introduces and discusses this particular text:

> The Western philosopher in the twentieth century A.D. finds himself in substantially the same position as the Egyptian thinker in the twentieth century B.C.: both the philosopher and the author of the "Dispute" are disturbed by the disorder of the age, they both are in search of a reality no longer alive in the surrounding images, and they both want to recover the meaning of symbols from their misuse in everyday debate.[12]

11 For a useful recent analysis of the dialogue (including a critical discussion of the question of suicide in it), see Yordan Chobanov, "A New Interpretation of 'The Dialogue of a Man and His Ba'," *Journal of Egyptological Studies*, Vol. IV (2015), 84–97.

12 Ibid., 64.

In other words, the philosopher is as disturbed by the disorder of his age as the "man" of the ancient Egyptian text. Therefore, he or she cannot avoid taking seriously—if one is truly a philosopher—experiences of meaning, life, death, the soul, and immortality: Is life worth living, and if so, what kind of life? And is there a life or a reality beyond this life that can correct or give some deeper meaning to the life we live here and now?

Understanding and articulating these experiences and the symbols that express them, found so compactly in the Egyptian myth, will even today imply a confrontation with the very reactions and expressions of meaning (or lack thereof) discussed by Voegelin: traditional pieties, dogmatic certitude, and—following upon the latter—deep-seated skepticism. And these are as pervasive today as they were in the age of the Egyptian "man" anno 2000 B.C.

Disorder

Before attempting to understand more fully the proper philosophical way to address this movement from experience through dogmatism to skepticism, we should ask what Voegelin means by the disorder of the age, arguably a Voegelinian *topos* that we as commentators too often leave unquestioned. After all, a basic premise in this as in many other of Voegelin's late essays is the existence of disorder and crisis. Some would question that assumption (say, a Stephen Pinker of present-day philosophical fame), saying that Voegelin lived in a democratic society that saw, at the time of writing, huge improvements in living standards, science, and health, and where the horrors of the world wars were rapidly becoming a thing of the past; a free society in which one could pursue philosophical and scientific discourse or the life of the spirit without fear of oppression and retribution. What is this deep disorder that Voegelin keeps returning to and lamenting?

The "Immortality" essay appeared as a lecture at Harvard and subsequently as an article in the mid-to-late 1960s (the lecture having been given in 1965 and the publication taking place in *Harvard Theological Review* in 1967). Given the timing, it is reasonable to assume that Voegelin—still residing in Germany and having delivered quite recently his lectures on Hitler and the Germans—has in mind the Second World War and National Socialism. However, more broadly and even more timely, he has in mind brutal totalitarian dictatorships, with the Soviet Union, Communist China, and North Vietnam being seen as the main threats to rule of law, peace, and human dignity by much of the West. In addition come weapons of mass destruction, deep-seated ideological quarrels even within democracies, and a rapidly developing skepticism, agnosticism, and even atheism in much of the world, some of it linked to a rebellious youth culture, all of which makes a truly articulate and serious discourse about spiritual phenomena difficult. Only a few of these concrete disorders of the time—most markedly the latter, about the lack of analytical philosophical tools within modernity—are expressly spelled out by Voegelin, which is why we as readers are forced to interpret what Voegelin actually means by disorder.

His lament that there is a severe lack of symbols and images to properly interpret and remedy the disorder is indeed crucial. Our time seems to lack the tools to discuss and analyze—internally and between ourselves—the disorder confronting us, according to Voegelin. With authoritarian and totalitarian ideologies being specialists in the art of spewing out statements, dogmas, and all-encompassing programs, the space for truly addressing the disorder becomes all the narrower and less secure.

By returning to the Egyptian case, we see that this is not only a modern state of affairs. In analyzing the Egyptian dialogue, Voegelin emphasizes the historical circumstance of a breakdown of political order, with the Pharaoh having ceased to function as the mediator of divine order to society. Hence, the man who encounters disorder around him—lack of trust, love, and fellowship is explicitly mentioned in the dialogue—has to become that mediator himself if he truly takes the disorder seriously. The divine status of living beyond this world, as a symbol and potential reality, represents a realization of that role. In short, the order in society that is supposed to mediate between the divine and man has broken down, and man himself thus comes face to face with the deepest questions and crises of life. He must take these upon himself. The only alternative is simply to accept or ignore the disorder.

Hence, the question of disorder, while certainly possible to define and delimit as I did above (enumerating twentieth-century phenomena from National Socialism via Vietnam to agnosticism), presents itself as an ever-present question about life as such, and not only a question about societal breakdown in the twentieth century. Disorder is, in short, part of the human condition (although Voegelin does not employ that particular phrase). Hence, the true and serious philosopher has the task of getting to the core of the problem of disorder not only by way of historical analysis but by way of psychological and philosophical analysis.

The Fallacy of Misplaced Concreteness

It is here that Whitehead's expression of the fallacy of misplaced concreteness becomes so central to Voegelin's analysis. The experience of disorder and the symbolism of immortality found in the Egyptian dialogue point to the structure of reality and human existence as such. But once the experience of disorder and symbols such as immortality are criticized skeptically because there is no certainty about what the experiences or symbols refer to, a category mistake is made, because the symbols in question refer to the experience of participation and existence, not to concrete physical realities. In Plato, this sense of participation in a reality beyond the physical and immediate is expressed through the symbols of the "in-between" (*metaxy*) and of the "spiritual man" (*daimonios aner*) who exists in and is conscious of the in-between nature of existence and therefore of the tension within which man exists. The skeptic, however, reacts to and ridicules the *concreteness* of the symbolization that is partly a result of the organizing of philosophical thought into schools and the organizing of religious belief into dogma. In turn, the dogmatic believer answers by further entrenchment and dogmatization, insisting on the absolute truth of the dogma to which he or she clings. The realm of non-existent reality is turned into a realm of concrete propositions or "things" to be debated and analyzed, verified or falsified. This is the fallacy of misplaced concreteness, and it has severe and fateful consequences.

What characterizes modernity is the way in which the skeptical reaction against dogma has itself been transformed into dogmatic ideologies, or as Voegelin puts it: "In the modern variant of the subfield we find a class of symbols that has no counterpart on the Egyptian scene, *i.e.*, the so-called ideological objections to doctrinal belief."[13] These ideological objections are prefigured by doctrinaire beliefs, a *topos* that goes back to the

13 Ibid., 67.

very beginnings of Voegelin's thought, such as his books on race (1933) and his book on political religions (1938). The point is that the understanding of the underlying or engendering experience—for instance, of immortality—moves from the compact to the differentiated, followed by the ever-present danger that the differentiated understanding (such as the *metaxy* or the transcendence of God) and with it recourse to the original experience underlying the differentiated symbols get lost, and all we end up with are doctrinaire beliefs. This happens when dogmatic assertions take the place of the open and searching quest which characterizes true philosophizing as well as religious faith. Indeed, dogma takes the place of faith in the sense of Hebrews 11:1, where faith is characterized as "the substance of things hoped for and faith in things unseen," or in the sense of Anselm of Canterbury's dictum "faith seeking understanding," i.e., a movement towards an understanding of reality where faith and philosophy seek to complement each other in an open process of understanding and quest for truth. When symbols such as "immortality," "soul," "spirit," or even "God" instead become dogmatic assertions, unmoored from the engendering experiences in which they were grounded, the skeptic or ideologue can demolish the symbols as meaningless, and replace them with symbols that seem more immediate, more fulfilling, and less tension-filled. In place of hope and faith come positive science (which is ideally seen to be "value-free," thus replacing all the illusory values of yesteryear) or political programs, promising a total understanding of the whole or, for that matter, a classless society or the Third Reich.

Voegelin sums up the modern attack on faith and symbols such as immortality by coining a critical phrase he sees as characteristic of the whole modern enterprise: "the experience is an illusion."[14] The phrase summarizes the view that the contents of certain experiences are merely figments of the imagination. The subject of the experience(s) simply does not exist. God is, in short, dead. However, as Voegelin puts it, "a judgment of illusion can pertain only to experiences of existent objects, not to experiences of participation in nonexistent reality."[15] By criticizing what is in essence a dogmatic hypostatization of nonexistent reality, the skeptic or ideologue will claim

14 Ibid.
15 Ibid., 68.

that what we can broadly call religious experiences and symbols refer to nothing but an illusion.

The problem is: religious experiences and symbols do not go away, to the skeptic's and the ideologue's great frustration. Voegelin refers to Feuerbach and claims he was disturbed "by the fact that dogmatic propositions, be they theological or metaphysical, survive socially, even when their fallacious character has been thoroughly analyzed and exhibited to public view."[16] Which reality, then, engenders them? Since neither the skeptic nor the ideologue can accept the possibility of a nonexistent reality towards which human beings live in a tension—there can be no intersection between time and the timeless, since the latter has been excluded from view—the engendering reality must exist within the world. The experiences and symbols we refer to as religious or spiritual must therefore have a world-immanent cause, which is exactly the point of thinkers from Feuerbach through Marx to Freud.

History and Human Consciousness

The anti-doctrinaire skeptic or ideologue thus arrives at the conclusion—meant to be the death blow to all religious doctrines—that each form of mythical or religious belief, or belief in a Ground of Being beyond this world, constitutes but "a phase of human consciousness"[17] taking place within a specific historical dispensation. The definitive sciences—say, the historical science of Marx or the psychological science of Freud—will be able to reveal all the former states of human consciousness as illusions created by historical or mental states of affairs, now to be superseded by the revelation that they were all illusions. From this follows quite naturally theories of historical epochs, each with its set of beliefs that all have a world-immanent cause. The idea of a "post-Christian age"[18] is an example of this sort of theoretical construct.

Neatly, then, the "carver" of history,[19] as Voegelin calls him, who performs the trick of carving history into phases or states of consciousness, can

16 Ibid.
17 Ibid., 69.
18 Ibid., 79.
19 Ibid., 71.

place his own consciousness "at the top of the ladder."[20] "The ideologue appeals to the reality, not of truth experienced, but of the world,"[21] continues Voegelin. The modern ideologue becomes the mirror image of the religious literalist, drawing all truth together into seemingly all-encompassing, scientific doctrines. This is the *libido dominandi* set free from all sense of an existential tension between the physicality of human power and this-worldly reality on the one hand and participation in a timeless, divine ground of being on the other. This is the world in which the ideological leader can dominate the world and kill whoever does not belong to his dream world—and claim to do so in the name of historical or natural science.

Prohibition of Questions and Denial of Phenomena

Voegelin, in the almost contemporaneous but more rhetorical essay "Science, Politics, and Gnosticism" speaks of the "prohibition of questions" as one of the key features of modern scientist or authoritarian ideologies.[22] In the "Immortality" essay he touches on the same problem when he holds that what happens when symbols such as immortality are employed and critiqued as if they were either physical things or mere figments of the imagination, created historically through mental, inner-worldly processes, with no referent to any other part of reality, is in essence *a denial of cognizance* to a whole class of phenomena.[23] When these phenomena nonetheless manifest themselves in reality, through religious belief or symbols of transcendence and immortality, they must be explained away. Thus, philosophical teachings or religious beliefs are either criticized as illusions of the past or as actually expressing a doctrine suited to the ideological movements of the present. Plato, for instance, Voegelin bitingly points out, would be (and has indeed repeatedly been) understood according to "the doctrinaire

20 Ibid.

21 Ibid., 75.

22 Eric Voegelin, "Science, Politics, and Gnosticism," 261; in *Modernity Without Restraint*, ed. Manfred Henningsen, *CWEV* Vol. 5 (Columbia: University of Missouri Press, 2000), 251–92.

23 Ibid., 71.

fashions of the moment," leaving him to be "flattened and crushed until nothing but a rubble of doctrine is left."[24]

What we can call, to return to William James's formulation, the varieties of religious experience thus come to represent a field of truth "whose symbols have become opaque and suspect."[25] This field of truth cannot be saved by what Voegelin calls "doctrinal concessions to the Zeitgeist."[26] Voegelin seems to have in mind, as examples of such concessions, some forms of liberal theology and the theological "God is dead" movement. The only way to recover the truth is by a return to the experiences, the very real experiences—even if expressed in the compact form of the myth—which engendered the symbols in the first place. We must approach the experiences and the symbols through an exegesis which is critical but open. It must be critical in the sense of being accurate, concise, and sensitive to historical and linguistic distance, but also open in the sense of Bergson's "open society," that is, open to the wholeness of reality, and thus to the tension between this-worldly and nonexistent reality, the tension between time and the timeless. To be human is to partake of both "time and eternity" and therefore of not wholly belonging "to the one or the other."[27] And it is exactly basic humanity that is lost when this fact is denied.

This Voegelinian understanding of life in the tension of the *metaxy* has some important implications for the articulation of religious doctrine, and Voegelin indeed spends some time on this in the "Immortality" essay. Fittingly, in an essay that takes the symbol of immortality as its point of departure, Voegelin chooses the "truth of salvation and immortality through faith in Christ" as his example of a teaching which, if taken purely literally and in a chronological, historical fashion, would exclude and condemn to hell "all mankind that happened to live before Christ."[28] Quite apart from the ethical problems of such a doctrine, the philosopher will struggle with it because it takes the human tension of faith toward God, which is a trait of human nature witnessed in myriads of mythologies and religious

24 Ibid.
25 Ibid., 73.
26 Ibid.
27 Ibid., 77.
28 Ibid., 77–78.

symbolisms through history, and seemingly turns it into "a Christian privilege."[29] Philosophers such as Augustine, Thomas Aquinas, or the authors of the Definition of Chalcedon, about the union of divine and human nature in Christ, were all aware of this and saw the historical symbols we attribute to Christ and other Biblical stories—such as the Exodus and Babylon—as expressive of the ever-present "movement of the soul when it is drawn by love toward God."[30] Christ is, then, *both* the historical Christ *and* "the divine timelessness, omnipresent in the flow of history."[31]

And so, this is where man finds himself (and, let us add, even if Voegelin does not do so explicitly, *her*self): as a being who partakes in the timeless. Nothing so strongly expresses this tension between time and the timeless as the tension between life and death, between the mortal and the immortal. This symbolism is not peculiar to Christianity. As we have seen, we find it in Egyptian mythology and in a host of other mythological, religious, and philosophical traditions.

Historically, the symbol of immortality is presented in two different modes of experience. Firstly, there is the mode of the primary experience of the cosmos, where immortality is seen as the opposite of mortality, and where it is predicated as a quality to certain entities, such as the gods or the soul. Secondly, there is the existential tension of existing in this world but *at the same time* participating in the timeless. In Aristotle, we find a prime example of a thinker who experiences a transition from the first to the second mode of experience. In his work (such as the *Nicomachean Ethics*, X, vii), there is still the dichotomy of the different entities: mortal men and immortal gods. The differentiation of the tension between the divine and the worldly has not yet been fully articulated. But at the same time, there is in Aristotle the recognition of divine presence in man. There is something in man—namely, a participation in *nous*—so high and dignified that we should rightly conceive of it as something immortal.

By showing and indeed emphasizing the gradual movement from mythical to philosophical symbolism, Voegelin shows us the complexity of the process. He takes care to point out that the compact symbolism of the myth and the differentiated symbolism of participation and tension "do not pertain

29 Ibid., 78.
30 Ibid.
31 Ibid.

to different realities but to the same reality in different modes. The experience of cosmic reality includes in its compactness the existential tension; and the differentiated consciousness of existence has no reality without the cosmos in which it occurs."[32] It follows from this that the language and imagery of myth has an important part to play even in philosophical and religious texts and traditions which seemingly have moved beyond the compactness of the cosmological myth. Voegelin succinctly summarizes this insight when he says that the compact symbolisms of the myth "may become obsolete in the light of new insights, but the reality they express does not cease to be real for that reason."[33] In short, the Egyptian man and the philosopher of the twentieth—or for that matter twenty-first—century do live in the same world.

It is to this class of "compact symbolisms" that immortality belongs: expressive of a basic, one could probably say primordial experience of human beings, which is articulated in myths and symbols and gradually finds its way into the philosophical analyses of individuals who are open to the larger field of reality that these experiences point to. The transforming of them into doctrines or dogmas and the subsequent skeptical or ideological attack on such dogmas as illusions constitute the real tragedy, because the reality that these experiences make us open to—what Voegelin calls nonexistent reality—is instead closed to us. The modern natural and psychological sciences, themselves easily turned into ideologies (or at least handmaidens of ideologies), will claim a monopoly in scientific enquiry, and all that belongs outside of them is then merely illusion, which the ideologues can claim to have revealed and defeated. This is the existential drama that Voegelin alerts us to, and indeed it is the source of the worst sorts of disorders, since it removes the divine or the Ground of Being from the purview of scientific enquiry and existential understanding—and thereby it way too easily puts the ideologue in place of God.

Conclusion

"Immortality: Experience and Symbol" masterfully argues that the scientist and ideological movements of modernity in essence express a "despair

32 Ibid., 93.
33 Ibid.

caused by an acute state of alienation."[34] Alienation is used as a key term by Voegelin to describe the sense of being strangers to the reality—or part of the reality—in which we live. The experience of timelessness and of a beyond that structures our existence belongs to the most basic facets of human existence. Immortality is a key symbol engendered by the experience of the tension between life and death. The symbol has developed from the compact mythical level to the differentiated philosophical level, all the time engendered by a basic experience of the cosmos. Once that experience is hypostatized into dogmatic assertions which in turn are analyzed and found wanting, since they do not conform to a narrow understanding of world-immanent reality as the only possible reality, we essentially alienate ourselves from the most basic structure of existence. We lock out one part of reality, we ridicule it, deconstruct it, psychologize it, and then throw it out the window, with nothing seemingly having been lost or destroyed, since there was nothing there to begin with. In his dramatic response to this, Voegelin urges us to go back to the engendering experiences that gave rise to the symbols of God and immortality. This is the task of the philosopher, and it is directly relevant to the problems and disorder of our age—or as Voegelin puts it at the very end of the essay: "These remarks, though they can be no more than the barest hints, will perhaps suggest a new understanding of some problems that move the age."[35]

34 Ibid.
35 Ibid., 94.

–4–
Voegelin's "Configurations of History"

Paul Kidder

Composed as a lecture that Eric Voegelin gave at Grinnell College in the spring of 1963, "Configurations of History" marks a stage in the process of development toward *The Ecumenic Age*, the fourth volume of *Order and History*, a process that caused that volume to take a new approach to *Order and History*'s overall project of identifying symbolisms of order in human history and politics.[1] The "Configurations" article, I would suggest, participates in three distinct but very much related trajectories in the movement toward *The Ecumenic Age*. A first trajectory has to do with Voegelin's developing sense of the relationship of philosophy, political theory, and history. This development proceeds by working through a set of problems that are voiced in this essay and related writings, such as "What is History?," "Eternal Being in Time," and "Equivalences of Experience and Symbolization in History,"[2] studies that contribute to the refinement of what I shall call

1 Eric Voegelin, "Configurations of History" (1968) in *Published Essays 1966-1985*, ed. Ellis Sandoz, *CWEV* Vol. 12, 1990, 95–114. Hereafter cited as Voegelin, "Configurations." Eric Voegelin, *Order and History, Vol. IV: The Ecumenic Age* (1974), ed. Michael Franz, *CWEV* Vol. 17, 2000. Hereafter cited as Voegelin, *Ecumenic Age*.

2 Eric Voegelin, *What is History? And Other Late Unpublished Writings,* ed. Thomas Hollweck and Paul Caringella, *CWEV* Vol. 28, 1990; see also the "Editors' Introduction" to this volume, xvi; "Eternal Being in Time" (1964) in *Anamnesis: On the Theory of History and Politics* (German edition 1966), ed. David Walsh, *CWEV* Vol. 6, 2002; "Equivalences of Experience and Symbolization in History" (1970) in *Published Essays 1966-1985*, ed. Ellis Sandoz, *CWEV* Vol. 12, 1990, 115–33. Hereafter cited as Voegelin, "Equivalences of Experience."

(using a term from Hans-Georg Gadamer) Voegelin's philosophical hermeneutic.[3] "Configurations of History" displays Voegelin's deepening grasp of the fact that historical phenomena exist simultaneously as events and interpretations of events. The historian, who also comes to the historical record as an interpreter, must learn how his or her interpretive assumptions both open and limit the possibilities for understanding the objects of study. The historian must be equal to the task of understanding the self-interpretations of historical agents, a task which may make great and broad-ranging intellectual demands.

A second trajectory in which "Configurations" participates has to do with the promised topic for Volume IV of *Order and History*. Having dealt with ancient Greek symbolisms of order in Volumes II and III,[4] the next subject was to be the "Age of Empires" and the rise of Christianity, spanning roughly the period from the emergence of the Persian Empire in the sixth century B.C. to the fall of the Western Roman Empire in the fifth century A.D. (or, as Voegelin broadly puts it in "Configurations," from the eighth century B.C. to the eighth century A.D.).[5] But a variety of complications interfered with this program. For one, the category of "empire" began to seem insufficient for capturing the operative symbolic dynamics of the period. Equally important were the symbols of "exodus" that evidenced an inherent failure of empires to symbolize adequately the unity and order that they sought to bring to the political world.[6] For this reason Voegelin preferred to call the period "the ecumenic age," so as to name it by its guiding symbolic ambition—to unite the whole of mankind under ultimate symbols of order—rather than by the partial and problematic realizations of that ambition in empires.

Voegelin, furthermore, was questioning the implicit assumption of progress over time that historians typically bring to the interpretation of history—an assumption that he came to believe was coloring the program

3 Hans-Georg Gadamer, *Truth and Method*, 2nd rev. ed., trans. J. Weinsheimer and D. G. Marshall (New York: Crossroad, 1990).

4 Eric Voegelin, *Order and History, Vol. II: The World of the Polis* (1957), ed. Athanasios Moulakis, *CWEV* Vol. 15, 2000; *Order and History, Vol. III: Plato and Aristotle* (1966), ed. Dante Germino, *CWEV* Vol. 16, 2000.

5 Voegelin, *Ecumenic Age*, 167; "Configurations," 98.

6 Voegelin, "Configurations," 104–8.

of his own study. To create the possibility of uprooting this assumption he was beginning to give the patterns of symbolic meaning (and his own hermeneutical self-reflections on them) more control over the analysis than the timeline per se, so that the meanings discernable in the ecumenic age are analyzed not only in the context of the historical period in question but also in their earlier instantiations and their later transformations up to the twentieth century. The term "configurations" in the essay aims to name a complex of associated patterns in which related symbolic meanings cohere, patterns that can recur in multiple historical contexts.[7] But Voegelin proceeds in this direction cautiously and reflectively, problematizing the term "configurations" even as he puts it to use in analyzing the ecumenic age.

A third line of trajectory has to do with the growth in Voegelin's understanding of what it means to pursue an ontological philosophy of history. From the beginning of *Order and History* it was clear that the great insights, in human history, into the nature of order constituted "leaps in being,"[8] but the later Voegelin goes further in ontological thinking, coming to grips with the implication that the ultimate subject of the study should not be the leaps but being. The claim may seem to be an odd one, given the abstractness of the notion of being when compared to the concreteness of historical events, persons, and societies, but the assertion represents a culmination of Voegelin's thinking that deepens his Platonic and Aristotelian inspirations and puts him in league with the very spiritual outbursts with which he is concerned. The ultimate constant in human history is the situation of human life in the presence of being in both its immediacy and mysterious transcendence. To see that the movement of human history is movement within this selfsame ontological situation is to recognize the dynamics through which any normative order must emerge. It is to comprehend the irresolvable tension of existence in history to which all conceptions of intramundane order may aspire or fail to aspire.

As these three trajectories appear in "Configurations of History" in the same order that I have adumbrated them, I shall explore them further in

7 Voegelin, "Configurations," 96–7.

8 Voegelin, Eric Voegelin, *Order and History, Volume I: Israel and Revelation* (1956), ed. Maurice P. Hogan, *CWEV* Vol. 14, 2001, "Introduction," e.g., 49.

that sequence, beginning with the hermeneutical issues, moving on to the question of configurations associated with empire, and ending with questions as to the nature of ontological philosophy of history.

I. Philosophical Hermeneutics

The historian is obliged to communicate information regarding the past "with a minimum of error," as Voegelin puts it in "Configurations of History."[9] There is an empirical dimension to this obligation: one must assemble the relevant data, learn how to grasp its content, and report on the intelligible patterns discernable within it. Thus far the model resembles natural-scientific empiricism, yet to embrace that analogy too thoroughly is so objectionable to Voegelin that he resists the very use of the term, "pattern." A natural scientist seeks patterns in intelligible but non-intelligent phenomena, but because the historian's data are the product of human minds that are at least as intellectually proficient as that of the historian, the historian must be an interpreter of interpretations. He or she does not simply seek patterns but must attempt to understand how they might have held significance for those who produced the data, how they might offer meaning for a present generation, and how the historian might function as an intermediary between the historical and contemporary worlds of meaning. A natural scientist exists, in a sense, outside of the phenomena that he or she studies because the scientist is not merely intelligible but intelligent. This fact provides a vantage point that is relatively unaffected by the data themselves: an intelligent mind makes sense of the patterns in intelligible data. But a truly self-aware historian realizes that he or she never stands apart from history in this way, that history must somehow be conducted from within its flow, that the historian's interpretative categories may themselves reflect the patterning of historical movements and symbolisms.

To imagine that one can somehow step out of history to interpret history is certainly an error of positivist historiography—the belief that a method modeled on natural science could free one from prejudice and historical situatedness; but one errs equally in claiming a privileged vantage point by virtue of being at the end of history, or by having somehow

9 Voegelin, "Configurations," 98.

reached a state of self-consciousness or a theory of the meaning or purpose of history that makes one an autonomous, ahistorical interpreter. Such assumptions, which Voegelin found so irksome in the philosophies of Comte, Hegel, and Marx, and which he came to range under the category of "historiogenesis," had a much earlier origin, he found, in writings that go as far back as the Sumerian King List of the middle Bronze Age, which was prepared not simply to provide a record, but to legitimate the authority of reigning rulers.[10] That authority is gained not merely by later rulers having taken the place of previous ones, but by virtue of the later rulers having the knowledge of the genealogy and being able to produce it in writing. Even in such primordial instances of historical thinking, one finds the significance of the past being asserted by writers of the present, and their authority to do so being assumed by virtue of coming at the end of the tale that they tell. All such assumptions, however, indulge in abstraction from the reality of historical existence, because as long as humanity exists no one can stand at the end of human history. Here lies the root of Voegelin's resistance to any search for the "meaning" of history; the very project is born of the biases of historiogenesis. Yet what the alternative would be—the attempt to select what is significant in the record of the past in light of an acute awareness of one's own immersion in ongoing traditions with uncertain futures—is something that would seem to have few precedents.

To the limitations of the investigator's historical situatedness we must add the limits of his or her understanding. An interpreter cannot interpret meanings that he or she has not grasped or explain insights that he or she has not had, even if the interpreter can reproduce all of the language in which these insights were originally formulated. The awareness of this fact forces the hermeneutically-minded historian to become an inquirer alongside his or her subjects of inquiry. One cannot come at the historical record armed with predetermined categories of significance and be accurate; rather, the emergence of significant patterns must be part of a process of being

10 Voegelin, "Configurations," 96, 102; *Ecumenic Age*, Introduction, Ch. 1. See also Barry Cooper, "Voegelin's Conception of Historiogenesis," *Historical Reflections/Réflexions Historique* 4 (1977), 231–51; Glenn Hughes, *Transcendence and History: The Search for Ultimacy from Ancient Societies to Postmodernity* (Columbia, MO: University of Missouri Press, 2003), 94–6.

educated by the record. Voegelin extends this insight to the study of symbols: if symbols are born of the experiences that engender them, and if one has not had those experiences, one is at a loss to say what they can mean unless and until one becomes open to comparable experience within one's own realm of possibilities—a realm that may indeed be expanded through the study of one's sources.[11]

To interpret the past is always also to draw upon the past, for the present from which one interprets is shaped by the past. The categories within which one thinks and speaks are to some extent the fruit of one's individual effort and skill, but to a far greater extent they reflect the social order of one's day and the ordering symbols of one's culture. Thus the situation of the historical inquirer is itself a product of historical processes, often including the very processes that one is investigating. What Voegelin realizes with particular acuteness is that one's social, political, and intellectual milieu may not be a normative product of history but may very well constitute a deformation, such as Voegelin experienced in the perversion of political symbols and the human sciences under twentieth-century totalitarian regimes in Europe.

The terms in which Gadamer expresses the hermeneutic realities that I have been describing are well known. For Gadamer, the set of questions, assumptions, background knowledge, biases, and intellectual influences, habits, and idiosyncrasies that one brings to the interpretive task constitute a "horizon," such that one can speak of the horizon of the interpreter and that of his or her sources. While the interpreter's horizon forms the only means of his or her access to other horizons, it is also the source of the limitations that generate misinterpretations, so that only an interpretation that both seeks to become aware of the contours of its horizon and puts that horizon at stake in the course of interpretation can hope to overcome at least some degree of bias in the process. At the same time, because a historical source only becomes meaningful through the interpreter's own horizon, the goal of historical inquiry can never be to enter the horizon of one's sources, as the earlier hermeneutics of Schleiermacher sometimes appear to contend. Rather, success in interpretation produces a *tertium quid*, something that is

11 See Voegelin, "Equivalences of Experience" and Glenn Hughes' analysis of it in the present volume.

neither the historical horizon as it was lived out by historical subjects nor the contemporary horizon of the interpreter, but is rather a means of translating and articulating equivalences across horizons.[12]

Fred Lawrence has suggested that parallels between Voegelin's thought and Gadamer's are traceable to the profound influence of Plato's *Dialogues* on both of them. It is an influence, in both cases, shaped by Paul Friedländer's emphasis on the crucial role that the dramatic characterizations and action of the *Dialogues* plays in their philosophical purport. The Socratic element in Gadamer's hermeneutic theory is decisive.[13] Socratic ignorance is not a matter of knowing nothing, even if Socrates might occasionally make exaggerated claims to that effect. Socrates' accumulated insights actually constitute a very firm basis for his questioning and he could be quite stubborn in his convictions. What really constitutes the "ignorance" is the humility by which he is willing to put all of these convictions at stake in every conversation that he undertakes, even those where there is little reason to expect much wisdom from his interlocutor. Socrates understands that the normativity of inquiry can be nowhere but *within* inquiry, and that this normativity can function only by continually putting what seems obvious or settled to a new round of interrogation, adapting a debater's techniques of argument and refutation, no longer for the purpose of winning arguments and persuading audiences, but in a shared effort of seeking truth. The spirit of Platonic dialectic inspires the hermeneutic claim by Gadamer that normativity in historical inquiry derives from the ability to put one's horizon at stake rather than by ignoring one's horizon or pretending that one can step out of it and just see the facts as facts.

That Voegelin's philosophical hermeneutic has Platonic roots helps to explain the frequent returns to Plato in Voegelin's later writings. Certainly

12 Gadamer, *Truth and Method*, Part II.

13 Fred Lawrence, "Voegelin and Gadamer: Continental Philosophers Inspired by Plato and Aristotle," in *Eric Voegelin and the Continental Tradition: Explorations in Modern Political Thought*, ed. Lee Trepanier and Steven F. McGuire (Columbia, MO: University of Missouri Press, 2011), 192–217. See also Frederick G. Lawrence, "Voegelin and Theology as Hermeneutical and Political" in *Voegelin and the Theologian: Ten Studies in Interpretation*, ed. John Kirby and William M. Thompson (NY and Toronto: The Edwin Mellen Press, 1983), 314–55.

it is legitimate to read the spiritual outburst of Platonic thought as an event in time with a historical before and after. *Nous* (mind) becomes a unique means of articulating the primordial in-between of human existence, its finite but open orientation to the mysterious beginning and beyond of the cosmos. But the noetic differentiation of consciousness is also a permanent achievement, in that it may always serve as a framework through which one approaches the study of human meaning. As Voegelin increasingly understood that historical research is inevitably hermeneutical—as his analysis came to "move backward and forward and sideways"[14] through the hermeneutic circle—he appropriated more profoundly, one might say, the noetic nature of his own enterprise, and this reflection naturally moved him more deeply into the Platonic texts.

II. The Ecumenic Age as Configuration

"Configurations of History" strikes a Socratic tone from its very opening, where Voegelin announces, first, that the essay will not follow the usual pattern of defending a position and, second, that one should expect an author (his example is Toynbee) to change his views in the course of decades of research. The piece is indeed an exploratory one, challenging standard ways of approaching the "Age of Empires," and considering alternative interpretive approaches. A key matter at stake is what Voegelin has called "the problem of the object": the reasons for naming the historical period in question the "Age of Empires" is clear enough, given the number and staggering size of those that emerged across the Eurasian continent; but as to whether the category of "empire" or the distinctions among "civilizations" of the period are adequate categories is another question—and, not surprisingly, a hermeneutical one. It is in this connection that Voegelin draws on Jaspers' famous distinction of the "axis period" in human history—the period between the eighth and second century B.C. that saw the rise of "prophetism, Zoroastrianism, Taoism, Buddhism, and philosophy"—but draws on it less as an interpretive solution than as a way of framing the question at stake.[15] As an interpretive solution Jaspers' category comes up short (as Toynbee

14 Voegelin, *Ecumenic Age*, 106.
15 Voegelin, "Configurations," 101.

complained) in leaving out the spiritual contributions of Moses prior to the period and Jesus afterward. Still, it poses the interesting puzzle of the parallelism of development among seemingly unrelated parts of the world, and the even more important suggestion that the spiritual outbursts of the period are of at least as much significance as the conquests of peoples and territories that reshaped the demographic and cultural makeup of the world. The regular phenomenon of spiritual breakthrough within the context of imperial expansion convinced Voegelin that the two must be interpreted together, whether or not one chooses to posit a causality between the two. They are conjoined sufficiently often to form a pattern and this pattern provokes important interpretive considerations.

The pattern results not merely from the observations of the historian but from the self-interpretations of historical agents. One form of self-interpretation is the self-conception of the empires of the period as "ecumenic"—that is, as potentially encompassing the whole world or the whole of humanity, at least to the extent that such a whole could be imagined. A second form of self-interpretation is found in symbolisms of exodus, whether in movements seeking to find earthly territory free from oppression, or a temporal future of complete spiritual transformation, or a transcendent destiny (as in Augustine's Kingdom of God) toward which one moves through transformation of the inner life. A third is in the spiritual outbursts that articulate not only the normative situation of human existence in the cosmos but also guide the process of self-interpretation itself.

Here we have the elements for grasping what Voegelin means by the term "configuration," and for understanding the particular configuration he is identifying, in this article, for the purposes of *Order and History*'s program. The category of "empire" cannot by itself form the subject in question. The configuration is the complex of competing ideas and movements around a central symbolic problematic. At the core of the age is the symbolism of the ecumene, of a unified humanity. In this light Voegelin sums up the components of the dynamic succinctly: the age is one wherein

> (1) ecumenic empires were founded, (2) a theory of ecumenic empires was developed, and (3) it was realized that ecumenic

> empires were not the solution to organizing mankind as a unity.[16]

The configuration in question is the complex of these three elements, and since they cluster around aspirations for a unified humanity, Voegelin replaces the language of the "age of empires" with the term "ecumenic age."

If one can grant that these reflections by Voegelin are seeking an adequate way of questioning rather than defending a position, still one is likely to notice that Voegelin is very much pursuing a founding hypothesis of his major work: that the most legitimate forms of social order arise from the adequate symbolization of primary experiences of the existential situation of human life within the cosmic order. Ecumenic empires fail in an obvious way to unite humanity when they truncate the goal of the ecumene into the political control of people through the slaughter of many and the subjugation of the rest, but at the level of symbolism the flaw lies in the belief that the power to unite universally is within the power of human beings in the first place. Out of this folly the rise and fall of ecumenic empires is normally accompanied by the deceptive dream that the new empire will be the everlasting one. Voegelin offers as an early example the pseudepigraphic *Apocalypse of Daniel*, wherein a fifth empire is prophesied to follow the Assyrian, Persian, Greek, and Roman that would be the kingdom of God filling the entire Earth.[17] The model of an immanentized imperial salvation he finds repeated in many forms, including modern theories of history such as the aforementioned ones of Comte, Hegel, and Marx.

The spiritual outbursts that reveal the failings of empire represent the movement of exodus, Voegelin says, in the biblical sense. It is, for example, the movement of Moses that begins with insight into the potential community of the people of Israel; it is the movement of the heart identified by Augustine, where the love of God initiates an exodus out of Babylon

16 Voegelin, "Configurations," 98. See also Eric Voegelin, "World-Empire and the Unity of Mankind," (1962) in *Published Essays 1953-1965,* ed. Ellis Sandoz, *CWEV* Vol. 11, 2000, 134–55. Hereafter cited as Voegelin, "World-Empire." See also *Ecumenic Age*, Ch. 4 and the "Editor's Introduction" to the volume by Michael Franz.

17 Voegelin, "Configurations," 102.

and toward the City of God.[18] In such movement there is a productive tension between the old order and the new insight out of which critique and reform may emerge; but the effort may fail, may be blunted by fantasies that locate the terminus of the exodus in an objective period in the future or (in the Gnostic variation) to a spiritual realm utterly beyond the world. Objectifications of this sort repeat the imperial error of valuing only the ultimate goal and not the productive tension with which one lives with the vision of ordered reality in a disordered world.

On the subject of empire one might say that Voegelin's "World-Empire and the Unity of Mankind" is more systematic in its treatment of the symbols than "Configurations of History," and *The Ecumenic Age* is far more complete, but "Configurations" uniquely allows us to see how the term "configurations" grows out of hermeneutic reflections that accompany the historical task at hand. The category of "configuration" goes "beyond causality"[19] in that it identifies relations of symbols that evoke questions about those symbols, rather than asserting that one symbol will invariably cause another. The type of analysis that centers on configurations permits hermeneutic reflection to enter at any point of the process, which is what not only explains but also justifies the backward-forward-sideways analytic style of Voegelin's late writing.

III. Ontological Philosophy of History

As "Configurations of History" opened curiously, with the author's forfeit of any defense of a position, so it ends curiously, with the author questioning the sense of his essay's title. The term "configurations of history," Voegelin now suspects, might imply (in the manner of Aristotelian metaphysics) that history is a kind of matter that receives the formal causality of configurations. But it would be more accurate to say that history is nothing other than its configurations. Because it only exists to the extent that it is intelligible, its reality is entirely relational. The positing of a material substrate need make no difference to the actual conduct of historical study.[20]

18 Voegelin, "Configurations," 105–6.
19 Voegelin, "World-Empire," 136.
20 Voegelin, "Configurations," 113.

In light of this insight Voegelin rejects standard conceptions regarding the question as to the subject of history. The subject cannot be individual human beings because history's patterns are patterns of human relations; it cannot be single societies because there exist multiple societies; it cannot be civilizations because one must also account for the forces that work against the perpetuation of any given civilization; it cannot be mankind as a whole because that is a concept that grows out of a particular period of history.[21] All of these answers are looking for a substrate that would underlie the relations of history as Aristotelian matter underlies Aristotelian form, a search that is not only unnecessary but distorting if the nature of history is, in truth, entirely relational.

Voegelin's odd-sounding alternative is to say that "Being itself" is the subject of history.[22] "Being" is a word to which are attached many ancient puzzles. Being is not *a* being, obviously, because it must function as that by which any being *is*. One might want to say that it is the totality of beings, but to that one would have add all of the relations among beings, both actual and possible—and still being would not be identical with these, for it would again transcend them as that by which all of this intelligibility can come to exist. Forms of the word "being," such as "is" and "was," can behave like predicates, but in a manner unlike any other kinds of predicates. Being is not a quality like "green" or "obstreperous" because these define the object particularly whereas being applies to everything about the object. Being is not a highest genus because it does not determine the nature of things but simply that they—whatever their natures might be—exist. Being is the most familiar of notions, in that one can question at all only because one exists among things that exist; but it is the most mysterious of notions in that the intelligibility of all that is quickly outstrips human powers of comprehension. Being would seem to transcend space and time inasmuch as both of these are said to exist; space and time rely, like all other qualities, upon being for their existence; they participate in being rather than being participating in them. Being may seem like the most abstract and empty of concepts when one takes it simply as a concept, but as the actuality of actual things one might say that so far from being abstract it is concreteness itself.

21 Ibid.
22 Ibid.

The notion of being, then, has been central to Western philosophy for both its obviousness and obscurity. At one time ontology was considered a field within metaphysics, the field specializing in the most general metaphysical category of all; but in twentieth-century Continental thought it came to be used as a kind of foil for metaphysics. A metaphysics, for example, that attempts to put the whole of reality in a set of logical categories ignores the fact that being transcends what we know of it through logic or through any other means. As the notion of being always straddles the known and the unknown, ontology must remain, as it seems to have been for Plato, an open-ended form of thinking, anticipating changes in thought that might undermine seemingly conclusive ways of categorizing reality, oriented to the circumstances of human knowing and unknowing—or, in Voegelin's appropriation of Platonic terminology, the *metaxy*.[23]

The idea that time is within being rather than being within time forms a central theme in the meditations by which Voegelin moved more deeply, over the course of his career, into an ontological philosophy of history—or, we might say (invoking Gadamerian language), his philosophical hermeneutics came to be more fully grounded in hermeneutic ontology. Eventually Voegelin became frustrated with the dominance of the timeline in the interpretation of history, and the language of "vertical" and "horizontal" dimensions of history that one finds in "Configurations" and related writings reflects his efforts to break free of this domination. To the extent that meaning emerges in history it is less significantly a progression along a timeline than the waxing and waning of "being becoming luminous to its truth," i.e., the experience of being as both immanent and transcendent, both known and unknown, revealed in the conscious tension of existence. Being encompasses both the historian and his or her subjects of study, so that to say that the ultimate subject of history is being is to summon the historian to the very limits of every kind of thinking, including the philosophical. To be a

23 See Voegelin, "Equivalence of Experience," 119–23; Eric Voegelin, "Reason: The Classic Experience," in *Published Essays 1966-1985*, ed. Ellis Sandoz, *CWEV* Vol. 12, 1990, 265–91. See also William Petropulos' discussion of this piece in the present volume, and David J. Walsh, "Philosophy in Voegelin's Work," in Ellis Sandoz, ed. *Eric Voegelin's Thought: A Critical Appraisal* (Durham, NC: Duke University Press, 1982), 135–56.

historian in the fullest sense is to be also a philosopher engaged with the thinking of being.

To put the point in Gadamerian terms, philosophical hermeneutics is a result of the existential situation of human consciousness within being. The understanding of another horizon requires the appropriation of one's own because both horizons are within being—being that is both known and unknown. The Gadamerian and Voegelinian approaches to the unknown of being are different, but this is a philosophical disagreement within their agreement that history and hermeneutics must be ontological. Gadamer insists that human consciousness is so thoroughly bound by its temporal nature that any talk of eternity must be called speculative in the pejorative sense, and this is most likely how he would characterize *Order and History*—as a speculative Platonic-Christian interpretation of history. Where Voegelin sees, for example, the Augustinian symbolism of the city of God as an articulation of the tension of existence, Gadamer would regard it as resolving that tension in a presumed knowledge of the beyond. Voegelin, for his part, would have to consider paradoxical and obscurantist the demand that one think being beyond subjectivity while yet doing so entirely within the confines of finitude.[24] For Voegelin, if being transcends human finitude, that transcendence becomes a pole in the tension of existence, a tension that may certainly be lost by treating the beyond as knowable, but equally by failing to allow symbols of transcendence to influence the tension in an active way. Symbols of the beyond are not speculative to the extent that they express the tension rather than asserting knowledge, and the assertion that only the immanent can be known constitutes an assertion of knowledge just as suspect, for Voegelin, as the speculative. The disagreement here, again, is a philosophical one, and part of the importance of noting the hermeneutic theory at the heart of "Configurations of History" is to show that the disagreement is indeed grounded in philosophy rather than resulting from hermeneutic naiveté on the part of Voegelin.

24 Cf. Lawrence, "Voegelin and Gadamer," 209–12; and Jürgen Gebhardt, "The Vocation of the Scholar," in *International and Interdisciplinary Perspectives on Eric Voegelin*, ed. Stephen A. McKnight and Geoffrey L. Price (Columbia, MO: University of Missouri Press, 1997), 29–30.

"Configurations of History," then, though relatively brief and transitional among the works in Voegelin's later corpus, can be read as a distinctive contribution to historical study, to historiography, and to ontology. To all three types of contribution it brings hermeneutical reflection that transforms the work of those fields even as it draws them together into a single movement of thinking. To emphasize the hermeneutic dimension in the essay can help to highlight the hermeneutic sophistication of Voegelin's late work, a sophistication that is insufficiently appreciated among thinkers and scholars beyond the circle of Voegelin specialists.

–5–

Voegelin's "Equivalences of Experience and Symbolization in History"

Glenn Hughes

"Equivalences of Experience and Symbolization in History" (1971)[1] is one of Eric Voegelin's six most important stand-alone essays, along with "Immortality: Experience and Symbol" (1967), "The Gospel and Culture" (1971), "Reason: The Classic Experience" (1974), "The Beginning and the Beyond: A Meditation on Truth" (written 1974–77), and "Wisdom and the Magic of the Extreme: A Meditation" (1983). It is a writing with relatively few textual references, consisting almost exclusively of a sustained exegesis of the nature and structure of human consciousness in history. Despite its being the briefest of these essays, "Equivalences" addresses questions about so many issues central to philosophy—concerning experience, language and symbols, truth, reality, values, divine being, history, and the structure of consciousness and its historical development—that a proper exposition and "reader's guide" to the essay would have to extend to the length of a book, and not a short book at that.

In what follows, I will illuminate the argumentative trajectory of Voegelin's essay, and identify most of the concerns propelling it, by bringing all exposition to bear on one of its crucial themes: the notion of a cosmic "depth." For Voegelin, the "depth of the cosmos"—or what he also calls "the underlying oneness of reality"—is an elementary fact; further, it is a fact that requires of and for each of us adequate expression, or "symbolization," if we are to successfully orient ourselves in existence.

1 Eric Voegelin, "Equivalences of Experience and Symbolization in History," in *Published Essays 1966-1985*, ed. Ellis Sandoz, *CWEV* Vol. 12, 1990, 115–33. Hereafter cited as Voegelin, "Equivalences."

After following Voegelin's own exploration of this theme to the final soundings of his essay, I will advance some considerations of my own prompted by his conclusions. First, I will elaborate on Voegelin's indicating that symbols of the cosmic depth may be *more adequate or less adequate* to the reality of this depth in light of modern, differentiated experiences and insights—and thus, we may conclude, in certain cases will be found philosophically wanting. Second, continuing to elaborate the same point from another angle, I will suggest that one symbol of the depth that *is fully adequate* to modern, differentiated experiences of reality is the symbol *Love*—a symbol that can play a crucial role in our being confident that there are knowable constants of existential truth, and that our striving to "live in truth" is meaningful.

I

I will begin with a few comments about the first word in the title of Voegelin's essay—about what the word "equivalences" means and implies.

To affirm that two or more words, symbols, experiences, or events are "equivalent" to each other is to say that they share an identity in meaning or function, derived from their relationship to an underlying "sameness" of meaning or truth which must be one and constant if the notion of "equivalence" is to be valid. Only the assumption of such an underlying "sameness," as Voegelin writes at the start of his essay, "justifies the language of 'equivalences' . . ."[2] For example, to say that the words *destruction* and *ruination* can function as equivalent terms means that they both may be understood to represent the same experience or idea which makes the two words effectively equal in meaning and import. For another example: to state that the purpose of *haruspication* is equivalent to the purpose of *scrying* is to affirm that there is a constancy and sameness of meaning defining the aim of each activity—which is the aim of foretelling what is yet to come, enabling prediction of future events. The notion of equivalent symbols, then, depends upon an underlying reality of a constant of meaning that validates recognizing them as equivalent expressions of it.

Now, Voegelin's principal aim in this essay is to determine the location,

2 Voegelin, "Equivalences," 115.

so to speak, of the unchanging constants of *truth* that would justify the assertion that different, and historically differentiating, symbolizations of significant truths about existence, reality, history, society, the world, or divine being, are "equivalent," even if some articulations are superior to others in representing a more refined or more differentiated understanding of a particular truth. Voegelin's concern, as usual, is with the most important symbolizations of truths about what it means to be a human being, and about the nature and order of reality, as these have emerged in the historical unfolding of the human search for knowledge. These most-important symbolizations of truth have all derived from human *seeking*; so, to describe his *own* search for an understanding of how human seeking has historically brought forth symbolizations of truth among which the philosopher can discern genuine equivalences of meaning, Voegelin refers to his investigation here as a "search of the search." This, he goes on to explain, will consist of an effort to grasp the nature of what is *constant* in both the human search for order and a few of its more notable results. It results, as we shall see, in Voegelin's explaining as carefully as possible that we may *reasonably affirm* that there are differing, equivalent symbolizations of key truths concerning existence and reality because we can *reasonably affirm* that, underlying those symbolizations, there are indeed constants of meaning.

An accurate and nuanced understanding of Voegelin's investigation in this essay is not easy to achieve. In part this is because "Equivalences" is, like a number of Voegelin's late essays, a "meditation." That is: it is not a systematic analysis and presentation of the meaning of one or more texts or events in political or cultural affairs, nor is it about problems of logic or formal structures of rational analysis. Rather, it is a personal effort on the part of the philosopher to re-enact and reconstruct in his own consciousness certain experiences in which crucial philosophical symbols or articulations of truth emerged in the psyches of earlier thinkers, and at the same time to encounter and follow the lead of question after question relevant to consciousness's understanding of itself and its participation in reality as these arise in the course of the re-enactive meditation. The purpose of such a meditation is thus both to arrive at a more discerning understanding of how certain key philosophical insights and articulations have come into historical being, and also to introduce *new insights and formulations* that carry the understanding of a complex of philosophical insights a stage further, as the philosopher's consciousness suffers clarification and differentiation, within itself, of the matters under investigation.

Because such a meditation uncovers new aspects of the subject under investigation, as it proceeds it alters the landscape of the problematic in such a way that fresh and original questions arise; the journey of thought moves in unexpected directions due to new insights; themes already touched on in the meditation are revisited, as new insights retrospectively adjust meanings and implications; and a continual revising of thoughts take place due to the meditation's advances in discovery and clarification. The written work resulting from such a meditation thus has the character of an adventure in self-illuminative thought, rather than the character of a philosophical essay that systematically explains the meaning and implications of a text or other "external" data. Voegelin calls this written work a "meditative exegesis," to distinguish it from anything like a "textual exegesis."[3] And due to its character as a journey of thought that undergoes in its course recurrent adjustments of understanding, expression, and focus, the work should be approached as being written from what the philosopher Bernard Lonergan calls "a moving viewpoint," in that some questions and assertions introduced earlier in the piece, because of later insights and viewpoints, require re-contextualization and re-formulation, sometimes with the later formulations contrasting with—or even seeming to contradict—earlier formulations.[4]

The reader of such a work, then, must be willing to do her best to follow the philosopher's meditation, re-enacting in her own consciousness the

3 For Voegelin's account of his analysis in this essay as a "meditative exegesis," see "Equivalences," 131.

4 "[A philosophical work] may be written from a moving viewpoint, and then it will contain, not a single set of coherent statements, but a sequence of related sets of coherent statements. . . . It cannot begin by presupposing that a reader can assimilate at a stroke what can be attained only at the term of a prolonged and arduous effort. On the contrary, it must begin from a minimal viewpoint and a minimal context; it will exploit that minimum to raise a further question that enlarges the viewpoint and the context; it will proceed from the enlarged viewpoint and context only as long as is necessary to raise still deeper issues that again transform the basis and the terms of reference of the inquiry . . . ." Bernard Lonergan, *Insight: A Study of Human Understanding*, Vol. 3 of *The Collected Works of Bernard Lonergan*, ed. Frederick E. Crowe and Robert M. Doran (Toronto: University of Toronto Press, 1992), 18; see 18–20.

questions, insights, and discoveries that make up the meditation, and moving along with—and not becoming unnerved or confused by—the moving viewpoint of the meditation as it proceeds on its journey.

For example, in the second paragraph of his essay, Voegelin explains that if "symbolizations" of experiences may be truly said to be "equivalent," the theoretical implication is that there are "constants of engendering experience" underlying such symbolizations, and that these constants must be the "true subject matter of our studies."[5] But later, on the basis of meditative developments, he concludes that it is a theoretical "fallacy" to consider any "engendering experiences" to be themselves "constants," and that it is philosophically necessary to "speak of the equivalence not only of symbols, but of experiences as well."[6] Again, early in the essay, Voegelin asserts that what "is constant in the history of mankind . . . is the structure of existence itself"—that is, the structure of each person as a seeker of truths about existence and reality.[7] But later, toward the end of the essay, Voegelin states firmly that "[t]here is *no constant to be found in history*, because the historical field of equivalents is not *given* as a collective of phenomena which could be submitted to the procedures of abstraction and generalization."[8] That is, no one can validly claim to possess the truth of a constant regarding "the structure of existence" on the basis of having had *empirical experiences* of the consciousnesses of all persons in history. Thus, it can seem to the reader who is not following the essay precisely *as* a meditation, and consequently not attempting to re-enact in her own consciousness the philosopher's meditative journey, that Voegelin corrects himself along the way to the point of self-contradiction, and that the essay as a whole may finally be a muddle. After all, either there are "constants of engendering experience" or there are not; and either there is a "constant in the history of mankind" or there is not.

And yet, to the attentive and careful reader, Voegelin's assertions, as the meditation proceeds, each make sense in their context; this moving context constitutes the genuine adventure of the essay; and Voegelin's conclusion

5 Voegelin, "Equivalences," 115.
6 Ibid., 123.
7 Ibid., 120.
8 Ibid., 131 (emphasis added).

to his inquiry into the constants that *must* exist if the language of equivalent symbolizations in history is to be justified may be summarized as follows: It is indeed the case that there are no constants or absolute truths in history that can be *empirically,* or *experientially*, verified; but, nevertheless, we are justified in affirming the truth, and the equivalence, of important philosophical symbols and propositions concerning existence and reality, because we can be confident that they are indeed founded upon constant or absolute truths *that lie beyond our empirical experience.* The meditative exegesis is finally concerned, then, with the precise nature and character of this reasonable confidence—this "trust" or "faith," as Voegelin calls it—that we may have in a constancy of truth beyond experience itself.

II

This much established, a few more comments about the essay as a whole should be made before following the path of those elements in Voegelin's meditation that lead to its key theme of "symbols of the depth."

Hans-Georg Gadamer has emphasized that, in interpreting an important text, the reader must try to understand as far as possible the author's *horizon of questions and concerns* that motivated the writing of the text. It will be useful to identify two of the principal concerns that drive Voegelin's meditative journey in "Equivalences." Both of these derive from his being a philosopher living and writing in the middle of the twentieth century, and both of them are mentioned in the text—but not mentioned in such a way that their overriding importance for Voegelin's engagement in this particular meditation is highlighted.

The first concern pertains to the rise of historical consciousness in modern centuries—the increasing cultural and intellectual focus on human *historicity*, or historical-situatedness, and a consequent deepening preoccupation with all of the implications of historicity for properly understanding the nature of language, social institutions, cultural insights and artifacts, self-interpretations, and truth-claims—especially truth-claims pertaining to moral, legal, and religious matters. One consequence of this focus and preoccupation has been particularly problematic. During the nineteenth century and after, the growing emphasis on historicity has led, in some intellectual, academic, and cultural circles, to its "absolutizing" in doctrines of *historicism*—that is, doctrines claiming that a human being is only and completely a historical or history-bound creature, with no element or dimension of a person's being or consciousness transcending the material, temporal, and cultural conditions of existence. In Voegelin's language, in the view of such historicist doctrines, a person is a purely "*world-immanent*" being.[9] A purely world-immanent being could have no access to any truth that transcends the physical, biological, biographical, cultural, and linguistic circumstances and conditioning factors of her existence, and in such a case all understanding of truth could only be historically relative. From the historicist perspective, no one could validly argue that any recognition of a genuine good or value, or any insight into how life should properly be lived, or any articulations or symbolizations concerning the order of reality or existence, is a truth that holds constant across the boundaries of cultures, languages, and epochs. Needless to say, this view of human existence is, for Voegelin, misleading and dangerous. And "Equivalences" is, in fact, both his most sustained meditation on historicity and at the same time his most deeply-elucidated rebuttal of historicism's claim that we cannot know transhistorical truths. Or, to put it another way, it is Voegelin's most sustained philosophical defense—in response to the challenge of historicism—of the view that the human search for enduring truths about existence and reality is not, and has never been, an unfounded and vain enterprise. Voegelin himself describes this elemental purpose of "Equivalences" in a somewhat casual sentence, whose importance the reader could easily overlook, at the end of the essay's brief introduction, where he writes: "The following reflections intend to clarify, as far as that is possible within the limits of a paper, the principal problems of the new historical consciousness."[10]

A second concern that propels Voegelin's meditation is one familiar to his regular readers: the delusion and harm caused, over the known centuries of history, by the confidence on the part of a leader and his followers, a thinker and his acolytes, or a powerful group or institution and its members or believers, that they alone possess the *absolute and final truth* about the

9 See, for example, Eric Voegelin, "The Drama of Humanity," (1967) in *The Drama of Humanity and Other Miscellaneous Papers 1939-1985,* ed. William Petropulos and Gilbert Weiss, *CWEV* Vol. 33, 174–75.

10 Voegelin, "Equivalences," 116.

meaning of human existence, the nature and order of reality, the factors determining the worth of individuals and the ultimate outcome of individual destinies, the purpose and goal of history, the right order of political life, the manner in which people should live, and which specific set of values and traditions should be revered by all people of all times as humankind's highest moral and cultural achievement. The conviction that *final knowledge of ultimate truths* has been attained and is possessed by the privileged, Voegelin argues, leads their presumed possessors into deluded viewpoints and degraded existential postures, which undermine the ability to make headway in the unending struggle against existence in untruth, and tends also toward the promotion, more or less active, of social and political disorder. In its most destructive manifestation, it is a delusion that leads to the use of force to punish or even kill those whose lives and convictions clash with the dictates or precepts derived from the "ultimate knowledge" of its presumptive possessors.

In modern centuries, the impact of doctrines and zealous activities on the part of self-proclaimed possessors of ultimate and final truth have become existentially and physically destructive on a scale much larger than earlier in history. This is due partly to technological advances (in communications, transportation, weaponry, etc.), and partly to the emergence of ideologies built on world-immanent interpretations of existence and history that view the necessary goal of historical process as both 1) known absolutely, and 2) dependent for its realization upon the concerted activities of the "possessors of ultimate truth" to force non-believers either to conform to the doctrine's vision or be put out of the way. Voegelin, who narrowly escaped Nazi arrest and almost certain internment, spent much of his energies as a political philosopher (and philosopher of history) analyzing the origins, character, and meaning of modern secular political ideologies and regimes founded on the presumed possession of ultimate truths and values, and of modern theoretical and philosophical systems, such as those of Hegel and Marx, that claimed also to have attained a "final" and "absolute" knowledge of ultimate truths and values. There is no doubt that a key passion guiding the meditation of "Equivalences" is Voegelin's abhorrence and rejection of all human claims to possess knowledge of ultimate truths about the final whys and wherefores of existence, about the final purpose and goal of history, and about what reality as a whole finally is. It is an abhorrence that finds articulation a few times in the essay, beginning in section I, which diagnoses the specific "deformation" of human thought and existence involved when persons believe that *ultimate truth* can be summarized and possessed in a fixed doctrine composed of true propositions. But it is most clearly and forcefully stated in a sentence near the start of section II, where Voegelin flatly states: "Ultimate doctrines, systems, and values are phantasmata engendered by deformed existence."[11]

Now, Voegelin's acceptance of the "new historical consciousness," with its emphasis on the historical situatedness of human experiences and utterances, on the one hand, and his rejection of the idea that human beings can possess ultimate truths about such matters as the purpose of existence and history's outcome, on the other hand, are fully compatible philosophically—and compatible with the view of any historicist, as well, who would instantly agree with Voegelin both that all human experiences and formulated understandings are historically situated and that ultimate doctrines, systems, and values are "phantasmata." But then Voegelin would also argue that these positions may and must be embraced without succumbing to the outlook of *historicism*. In other words, Voegelin accepts human historicity while rejecting historicism's argument that we cannot claim knowledge of *any* trans-historical truths. Voegelin argues that, in fact, we *can* be confident in our knowledge of many fundamental, permanent truths about human nature, about the right order of existence, and about the structure of reality, even while we must acknowledge that these do not constitute a possession of final or ultimate answers regarding the meaning of human existence, the purpose and goal of history, or why there is a reality at all.

As already mentioned, the path of Voegelin's meditative journey leads to the reasons *why* a philosopher may confidently claim to have knowledge of certain "constants" concerning existence and reality, as well as why *the precise nature of our relationship with these constants* leaves us, as humans, still and forever engaged in the ongoing search for a deepening understanding of how to order our individual and social lives; of history's structure and direction; and of the order of reality as a whole. So let us now move through the stages of Voegelin's meditation and examine the *basis* of these conclusions of Voegelin—an examination that will entail addressing the

11 Ibid., 120.

human need for "symbols of the depth" of reality for our proper philosophical and existential orientation.

III

Voegelin begins his essay by explaining that the search for constants of truth about human order in society and history will not be found at the level of symbols, that is, in spoken or written words or other expressions of meaning. The historical process of the human search for order throws up successive symbolizations (formulations) of truth; symbolizations emerge that are superior in their complexity and differentiation to earlier symbolizations; but at the level of expression or formulation or proposition, truth is multiform, adaptational, shifting, unstable. There is no one absolute symbolization of any important truth, only "equivalent" symbolizations of significant truths. Thus, the person who wants possession of a constant truth about human order will not find it in any particular set of propositions, or a written catalogue of permanent values, or in any doctrine, religious or secular, concerning the meaning of existence or history.

We are tempted to look, then, to the experiences that have given rise to, "engendered," the varying and equivalent symbolizations for what is "constant" in human discoveries about truths concerning existence and reality: we may hope, that is, to find *experiential constants* of truth. For example, the Chinese symbol of the *Tao* and the Upanishadic symbol of *Brahman* may well be understood as equivalent symbolizations of a truth that, "beyond" the world intrinsically conditioned by space and time, there is a transcendent and ultimate reality, unconditioned by space and time, which is more real and more enduring than worldly reality. One may be ready to affirm that, not the symbols, obviously, but the *experiences* that gave rise to them are the same—are a constant—to be found wherever and whenever a person undergoes the experience producing the insight expressed in the affirmation of such a transcendent reality.

But this, Voegelin explains, would be a theoretical error, for two reasons. First, human experiences, like human symbolizations, are part of a reality that is continually in process, continually in movement, so that each human experience is a *distinct and different involvement* in the movement of a consciousness participating in the process of reality, and is thus not the "same" as any other. Every experience is that of a distinct person, of reality becoming luminous for an experience at the emergent site of that particular consciousness, and each such experience has a unique position in the movement of the historical process; each is historically conditioned and distinct from any other.

Second—and unlike the former point, this is a point Voegelin emphasizes—it is theoretically untenable to separate an *experience of truth* from the *symbolization of the truth* of that experience. This is because there is no human experience of "truth" without both *an act of understanding that grasps the meaning* of that experience and *some inward or outwardly expressed formulation of that meaning* in some type of symbolization. Therefore an "experience of truth" is always an experience-understanding-and-symbolization of truth. Experience-understanding-symbolization—the hyphenated complex is my own linguistic formula, not Voegelin's, but it clarifies his point—is an inseparable unit *insofar as any discovery or emergence of truth* is concerned, such that to separate out "experience" from that complex is a misleading hypostatization.[12] If we were to assert that some type of *experience* that has engendered important "equivalent" symbols of truth is itself a constant, then we will have fallen into the trap of ignoring the indivisible unity of the complex experience-understanding-symbolization with respect to human discoveries of truth. As Voegelin explains: "[The supposedly] constant experience, in order to be *identified*, would have to become *articulate*, and once it has been articulated the result would be a *symbolism* claiming to be exempt from the fate of being one more historically equivalent truth."[13]

Voegelin sums up the preceding points by saying that what "we call *experiences*, as well as the *symbols* engendered by them, are part of reality *in process*," and in consequence he concludes that "we must *extend the differences* of the symbols [concerning important truths] *into the engendering*

12 Such an error is analogous to thinking of "transcendence" as a reality that is apprehended in some way other than in its interpenetration or fusion with immanent reality in conscious existence in the *metaxy*, the in-between of immanence and transcendence that is the ontological condition and ambience of *all* human consciousness and experience—a mode of thinking that unwarrantedly hypostatizes "transcendence."

13 Voegelin, "Equivalences," 123 (emphasis added).

experiences and, consequently, speak of the *equivalence not only of symbols, but of experiences as well.*"[14] Bernard Lonergan has put this point, which essentially concerns the historicity of human truth, in a striking way by curtly stating: "concepts have dates." That is, every human act of insight, and every idea resulting from it, and every articulation of that idea, occurs at some moment in the historical process; and it is both false and futile to claim that any insight, concept, or doctrine has entered consciousness from beyond the historically-embedded activities of human consciousness. The person who claims to possess knowledge of a truth that has not been uncovered through historically situated human experience, language, and interpretation is simply ignoring human historicity, i.e., the temporally-conditioned and situation-specific character of human existence with respect to any experience, discovery, and articulation of truth.

Where does this leave us, then, in the search for *constants* of human order in society and history, in the light of whose truth we attempt to orient our lives in confidence that we are moving in the direction of living more well-ordered and less deformed existences? It leaves us looking for some *level of reality* that is more enduring and profound than the historically conditioned variables of experiences and symbolizations. And any claim that humans can attain *any* knowledge of genuinely enduring truths about existence and reality depends on our discovering such a level of reality; for, as we recall, the language of "equivalent truths," whether applied to symbolizations or to experiences, requires for its validity an *underlying sameness or constancy of truth* with respect to which the experiences and symbols may be understood to be related *as* equivalents. As Voegelin writes at this point in his meditation: "The constant that will justify the language of equivalent experiences and symbols must be sought on a level *deeper* than the level of equivalent experiences which engender equivalent symbols."[15]

We are searching, then, for a reality that in some sense can be understood to "underlie" all human experiences of what Voegelin calls "the primordial field of reality [consisting of the community of] God and man, world and society";[16] all experiences of existential tension; and all experiences

14 Ibid., 121, 123 (emphasis added).
15 Ibid., 123–24 (emphasis added).
16 Ibid., 126.

of participation. And indeed, Voegelin writes, such a reality has long been philosophically identified: it is the "depth" from which consciousness experiences itself as emerging into illuminated, self-aware questioning and understanding. It is that dimension of the human psyche, Voegelin explains, that lies "below" conscious experience and from which, through inward exploration and meditation, "new truth[s] of reality can be hauled up to conscious experience," but which *in itself*, as the "depth" of the soul or psyche, always remains "beyond articulate experience."[17] This "depth of the soul," which has been symbolized since the time of the Hellenic philosophers as a *boundless extension of the psyche into the depth of reality*, is understood to have ontological continuity with consciousness—to be reality of the "same nature as the reality of consciousness"—but to which one cannot validly attribute any "substantive content," since any psychic depth that has come to light in conscious experience as images, insights, or symbols, no longer belongs to the psyche's "depth" but to consciousness.[18] As Voegelin explains:

> We experience psyche as consciousness that can descend into the depth of its own reality, and the depth of the psyche as reality that can rise to consciousness, but we do not experience a content of the depth other than the content that has entered consciousness.[19]

The content of the "depth" that *remains* below consciousness remains unfathomable, because it is by definition not experienced. Therefore, we cannot validly attribute to a person's *experience* of the depth of the psyche any truth-content that would constitute a permanent or constant truth of meaning that underlies the historical field of experiences and symbolizations. Every *experience* of the depth of the psyche, of the boundary-area where depth and consciousness meet as self-exploration succeeds in bringing new images, insights, or symbols into the light of conscious experience,

17 Ibid., 124.
18 Ibid., 124, 126.
19 Ibid., 126. It should be noted that such a "depth" of psyche or consciousness (or "self") has also been symbolized in Eastern thought since the time of early Buddhist and Upanishadic writings.

is personal, and governed by historical conditions; in other words, there is no such thing, Voegelin writes, as an "autonomous depth" *experienced*, but "only a [specific] consciousness in continuity with its own depth."[20] Therefore the search for a constant of truth that would justify the language of "equivalent symbolizations of the truth" must be extended even beyond *experiences* of the depth. The search for a constant *in the history of experiences and symbolizations* has ended in failure: "There is no constant to be found in history . . .," Voegelin concludes.[21]

But Voegelin's meditative search for constants of absolute truth has not, in fact, reached a dead end. For while the search has found no constant *in history*, it has disclosed a depth of reality below consciousness and history, a depth that is not *merely* an "individual" depth, restricted as a localized continuation of this or that specific consciousness, but rather to be identified also as *the one depth underlying all reality experienced in the primordial field of God and man, world and society*. For when a person asks, what kind of reality "is touched when man descends into the depth of his psyche," Voegelin writes, he will recognize that, since truths brought up from its depth affect his understanding of the field of partners as a whole, this depth cannot be identified with any one of these partners in the community of experienced being including himself, "man," but only with "the underlying reality that *makes them* partners in a common order, *i.e.*, with the substance of the Cosmos."[22] That is: the depth underlying consciousness is the one depth of "substance" underlying *all* experienceable realities. To grasp why this must be so, it is crucial to remember that every human consciousness is ontologically *a mode of participation in the process of reality as a whole*—a "site" in the process of reality where this becomes consciously luminous; thus, the depth from which the consciousness of one partner emerges (a "man") can *only* be the depth of reality as a whole. And because it is contrary to reason to imagine there being a "depth below depth in infinite regress," this depth must be understood as the "underlying oneness of reality" that gives reality *as humanly experienced* its coherence, order, and intelligibility, and also such constancies of structure as are repeatedly and universally

20 Voegelin, "Equivalences," 129.
21 Ibid., 131.
22 Ibid., 126 (emphasis added).

experienced in the historical field—constancies such as the unvarying four partners in the primordial community of being (God and man, world and society), and the human universality of the search for meaning and order.[23]

It is important to note this is not a claim that we have *experiential access* to this "substance" *as* a oneness that underlies all reality experienced. In clarifying this point, Voegelin takes care to explain both the genesis of symbols that express this "underlying oneness," and the status of all such symbols.

The genesis of such symbols Voegelin describes as follows. First, there is the experience by consciousness of "touching" and "descending into" its own depth, which we understand can only be, also, the depth of reality as a whole. Second, symbols emerge, or are chosen, to signify the underlying oneness of reality through *bringing together insights* arising from 1) this experience of the depth of the psyche, and 2) experiences of the entirety of the primordial field of God and man, world and society. Once *both* types of experience have been undergone and understood, the consequence is that through an act of "imaginative fusion" symbols are created that trustingly unite *the experience of depth* with *experiences of the primordial field of reality*. That is, such symbols representing an "underlying oneness of reality" are generated through *trusting* that all the discrete intelligibilities experienced in the primordial field are grounded in an ultimate metaphysical oneness—which is also a trust that reality as a whole is *fully intelligible*, absent which fact human experiences of "cosmic order" would be grossly deluding, and the human *search* for order, which is existentially predicated on the assumption that reality is in the end fully intelligible, would be unfounded and finally meaningless.[24]

As to the status of imaginative symbols of this underlying oneness or "depth," Voegelin is clear on the point that they have the status of "myth"—that they are the creative product of mythopoetic imagination. As we shall see, symbols of the depth are a type of mythic symbol that differentiated

23 Ibid., 127, 129.

24 Voegelin makes clear that, in Hellenic thought, the emergence of the symbol of a "psyche" that has "depth" runs parallel to the emergence of the symbol "cosmos" as a symbol of the underlying oneness of reality. See "Equivalences," 127–28.

consciousness cannot do without; and the most important of them all, Voegelin points out, is the symbol *Cosmos* itself, through which was first expressed, by Hellenic thinkers, reality's ultimate oneness, intelligibility, coherence, lastingness, and constancy of structure.

So here we find, at last, the source of justification for the affirmation of equivalences of symbolized truth: the constancy of truth that cannot be found in the history of experience may be assumed, in trust and faith, to be "located" in the "depth of the cosmos," in the underlying oneness whose ultimate coherence, intelligibility, and constancy of structure are the guarantee for the truth of the equivalent experiences and symbolizations that appear, and differentiate, in the historical drama of human consciousness. Therefore the human search for truth—for significant and enduring truths about society and history, about existence and world, about consciousness and God—*does* make sense; and we *can* be confident that such important truths as we arrive at, verified by their recurrent discovery through the millennia of history, are not transient ephemera without trans-historical significance, as a radical historicist would argue. Voegelin's conclusion, at the end of his meditation, is that the "search for truth makes sense *only under the assumption* that the truth brought up from the depth of his psyche by man, though it is not the *ultimate* truth of reality [which, as historically conditioned, it could never be], is *representative* of the truth in the divine depth of the Cosmos." In other words, a truth expressed by different but equivalent symbols that has been discovered, across cultures and in the historical course of differentiation, to consistently illuminate existence and reality, may rightly be trusted, Voegelin says, to be "representative of a truth that is more than equivalent."[25]

It is significant, and worthy of our close attention, that Voegelin in the last paragraph of his essay (quoted above) suddenly refers to the underlying oneness of reality as the "*divine* depth of the Cosmos." For what occurred historically when the experience of psychic depth was united with experiences of the primordial field to create, through imaginative fusion, symbols articulating an underlying oneness of reality—an historical development of experience and symbolization that Voegelin has re-enacted in his meditation—was that the *traditional mythological account* of the divine within

25 Voegelin, "Equivalences," 133 (emphasis added).

cosmic reality, represented by a plurality of gods and goddesses, nature-divinities, and multivarious minor deities and numinous presences, was replaced by a *philosophical mythological account* of the divine within cosmic reality as the "underlying oneness" of the cosmos. In Voegelin's rather compact words: "The depth of the psyche is . . . the quite authentic understanding of divinity present in the order of the cosmos peculiar to the philosophy on the depth emerging from myth."[26] This means that the origin and guarantee of an ultimate order, intelligibility, coherence, and constancy of structure in experienced reality has historically shifted, in this development, from "the gods" as portrayed by traditional myth to the "underlying oneness" of reality as mystically apprehended in experiences of the depth of the psyche and articulated by the philosophically mythic symbol of *Cosmos*.[27]

This raises some important questions. If the "depth of the cosmos" is a symbol of divine reality, occasioned by philosophical insights into the order of reality, which replaces—for differentiated understanding—traditional myths about the gods, then what is the relationship of that insight and development to the philosophical discovery, in the same Hellenic milieu, of the *transcendent* nature of divine reality—e.g., the "being beyond being" of Plato's *Republic*—which "dissolves" the one cosmos into 1) world, and 2) transcendent divinity? How can these two developments be brought into explanatory conjunction? Where, one might ask, *is* the divine: is it the "underlying oneness of reality" symbolized as cosmic depth, or is it transcendently beyond the

26 Eric Voegelin, letter of July 30, 1969, to Stephen J. Tonsor; published in Voegelin, *Selected Correspondence, 1950-1984*, trans. Sandy Adler, Thomas A. Hollweck, and William Petropulos; ed. Thomas A. Hollweck, *CWEV* Vol. 30, 2007, 619. In June, 1969, Voegelin finished revising the text of "Equivalences" (originally a paper given in Rome in October, 1968) for publication, and sent copies to a number of people, including his former assistant and colleague Professor Manfred Henningsen, at the University of Hawaii at Manoa, and Professor Stephen J. Tonsor at the University of Michigan. In his replies to their written responses to the text, specifically in four letters to Henningsen and one to Tonsor, Voegelin expanded on the meaning of the symbol of the "depth" in a manner that is especially illuminating. See *Selected Correspondence, 1950-1984*, letters 314, 317, 318, 319, and 321 (604–06, 611–16, 618–19).

27 Voegelin refers to the apprehension of the depth of the cosmos, through experiences of psychic depth, as a type of "mysticism" in a letter of July 10, 1969 to Manfred Henningsen; see *Selected Correspondence, 1950-1984*, 614.

world? And how are the later Christian mystical differentiations and symbolizations of the *transcendent* God related to the "cosmological" apprehensions of a divine depth that, according to Voegelin, "has remained a constant in Western history from the *Timaeus* through Neoplatonism of Antiquity, and the Renaissance into the Neoplatonism of the German Pietists, Jakob Boehme, and Hegel"?[28]

The core component in Voegelin's response to these and related questions is that there always remains, for differentiated consciousness, two basic approaches to understanding our human relation to divine reality, and two basic sets of symbolizations corresponding to these. First, there is the approach that he calls the "mysticism of the 'height'" through which the *transcendent* being of the divine is apprehended—which provides, writes Voegelin, a "partial experience of God." Second, there is "the mysticism of the soul of the 'depth'," in which one apprehends the divine as the "underlying oneness of reality," which provides "another partial experience" of God.[29] These two distinct types of mystical approach to divine reality, Voegelin indicates, are compatible and complementary, and—more important from a philosopher's point of view—both types of apprehension and symbolization of divine being "*must* be taken into account in any philosophy of the human condition that wants to be *complete*."[30]

These comments will bring to mind, among Voegelin's readers, the opening passage of his later meditation, "The Beginning and the Beyond: A Meditation on Truth," which states: "Divine reality is being revealed to man in two fundamental modes of experience: in the experience of divine creativity in the cosmos; and in the experience of divine ordering presence in the soul."[31] That the "divine ordering presence of the soul" is identified with the God of "the Beyond" (i.e., transcendence) and thus with the God

28 Voegelin, letter of July 30, 1969 to Stephen J. Tonsor, in *Selected Correspondence, 1950-1984*, 619.

29 Voegelin, letter of July 10, 1969 to Manfred Henningsen, in *Selected Correspondence, 1950-1984*, 613–14.

30 Voegelin, letter of July 30, 1969, to Stephen J. Tonsor, in *Selected Correspondence, 1950-1984*, 619 (emphasis added).

31 Eric Voegelin, "The Beginning and the Beyond: A Meditation on Truth," (1977) in *What Is History? and Other Late Unpublished Writings*, ed. Thomas A. Hollweck and Paul Caringella, *CWEV* Vol. 28, 1990, 173.

of the "height" is clear. Just how the "divine creativity in the cosmos," here identified by the symbol of "the Beginning," is associated with the God of the "depth of the cosmos" is less obvious, and would perhaps require a separate paper to explore and explain. But three facts resulting from Voegelin's philosophical reflections on the differentiated understanding of divine reality may be stated clearly. First, in a general philosophical account of how human beings approach and understand their relation to the divine, we must remember that divine reality is apprehended and symbolized in two different fundamental modes. Second, the "depth" of the cosmos is a *theological* symbol, originating in the search for and discovery of *a differentiated apprehension of divine reality* beyond the symbols of traditional myth, and thus *valid* symbols of the depth will always have a theological character.[32] Third, human beings require valid symbols of the depth if they are to succeed in existentially orienting themselves in relation to divine reality, as well as in relation to the meaning of personal existence as a mode of participating in reality.

The underlying oneness of reality can be, and has been, symbolized in many ways. In "Equivalences," Voegelin discusses how Plato, in his *Timaeus*, introduced the mythic symbol of the *anima mundi* (world soul) to articulate his imagining of the divine depth, and comments that this symbol and its meaning-equivalents have had "a prodigious career" of employment by Western philosophers and mystics from the classical Neoplatonists down to such modern thinkers as Boehme, Schelling, and Hegel (and we should not forget Emerson).[33] But also in modernity we see the emergence of explicitly anti-theological immanentist and materialist worldviews that lead inevitably to the introduction of immanentist symbols for the underlying oneness of reality. Many Enlightenment and Romanticist writers, for example, embraced the symbol *Nature* as an appropriate symbol of the depth—a symbol in which (whatever the specific view of this or that thinker) the presence of the divine is not explicit, and one that was used by many anti-religious Enlightenment figures as a *replacement* for the conception of a divine foundation

32 Voegelin, letter of July 10, 1969, to Manfred Henningsen, in *Selected Correspondence, 1950-1984*, 614–15.

33 Voegelin, "Equivalences," 126–28; letter of July 30, 1969, to Stephen J. Tonsor, in *Selected Correspondence, 1950-1984*, 619.

of reality. Schopenhauer's *Will* and Nietzsche's *Will to Power* likewise symbolize the depth in its oneness—and again, considering Schopenhauer's understanding of *Will* as a blind unconscious striving and his ethics of pessimism, and Nietzsche's explicit atheism, we find authentically theological symbols of the depth replaced by, as Voegelin calls them, mere de-divinized "metaphors."[34]

In the twentieth century, in light of the development of theoretical physics, many would be satisfied to symbolize the oneness underlying all reality by the term *Energy*. Here, too, we recognize the impact of the de-divinization and immanentization of reality; for the symbol *Energy*, as it is generally understood in modern culture, has no theological meaning or implications. In fact, for most people, if embraced or employed as a symbol of the depth, *Energy* functions simply as a more sophisticated and highly etherialized version of *Matter*—that symbol of the underlying oneness of reality so dear to materialists and immanentists of all persuasions.

A brief consideration of the symbol *Matter* in its function as one of the most popular modern symbols of the depth of the cosmos will help to explain why the immanentist doctrines and ideologies of modernity—metaphysical, political, cultural, and existential—are both disorienting and dangerous. First: because almost all usages of *Matter* as a symbol of the depth are not only *non*-theological but *anti*-theological, a person's casual or passionate embrace of it as such a symbol obstructs the ability to imaginatively experience his or her own psyche as emergent from, and constantly grounded in, divine being. It establishes a blind spot precisely at the center of self-understanding where one seeks to discern the deepest core of one's human identity. Thus it is one of those pervasive and powerful modern symbols that "eclipses the reality of man's existence in the Metaxy" of which Voegelin writes so powerfully at the end of his Introduction to *The Ecumenic Age*, part of the "great obstacle" of accumulated symbols preventing our return to the experiential insights that would reveal to us our true human situation as participants in a divinely ordered reality.[35] Second: we must

34 Voegelin, letter of July 10, 1969, to Manfred Henningsen, in *Selected Correspondence, 1950-1984*, 614.

35 Eric Voegelin, *Order and History, Volume IV: The Ecumenic Age* (1974), ed. Michael Franz, *CWEV* Vol. 17, 2000), 107.

remember that an adequate symbol of the depth is a *myth*—and what the soul seeks and needs is a "likely myth," in the phrase that Plato uses in the *Timaeus* to describe his symbol of the *anima mundi*. In "Equivalences," Voegelin explains exactly what makes a mythic symbol or story "likely": the "degree of *likeness* will depend on the amount of disparate experiences it has achieved to unify persuasively in its imagery."[36] Considering this criterion, *Matter* is a profoundly "unlikely" symbol for signifying the underlying oneness of reality, since its imagery leaves inexplicable, ignored, or fragmentarily disassociated, some of the most important types of experience available to conscious existence—one of these being experiences of loving encounter with the boundless spiritual presences of other persons (Buber's I-Thou encounters), and another being the many varieties of the experience of transcendence that existence in the *metaxy* provides.

To embrace the symbol *Matter*, or any of its meaning-equivalents, as representing the cosmic depth has therefore genuinely harmful existential consequences. For symbols of the depth are, however consciously or tacitly they function for us, symbols through which we interpret the essential being of the cosmos, and by which we orient our lives. They shape our appreciation of what consciousness is and might grow toward; the imaginative trajectory of our existential hopes and yearnings; our sense of what the human search for meaning is ultimately for; and our assumptions or beliefs concerning why human beings—and the cosmos itself—have come into being. Indeed, the symbolization of the depth provides a person with the most basic understanding of his or her identity, since it imaginatively represents the depth from which every human consciousness has emerged—"the depth by which experience lives."[37]

Voegelin does not in "Equivalences" directly address the problem of misleading and dangerous symbols of the depth. But it is a problem whose

36 Voegelin, "Equivalences," 128 (emphasis added). Just prior to this statement, Voegelin discusses the fact that Plato in *Timaeus* "wavers" in his description of the type of truth expressed in the symbol of the *anima mundi,* calling it both an *eikos mythos* (likely myth) and an *alethinos logos* (true story). The key fact, for Voegelin, is that Plato "was sure that the symbolism had not been engendered through articulation of an *experience*" but was consciously a "philosopher's myth" (127; emphasis added).

37 Voegelin, "Equivalences," 129.

solution he alludes to when he describes how, in the development of a life (or a culture), the images or stories that have previously been felt to successfully symbolize the depth *lose their persuasiveness*, and need to be replaced through discovering a more adequate symbolization, a more "likely" myth. In this development, Voegelin writes, "the truth of the depth has drained from the symbols by which [a person] orients his life," and a return to an explorative concern with the depth of the psyche, together with renewed reflection on experiences of the primordial community of being, will *normatively* bring forth a new "imaginative fusion" in the form of a mythic symbolization of the depth that will again—in its being more profoundly or differentiatedly "true"—be existentially persuasive and reassuring.[38]

The person who undergoes such a transition, or transformation, will be someone who has not abandoned the existential search for truth and right order—someone who heeds the fact that existence is "participation in a movement with a direction to be found or missed," and understands the degree to which the struggle for existence in truth depends on finding convincing and inspiring symbolizations of the underlying oneness of reality.[39] It will be a person who recognizes that his or her role in the drama of humanity is part of a more comprehensive "play"—the play or drama of the cosmos itself as it unfolds through the eons. And above all, a person who cares passionately about orienting herself through symbols of the depth that are persuasively adequate will be someone who consistently remembers that she is a luminously conscious participant in a cosmic drama whose ultimate "plot" or purpose can only be apprehended through mythic elaboration, an elaboration based on extrapolating some design of its mystery from the fullest possible range of available experiences 1) of the primordial field, 2) of existential tension, 3) of experiences of psychic depth, and 4) of known historical developments. Voegelin summarizes all this by stating that the person whose outlook is informed by such insights and who *does* find trustworthy mythic elaborations for guidance—his example is Plato—will recognize that "the most intimate truth of reality, the truth about the meaning of the

38 Ibid., 125.

39 Eric Voegelin, "The Gospel and Culture," (1971) in *Published Essays, 1966-1985*, 176.

cosmic play in which man must act his role with his life as the stake, is a mythopoetic play linking the psyche of man in trust with the depth of the Cosmos."[40] The symbol of the depth that is embraced by a person undeluded by immanentism, and attuned to the fact that cosmic reality is a divinely ordered "play," is of such existential importance because *it must be linked to*, and radiate a meaning in harmony with, a more comprehensive "likely story" that expresses, through myth, why there *is* such a cosmic "play" at all, and what it might ultimately be about.

I would like to suggest that there is one most important condition for recognizing and embracing a proper and salutary "mythopoetic play" that links our understanding of our personal struggle for existence in truth with our mythic apprehension of both the cosmic "depth" and the process of reality as a whole. That condition is a loving openness toward reality in all its dimensions. Such loving openness allows us to acknowledge, and investigate the history of insights into, all four partners in the primordial field, God and man, world and society; it allows us to commit ourselves to the meaningfulness of our own personal search for truth and order; and in conformity with that commitment, it leads us to have faith in an underlying oneness of reality that ensures the coherence and full intelligibility of the cosmos, as well as in the divine constancy in the depth that justifies claiming that equivalent symbols of truth found in history are representative of a truth that is more than equivalent. Finally, it enables us to love the fact that we *belong* to the cosmos as luminous sites of participation in its process, and to recognize that all human beings deserve our respect and love as also belonging, in their ontological constitution, to the one cosmos in the same manner as ourselves. Without a loving openness to reality in its fullness, one might be led to ignore some part of the primordial field (such as God); or to become alienated from the human search for order and conclude that it is meaningless; or to refuse to accept the reasonableness of affirming an underlying oneness of reality, since such a oneness cannot be empirically experienced, and thus to view phenomena and persons as essentially fragmented, essentially heterogeneous, incoherent, and historically disconnected. Without it, in other words, one might become a radical historicist, an immanentist, a moral relativist, a cynical ironist, a

40 Voegelin, "Equivalences," 128.

xenophobic nationalist, a nihilist, or one of the more shoddy and shallow types of philosophical or literary postmodernist.

If, however, one were—through sufficient loving openness—to discover this to be the most important condition for orienting oneself aright in relation to existence and reality, one might be tempted to identify this dynamic core of one's search for truth (that is, love) with "the process in the depth"[41] that underlies our personal experience of the process of reality in the mode of presence, and proceed to mythically symbolize the depth of the cosmos as *Love*. This is a symbol that would unify a vast range of disparate experiences in its imagery, and is properly theological in linking the cosmos to its divinely transcendent ground differentiatedly understood and symbolized as the God who is Love (1 John 4:16-21). It is a symbol that would mythopoetically interpret the "cosmic play," to which we link our own psyches in trust, as a universal movement of love that is self-illuminative in humans and is heading, historically, toward its ever-more illumined fulfillment. In light of such a mythopoesis, one would be drawn to identify the factors that most *impede* the movement and actualization of love as evil, fear, and sin, and to conclude that faith in the ultimate coherence and intelligibility of the cosmos must also entail faith in a divinely redemptive power in the cosmic process that would ensure Love's illuminative fulfillment. With such thoughts in mind, one might scan the cultural scene for a mythopoetic play of the cosmos, arising from reality's luminous emergence as self-presence in history, in which all of these factors are "imaginatively fused." And that could provide a "likely story" of the cosmic play whose meanings and images one could rely on for guiding one's struggle for existence in truth.

IV

The general truth to be drawn from Voegelin's meditative conclusions in "Equivalences" pertinent to the foregoing reflections on love is that—living, as we are, in the epoch after the philosophical differentiation of the four partners of the primordial field, including the transcendent God—*mythopoetic symbolizations* of the "depth by which experience lives" and of the

41 Ibid., 130.

"meaning of the cosmic play in which man must act his role with his life as the stake" are necessary to help guide us if we are genuinely committed both to the struggle to make sense of our lives and to the struggle against existence in untruth.[42] Two further general truths may be drawn from his conclusions as well, both of which pertain to the two concerns identified earlier in this paper as dominating Voegelin's meditation: the challenge of historicity to our search for, and our claims to know of, "constants" pertaining to human nature and human existence; and the delusory supposition that humans can arrive at *possession of ultimate truths and systems of explanations* about existence, history, and reality.

First, because the human search for order and truth—and thus personal existence—is itself meaningful only if there is a "constancy of structure, order, and intelligibility" in the depth of the cosmos, a constancy of truth it is reasonable to have faith in, we may reasonably extend that faith into a confidence that truths about the structure of human nature and existence discovered and symbolized, with increasing differentiation, over the known historical millennia may be granted the status of constants.[43] For instance, to use Voegelin's example from the end of his meditation, it is a constant, of which we can be sure, that "all men by nature desire to know," as Aristotle put it. Why? Not because we have empirically experienced the interiority of the consciousnesses of all persons, but rather because 1) the empirical evidence we do have of this structural element of human nature—the human search for meaning—is consistent through all known history, and 2) our faith in the constancy and lastingness of structure in the depth of the cosmos allows us to accept that this historically situated and equivalently symbolized truth—"*the desire to know is constant in human nature*"—is truly representative of a truth that is more than situatedly conditional and more than equivalent.[44] The same argument holds for a number of truths about the structure of human existence, as Voegelin

42 Ibid., 128, 129.

43 Ibid., 127.

44 If there were to emerge, in being, a creature in whom the process of reality came to luminous self-awareness in the mode of presence and *was not characterized by a desire to know at the core of its consciousness*, then that creature would not be human; it would be another kind of being; but I would hazard to say that such a luminously self-aware creature is rationally unimaginable.

indicates in a series of propositions near the start of section II of his essay—for example: "Man participates in the process of reality"; "Man is conscious of reality as a process . . . and of his consciousness as a mode of participation in its process"; "While consciously participating, man is able to engender symbols which express his experience of reality...."[45] We may affirm with confidence that these, too, are constant truths of human nature. All of these constants may be understood to be implicit in the assertion at the end of Voegelin's meditation when he states that his search into the history of the search for order has revealed, above all, *the constancy of the process of reality "in the mode of presence."* That is: his "search of the search" has revealed the constancy of the human luminous search for and symbolization of truth—the constancy of human nature itself—which has left behind it the "trail of equivalent symbols in time and space" that collectively constitute what may be called "history."[46]

Second, a distinction must be drawn between discoverable truths that are constants pertaining to the human search for meaning, the structure of human participation in reality, the features of existential tension, the primordial field of historical experience, and basic criteria distinguishing between existence in truth and existence in untruth, on the one hand, and on the other hand, truths concerning—for example—the final meaning and goal of history; the ultimate outcome of individual moral and spiritual striving; why reality exists (and has the structure it has); or why humans exist (and have the structure they have). In these latter cases, no answers in the forms of philosophical truths or propositions are possible; they remain mysteries. Thus, a temperate and mystery-respecting philosophy of consciousness such as Voegelin's may, indeed, accurately be said to include many *true statements and propositions.* Two philosophical essays on the structure of consciousness replete with such propositions are "Equivalences" itself and "What Is Political Reality?" in *Anamnesis.*[47] But the only valid

45 Voegelin, "Equivalences," 120.

46 Ibid., 132–33.

47 See Eric Voegelin, "What Is Political Reality?" (1965) in *Anamnesis: On the Theory of History and Politics*, trans. M. J. Hayak based upon the abbreviated version originally translated by Gerhart Neimeyer, ed. David Walsh, *CWEV* Vol. 6, 2002, 341–412.

means of articulating suppositions about *ultimacies of meaning*—concerning, for example, why there is a cosmos at all, and why human beings have emerged within it, or what the purpose and goal of human history are—is mythopoetic elaboration, that is, the presenting of a "likely story" whose persuasiveness and helpfulness will be based precisely on how well it harmonizes with our experiences of psychic depth and with what we know about the primordial field of experienced reality, as well as on how successfully it protects insights into what it means to live a well-ordered existence in attunement with what history has revealed of "the divine drama of truth becoming luminous."[48]

48 Voegelin, "Equivalences," 133.

–6–

Voegelin's "On Henry James's *Turn of the Screw*"

Charles R. Embry

With the publication in *Published Essays, 1966-1985*[1] of "On Henry James's *Turn of the Screw,*" which includes two parts—the 1947 letter to Robert B. Heilman in which Voegelin analyzes *The Turn of the Screw* and a "Postscript" to that letter—we are presented with two instances of Eric Voegelin's approach to literary criticism. These examples are separated by twenty-two years.[2] Although Voegelin read extensively in what is conventionally called "literature," these two pieces are the only fully developed interpretations of a work of modern fiction. Here Voegelin not only presents us with interpretations of James's novella, but articulates several interpretive principles of his literary criticism. The articulation of these interpretive principles, as well as additional principles that he articulates in his correspondence with Heilman and Donald Stanford, invites us to survey and comment on their application to *The Turn of the Screw*.[3]

1 Eric Voegelin, "On Henry James's *Turn of the Screw,*" in *Published Essays, 1966-1985*, ed. Ellis Sandoz, *CWEV* Vol. 12, 1990, 134–71. Hereafter cited as Voegelin, "On Henry James's *Turn.*"

2 Even though "Postscript: On Paradise and Revolution" was published in 1971, it was finished in late 1969. I am, therefore, using dates that reflect the writing of each source.

3 In Charles R. Embry, ed. *Robert B. Heilman and Eric Voegelin: A Friendship in Letters, 1944-1984* (Columbia, MO: University of Missouri Press, 2004) twelve letters (seven written by Heilman and five by Voegelin) discuss—in philosophical/theoretical and/or procedural terms—the 1947 Letter and "Postscript" and their publication in *The Southern Review*. If we add the original 1947 letter itself, then thirteen of the 152 letters deal with James's novella. Hereafter cited as Embry, *A Friendship in Letters.*

Before we focus our attention on Voegelin's "literary criticism" as applied in "On Henry James's *Turn of the Screw,*" we briefly survey the genesis and historical-biographical context from which the publication in *The Southern Review* emerged.

Genesis of "On Henry James's *Turn of the Screw*"

His friendship with Heilman not only gave Voegelin the opportunity to develop his proficiency in the English language (Heilman often read important manuscripts and advised Voegelin on his writing[4]) but supplied an energetic interlocutor and advocate for Voegelin's work. After he received the original 1947 letter on *The Turn of the Screw*, Heilman supported its publication from time to time.[5] When the editor of *The Southern Review*, Donald Stanford, asked Heilman if it was true that Voegelin had written on James Joyce, Heilman replied that he did not know of such a commentary, but that he could "supply" "Voegelin-on-James." About the same time, Stanford had written Voegelin with the same question and was offered the 1947 letter on James.[6] Heilman's participation continued when Stanford asked him to write a Foreword for the *Review*'s publication of the original letter and the additional "Postscript."

Since the publication of "On Henry James's *Turn of the Screw*" in *Published Essays, 1966-1985*, stands alone as a *fait accompli*, the reader is presented an incomplete picture of the historical context from which it emerged. The Table of Contents of the January 1971 issue of *The Southern Review* lists the publication as: "*The Turn of the Screw*, Eric Voegelin." This published "unit" included not only "A Letter to Robert B. Heilman" dated November 13, 1947, and the "Postscript: On Paradise and Revolution,"

4 In point of fact, Voegelin wrote to Heilman in May 1952 "with a humble request" to read the MS that would become the Introduction to Volume I of *Order and History*. See Letter 37, May 3, 1952, in Embry, *A Friendship in Letters*, 107. Heilman read and annotated the MS with comments and suggestions to clarify Voegelin's language. A holograph of this MS with Heilman's annotations may be found in the Hoover Institution Archives, Box 65, File 1 of the Voegelin Papers.

5 Letter 115, September 23, 1969, Embry, *A Friendship in Letters*, 251.

6 Letter 116, September 26, 1969, Embry, *A Friendship in Letters*, 252–53.

but also "A Prefatory Note" by Donald E. Stanford, Co-editor of *The Southern Review*, and a "Foreword" by Heilman himself. These prefatory pieces provide introductory and historical comments that introduce Voegelin's work to *Southern Review* readers and place his original letter and subsequent postscript in a larger context.

In his "Prefatory Note," Professor Stanford writes that

> Voegelin's 1947 letter to Heilman was not intended for publication, but it achieved, nevertheless, an "underground" circulation in manuscript.... When Voegelin was approached on the possibility of permitting this letter to be published in *The Southern Review* he agreed with the proviso that he be allowed to add a postscript. The "postscript" turned out to be even more far-ranging and profound than the original letter.[7]

In his "Foreword" Heilman remembered not only the situation that resulted in the original letter to him but also the place that Voegelin's study of *The Turn of the Screw* occupied in the context of the contemporary studies of Henry James. Stanford and Heilman, both literature scholars, praised Voegelin's interpretations of the novella—especially that of the "Postscript"—as significant contributions to the then-current James scholarship. Heilman remarked that Voegelin was his colleague—he in the Department of English and Voegelin in the Department of Government—at Louisiana State University, and that by 1947 they

> ...had been acquainted for about five years. I was the regular beneficiary in conversations in which many subjects were brilliantly illuminated by the wealth of learning (in political theory, law, philosophy, theology, literature and the arts) under Voegelin's easy and unpedantic control.
>
> It was in [the role as native informant on the American scene] . . . that I suggested *The Turn of the Screw* to him—in answer to a request. Voegelin had become aware of the "James

7 Donald E. Stanford, "A Prefatory Note," *The Southern Review*, Vol. VII, New Series, January 1971, Number 1, 4–5.

> Boom" then in progress and said, approximately, "Everybody is talking about James. I must learn something about him. What should I read?" . . . I had been teaching *The Turn* and had written a little about it; I named it almost without thinking, and at the same time, doubtless also without thinking, sent my articles along to him.
>
> Voegelin's response to *The Turn* was immediate, enthusiastic, and at the same time profoundly critical. His epistolary essay reached me, I think, no more than three days after I had named the book to him. My impression is that it was written at a single sitting almost immediately after his reading of *The Turn.* Aside from the more formal criticism in his essay, Voegelin made a number of comments in conversation. One of these, or at least the spirit of it, I remember very clearly: "It is a great book. It reveals an aspect of American consciousness that I did not know about. If I had known of it, my book about America would have been different."[8]

For Voegelin scholars, the inclusion of "On Henry James's *Turn of the Screw*" in *Published Essays, 1966-1985*, represents a rare opportunity to compare two examples of Voegelin's literary criticism interpreting a single work. These examples are separated, of course, by a significant span of time. The period between the original letter to Heilman and "Postscript: On Paradise and Revolution," from 1947 to 1969, spans a time of important changes and philosophical breakthroughs in Voegelin's work and thought. During this time, Voegelin abandoned his contracted *History of Political Ideas*, wrote and published *The New Science of Politics*, recast his *History* as *Order and History* and published volumes I, II, and III of *Order and History*, published the German edition of *Anamnesis*, and completed numerous essays, which appeared later as chapters 1-4 of volume 12 of *The Collected Works.* While working on these various projects he also was developing a mode of reading texts that Athanasios Moulakis would designate in 2000 as *pia interpretatio*. This mode of reading texts depended upon a "participatory disposition" in order to

8 Ibid., 4–5.

imaginatively re-enact the experiences that are symbolized in the language of the text.[9]

Although it is clear that Voegelin was making interpretive advances in his search for the order of history, he was also struggling to complete volume IV of *Order and History, In Search of Order* (as volume IV was tentatively entitled at the time). Voegelin anticipated that the letter and "Postscript" would be part of his analysis of modernity. In a letter dated January 30, 1971, to Leslie E. Phillabaum, Assistant Director and Editor of Louisiana State University Press, he included a table of contents that outlined the organizational structure of the proposed volume. Part III to this table of contents he titled "The Eclipse of Reality" and included in this section four "chapters" focused on modernity and the "reduced" self: "The Eclipse of Reality," "On Hegel," "On Schelling," "On Nietzsche and Pascal," and "Henry James."[10] At the time the letter was written only two essays and part of another had been published. One of these was the *Southern Review* publication on James's novella. Clearly, Voegelin understood that the eclipse of reality that characterizes modernity may be symbolized in various genres.

Voegelin was not unfamiliar with literature as is evident from reading not only the posthumously published *History of Political Ideas*, as well as his five-volume *Order and History*, not to mention the plethora of essays that he published and the hundreds of letters that he exchanged with hundreds of correspondents. One notes that he read and interpreted written texts to include the sacred scriptures of various cultures, epics, ancient and Renaissance drama, myths, philosophical fragments, and philosophical and theological works. In various essays or letters, he frequently commented on works of modern literature by various authors including Proust, Baudelaire, Henry James, Shakespeare, Thomas Mann, Dostoyevsky, Cervantes, Doderer, Camus, Sartre, and Musil, among others. During this time he also had the opportunity to articulate and refine principles of literary interpretation in a

9 Athanasios Moulakis, "Editor's Introduction," Eric Voegelin, *Order and History, Volume II: The World of the Polis* (1957), *CWEV* Vol. 15, 24. Hereafter cited as Moulakis, *CWEV* 15. See below for more discussion of this participatory mode for reading texts.

10 Eric Voegelin, *What is History? and Other Late Unpublished Writings*, ed. Thomas A. Hollweck and Paul Caringella, *CWEV* Vol. 28, Appendix, 242–43.

1956 letter to Heilman, in the "Postscript," and in a letter to Donald Stanford.[11]

Principles of Literary Interpretation

After surveying Voegelin's *Collected Works*, I discovered that he articulated his principles of literary criticism in only four locations. Three of these fall within the orbit of "On Henry James's *Turn of the Screw*." These four principles include: (1) Primacy of the Text; (2) Submission to the Master and Exhaustion of the Source; (3) Provision by the reader of the Critical Consciousness of Reality; and (4) Recognition of the Existential Content of a Work. After a brief look at each of these principles of literary interpretation we examine how these are implemented in the two parts of "On Henry James's *Turn of the Screw*."

1. Primacy of the text

As we have seen, Voegelin's November 13, 1947, letter to Heilman resulted from Heilman's recommendation that he read James's novella. Heilman accompanied his recommendation with copies of two of his own articles—"The *Turn of the Screw* as Poem" and "The Freudian Reading of *The Turn of the Screw*." In articulating the literary principle—Primacy of the Text—that he followed in his reading of the novella, Voegelin asserted:

> Your own interpretation (for what my opinion is worth) looks most convincing to me. To follow the pattern of symbols, and see what emerges by way of meaning, is certainly the proper method to be employed.[12]

After recognizing that his interpretation of the novella doesn't follow the lines of interpretation suggested in various statements by James, Voegelin articulates the principle he follows:

11 Eric Voegelin to Donald Stanford, Letter 357, September 15, 1970 in *Selected Correspondence, 1950-1984*, ed. Thomas Hollweck, *CWEV* Vol. 30, 2007, 665. Hereafter cited as Voegelin, *Selected Correspondence, 1950-1984*.

12 Voegelin, "On Henry James's *Turn*," 134 (emphasis added).

> the basis for the analysis of a literary work must be the work itself; if the author has expressed himself on the meaning of his work, such utterances are most valuable if they clear up obscure points; but if (as it seems to be in this case) the utterances of the author are in open conflict with the text of his work, then the meaning offered by the text has to prevail.[13]

Voegelin closes his 1947 letter with an apology to Heilman for "pestering" him with his long, presumptuous letter after only recently reading the story, but, he declares: "Nevertheless, I think you will have seen that just now I am lying prostrate in admiration for James."[14] This declaration by Voegelin of his admiration for James anticipates the second principle of literary criticism: Submission to the Master.

2. Submission to the Master and Exhaustion of the Source

Although the second of Voegelin's principles does not occur directly in the context of the present focus, it does supply a principle that is related—by implication—to the "Postscript." In responding to Heilman's dedication to him of his book, *Magic in the Web: Action and Language in "Othello,"* Voegelin complimented the work on its demonstration and application of interpretive principles:

> . . . the principle of exhaustion of the source. The interpretation of a literary work by a first-rate artist or philosopher must proceed on the assumption that the man "knew" what he was doing. . . . Under that assumption the interpretation will be adequate only, if every "part" of the work makes sense in the comprehensive context. Moreover, the sense must emerge from the texture of the linguistic corpus, and it must not be prejudged by "ideas" of the interpreter. No adequate interpretation of a major work is possible, unless the interpreter assumes the

13 Ibid., 134–35.
14 Ibid., 149.

> role of the disciple who has everything to learn from the master.[15]

Voegelin pointed out how Heilman had not only exhausted the content of Shakespeare's drama but had translated into "the rational order of his work" the meaning that the poet had developed in the "action and language of the poem."[16]

> This conception of the whole of human nature, that in the poem is carried by the magic in the web, must now be carried by the magic of the system. And here I am now full of admiration for your qualities as a philosopher.[17]

3. Provision by the Reader of the Critical Consciousness of Reality

By 1969 Voegelin could admit in the "Postscript," that in 1947 he "was uneasily aware of an incongruence between the meaning I tried to establish in terms of God and man, the Puritan soul and common sense, the passion of self-salvation, grace and damnation, and the Jamesian symbols which carried these meanings distinctly but surrounded by a ghostly aura of indistinctness."[18] He concluded in the "Postscript" that the indistinctness and ambiguity he noticed in his first reading can be understood as the result of a symbolistic deformation of reality.

15 Embry, *A Friendship in Letters,* 150. This principle must be understood in the context of Voegelin's admiration for Shakespeare as a literary master. In "Wisdom and Magic of the Extreme" (1983), he quotes and analyzes Sonnet 129 by Shakespeare. Introducing that analysis, Voegelin wrote: "A first understanding of the 'magic of the extreme' can be gained by confronting the self-interpretation of the magicians with the self-analysis by the master of dream and reality, of their tension, and of the language of their conflicts—by Shakespeare." Voegelin, "Wisdom and Magic of the Extreme," in *Published Essays, 1966-1985, CWEV* Vol. 12, 1990, 328.

16 Ibid., 151–52.

17 Ibid., 152.

18 Voegelin, "On Henry James's *Turn,*" 150.

> Works of this kind are not always easy to understand. The reader, in order to extract the full meaning, must supply the critical consciousness of reality, as well as of the range of its possible deformation, which in the work itself does not become sufficiently thematic. . . . [T]he conscientious interpreter is faced with a critical task indeed. He cannot simply follow the symbolism wherever it leads and expect to come out with something that makes sense in terms of reality. He must rather ascertain, first, what kind of reality has become the victim of deformation and, second, what kind of deformation it has suffered.[19]

Although "Provision by the reader of the Critical Consciousness of Reality" seems to be a substantive revision of the first principle, "Primacy of the Text," Voegelin remained committed to the primacy of the text even in his interpretation of the "Postscript," a comprehensive interpretation that ultimately relied upon Voegelin's original letter. Without granting primacy to the text, the *pia interpretatio* could not penetrate to an adequate understanding of the story of *The Turn.*

4. Recognition of the Existential Content of a Work of Art

Writing to Donald Stanford in 1970, Voegelin recalled a "splendid evening" in the course of which

> you stressed very strongly that the formal quality of a work of art is the one and only quality a literary critic has to take into account. And, if I remember correctly, I expressed equally strongly the opinion that in a critical judgment there must also be taken into account the existential content.[20]

The existential content of a work of literature that Voegelin emphasizes should be understood as those components in a particular work that

19 Ibid., 152.

20 Letter 357, September 15, 1970. Voegelin, *Selected Correspondence, 1950-1984*, 665.

symbolize the habitat of humanity or the reality in which human beings exist. Elsewhere Voegelin has formulated two modes of existence variously styled as "existence in truth" or "existence in untruth" and as the "truth of existence" or the "untruth of existence." In the "Postscript," Voegelin uses the terms "openness of existence" or "closure of existence" to designate the meanings that underlie the earlier terms; that is, the three sets of terms are equivalent symbolizations in Voegelin's work on modernity. In "On Debate and Existence," he defines "the truth of existence" as "the awareness of the fundamental structure of existence [reality] together with the willingness to accept it as the *condicio humana*. Correspondingly we shall define untruth of existence as a revolt against the *condicio humana*. . . ."[21] Voegelin relies upon the "fundamental structure of existence" (or "reality") as symbols of the experience that becomes luminous in the consciousness of a human being and is then recorded in written texts—whether literary, philosophical, religious, or mythic. These texts record the existential experiences of specific human beings and remain as an historical record of man's search for order. A philosopher who has been moved to search for the truth of his own existence, i.e., Voegelin, can then declare, as he does in the opening sentence of his Introduction to *Israel and Revelation*, that "God and man, world and society form a primordial community of being."[22]

Supplementing this view, Voegelin asserted in a 1978 lecture that in "the analysis of a work of art as a work of art by literary criticism, one shouldn't forget that *works of art also have a content referring to man's existence, and that they should be viewed under that aspect, and be valued under that aspect, and read under that aspect.*"[23]

21 Voegelin, "On Debate and Existence," in Voegelin, *Published Essays, 1966-1985*, 49.

22 Voegelin, *Order and History, Volume I: Israel and Revelation* (1956), ed. Maurice P. Hogan, *CWEV* Vol. 14, 2001, 39. Hereafter cited as Voegelin, *Israel and Revelation*.

23 According to Zdravko Planinc, the original editor of Voegelin's "Structures of Consciousness" lecture, this passage appears in his remarks on *paranoia/pronoia* from the panel on "Literary Criticism (November 24, 1978), representing section 6 of the "Structures of Consciousness" lecture. Voegelin, *The Drama of Humanity and Other Miscellaneous Papers, 1939-1985*, ed. William Petropulos and Gilbert Weiss, *CWEV* Vol. 33, 2004, 383 (emphasis added).

It will become apparent that while the principles of literary criticism *may be* clearly delineated, the early principles (dated to 1947 and 1956) are significantly transformed and supplemented by the latter two principles announced in the "Postscript" and the letter to Stanford. Beneath all of Voegelin's interpretations of texts, however, lies an unarticulated approach to reading. In the *New Science of Politics* (1952), when describing qualities required of the theorist who is searching for the truth of existence, Voegelin writes that

> The theorist need perhaps not be a paragon of virtue himself, but he must, at least, be capable of imaginative re-enactment of the experiences of which theory is an explication; and this faculty can be developed only under certain conditions such as inclination, an economic basis that will allow the investment of years of work into such studies, and a social environment that does not suppress a man when he engages in them.[24]

As mentioned above, this mode of reading texts is described by Athanasios Moulakis as *pia interpretatio*. In his Introduction to *The World of the Polis,* volume II of *Order and History*, Moulakis writes that like Marsilio Ficino who enjoined readers of Plato's dialogue *Parmenides* "to adopt a Platonic frame of mind" when approaching the text, Voegelin "invites his reader to a *pia interpretatio* of the decisive documents, which does not mean the recognition of external authority or verities to be accepted on faith, but an inner preparation, a participatory disposition of the interpreter."[25] This mode of reading enabled Voegelin to "sense" incongruent elements that are not readily discernible through a straightforward description of the various components of the stories themselves. This sensibility is especially important to Voegelin's interpretation of *The Turn of the Screw*—a modern novella—in "Postscript: On Paradise and Revolution."

24 Eric Voegelin, *The New Science of Politics* (1952) in *Modernity Without Restraint: The Political Religions; The New Science of Politics; and Science, Politics, and Gnosticism,* ed. Manfred Henningsen, *CWEV* Vol. 5, 2000, 139. Hereafter cited as Voegelin, *New Science.*

25 Moulakis, "Editor's Introduction," *CWEV* Vol. 15, 24.

Initial interpretation of *The Turn of the Screw*: A Letter to Robert B. Heilman

What we find in the bulk of the 1947 Letter is an unambiguous expansion of Heilman's qualified interpretation of James's novella as a symbolization of the "Christian dualism of good and evil."[26] In the article that he sent to Voegelin, Heilman had written: "by now it must be clear from the antipodal emphasis of the story that James has an almost religious sense of the duality of man, and, as if to manifest an intention, he makes that sense explicit in terms broadly religious and even Christian."[27]

Voegelin writes that he agrees with Heilman's interpretation, but that in his opinion Heilman "is not going far enough."[28] He then proceeded, in what I would call a "strong reading," to interpret the religious elements of the story by asserting that the novella is "a study, not of the mystery of good and evil only, but of this mystery in relation to the complex of consciousness-conscience-virtue" as a Puritan variant of the tensions within the soul. Then he described the characters of the employer, the governess, and the housekeeper in order as symbols of "God, the soul, and the earthy, commonsense existence," pointing out that "the soul is released by God to enter on its struggle with forces of good and evil

26 In Gerald Willen, ed., *A Casebook on Henry James's "The Turn of the Screw"* (New York: Thomas Y. Crowell Company, 2d ed., 1969), 183.

27 Ibid., 181.

28 Voegelin, "On Henry James's *Turn*," 134. When Voegelin declares in the first few paragraphs of the 1947 letter that he agrees with Heilman's interpretation, but that Heilman did not go far enough, he seems to allude to a difference—dimly perceived perhaps?—between Anglo-American and Continental European literary styles—both of creation and criticism. He does not make this difference specific, however, until the "Postscript" that he wrote ca. 1969. There he identifies and briefly discusses the Anglo-American form of understatement that characterizes and colors not only James's novella but also Anglo-American philosophical and literary works in general. Since he only touches briefly upon this style in Henry James in the "Postscript," it is "left" to Heilman to "invite" Voegelin to expand this point in a letter that focuses on the "Postscript." Voegelin responds to Heilman's "request" with a more complete exposition of Anglo-American understatement and the Continental European style of interpretation. Cf. Letters 122 and 123 in Embry, *A Friendship in Letters*, 257, 258–60.

(children and apparitions). . . . The central problem of the relation between God ["the young man in Harley Street"] and the soul [the governess] is the problem of communication."[29] Section I of the letter closed with the following sentence:

> From the beginning, James has defined his study carefully as a study of the demonically closed soul; of a soul which is possessed by the pride of handling the problem of good and evil by its own means; and the means which is at the disposition of this soul is the self-mastery and control of the spiritual forces (the symbol of the governess)—ending in a horrible defeat.[30]

Throughout §§II-VII, Voegelin supplied the details from James's story that address the central problem of communication between God and the soul[31] and the struggle of the governess to combat and save the souls of the children—Miles and Flora—from evil symbolized in the apparitions of Quint and Miss Jessel. He then followed the details of the failed attempts of the governess to guard the children—in their assumed innocence—from succumbing to the temptations proffered by Quint and Miss Jessel. Finally, in §VII Voegelin addressed the problem of incest that permeates "all the levels of the symbolic structure." Commenting upon the incestuous relations between various pairs of characters in the story (Quint—Miss Jessel; Uncle—the governess; Miles—the governess; and, Miles—Flora), Voegelin suggested that the "prehistory" of the story is simply the

> repetition (in the sense of the psychology of the myth) of the paradigmatic fall—culminating in the incest of the last scene. . . . If I do not misunderstand the relations of these symbols completely,

29 Voegelin, "On Henry James's *Turn*," 135.
30 Ibid., 136.
31 In *The Turn*, the young man in Harley Street hires the governess to care for his niece and nephew in the garden of the estate on the condition that she is forbidden to communicate with him. In order to please the young man, not only does she obey his command but she intercepts letters written by Miles to his uncle. Thus the governess symbolizes the soul cut off from the divine and the garden symbolizes the post-exilic Garden in which the self has become autonomous and responsible for combating evil on her own.

> I would say that the ultimate, metaphysical conception of James goes back to a vision of the cosmic drama of good and evil as an incestuous affair in the divinity.[32]

Asserting that "James is simply dealing with the problem of 'self-salvation' through the demonically closed human will that plagued everybody in the nineteenth century, particularly Nietzsche," Voegelin concluded his initial interpretation of the novella.[33]

Interpretation of *The Turn of the Screw* after 22 years: "Postscript: On Paradise and Revolution"

In the 1947 letter, Voegelin already sensed the direction that an expanded interpretation would have to take, i.e., the problem of the Puritan soul and its self-salvation. But as he indicated in the opening pages of the "Postscript," he did not have access in 1947 to studies on symbolization and the modern deformations of reality, as well as to a changed understanding of "modern ideological and literary movements" that would have permitted him to arrive at a more complete understanding of *The Turn of the Screw*. With the advancements available to him when he came to write the "Postscript" in understanding problems of symbolization, as well as of modernity in general—advancements that may be largely attributed to Voegelin's work itself—he proceeded to expand his initial insight (influenced, of course, by Heilman's work on James) that the novella is a "study of the Puritan variant of the generic problem."[34]

Hence the reader of the "Postscript" must recognize that "the critical consciousness of reality" that informs Voegelin's interpretation of the novella as a literary symbolization of deformation depends both upon the work that he completed and published between 1947 and 1969, and the progress that contemporary scholars had made in understanding modern literature. Especially important for understanding the background against which

32 Ibid., 148.
33 Ibid., 149.
34 Ibid., 135.

Voegelin provides this "critical consciousness of reality" are two sentences from *Israel and Revelation*, volume I of *Order and History* (1956). The Preface begins with the assertion "The order of history emerges from the history of order"; and the Introduction begins with the declaration that "God and man, world and society form a primordial community of being."[35] With these sentences Voegelin focuses his project *Order and History* and announced the discovery that the first three volumes of *Order and History* elaborate. With the simple declarative sentence that opens the Introduction, Voegelin articulates the ontological-interpretive basis for all his future meditations on "typical features in the process of the symbolization" of the order of reality, as well as the process of the symbolizations of disorder—symbolizations that in this essay he designates collectively as the "deformation of reality" that occurs when one of the partners of the community of being is excluded or is absent as in *The Turn of the Screw*.

Several essays—especially "On Debate and Existence" published in 1967 and "Equivalences of Experience and Symbolization in History" published 1970 but completed during the time he was preparing the "Postscript" for publication—supplement his "Introduction" to *Israel and Revelation*. Additionally, as we will see presently Voegelin relied

35 Voegelin, *Israel and Revelation*, 19. God, man, world and society constitute the quaternarian structure of reality as it has been experienced and symbolized in the history of the human search for the order of history. Voegelin amplified, and thus clarified, how he understood this introductory sentence. He wrote: "The community with its quaternarian structure is, and is not, a datum of human experience. It is a datum of experience in so far as it is known to man by virtue of his participation in the mystery of its being. It is not a datum of experience in so far as it is not given in the manner of an object of the external world but is knowable only from the perspective of participation in it." Voegelin, *Israel and Revelation*, 39. In the "Postscript" Voegelin pointed out that the critical reader who is faced with the ambiguity inherent in *The Turn* knows—in the sense of existentially experiencing—that reality becomes luminous in the consciousness of man. This statement written in 1969 foreshadows in an inchoate form Voegelin's meditation on consciousness in the first chapter of *In Search of Order*, but only published posthumously. Cf. Voegelin, *Order and History, Volume V: In Search of Reality* (1987), ed. Ellis Sandoz, *CWEV* Vol. 18, 2000, Chapter 1: "The Beginning of the Beginning," 27–62.

upon the analyses of "the androgynic eroticism in the constitution of modern Edens" by Mario Praz, Mircea Eliade, and Hans H. Hofstätter in order to understand and explicate the "Puritan variant" found in *The Turn*.[36]

When Voegelin read James's novella for the first time in 1947 he had been working through historical documents of human history extending back to the ancient Orient and Greece for his *History of Political Ideas* and subsequently interpreted in the first three volumes of *Order and History*: *Israel and Revelation*, *The World of the Polis*, and *Plato and Aristotle*. The participatory mode of reading and interpretation permitted Voegelin to "sense" something was amiss in *The Turn*. In fact, in the introductory paragraphs of the "Postscript," he asserts:

> Even while writing the letter, I was uneasily aware of an incongruence between the meaning I tried to establish in terms of God and man, the Puritan soul and common sense, the passion of self-salvation, grace and damnation, and the Jamesian symbols which carried these meanings distinctly but surrounded by a ghostly aura of indistinctness. Even worse, when later I tried to pursue the symbols through the labyrinth of the story, the distinct core tended to be shrouded by the fogginess of meaning that pervaded the work as a whole.[37]

By the writing of the "Postscript," Voegelin realized that the "indistinctness and ambiguity" which so disturbed him in the first reading in 1947, "are inherent to the symbols which express deformed reality."[38] He recognized too that the artists who represent the movements of Mannerism, Romanticism, and Symbolism "place themselves in the situation of deformed existence and develop symbols that will express their experience, as it were, from within

36 The works of these writers are: Mario Praz, "*Romantic Agony* (1930; 2nd English ed., 1951), Mircea Eliade's *La Coincidentia oppositorum et le Mystère de la totalité* (1959), and Hans H. Hofstätter's *Symbolismus und die Kunst der Jahrhundertwende* (1965). Voegelin, "On Henry James's *Turn,*" 168.

37 Ibid., 150.

38 Ibid., 151.

the deformation."[39] In the final paragraph of the "Postscript," Voegelin quotes James's description of himself as an artist in a letter to Henry Adams. There James writes: "I am that queer monster, the artist, an obstinate finality, an inexhaustible sensibility."[40] James's "inexhaustible sensibility," suggested to Voegelin the literary and philosophical traditions to which James was heir. As Voegelin pointed out, the "fuzziness of the symbols, as well as the general fogginess of meaning pervading the work, is caused . . . by a certain deformation of personal and social reality that was experienced as such by artists at the turn of the century and expressed by means of symbolistic art."[41] "The deformation of which I am speaking," he then writes, "is the fateful shift in Western society from existence in openness toward the cosmos to existence in the mode of closure against, and denial of, its reality."

> As the process gains momentum, the symbols of open existence—God, man, the divine origin of the cosmos, and the divine Logos permeating its order—lose the vitality of their truth and are eclipsed by the imagery of a self-creative, self-realizing, self-expressing, self-ordering, and self-saving ego that is thrown into, and confronted with, an immanently closed world.[42]

Placing James within the Symbolist movement, Voegelin described the history of the deformation from its origins in the seventeenth century and traced it through the nineteenth and twentieth centuries in which James lived and wrote. Expanding upon "the Puritan variant of the generic problem" of self-salvation, Voegelin focused first on Milton's transformation of the cosmos into a Godless Eden whose perfection depends upon the actions of human beings expelled from the original Eden and cut off from communication with the divine. He argued that Milton

39 Ibid., 151.

40 Ibid., 171. Even though Voegelin cites this assertion by James in the final paragraph of the "Postscript" in his summative assessment, it underlies the approach that Voegelin develops from the beginning of his essay, i.e., to supply the history of literary-artistic and philosophical deformations of which James is heir and to which he responded sympathetically.

41 Ibid., 151.

42 Ibid., 151.

> introduced the ambiguities of paradise into the tradition in which James moved. The paradise lost by Milton has the peculiar aura of 'forget about it.' Adam and Eve were expelled from it with the assurance that from their seed will spring the Savior; and with the acquisition of Christian virtues:
>
> wilt thou not be loth
> To leave this Paradise, but shalt possess
> A Paradise within thee, happier far.[43]

Voegelin pointed out that in *Marriage of Heaven and Hell* (ca. 1790) William Blake recognized this deformation of Christian Trinitarian symbols when he wrote: "But in Milton, the Father is Destiny, the Son a Ratio of the five senses, and the Holy-ghost, Vacuum."[44] In other words: God has been absorbed into the destiny of man who possesses "A Paradise within," the human being has been reduced to his material, sensory self, and the Holy Ghost—reduced now to a Vacuum—is no longer accessible to human beings. This deformation Voegelin then traced through Schiller's character, Karl Moor, in *Raeuber* (1781) and into Hegel's recognition of it in his *Philosophie des Rechts* (1821). This historical description of the deformation culminates with references to T. S. Eliot's existential state of the self-actualized man in *The Waste Land* (1922) and "The Hollow Men" (1925) to finally find expression in Jean-Paul Sartre's *Huis Clos* (1944). But before the twentieth-century manifestations of the deformation, the garden that provides the setting for Henry James's novella has become the new habitat of man who is cut off from and ordered to maintain his independence from the Divine.

After explicating the tradition of deformation to which James was heir, Voegelin located James historically between the "exuberant creation of new worlds in the wake of the French Revolution and the explosion of hell beginning with the First World War."[45] James, he noted, participated fully in the Anglo-American cultural ambience that occupied a peripheral position to the violent, revolutionary upheavals that followed the French Revolution;

43 Ibid., 153.
44 Ibid., 156.
45 Ibid., 160.

the garden of *The Turn* "is located in the outer fringe of the storm, in America and England. . . . [and has become] the park surrounding an English country house."[46] From within this Anglo-American sphere, James partook fully in an Anglo-American mood of understatement. The symbols that James used to portray the drama and personae of *The Turn* are understated in order to distort reality "by veiling or subduing its starkness."[47] The crucial importance of understatement resides in the desire to ameliorate the starkness of the realization that the human condition includes the imperfection of human beings, the presence of evil, and the inevitability of death. Through understatement, understood by Voegelin as James's "fastidious restraint" and commitment to what James called his "good taste," James can invite his readers to avoid facing that realization. Consequently, his readers are left with a vague sense that something in the story is disturbing, i.e., the readers are disturbed but not enlightened. It becomes the responsibility of the reader with a critical consciousness of reality to penetrate the veil of understatement and recognize the inevitable outcome of the governess's dependence on her own spiritual "power" and the inevitable outcome of her independence. The effect of James's "Edenic mood of understatement," writes Voegelin, "will allow neither for the outcry of suffering, nor for the defiant symbolization of man in revolt."[48]

46 Ibid.

47 Ibid.

48 Ibid., 164–65. Responding to a letter from Heilman in which Heilman asked Voegelin to expand on the point he had made about Anglo-American understatement, but more especially about English understatement, Voegelin pointed out that after the Glorious Revolution, the content of English thought changed from the rigor displayed in the works of Hobbes, Locke, and Berkeley into the "common sense" philosophy of Reid and his successors. The common sense tradition represents a toning down of philosophy to the level of "the common man who does not engage in philosophical meditations. He wrote that "The common sense man of the Scottish philosophers is a man who holds the same truths with regard to man and his ethical conduct as a philosopher but without the philosophical apparatus." Furthermore, Voegelin pointed out that even Edmund Burke engaged in this type of understatement in his *Reflections on the Revolution in France* in which he used progressivist language ("man is a creature of his own making") even though he was writing from within the classical tradition that understood man as living in the "classical

Consulting five of James's other works, Voegelin discovers that the dustiness of symbols and ambiguity characteristic of *The Turn* is not an aberration in James's oeuvre.[49] Even though James carefully guards with understatement and restraint his writing, Voegelin discovers the *cri de coeur* of existential closure in *The Wings of the Dove* (1902). The character asks:

> Why should a set of people have been put in motion, on such a scale and with such an air of being equipped for a profitable journey, only to break down without an accident, to stretch themselves in the wayside dust without a reason?[50]

This striking expression of existential derailment was not, observed Voegelin, "the problem of Henry James alone; it is the mark the 'age' threatened to stamp on more than one of its public figures."[51]

While Voegelin maintained that there was "no certain answer" to the existential question posed by James's character, his discussion of incest in the "Postscript" of 1969 may suggest a path to understanding. When Voegelin

tension between potentiality and actualization." Burke's formulation in the *Reflections* "blurs the intellectual structure of the problem." The "fuzziness" in James's symbols is also characteristic of Burke's writing. Voegelin concluded: "It is an English style of messing up the Logos of reality that goes parallel with the development of the symbols 'understatement' and 'gentility.'" Voegelin then draws a political lesson from this English commitment to understatement: "The deliberate refusal to enter into explicit intellectual debate has proved an effective preservative for the substance of common sense in England and America. The French and German adventures in more penetrating thought have proved disastrous in their social consequences." Cf. Letters 122 and 123 in Embry, *A Friendship in Letters*, 257, 258–60.

49 There is no indication that Voegelin read the complete stories of James, but we do know that he discovered that dustiness or fogginess beclouds the characters of four of James's short stories or novellas—in addition to *The Turn of the Screw* (1898)—and one of his novels. These include: "An International Episode" (1878), "Daisy Miller" (1878), "The Aspern Papers" (1888), the novel *The Wings of the Dove* (1902), and "The Beast in the Jungle" (1903). Note that all these stories are written in a twenty-five-year period from 1878 to 1903 and that *The Turn* is situated relatively late.

50 Ibid., 166.

51 Ibid.

recognized in 1947 the issue of "incest" and androgyny in *The Turn* he did not associate this component with what he then knew of Immanuel Swedenborg's myth of the perfect man with its androgynic element and the fact that James's father was a Swedenborgian. Consulting modern studies of the role of the androgynic myth in the construction of modern Edens, Voegelin realized that symbols derived from the ancient myths that aimed to symbolize the mystery of existence could be degraded in a Symbolist work of art and used, as did James did, in the construction of his modern Eden.[52] And since he had not completed his studies "of experience and symbolization, of compact and differentiated experience, of open existence and closure" he was also not aware in 1947 "of the possibility that prephilosophic symbolization in the mode of open existence, and postphilosophic symbolization in the mode of closure, could have the same structure of a spectrum in which symbols can combine and blend."[53] The essential difference between the prephilosophic, i.e., mythic symbolizations in the mode of openness and the postphilosophic symbolizations of order in the mode of closure hinges on the fact that the mythic forms of symbolization sought only to understand the mystery of the ground of being in a cosmos that was accepted as the lot of man, i.e., the inevitability of suffering and death and the existence of male and female. The makers of myth did not seek to perfect the habitat of man. The postphilosophic symbolizations in the mode of closure, on the other hand, appropriate the symbols of openness created in response to experiences of the divine ground of being achieved by Judaism, Greek philosophy, and Christianity to their own end of perfecting the habitat of humanity. When the different symbols of oneness in diversity such as God and Satan, good and evil, and the Christian paradise before the fall and death, are viewed not as

> Isolated phenomena [however] . . . but as symbols which derive their meaning from the mode of closure they express, the connection between a Miltonian paradise, a Swedenborgian perfect man, a God who is Satan, and a Jamesian soul who has lost itself to its pride becomes clear.[54]

52 See above, Footnote 31.
53 Voegelin, "On Henry James's *Turn*," 171.
54 Ibid.

While Voegelin knew the answer to the question asked by the character of *The Wings of the Dove*, he suggested that James also knew, i.e., that the Edenic existence of his creation in *The Turn* was "the hell of living death."

By now it should be apparent that the form of literary criticism that Voegelin displays in the "Postscript" has moved beyond the earliest articulated principles. It is impossible to demonstrate how Voegelin relied upon the first two principles—Primacy of the Text and Submission to the Master and Exhaustion of the Source—as he understood them in 1947 and 1956 in the "Postscript" of 1969. The third identifiable principle—that the reader must supply the Critical Consciousness of Reality—actually absorbs the first two principles, as well as the fourth principle—recognition of the existential content of *The Turn*. The recognition or determination of the existential content of a work depends upon a Submission to the Master that rests upon Voegelin's *pia interpretatio* all the while maintaining what Voegelin has called "reflective distance." When Voegelin articulated this principle of Submission to the Master and Exhaustion of the Source, he was complimenting Heilman's work on Shakespeare's *Othello* in which Heilman had exhausted the content of the drama in order to demonstrate the completeness of Shakespeare's understanding of the human condition. In other words, the principle of exhaustion that depends upon the interpreter submitting to the master as disciple, only succeeds when the work itself is written by an author who recognizes and dwells in the openness of existence. When Voegelin first read *The Turn*, he attempted in his 1947 letter to Heilman to directly translate the elements of the story into philosophical symbols. This attempt failed. Voegelin admitted in the "Postscript" that he had sensed an incongruence in the story that would not yield to the application of the principle of direct translation into philosophy. Therefore, in order to penetrate to the existential content of James's story, Voegelin silently transformed the principle, Submitting to the Master,[55] while maintaining a reflective distance since he now knew that "in the consciousness of man reality becomes luminous to itself; and . . . that reality does not

55 It is clear that Voegelin continued to admire James as a writer, for he asserted "That James chooses a 'ghost story' for expressing the mood of this understated Eden is a superb stroke of realism." Ibid., 160.

cease to be luminous when a man contracts his existence."[56] In "The Beyond and Its Parousia," published in 1982, Voegelin wrote: "We can reflectively distance ourselves from the paradox in which we are involved and talk about it—and such talk is called *philosophy*."[57] Even though Voegelin had not articulated his understanding of the nature of reflective distance at the time he wrote the "Postscript," I think that he depended upon his reflective distance as an essential element of his unarticulated *pia interpretatio*.

Voegelin's type of literary criticism is not an easy matter to undertake or even to understand, for it places upon the critic (and a reader) the responsibility to master not only the text of the particular work, but the texts of the author's oeuvre and indeed the texts of human history that have symbolized man's search for order. Voegelin committed his life to understanding, explicating, and transmitting to future generations his insights concerning the search for the truth of human existence. His discoveries in that search enabled him to expand his original reading of *The Turn* to that of the "Postscript: On Paradise and Revolution."

Final Remarks

The reader of the "Postscript" may well be overwhelmed by Voegelin's "command" of the elements of modern European literary and philosophical traditions to which Henry James was heir and in which he participated, yet he has created a context in which James's novella can be understood as the creation of an artist who is cognizant that he is creating a closed cosmion from which the divine is excluded and the human is elevated—and burdened with—the responsibility for combating evil.[58] It is indeed a magisterial performance. Even though Voegelin has demonstrated the necessity

56 Ibid., 164.

57 Voegelin, "The Beyond and Its Parousia," (1982) in *The Drama of Humanity and Other Miscellaneous Papers, 1939-1985*, ed. William Petropulos and Gilbert Weiss, *CWEV* Vol. 33, 2004, 399.

58 Voegelin, in answer to the critics of the first edition of his *The Political Religions*, writes: "One cannot fight a satanical force with morality and humanity alone." Eric Voegelin, *Modernity Without Restraint: The Political Religions; The New Science of Politics; and Science, Politics, and Gnosticism*, ed. Manfred Henningsen, *CWEV* Vol. 5, 2000, 24.

of such a context for understanding *The Turn of the Screw*, the reader of the "Postscript," in order to appreciate Voegelin's interpretation cannot depend solely upon the "Postscript" itself. Instead the reader must complete three labors. First, he must not only familiarize himself with the novella but must adopt a participatory mode of reading, and thereby enter into the world of its Garden. The reader must, however, simultaneously guard himself from succumbing to the temptation to accept the closed cosmos that *The Turn* symbolizes. The reader may indeed permit the "Postscript" to function as an inoculation against the seductive power of James's writing. Second, he must read (or rather reread) Voegelin's 1947 letter in order to understand how Voegelin approached and interpreted the story after his initial reading. Third, he must closely follow the intricacies of Voegelin's argument from his opening description of deformation that characterizes Western modernity through the concluding discussion of the spectrum of the androgynic myth and its relevance for *The Turn*. It is only at this point that the reader can determine if Voegelin's interpretation has penetrated to the essence of James's creation.

–7–

Voegelin's "The Gospel and Culture"

Thomas Heilke

An informed reader might reasonably harbor an expectation or two of an essay entitled "The Gospel and Culture."[1] The essay was published in 1971, during a decade that saw a remarkable proliferation and endurance of historical Jesus studies that have not abated a half-century later. One might, therefore, expect manifold references to the person or the teachings of Jesus of Nazareth, the central subject of all known Christian gospels. Instead, a direct approach to either topic is not apparent. This absence in an essay that includes "gospel" in its brief title, written by a foremost political philosopher of the twentieth century with a prevailing concern for the place of the life of the spirit in the political, therefore raises one's curiosity.

The Philological Context of "The Gospel and Culture"

Commenting on the import of Voegelin's posthumous, just-published fifth volume of *Order and History*, a late friend observed that, "As they get old, political philosophers start to worry about dying and forget about politics." "The Gospel and Culture" is a late essay, one of twelve that Voegelin published between the appearance of the first three volumes of *Order and History* (1956/57) and his death twenty-eight years later. Brought together in

1 Various drafts of this essay were presented at the Annual Conference of the American Political Science Association (2014), the Annual Meeting of the European Association of Biblical Studies (2015), and the Congress of Learned Societies: Canadian Political Science Association (2016). My thanks to the discussants on all three occasions for their helpful comments, and especially to Michael Franz for originally suggesting the study.

Volume 12 of Voegelin's *Collected Works,* several of these twelve arguably belong to this seemingly unpolitical category of inquiry into matters of meaning and mortality to which my friend alluded and that struck him as distant from the quotidian concerns of politics or even political philosophy.

One might observe that Voegelin was a self-described mystic philosopher in a rapidly demystifying academic guild. Even so, several essays of Volume 12 stand in marked contrast to much of his earlier published work, which is consistently and readily recognizable as pertaining to political science or political philosophy: topics such as the Gospel and culture, Hegelian sorcery, immortality, or equivalences of experience do not seem the stuff of political science. This puzzle is not merely taxonomic or biographical. Voegelin's work concerning the problem of spiritual disorder in politics, representations of meaning, and the like, was extensive. It included *The New Science of Politics* (1952), *Science, Politics, and Gnosticism* (1968), and the published essays that emerged around the time of these two works. The first three volumes of *Order and History* are consistent with Voegelin's ongoing line of interpretation during this period. Other materials from this period include *Anamnesis* (1966), the German lectures, "Hitler und die Deutschen" (1964), and a sizeable quantity of unpublished materials in the form of lectures, discussions, fragments, and nearly-polished pieces.[2] Voegelin published the fourth volume of *Order and History* in 1974 and continued work on a fifth, of which a surviving fragment appeared posthumously in 1987. What role does the published overflow of *CWEV* Volume 12 play amidst this sizeable body of work, in particular the meditative essays less immediately recognizable as political philosophy?

I make no argument here for the relative importance of one essay over any other in a full interpretation of Voegelin's work, nor do I propose in the few pages assigned to me to offer such an interpretation. Rather, I propose that the topic and approach of "The Gospel and Culture" stands in its own right as a portal to understanding Voegelin's approach to a central

2 An extensive selection of these latter materials can be found in Voegelin, *What is History? And Other Late Unpublished Writings,* ed. Thomas Hollweck and Paul Caringella, *CWEV* Vol. 28, 1990, and Voegelin, *The Drama of Humanity and Other Miscellaneous Papers, 1939-1985,* ed. William Petropulos and Gilbert Weiss, *CWEV* Vol. 33, 2004.

question of Western Civilization, an approach that pervades his work after *The New Science of Politics*. That question, its framing, Voegelin's specific "take" on it, and its import for an understanding of the modern West are the topics of what follows.

The Argument of "The Gospel and Culture"

The central question, its parameters, its importance, and the outline of a response are delivered to us in the first two pages of Voegelin's essay, which begins with a statement of the invitation—one might say the assignment—that motivates it. Voegelin's hosts "wanted to hear what a philosopher has to say about the Word's difficulty to make itself heard in our time and, . . . to make itself intelligible to those who are willing to listen."[3] Five questions follow from this assignment:

1. What were the reasons for the success of the Gospel in the Hellenistic-Roman environment in which it originated?
2. Why did the Gospel "attract an intellectual elite who restated the meaning of the gospel in terms of philosophy and, by this procedure, created a Christian doctrine?"
3. How was it possible that the doctrine developed in this process could become "the state religion of the Roman Empire?"
4. "How could the church, having gone through this process of acculturation, survive the Roman Empire and become the chrysalis, as Toynbee has called it, of Western civilization?"
5. What "blighted this triumphant cultural force, so that today the churches are on the defensive against the dominant intellectual movements of the time, and shaken by rising unrest from within?"[4]

It is not possible in my allotted space to engage fully with the swarm of assumptions and embedded historical arguments contained in these five

3 Eric Voegelin, "The Gospel and Culture," (1971) in *Published Essays, 1966-1985,* ed. Ellis Sandoz, *CWEV* Vol. 12, 1990, 172–212, at 172. Hereafter cited as Voegelin, "Gospel and Culture."
4 Ibid.

questions. Leaving aside their implicit historical, political, and sociological assumptions and silences, several of which are—to a greater or lesser extent—contestable in current scholarship, let it suffice to say that the five questions circle round a principal Voegelinian assertion:

> By absorbing the life of reason in the form of Hellenistic philosophy, the gospel of the early *ekklesia tou theou* [became] the Christianity of the church. If the community of the gospel had not entered the culture of the time by entering its life of reason, it would have remained an obscure sect and probably disappeared from history: we know the fate of Judaeo-Christianity.[5]

At the conclusion of the essay that ensues from this rich claim, we find Voegelin attempting to rescue Christianity from itself by means of philosophy. It might surprise us that the Gospel needs such a recovery, but if the core contemporary problem of the Gospel is philosophical, as Voegelin argues its ultimate reception was in the first several centuries, then the claim gains intelligibility. What have the stewards of the Gospel lost that a rescue is needed? How does Voegelin intend to effect it, and of what interest is this rescue attempt to a political scientist?

Voegelin's philosophical rescue entails first and foremost the recovery of a life of reason in the context of Christianity. The most important quality of that life is its activity of questioning. Properly understood, this activity comprises most especially an adequate understanding of what are the ultimate questions for human beings and, following upon those, what are the appropriate orientations and procedures for answering them, or—more precisely—for understanding their meaning? It is Voegelin's objective to rescue Christianity from its contemporary state of having lost the ability to ask the fundamental questions that a life of reason demands.

This state of loss has come about through the "hardening" of the gospel message "into self-contained doctrine" to such an extent that "the raising of the question to which [the gospel] is meant as an answer can be suspect as 'a non-Christian attitude'."[6] Voegelin contends that "the gospel as a

5 Ibid., 173.
6 Ibid., 174.

doctrine which you can take and be saved, or leave and be condemned, is a dead letter; it will encounter indifference, if not contempt, among inquiring minds outside the church, as well as the restlessness of the believer inside who is un-Christian enough to be man the questioner."[7] Anticipating the usual sorts of doctrinal objections such a Christian might make, Voegelin points to the example of Justin Martyr, who, among the third generation of Christian believers, "started as an inquiring mind and let his search, after it had tried the philosophical schools of the time, come to rest in the truth of the gospel."[8] The gist of Voegelin's response to his hosts is to articulate this truth of the gospel in philosophical terms such that the core of the gospel is understood as an articulation of and answer to the perennial Question that animated not only the philosophical inquiries of the Hellenes, but also the cosmological myths of pre-philosophical humankind. The recovery of this trans-historical, trans-cosmic, and trans-religious core will furnish a therapeutic for the (Christian) believers of today, many of whom—in contrast to Justin and other early Christians with an inclination toward philosophical inquiry—"are at rest in an uninquiring state of faith." The "intellectual metabolism" of these believers "must be stirred by the reminder that man is supposed to be a questioner, that a believer who is unable to explain how his faith is an answer to the enigma of existence may be a 'good Christian' but is a questionable man."[9]

Voegelin is not addressing fundamentalist Christianity, where we might anticipate most easily finding the kind of dogmatism and anti-intellectualism that he appears to be confronting. His hosts are not of this group. Nor—in the 1970s—is it the fundamentalist and conservative churches teaching some version of either a traditional orthodox or modernist conservative doctrine that are seeing declines in membership. It is the so-called "mainline" churches whose membership is gradually entering free-fall.[10]

7 Ibid., 174–5.

8 Ibid., 174.

9 Ibid.

10 The literature concerning this phenomenon is legion. See, for example, Reginald W. Bibby, *A New Day: The Resilience & Restructuring of Religion in Canada* (Lethbridge: Project Canada Books, 2012); Kurt Bowen, *Christians in a Secular World: The Canadian Experience* (Montreal and Kingston: McGill-Queen's University Press, 2004), 49–50.

The difficulties surrounding an identification and articulation of the problem to which Voegelin points will be familiar to his readers: "doctrinal hardening," "loss of the question," "intellectual distortions," and prejudicial premises are all aspects of the core problem that "the question concern[ing] the humanity of man" is no longer available as the beginning point of a search for the (divine) ground of being.[11] That search, and the experiences and consequent questions that animate it, are "the same today as [they] ever [have] been in the past."[12] It is that sameness, that universality of the question, that gives Voegelin the entrée to his rescue mission: He is able not only to trace a history of a Western crisis in the life of reason informed by the Hellenic and Christian inquiry that originally opened us to a philosophical articulation of the Question and a search for its answers, but also to point to a panoply of examples of the Question in pre-philosophical, cosmological cultural settings. This comparing and contrasting of noetic insights with the (philosophical) message of the Gospel makes up the bulk of Voegelin's essay. The universality of the question regarding the meaning of existence enables him to address the message of the Gospel as one articulation of the Question and a response to it, and compare it to other articulations and responses, especially that of Hellenic philosophy. The latter developed into a tradition of inquiry that—according to Voegelin—the Mediterranean stewards of the Gospel message were able in various ways to absorb into their theological inquiries and "systems," and which thereby formed the spiritual/noetic basis for at least two major historical civilizations (Byzantine/Orthodox and, later, Latin/W. European). In response to my late friend, Voegelin's effort has political import, because "The life of reason [is] the ineluctable condition of personal and social order."[13]

Voegelin's philosophical response to the problems of the difficulty of the Word of the Gospel making itself heard is, therefore, based on a specific conception of the universality of the claims of the Gospel. In his response to a review of the fourth volume of *Order and History*, he noted that he was "very conscious" in that work "of not relying on the language of

11 Voegelin, "Gospel and Culture," 174 and 175.

12 Ibid., 175–6.

13 Eric Voegelin, "On Classical Studies" (1973), in *Published Essays, 1966-1985*, *CWEV* Volume 12, 256–64, at 257.

doctrine." He was, at the same time, "equally conscious of not going beyond the orbit of Christianity," when, for example, he gave preference to "the experiential symbol divine reality" in contrast to "the God of the Creed, for *divine reality* translates the *theotes* of Col. 2:9." This specific term was particularly valuable for expressing the universality of the Christian language and Gospel claims: "The *theotes*, a neologism at the time, is a symbol arising from experiential exegesis; its degree of generality is so high that it can be applied, not only to the specific experience of divine reality becoming incarnate in Christ and the Christian believers . . . but to every instance of *theotes* experienced as present in man and forming his insight into his nature and its relation to the divine ground of his existence." Voegelin's "inquiry into the history of experience and symbolization" thereby included every kind of faith seeking understanding by reason, not solely the Christian variety. He asserted that, at the same time, such an experience did not "go beyond 'Christianity,'" because universalist statements consistent with this principle can be found as core statements of Christian doctrine. "In practice," such core statements mean "that one has to recognize, and make intelligible, the presence of Christ in a Babylonian hymn, or a Taoist speculation, or a Platonic dialogue, just as much as in a Gospel."[14] Accordingly, Voegelin could summarize in succinct form the identification and pursuit of the "Question" in the context of Greek philosophy—represented most especially in the recorded inquiries of Plato and Aristotle—and the identification and pursuit of the question concerning the meaning of human existence in the context of Israelite and early Christian history as being one and the same:

> The noetic core, thus, is the same in both classic philosophy and the gospel movement. There is the same field of pull and counter-pull, the same sense of gaining life through following the pull of the golden cord, the same consciousness of existence in an In-Between of human-divine participation, and the same experience of divine reality as the center of action in the movement from question to answer. Moreover, there is the same

14 Eric Voegelin, "Response to Professor Altizer's 'A New History and a New but Ancient God?'" in *Published Essays 1966-1985*, *CWEV* Vol, 12, 294.

> consciousness of newly differentiated insights into the meaning of existence; and in both cases this consciousness constitutes a new field of human types…[15]

To make his case that various derailments with regard to the Question—including dogmatic hardening among Christians—can be ameliorated by the message of the Gospel, Voegelin must show how that message is, in fact, an articulation of the Question and ultimately a substantive answer concerning the puzzle of human existence. He must then show how that articulation and response is, at least in its most significant respects, parallel to similar articulations and responses in the cosmological mythologies of pre-philosophical societies and in the philosophical explorations of the Greeks. The tenuous character of this articulation and answer (and its vapor-like yet core role in civilizational formation) is brought to light in Voegelin's startling remark that "existence is not a fact":

> If anything, existence is the nonfact of a disturbing movement in the In-Between of ignorance and knowledge, of time and timelessness, of imperfection and perfection, of hope and fulfillment, and ultimately of life and death. From the experience of this movement, from the anxiety of losing the right direction in this In-Between of darkness and light, arises the inquiry concerning the meaning of life. But it does arise only because life is experienced as man's participation in a movement with a direction to be found or missed; if man's existence were not a movement but a fact, it not only would have no meaning but the question of meaning could not even arise.[16]

Only from the vantage point of this insight, alongside the insight concerning the basic Question of existence, can Voegelin's characterization of the life of Jesus as a "historical drama of revelation" in which "the Unknown God ultimately becomes the God known through his presence in Christ"[17]

15 Voegelin, "Gospel and Culture," 192.
16 Ibid., 176.
17 Ibid., 199.

be met with intelligent assent. It is because existence is a *movement* that "tearing the drama of participation asunder into the biography of a Jesus in the spatiotemporal world and eternal verities showered from beyond would make nonsense of the existential reality that was experienced and symbolized as the drama of the Son of God."[18] By providing a philosophical analysis of a number of episodes from the Gospels, their predecessor Hebrew scriptures, and several of the early Christian epistles, and keeping carefully in view the pre-philosophical cosmological myths, Voegelin demonstrates that

> The imaginative play of the *alethes logos* is the "word" through which the divine Beyond of existence becomes present in existence as its truth. The Saving Tale can be differentiated beyond classical philosophy, as it has historically happened through Christ and the gospel, but there is no alternative to the symbolization of the In-Between of existence and its divine Beyond by mythical imagination.[19]

The Gospel and Hellenic philosophy can meet and meld in their mutual illumination of one another, because they are explorations and articulations of the same reality.

Voegelin saw one notable distinction between these two traditions of questioning and symbolization: "Though the noetic core is the same in the gospel, its spiritual dynamics has radically changed through the experience of an extraordinary divine irruption in the existence of Jesus."[20] It is because of this unique "divine irruption," that out of a common, complementary search we nevertheless see culturally and even politically influential differences:

> The movement that engendered the saving tale of divine incarnation, death, and resurrection as the answer to the question of life and death is considerably more complex than

18 Ibid., 201.
19 Ibid., 188.
20 Ibid., 192.

> classic philosophy; it is richer by the missionary fervor of its spiritual universalism, poorer by its neglect of noetic control; broader by its appeal to the inarticulate humanity of the common man; more restricted by its bias against the articulate wisdom of the wise; more imposing through its imperial tone of divine authority; more imbalanced through its apocalyptic ferocity, which leads to conflicts with the conditions of man's existence in society; more compact through its generous absorption of earlier strata of mythical imagination, especially through the reception of Israelite historiogenesis and the exuberance of miracle-working; more differentiated through the intensely articulate experience of loving-divine action in the illumination of existence with truth.[21]

The intricacies of this claimed complementarity amidst difference and its various philosophical and theological problems have been extensively explored, critiqued, affirmed, and disputed.[22] My objective here is neither to review this literature nor to rehearse its arguments, but to suggest a new perspective on what Voegelin understood himself to have been doing and why. If he proposed to provide a socio-political therapeutic, as "Gospel and Culture" seems to suggest, an examination of his approach to studies of the historical Jesus, the beginnings of Christianity, and the development of the biblical texts, combined with his philosophical interpretation of the meaning of Jesus and early Christianity will show whether—and in what ways—my late friend's critique of Voegelin's approaching-the-end philosophizing missed a political element in fact still present and standing in contrast to more typically "doctrinal" approaches. For anyone more closely interested

21 Ibid.,189.

22 See, for example: Bruce Douglass, "A Diminished Gospel: A Critique of Voegelin's Interpretation of Christianity," in Stephen A. McKnight, ed., *Eric Voegelin's Search for Order in History* (Baton Rouge: LSU Press, 1978); Murray Jardine, "Eric Voegelin's Interpretation(s) of Modernity: A Reconsideration of the Spiritual and Political Implications of Voegelin's Therapeutic Analysis," *Review of Politics*, Vol. 4 (Fall, 1995), 581–605; David Walsh, "Voegelin's Response to the Disorder of the Age," *Review of Politics*, Vol. 46 (April, 1984), 266-287

in Voegelin's work per se, an examination of this one particular essay from this one particular direction may suggest what several of Voegelin's later works add to the understanding of politics that he first (re)opened in *The New Science of Politics*.

This approach to Voegelin's work must begin with Voegelin's understanding that the extraordinariness of his historical appearance notwithstanding, Jesus is, while unique, also nontrivially like the great figures of philosophy or the prophetic tradition or the mystical tradition: he, like them, is a representative human being, a representative of humanity. Such a representative is someone who sets a "standard of knowledge" regarding how to realize one's humanity. In Aristotelian terms, such knowledge entails understanding how to "set goals entirely different from the goal of fulfilling [one's purely biological] nature," which means knowing how to become what one should be in accordance with one's ultimate and complete flourishing; in Kantian terms, it is to know what "ought to be willed";[23] in Christian terms, it is to know how to be an imitator of Christ. Each of these standards of knowledge are represented by historical figures who exemplify the standard, be it the *spoudaios* (Aristotle), the fully rational individual (Kant), or the pure in spirit (Christianity). The difficulty for these and any other representative form is that "in concrete historical societies . . . most human beings are little inclined to orient conduct to the models of representative humanity, but prefer other paths."[24] A number of political prescriptions follow from this fact, but the humanly representative characteristics of these leading figures nevertheless remains as an ordering force in those societies where, resistance and disinclination notwithstanding, they remain models for what it is to be fully human.[25] It is this theory

23 "Natural Law in Political Theory: Excerpts from the Discussion," (1963) in *The Drama of Humanity and Other Miscellaneous Papers, 1939-1985*, ed. William Petropolus and Gilbert Weiss, *CWEV* Vol. 33, 2004, 113. The quotes are from Voegelin's comments in the discussion.

24 Ibid.

25 For a fuller articulation of Voegelin's theory, see especially "What is History" (1963) in *What is History? And Other Late Unpublished Writings*, ed. Thomas Hollweck and Paul Caringella, *CWEV* Vol. 28, 1990, 47–51. Voegelin (at critical distance) outlined a Romantic version of this theory in *The History of the Race Idea from Ray to Carus* (1933), trans. Ruth Hein, ed. Klaus Vondung,

of representative humanity and Jesus as a uniquely, fully articulated exemplar of such that sets Voegelin's understanding of Jesus, the Christian church, and the civilizational role of Christianity apart from other interpretations. It also accounts for the silences we encounter in "Gospel and Culture" and for a distinctive ecclesiology that undergirds Voegelin's prescriptions in that address.

"The Gospel and Culture" and the Problem of the Historical Jesus

The study of or search for the historical Jesus is a branch of either history, philology, or theology that passes into philological, historical, and theological studies of the biblical canon. It has proliferated in the past 200 years into an academic cottage industry of an impressive size and lastingness. Accounting for all this bother with Jesus may be as complex as explaining why a man is shoveling in his front yard,[26] but after two centuries, and now persisting into the European so-called "post-Christian" era, we may reasonably marvel at its continuity. In notable measure, it has passed the era of "faith seeking understanding."[27] While that remains the project of scholars such as N. T. Wright, Marcus Borg,[28] I. Howard Marshall,[29] and Richard

CWEV Vol. 3, 1998. In chapters 17–19, Voegelin traced the genealogy of a new, post-Christian idea of the person, exemplified by the person of Goethe in the work of Carl Gustav Carus, that echoes in important respects Voegelin's later theory of representative humanity.

26 Alasdair MacIntyre, *After Virtue: An Essay in Moral Theory*, 2nd ed. (Notre Dame: University of Notre Dame Press, 1984), 206 (digging; gardening; taking exercise; preparing for winter; pleasing his wife; etc.)

27 Cf. James Crossley's recent emphasis in *Jesus and the Chaos of History*: "What I want to do is shift the focus to using Jesus as a means of understanding historical change and the ways in which power functions in human society, irrespective of whether his teaching is nice, terrible, weird, useful, or seemingly irrelevant." James Crossley, *Jesus and the Chaos of History: Redirecting the Life of the Historical Jesus* (Oxford: Oxford Scholarship Online, 2015), 11.

28 See Marcus J. Borg and N. T. Wright, *The Meaning of Jesus: Two Visions* (New York: Harper San Francisco, 1999).

29 I. Howard Marshall, *I Believe in the Historical Jesus* (Grand Rapids, MI: Eerdmans, 1977). Hereafter cited as Marshall, *Historical Jesus*.

Bauckham,[30] others explicitly disavow a motivation drawn from faith,[31] while yet others recognize the intersection of "faith, history, and hermeneutics"[32] in these studies and make transparent whatever methodological protocols they find best provide scholarly integrity whilst working at that intersection. Scholars such as N. T. Wright remain interlocutors for avowedly secular scholars, since they all share a commonly disputed interest that they contest on scholarly grounds.[33] That interest arises from a variety of motives: faith, the enjoyment of historical, philological, or other kinds of puzzles, or from a recognition that Jesus and the movement that he started are of civilizational importance for the West. As Northrop Frye cogently argued, Jesus and the biblical tradition in which he stands are a civilizational origin for us,[34] and this argument is tacitly or expressly accepted in much of the historical Jesus and biblical studies literature.[35] And if Christianity is waning in the West, it appears to be the fastest-growing religion world-wide, and certainly one of the *two* most widely influential and

30 Richard Bauckham, *Jesus and the Eyewitnesses: The Gospels as Eyewitness Testimony* (Grand Rapids, MI: Eerdmans, 2006). Hereafter cited as Bauckham, *Eyewitnesses.*

31 Examples include James Crossley, *Jesus and the Chaos of History*, and the work of the well-known New Testament scholar, Bart D. Ehrman.

32 James D. G. Dunn, *Jesus Remembered* (Grand Rapids, MI: Eerdmans, 2003), 12. Hereafter cited as Dunn, *Jesus Remembered.*

33 See, for example, Fernando Bermejo Rubio, "The Fiction of the 'Three Quests': An Argument for Dismantling a Dubious Historiographical Paradigm," in *Journal for the Study of the Historical Jesus*, Vol. 7 (2009) 211–53.

34 Northrup Frye, *The Great Code: The Bible and Literature* (Toronto: Academic Press Canada, 1982), xviii-xx, and *passim.* Frye is speaking first and foremost of the influence of the Bible on Western literature, but throughout his argument, we see influences well beyond the literary realm into the general thought-ways of the Western world, including natural science and the other arts. In back of Frye's claim stands a deep, broad, and occasionally contentious literature, the further claims and particulars of which I will not recite here.

35 As claimed or implied, for example, in two very different approaches to historical Jesus studies: James Dunn, *Jesus Remembered*; Bart D. Ehrman, *Jesus Before the Gospels: How the Earliest Christians Remembered, Changed, and Invented Their Stories of the Savior* (New York: HarperCollins Publishers, 2016), 289–95. Hereafter cited as Ehrman, *Jesus Before the Gospels.*

expanding.[36] Jesus of Nazareth, being the originator, if not the "founder," of this highly complex, variegated, and eminently durable tradition, therefore remains among scholars—of various confessions and none—a figure of intense interest. As long as Christianity remains a major religious tradition, interest in its historical founding is assured. The "assignment" that initiated Voegelin's "Gospel and Culture" is more narrowly defined than this broad interest, but his approach to the question necessarily stands in a clear, critical relationship to this wider story of the historical Jesus. The terms of Voegelin's critique are instructive for grasping the insights and limitations of his philosophical approach.

The Civilizational Jesus Disputed

Additional drivers in this civilizational mix continue to animate historical Jesus studies: the politically, ethically, or otherwise newly "relevant" historical Jesus and the Jesus, newly considered, who confirms or rejuvenates one of the Jesuses of Christian tradition. Relevant not because, in studies like that of Crossley, the socio-political context and socio-political outcomes of the Jesus movement may be instructive for other concerns, but because such study may reconfigure Christianity itself and thereby what we, its inheritors, take ourselves to be. Historical knowledge leads to contemporary recalibration, but not in the manner Voegelin wishes to foster. By way of brief example from among a multitude, we may compare the work of three very different scholars of the Jesus movement: Jacob Needleman, Elaine Pagels, and John Howard Yoder. While representing widely divergent positions, all three stand in illuminating contrast to Voegelin.

For Needleman, the recovery of a "Lost Christianity"—attested to in

36 For the current status of global Christianity, see especially Philip Jenkins, *The Next Christendom: The Coming of Global Christianity*, 3rd ed. (Oxford: Oxford University Press, 2011). Jenkins' description of the recent and current growth of Christianity in the South can be usefully contrasted with the remark of Paul Peachy in 1962 that "Christianity on the world scene represents a dwindling minority" (p. 8); Peachy, ed., *Biblical Realism Confronts the Nation: Ten Christian Scholars Summon the Church to the Discipline of Peace* (Pennsylvania: Fellowship Publications, 1963).

some part in recently rediscovered or long preserved but not validated "non-canonical" writings, in some part in the interpretive writings of early and more recent church leaders, and in some part in the New Testament writings themselves—is the recovery of a (lost) knowledge of how to be authentically human:

> When the issue reads out in these terms—spirituality vs. moral commitment, inner vs. outer—something fundamental has been distorted in the understanding of both inner development and moral action. The inner and outer world have been misunderstood, and this misunderstanding has had disastrous consequences both for Christianity and for modern culture.[37]

For Pagels, gnostic Christianity, as expressed in the documents discovered at Nag Hammadi but also as articulated in the documents of the (orthodox) New Testament—when read through an appropriate lens—represents an historically grounded alternative to the orthodox Christianity that developed into the bedrock religion of Western Civilization. The suppression of the gnostic alternative is a loss:

> Gnostic Christianity proved no match for the orthodox faith, either in terms of orthodoxy's wide popular appeal, what Nock called its "perfect because unconscious correspondence to the needs and aspirations of ordinary humanity," or in terms of its effective organization. Both have ensured its survival through time. But the process of establishing orthodoxy ruled out every other option. To the impoverishment of Christian tradition, gnosticism, which offered alternatives to what became the main thrust of Christian orthodoxy, was forced outside.[38]

37 Jacob Needleman, *Lost Christianity: A Journal of Rediscovery* (New York: Harper and Row, 1980), 217.

38 Elaine Pagels, *The Gnostic Gospels* (New York: Random House, 1979), 179. Nock's comment may be contrasted (*pace* Pagels) with G. K. Chesterton's contrary estimation that "The Christian ideal has not been tried and found wanting; it has been found difficult and left untried." (*What's Wrong with the World*, 1910, Part 1, Ch. V).

For Yoder, finally, the loss is not of a hidden Christianity, but of a Christianity and a Jesus that have largely been ignored since the political establishment of Christianity in the late Roman Empire. Since that time, "organized Christianity could be defined as the ever renewed effort to get around [the Sermon on the Mount] without repudiating Jesus."[39] Yoder argues that this circumvented ethic is not merely a personal ethic (an interpretation that is indeed a form of circumvention), but a social and political one. While "theologians have long been asking how Jerusalem can relate to Athens[,] here the claim is that Bethlehem has something to say about Rome—or Masada."[40] Accordingly, his study "claims not only that Jesus is, according to biblical witness, a model of radical political action, but that this issue is now generally visible throughout New Testament studies, even though the biblical scholars have not stated it in such a way that the ethicists across the way have had to notice it."[41] Yoder, in other words, claims throughout his work to find support for a Jesus of "significant oppositional impact" that Crossley finds rarely emerging among contemporary "radical historical Jesuses."[42]

Yoder's is but one example of a genus of versions of the Jesus of politics that are on offer in the contemporary cornucopia of Jesus or Christian movement studies. In it, we find many species: Jesus as revolutionary, as a teacher of peace, as decisively apolitical, as a Zealot, or idealist, or realist, or political naïf, and so on. Here, too, regardless of one's image of Jesus and its motivation, it remains incontrovertible that Jesus has played a nontrivial socio-political role as historical figure in Western Civilization and beyond. He and the multi-layered, variegated religious tradition that surrounds him therefore becomes a subject of inquiry not only for historians and theologians, but also for political scientists and political philosophers.

This plethora of historical Jesus and historical Christianity studies may quickly bring us with Philip Jenkins to a second-level "hermeneutics of

39 Walter Kaufmann, *The Faith of a Heretic* (New York: Doubleday and Company, Inc., 1963), 231, also 233, 235, and 242.

40 John Howard Yoder, *The Politics of Jesus: Vicit Agnus Noster*, 2nd ed. (Grand Rapids, MI: Eerdmans, 1994), 3.

41 Ibid., 2.

42 Crossley, *Jesus and the Chaos of History*, 8.

suspicion" in the tradition of either Friedrich Nietzsche or Thomas Hobbes.[43] Where Jenkins criticizes one stream of these studies, we can add others:

> . . . the rediscovered texts [of non-canonical Christian gospels] . . . in very few cases . . . reveal anything of significance about the times of Jesus and the apostles, or indeed about the first century of the Christian era. Even the few exceptions . . . tell us much less about the earliest ages than their advocates like to believe. . . . The alternative gospels are thus very important sources . . . for what they tell us about the interest groups who seek to use them today; about the mass media, and how religion is packaged as popular culture; about how canons shift their content to reflect the values of the reading audience; and more generally, about the changing directions of contemporary American religion.[44]

To add to the mix of scholarship, ideological drum-beating, controversy, and otherwise motivated investigation, it is not only such overtly

43 I am thinking here of the concept as articulated by Paul Ricoeur with regard to Nietzsche, Marx, and Freud: for a critical re-affirmation of Ricoeur's (naturalistic) conceptualization see Brian Leiter, "The Hermeneutics of Suspicion: Recovering Marx, Nietzsche, and Freud," in Brian Leiter ed., *The Future for Philosophy* (Oxford: Oxford University Press, 2004), 74–105; for the Hobbesian essentially political, structuralist, pre-genealogical version, see *Leviathan*, esp. XLVII.

44 Philip Jenkins, *Hidden Gospels: How the Search for Jesus Lost Its Way* (Oxford: Oxford University Press, 2001), 5. Jenkins makes no claims to expertise as a textual scholar, nor does he need to have any to make the arguments and evaluations posed in his book: they concern the sociology and American cultural fit of the quest for the historical Jesus based on "hidden gospels," and the paucity of "truly new information" that has emerged from them (22–26, 27–28, and *passim*). James Crossley encourages us to think "about the quest for the historical Jesus in . . . politicized and historicized ways" (*Jesus and the Chaos of History*, 5). I am unsure he would have Jenkins' approach in mind, but his critique of the "liberal" approaches to the study of the "Jewish" Jesus and of the liberal Jesus at which the studies of John Crossan and Marcus Borg arrive seem to run parallel to Jenkin's critique of the "American" characteristics of certain other approaches to the historical search.

anti-orthodox studies, but also more "traditional" historical Jesus studies that are occasionally thought to be corrosive to traditional (non-gnostic) Christian beliefs and faith.[45]

Voegelin, in contrast, seems intent on standing outside this fray. His interpretive approach sets out largely to bypass these debates, and he seems resolutely disinterested in the so-called "historical Jesus." The rationale for such a move is at least four-fold. First, as John Ranieri has pointed out in an extended argument in *Disturbing Revelation,*[46] Voegelin consistently treats the biblical texts strictly from a (Platonic) philosophical perspective. This approach allows the interpreter to ignore most of the debates outlined above. Second, Voegelin worked as a scientist. The noetic insights of Greek philosophy may themselves be the substance of a science, but the historical (in contrast to noetic) claims of faith are *not* themselves the substance of such an endeavor, but at best the *objects* of one. Third, insofar as the Jesus of history could play a non-philosophical role in the formation of communities and even civilizations, that role could be fulfilled along the lines of the Voegelin's concept of "representative humanity" that I have already sketched out. Finally, Voegelin largely sidesteps the question of an ecclesiology that will theoretically and practically do the work of bearing the civilizational undertaking that he has in mind. I take up these four inter-related aspects of Voegelin's approach in sequence.

Voegelin and the (Philosophical) Substance of Christianity

Recall that the noetic core of the Christian gospel and of the classical philosophy that Plato and Aristotle developed are the same, while the "divine irruption in the existence of Jesus"[47] changes the spiritual dynamic of that core. That change does not imply for Voegelin the central traditional Christian

45 I am aware of the looseness of the term "traditional," but use it advisedly, while bracketing the wide diversity within the "traditional." I. Howard Marshall's work is helpful for understanding the mainstream sensibilities of this category and its relationship to historical Jesus studies. See Marshall, *Historical Jesus.*

46 John J. Ranieri, *Disturbing Revelation: Leo Strauss, Eric Voegelin, and the Bible* (Columbia, MO: University of Missouri Press, 2009). Hereafter cited as Ranieri, *Disturbing Revelation.*

47 Voegelin, "Gospel and Culture," 192.

claim that the Divine reality can or should be understood as a personality who says "I am going to do something at this moment in space and time (history) to change the dynamic and meaning of the noetic core under which humankind has lived heretofore." On the contrary, when he considers the baptism of Jesus, for example, Voegelin sees in that story the expression of a prototype that reaches back to an ancient Egyptian symbolism:

> The Father-and-Son symbolism is an old Egyptian symbolism. Every pharaoh is the son of God. . . . Then you get, in the Exodus story, the transfer of the son of God from the pharaoh to the Chosen People . . . In the Gospel you get the further transfer: "This is my son, my first-born in whom I have my pleasure" . . . So you can trace that, and what it amounts to is the realization that the existential presence of God is experienced in existence in consciousness. And if you go beyond *that*, well, then you do one of these misconstructions.[48]

So, too, with the (occasional) Christian experience of the Divine breaking into concrete history. To imagine such an act is, for Voegelin, to engage in metastatic faith, a term that he coined to come to grips with a problem he perceived to have begun in the prophetic tradition of Israel and continued in the Christian movement:

> The tradition is always the structure of consciousness. That is reality. And in many respects, it is better worked out in [] classic philosophy than anywhere in Christianity. . . When you look, say, at the parable of the cave in the *Politeia*—where the man is turned toward the wall and then is *forced* to turn around and walk up toward the light in order to see the light—that is obviously a description of an experience of overcoming a

48 "Conversations with Eric Voegelin at the Thomas More Institute for Adult Education in Montreal," (1967) in Voegelin, *The Drama of Humanity and Other Miscellaneous Papers, 1939-1985,* ed. William Petropulos and Gilbert Weiss, *CWEV* Vol. 33, 2004, 293. Hereafter cited as Voegelin, "Conversations."

> resistance to turn around, being overcome by that pull of new force (by Divine Grace, or intervention, or whatever you wish to call it). Now what is the difference between this force compelling you to turn around, in Plato, and the vision of Saint Paul on the road to Damascus? I don't know what the difference is.[49]

In contrast to this pull in the psyche, we have Isaiah looking for a concrete act of the Divine in concrete human affairs. Such an expectation is a sign of metastatic faith, a "quasi-magical transformation of reality and the human condition,"[50] or "a vision of a world that will change its nature without ceasing to be the world in which we live concretely."[51] Metastatic faith appears in a variety of forms in the Israelitic and Christian traditions, but its common denominator is "to transform reality by means of eschatological, mythical, or historiographic fantasy, or by perverting faith into an instrument of pragmatic action."[52] On the one hand, it is easy to acknowledge the silliness—or, politically speaking, much worse—of a belief in a magical transformation of reality. On the other hand, Voegelin's insistence that the faith of Isaiah and Paul, both whom he accuses of metastatic inclinations, has "ontological implications"[53] deserves further attention.

It is not only Paul's theology, but all four gospels themselves that display metastatic tendencies, not merely with respect to the Resurrection, but also, for example, in the plenitude of miracle stories they contain throughout. John P. Meier argues that, whatever one may make of them, these stories are such a core ingredient of the gospel story that it is difficult to support a claim that they do not "go back to the time and ministry of Jesus

49 Ibid., 294.

50 q.v. in "Glossary of Terms Used in Eric Voegelin's Writings," in Eric Voegelin, *Autobiographical Reflections: Revised Edition with a Voegelin Glossary and Cumulative Index*, ed. Ellis Sandoz, *CWEV* Vol. 34, 2006, 168.

51 Eric Voegelin, *Order and History, Volume I: Israel and Revelation* (1956), ed. Maurice P. Hogan, *CWEV* Vol. 14, 2001, 506. For a thorough discussion of metastasis, which Voegelin introduced into philosophical discourse, see especially *Israel and Revelation,* 501–11.

52 Ibid., 507.

53 Ibid., 506, n6.

himself."[54] Meier avoids a Voegelinian critique of metastatic faith, however by limiting himself to the task of the historian, which is not "to decide the theological question of whether particular extraordinary deeds done by Jesus were actually miracles, i.e., direct acts of God accomplishing what no ordinary human being could accomplish," because "such a judgment ('this particular act is a miracle performed directly by God') goes beyond what any historian can legitimately assert within the limits of his or her own discipline."[55] At the core of the gospel claim, moreover, speaking concretely and historically, is a metastatic event—God becomes man. Voegelin responds that this claim should be understood symbolically, as the last of a long chain of similar symbolisms, being responses to a similar, repeated human experience of divine irruption, stretching back to ancient Egypt.

Voegelin understands Jesus to be someone in whom "the God speaks," just as He does through a (Platonic) philosopher.[56] In Jesus we see "the event of the divine Logos becoming present in the world through the representative life and death of a man,"[57] so that Jesus "embodies" "to the highest degree . . . the truth that the divine Beyond is present in each person."[58] In this sense—and this sense only—Jesus, like other exemplary human beings, is a representative of humanity. Voegelin does not regard the denial of the historicity of an actual resurrection (as contrasted with the vision of a "Resurrected One") or of other, seemingly "foundational" dogmatic claims of Christianity to be a rejection of its role as a civilizational underpinning, or of the role of Jesus as an extraordinary representative of humankind: Paul's vision of the "Resurrected One" is fundamentally equivalent to the theophanies of the earlier Hellenistic philosophers. Both kinds of theophanic visions are "open": they can accommodate a variety of

54 John. P. Meier, "The Historicity of Jesus' Miracles: The Global Question," excerpt from *A Marginal Jew: Rethinking the Historical Jesus, Volume 2: Mentor, Message, and Miracles* (New York: Yale University Press, 1994) in Werner Zager, ed., *Jesusforschung in vier Jahrhunderten* (Berlin/Boston: Walter de Gruyter GmbH, 2014), 473. Hereafter cited as Meier, *Historicity of Jesus*.

55 Meier, *Historicity of Jesus*, 473.

56 Voegelin, "Conversations," 301.

57 Voegelin, "Gospel and Culture," 190.

58 Ranieri (82) is here summarizing succinctly several characterizations Voegelin makes in "Gospel and Culture."

constructions to symbolize the basic "experience of divine presence in the myths of the intracosmic gods, in mytho-speculation, and in the noetic and pneumatic luminosity of consciousness."[59] Paul, along with the Christian "patres" of the first three centuries, worked in a "theophanic field" in which the "worrisome debates" about the "historicity" of Christ were "hardly an issue." Various "subordinationist construction[s]" to symbolize "the relation of the Son to the Father-God" were available and taken to hand as fit the need. Only as dogmatic constructions began to obscure the theophanic experience/event did the need to concern oneself with the historicity of Christ arise.[60] Accordingly:

> If the question of the "historicity" of Christ is raised with the "Christ" of dogma in mind, difficulties will inevitably arise. For the "Christ" of Nicaea and Chalcedon is not the reality of theophanic history that confronts us in the Pauline vision of the Resurrected; and to invent a special kind of "history," disregarding the theophanic reality on which the dogma is based, in order to endow the Christ of the dogma with "historicity" would make no sense.[61]

Because of this disconnection between historicity and civilizational role, brought about by an affirmation of the noetic core of Christianity that requires little attention to its historical claims, Voegelin proceeds as a scientist without needing to pay attention to the nexus of faith, history, and hermeneutics as much of traditional Christian theology stresses we must.

The Scholarship of the Text

It is not only this Platonic take on the biblical and patristic texts that leads Voegelin to discount the historical claims that the Christian community

59 Eric Voegelin, *Order and History, Vol. IV: The Ecumenic Age* (1974), ed. Michael Franz, *CWEV* Vol. 17, 2000, 326. Hereafter cited as Voegelin, *Ecumenic Age.*

60 Voegelin, *Ecumenic Age*, 325.

61 Ibid., 326.

has made from its earliest days. He paid close attention to the state of science in the areas in which he worked, as is immediately evident in the conversations with Old Testament scholars to which he refers in *Israel and Revelation*, and in his footnote apparatus throughout. There is nothing dilettantish in his scholarship: he did not consider his work possible without close attention to the state of science in those areas (like paleolithic, Old Testament, or Near Eastern studies, for example) in which he or his students were working.[62] Accordingly, the footnotes of *Israel and Revelation* are replete with references to the current scientific work on the general topics under consideration there. In his study of Paul, however, which appeared three years after "Gospel and Culture" in *The Ecumenic Age*, the references to then-current scholarship are far more slight; with regard to the question of the historical Jesus, they are non-existent. This approach, which Ranieri notes in his critique, receives support from those elements of New Testament scholarship of which Voegelin does seem to have taken note, most especially the work of Rudolph Bultmann, which he sharply critiqued in his 1965 "History and Gnosis." The critique is directed not at Bultmann's scholarship overall, which Voegelin judged to be "excellent,"[63] but at one specific problem: the denial of historical continuity between Christianity and its temporal predecessors, especially Judaism. It would be a fault of historical Jesus studies or Christian theological studies to deny it, and Voegelin's philosophical rejuvenation of Christianity partially relies on that continuity.

Voegelin's affirmation of history might encourage us to imagine that he is not so far from an engagement with studies of the historical Jesus or early Christianity as Professor Ranieri's and my reading of his work indicate. Both James Dunn and Richard Bauckham, for example, are proponents—contra Bultmann and others who take his approach—for maintaining a strong historical sense in our studies of Jesus. Bauckham argues that the gospel writers were keen to recount the "words and deeds" of God, not

62 Tilo Schabert, "Eric Voegelin's Workshop," in *Hunting and Weaving: Empiricism and Political Philosophy*, ed. Thomas Heilke and John von Heyking (South Bend: St. Augustine's Press, 2013), 232–51.

63 Voegelin, "History and Gnosis" (1965), in *Published Essays, 1953-1965*, ed. Ellis Sandoz, *CWEV* Vol. 11, 2000, 157.

merely the ageless philosophical-anthropological truths of human existence.[64] The Gospels are not philosophical treatises; from them, Voegelin extracts timeless philosophical truths, but one can also do that from a novel.[65] The eyewitness claims of the Gospel are something other than either treatises or literature. In the case of prophetic traditions of Israel, "the prophetic critique retains a strong sense of communal identity; if there is a universal dimension to the prophetic message, it is inseparable from the notion of a restored Israel."[66] In the case of the Christian writers, I would offer two comments. First, as Ranieri points out, the *particularities* of Paul's interpretation of his vision are not as proximate to Plato's framing of cosmic existence as Voegelin lets it appear to be. As a corollary to his critique of Isaiah's and Paul's metastatic faith, "Voegelin's criticism of Paul has as much to do with the apostle's apparent disregard for the role of perishing in determining the human condition."[67] Thus, "Voegelin follows [classical philosophers like] Anaximander and Plato in taking the reality of perishing for granted, so the issue becomes one of who best 'balances' the tension between *genesis* and *phthora*" (coming to be and perishing). Paul, however, contra this Greek philosophical conclusion, "rejects the very manner in which the philosophers have framed the issue":

> For Paul, the question is not how best to preserve the balance of consciousness within a divinely constituted order in which *genesis* and *phthora* are a permanent feature. Rather, the apostle has come to realize that God has nothing at all to do with death. The raising of Jesus from the dead testifies to this. From a Pauline perspective, Anaximander and Plato (and Voegelin) are mistaken in having the divine involved in any way with perishing.[68]

64 Bauckham, *Eyewitnesses*, 490.

65 This is how Ehrman seeks to restore some standing to the biblical texts he dismantles in his historical-philological critiques. Ehrman, *Jesus Before the Gospels*, 289–95.

66 Ranieri, *Disturbing Revelation*, 68.

67 Ibid., 88.

68 Ibid., 89.

That rejection, however, also entails a further affirmation: "So it is wonder that would be lost were we deprived of true Gospel testimonies that evoke the theophanic character of the history of Jesus." In Bauckham's estimation, this theophanic character is—on this account, and in contrast to all accounts that reject an actual and not merely visionary resurrection—directly related to "the way in which the Gospels relate the horror of the cross to this 'wonder-ful' exceptionality of the history of Jesus."[69]

Second, Voegelin, Bauckham, and Dunn do not all mean the same thing by an affirmation of history. Voegelin refers in his critique of Bultmann not to the abandonment of an historical Jesus—which he has left behind every bit as much as Bultmann—but to an historical *humankind* that Bultmann has abandoned as the "historical problem." This turn makes him a gnostic thinker in Voegelin's estimation. Human historicity is a quite different matter from the historicity of Jesus, nor is the solution to its problem the same. Bultmann has given up a search for the historical Jesus and had come to understand Christianity as a message concerning the human condition to which human beings are called to respond. Voegelin did not disagree with this interpretation. The point of contention was, instead, what to make of the historicity of humankind. While the particulars of the life of Jesus may not matter to the existential meaning and eventual socio-political success of the Christian movement, the existential historicity of that *meaning* does. While Voegelin can therefore follow Bultmann's abandonment of the historical Jesus question,[70] he cannot follow Bultmann into a de-historicizing existentialism. At the same time—and here

69 Bauckham, *Eyewitnesses*, 500. "We do well to be precise in our attention to what is at issue here [which is] not whether Voegelin's reading of Paul is in accord with church doctrine. Theologians and church authorities can determine whether Voegelin's account of Paul's encounter with the Risen Christ is compatible with Christian dogma. The question is whether Voegelin's interpretation does justice to the self-understanding of the biblical texts he analyzes." (Ranieri, *Disturbing Revelation*, 91).

70 This abandonment should be clarified with a caveat. Bultmann did not, on Dunn's account, reject any question of the historicity of the gospel, but rather, of the Liberal quest to write a modern biography of Jesus, which would include an account of the "personal life and development of the biographical subject"—Jesus (James D. G. Dunn, *Jesus Remembered*, 185; Cf. Rudolph Bultmann, *Jesus* (excerpt) in Zager, *Jesusforschung*, 289–90.)

again we see Voegelin's emphasis also—Bultmann, as he makes clear in the opening chapter of his *Theology of the New Testament*, is focused on neither the life nor deeds of Jesus, but his message and its meaning.[71]

This particular scholarship of the text adds credibility to Voegelin's insistence on treating the biblical texts strictly from a (Platonic) philosophical perspective. Ranieri identifies "The Gospel and Culture" as a key essay for observing Voegelin's approach of a "highly selective reading that tends to approximate the language of early Christianity to that of philosophy." He suggests further that this assimilation of the biblical text "to a philosophical perspective" contains a "risk" that the "specific character" of the text in question "may be lost," and that it "skirts the question as to whether philosophy itself is in need of a critique rooted in insights derived from the biblical text."[72] Voegelin's study of Paul in *The Ecumenic Age* three years after publication of "The Gospel and Culture" does not depart from this approach, and it offers no additional insights regarding the early Christian movement.

Reading the Gospel Story All Over Again for the First Time

As evidence for his argument that a philosophical interpretation of the Gospel is not the extraordinary move Christian believers might initially take it to be, Voegelin briefly referred in his address to the writings of Justin Martyr. Justin was an early second-century Jewish convert to Christianity whose winding road to Christian belief, recounted in his *Dialogue with Trypho*, took him first through various schools of Hellenic philosophy, culminating in the thought of Plato before arriving at Jesus. In Voegelin's interpretation of Justin's *Dialogue*, "Christianity is not an alternative to philosophy, it is philosophy itself in its state of perfection; the history of the Logos comes to its fulfillment through the incarnation of the Word in Christ," which means that "the difference between gospel and philosophy is a matter of successive stages in the history of reason."[73]

71 Bultmann, *Theology*, 3–32. As Meier has it, "The specific deeds of Jesus tend to disappear behind the 'naked word' of Jesus' message— which is characteristic of Bultmann's whole theological program." (Meier, "Historicity," 475 n4).

72 Ranieri, *Disturbing Revelation*, 92, 102.

73 Voegelin, "Gospel and Culture," 173.

There is no particular reason to dispute the basic outlines of this interpretation.[74] Justin himself argues that "Christ is the Word (*logos*) of whom every race of men were partakers" so that "those who lived reasonably (*meta logon* [in accordance with the Word or reason]) are Christians, even though they have been thought atheists; as, among the Greeks, Socrates and Heraclitus and men like them; and among the barbarians, Abraham and Ananias, and Azarias and Misael and Elijah and many others . . . ."[75] At the same time, Justin's defense of Christianity, both in the *Dialogue* and in his *Apology*, rests not only on philosophical claims, but also on exegetical and historical ones. Indeed, even in the passage just cited, Justin's aim is to show how it is possible to say that Jesus is/was "the Word," when he "was born one hundred and fifty years ago under Cyrenius," and more widely, when he seems to have been part of a much larger story of God and God's people in a prophetic tradition (*Apology*, XXXI-LXV; *Dialogue*, L-LIV, XCV-XCIX, CIV, etc.), in Hebrew temple worship practices (*Dialogue*, XL-XLII) and in the history of Israel (*Dialogue*, C, CXIII). Thus, Justin seeks to defend Christian claims in the context not only of a philosophical tradition, but also an historical one, i.e., in the context of a story. A rejoinder to this objection might be that Voegelin can criticize this aspect of Justin's "apology" from the same philosophical perspective that he criticizes Paul[76]: Justin has simply made a philosophical error. Justin's persistent linkages to historical incidents, persons, and tradition are not to be dismissed in one important respect, however: the need to consider the sociological and organizational substrate by means of which the Gospel message is sustained.

74 For a similar interpretation, see Arthur J. Droge, "Justin Martyr and the Restoration of Philosophy," in *Church History*, Vol. 56 (September 1987) 3, 303–19; George H. Gilbert likewise points out that at times, Justin's interpretation of biblical texts is philosophical, not exegetical. ("Justin Martyr on the Person of Christ," *The American Journal of Theology*, Vol. 10 (Oct., 1906) 4, 663–74 at 669.

75 Justin Martyr, *The First Apology of Justin*, XLVI in *Ante-Nicene Fathers*, Vol. 1, T*he Apostolic Fathers, Justin Martyr, Irenaeus*, ed. Alexander Roberts and James Donaldson (Peabody, MA.: Hendrickson Publishers, Inc., 1994 [1885]), 178. I have slightly modified the translation.

76 Gilbert's final criticisms of Justin's methods are pertinent here ("Justin Martyr," 668–9).

If so, then Voegelin ultimately leaves us not in biblical studies, quests for the historical Jesus, or philosophical theology, but in questions of ecclesiology.

By "questions of ecclesiology," I mean this: what will be the relationship between our philosophical claims and our *historical* claims—between a vision[77] and what we take actually to be empirical (historical) observations—on the one hand, and everyday practical concerns that we seek to address out of both our understanding of a vision and our historical claims on the other? Alternatively, how are the meaning and existential implications of a vision or of the words and deeds of a representative of humanity sustained over time? Voegelin was concerned that "the reality of the gospel threaten[ed] to fall apart into constructions of an historical Jesus and a doctrinal Christ," thereby discarding the essential "status of a gospel as a symbolism engendered in the *metaxy* of existence by a disciple's response to the drama of the Son of God."[78] Voegelin hints at the pragmatic elements involved in such a response: "The drama of the Unknown God who reveals his kingdom through his presence in a man, and of the man who reveals what has been delivered to him by delivering it to his fellowmen, is continued by the existentially responsive disciple in the gospel drama by which he carries on the work of delivering these things from God to man."[79] It is only a hint, however, and Voegelin does not concern himself with further particularities.

Much more concretely, claims concerning the historical words and deeds of Jesus are claims concerning what James Dunn—in part to avoid the usual dogmatics calisthenics—has called a "Jesus tradition." It is *that* tradition ("the work of delivering these things"), and not the abstraction of

77 Despite its acidic skepticism, quasi-doctrinal claims, and its intended popular audience, Ehrman's discussion of visions among the disciples of Jesus is, at the purely phenomenal level, consistent with Voegelin's interpretation. Ehrman, like most of the scholars in his guild, shows no interest in the kinds of existential philosophical (in contrast to hermeneutical, historical, or faith-related) implications that direct Voegelin's interpretation. Bart D. Ehrman, *How Jesus Became God: The Exaltation of a Jewish Preached from Galilee* (New York: HarperOne, 2014), 183–210.

78 Voegelin, "Gospel and Culture," 201.

79 Voegelin, "Gospel and Culture," 201.

a theophanic event, that provides the substance of "recollections of Jesus' teachings and manner of living and socializing" and that "evidently continued to serve the early Christian groupings as a *model* for any or all responsible living in community, as part of society." One can and should consider in what ways theophany validates the truth of the tradition, but it should also be clear that the philosophical experience of a Plato must be translated—is this not one of the lessons of Plato's allegory of the cave and an implication of Voegelin's description of the workings of the Gospel drama?—to become actualized in the quotidian concerns of the kinds of communities of believers that eventually formed the social and intellectual core of post-Rome Western civilization:

> . . . *through the Jesus tradition the would-be disciple still hears and encounters Jesus* as he talked and debated, shared table-fellowship and healed. In hearing the Jesus tradition read from pulpit or stage, in a sacred space or neighbor's sitting room, we sit with the earliest disciples and church groups as they shared memories of Jesus, nurtured their identity as his disciples, equipped themselves for witness and controversy, celebrated and learnt fresh lessons for life and worship from and in that celebration. Through that tradition it is still possible for anyone to encounter the Jesus from whom Christianity stems, the remembered Jesus.[80]

It is some distance from a community so constituted to the civilizational religion that became Christianity and that Voegelin describes. Yet we know that by the second century, small groups of philosophically-minded Christians did, in fact, constitute themselves in quasi-ecclesiastical communities to live a disciplined life as prescribed by philosophy, and that they engaged in "an intellectual discourse that proclaimed Christianity as the true and superior philosophy."[81] Voegelin is therefore on solid historical ground—

80 Dunn, *Jesus Remembered,* 893.

81 Winrich Löhr, "Christianity as Philosophy: Problems and Perspectives of an Ancient Intellectual Project," in *Vigiliae Christianae*, Vol. 64 (2010) 2, 160–88.

regardless of his Platonic philosophical argument—in his efforts to identify the philosophical luminosity of the Gospel message in its earliest days. The Christians so engaged, however, were a tiny minority among their fellow believers, who were themselves a small minority in the Empire for the first three centuries of the Christian movement. Thus, the language of *theotes* in Col. 2:9 and its analogues elsewhere ("before Abraham was, I am" [John 8:48]) in the Christian writings is preceded and followed by much more particular historical and ethical claims. Paul's readers were a particular gathering of believers in a particular place and time. He was eager to emphasize to them that they "walk in a manner worthy of the Lord," and he outlined in some detail what that "walk" entails. This particularity in the midst of universal claims may return us ever again to the question of the historical Jesus, but it also implies more immediate concerns regarding the nature of the community of believers who gather around claims about Jesus.

In contrast to Dunn's communally sustained "Jesus tradition" and to other practical ecclesiologies, Voegelin offered a political-scientific ecclesiology in his 1964 lectures, "Hitler und die Deutschen," that was centered on the transcendent representational role of the church in a given society. There being, in his estimation, "no theory of the church available," he distinguished six different levels of speaking about "church." Beginning with the two major German church organizations —Catholic and Evangelical— as social institutions, the six levels ended with the theological understanding of the church as the *corpus mysticum Christi* that Thomas Aquinas first identified, the mystical body of Christ that includes all human beings from the beginning of the world to its end.[82] At the common-sense level of the church as a social organization in a particular society, its role is to "represent the spiritual order of human beings toward God."[83] In a society like Germany of the 1930s, in which church membership and citizenship overlapped nearly entirely, one could say that "church people and German people are more or less identical," so that "the German people in politics and the German people in the church are the same; as human beings it

82 Eric Voegelin, *Hitler and the Germans,* ed. Detlev Clemens and Brendan Purcell, *CWEV* Vol. 31, 1999, 155–6. Hereafter cited as Voegelin, *Hitler*.

83 Voegelin, *Hitler*, 156. I have slightly amended the translation: "Menschen" is "human beings."

belongs to their constitution to be transcendentally oriented."[84] Accordingly, "The churches are nothing other than the representation of the spiritual transcendence of man. They are not anything else."[85]

At least two broad pressures militate against such representation. First, a church of the national type existing as Evangelical ("Lutheran") and Roman Catholic varieties in Germany in the early twentieth century is a large institution that can readily incubate an interest in sustaining itself purely and solely at the institutional level, thereby neglecting its representative role for the whole of humanity under God.[86] Second, "the contact with the reality of man in his individuality as *theo-morphes*, and thus his real human nature" can be lost under social, political, or intellectual (theological and philosophical) conditions that encourage such a forgetting. In an important sense, this second problem—their intellectual and spiritual decline—constitutes the gist of Voegelin's critique of the German churches before, during, and after the Third Reich.[87] The summary understanding of the church as "representative for order" is identical in these lectures to Voegelin's stated interpretation seven years later:

> Representative for order, therefore, are not only the covenant or the Sermon on the Mount or the formulations of the New Testament—handed on in apocalyptic expectation—but also the philosophic insight into the nature of man and the ideas of human and social order arising from it, as they were taken over from the pre-Christian philosophic complex.[88]

Voegelin leaves us with nothing like the Jesus of Dunn's communities of disciplines, but with the cosmic *logos* of philosophy, even if that *logos* is manifest through a particular "event in the drama of revelation," a "unit through the common presence of the Unknown God in the men who

84 Ibid.
85 Ibid.
86 Ibid., 208, 210.
87 Ibid., 157ff.
88 Ibid., 208.

respond to his 'drawing' and to one another."[89] How that representation and response to one another is manifested concretely is no concern of a Voegelinian "theory of the church," beyond the role of the church in representing human order through the ethical and political expressions and activities of its governing representatives in political society, which should, in turn, influence at some non-specified level the behavior of its members.

Let us accept Voegelin's Western civilizational account of Christianity, and especially his remedy for its philosophical closure among the acquaintances of those interlocutors who set his assignment for "Gospel and Culture." If the church is, nevertheless, not a philosophy seminar, but a community of believers, one should assume that stories, rituals, and even doctrine, not extensive philosophical investigation, will be the medium through which its representation of humanity will be expressed. The question then would become not how to eliminate doctrine and even dogma (or stories or rituals), but how to harness them to appropriate ends. If so, compelling questions remain. Two may be of particular interest forty-five years after Voegelin's address.

First, current major movements in global Christianity point to a possible working-out, not of a new Christendom, but of new articulations of the gospel message in new political contexts. If these new modes of Christianity do not lead to Christendom, what then? The "transmission" of what Voegelin takes to be that Gospel message is frequently messy, fraught, and "unphilosophical" in the extreme. It is not clear how strongly the experience of philosophical supersession that Voegelin identified in the thought of Justin Martyr drives us toward an anticipation of civilizational success. Insofar as, according to Voegelin, it is the philosophical attunement of Christianity that enables that success, we can at least suggest it is a key driver toward Christianity's civilizational role in his estimation. If, however, we consider current forecasts concerning Christian possibilities, there is a growing sense among significant numbers of theologians and historians of Christianity that Christendom is not merely a finished and discarded project, but that any currently foreseeable future with regard to a new Christendom is unlikely, and that the foreseeable future of the Christian Church will not

89 Voegelin, "Gospel and Culture," 201.

look like its European past.[90] One aspect of this conclusion is a growing awareness that—Voegelin's comments concerning the disappearance of Christianity in the absence of an imperial partnership notwithstanding—there have been significant and long-lasting Christian communities in history that did not require a Christendom arrangement to survive or, for that matter, to be culturally influential.[91]

A second confounding feature of this scholarship resides in the "messiness" it reveals concerning the Christian movement from its very beginnings. The inability to draw a straight line of development, whether in the development of European Latin and Eastern Orthodox versions of Christendom or the recent emergence of various streams of "Christianity without Christendom,"[92] lead us to ask outside of a specific Western or European context what the social, material, and political mechanisms are by way of which Christianity might become a civilizing force. How are these related to The Question? Why, in respect to The Question, might these mechanisms be interesting? How, if at all, does global Christianity outside of the Mediterranean and Atlantic regions illuminate these questions? These considerations bring several further questions to mind. (1) How, in the sociological and historical and political process, and especially in contrast to a waning liberal Christianity, does the question of the Unknown God reveal itself? (2) To what degree—if at all—do those conservative churches still thriving in the West and growing globally reveal this question to be part of their "winning strategy," i.e., an underlying force behind their growth? (3) To what degree and in what ways—if at all—do the globally growing churches reveal this question to be part of *their* "winning strategies"? (4)

90 See, for example, Brian Haymes and Kyle Gingerich Hiebert, *God after Christendom?* (Crownhill: Paternoster, 2015); Rodney Clapp, *A Peculiar People: The Church as Culture in a Post-Christian Society* (Downers Grove, IL: Intervarsity Press, 1996); or the essays collected in *The Church as Counterculture*, ed. Michael L. Budde and Robert W. Brimlow (New York: State University of New York Press), 20.

91 Among others, Syrian, Iraqi, Palestinian, and Egyptian Christian communities, all enduring minorities left over from the Ottoman Empire, come to mind. All are currently under threat or being systematically dispersed.

92 Andrew F. Walls, *The Cross-Cultural Process in Christian History* (New York: Orbis Books, 2002), 45.

What are the ways in which The Question is revealed in everyday church life and discourse, and in the various "post-Christian" Christianities that are alive and well across the globe? (5) What are the elements of church growth in this post-Christendom world, and what is their relationship to what Voegelin calls The Question?[93]

In his notable review of the non-European, post-Christendom Christianity(s) of the "Global South," Philip Jenkins depicts a Christian movement at times barely recognizable to the post-Enlightenment, rationalist Christians of the "Global North," namely Europe and North America. Demons, miraculous healings, ecstatic worship forms, salvation as present in the here and now and not merely in an afterlife, struggles against forceful paganism, doctrinally and ethically conservative readings of the scriptures, and a socio-economic background largely of impoverishment to which the Gospel is understood to respond, are prevalent themes and realities. So, too, are the abuses of charlatans and other "false prophets" associated with these practices and characteristics. At the conclusion of his study that describes the differences between Northern and Southern global Christianity and that paints a picture of a chaotic coat of many colors that is likely to appear quite alien to Northern Christians accustomed to a faith informed by Platonic, Aristotelian, Stoic, or Ockhamite sensibilities, Jenkins concludes:

> Amidst the horrors of the First World War, Karl Barth warned against attempts to find in the Bible answers to specific queries about politics, history, or culture; to seek anything grounded in the real-life experience of any society, past or present. Viewed

93 Two supplementary questions of interest that would likely send us too far afield might be: (1) What is the unique nature of Latin Christendom that contrasts it with post-Christendom Christianity? (2) What were the unique characteristics of the Constantinian settlement, and how did that settlement compare to the Carolingian version, especially with respect to the imperial motivations for getting the church involved in politics the way it did? What did Constantine want from the bishops, compared to what Charlemagne wanted? See, for example, H. A. Drake, *Constantine and the Bishops: The Politics of Intolerance* (Baltimore and London: The Johns Hopkins University Press, 2000).

> in this light, he said, the Bible would always disappoint. The danger is always in trying to understand the Bible by human standards and expectations, and not recognizing its fundamental difference from the experience of its readers. Always, "within the Bible there is a new world, the world of God." Reading the Bible through fresh eyes constantly reminds us of the depths that still remain to be discovered there.[94]

The proximity of Jenkins's conclusion to Voegelin's encourages the thought that reading Voegelin's "Gospel and Culture" in the context not of a Latin Christendom past, but of a global Christianity future, may help to illuminate the arguments of his explication of the Gospel in terms of a culture attuned to the question of transcendence. Voegelin's Christendom lacks contemporary adhesion: it is no longer consistent with our experience of the context of religious belief and practice, whether we are inside or outside the circle formed by such. But his identification of The Question as it is articulated in the Gospel may well still have attraction, if put into a new context of believers in community.[95]

94 Philip Jenkins, *The New Faces of Christianity: Believing the Bible in the Global South* (Oxford: Oxford University Press, 2006), 193.

95 As a footnote to return to our other theme, what will be the place of historical Jesus studies in all this? On the one hand, the historical status of the "Resurrected One" is uninteresting in the Platonic-philosophical and civilizational story of the Christian movement that Voegelin wants to tell. On the other hand, as alien as global Christian may look to (some) Western eyes, it has its roots in the same Gospel movement as Latin and Greek Christianities, and it will, therefore, carry with it not only the philosophical tradition of inquiry that Voegelin emphasizes, but also the rationalism of Aristotelian inquiry and the scientific skepticism that will likely follow close behind. It will also, of course, carry claims about Jesus: *pace* Voegelin, who mentions Jesus nearly not at all in his defense of the Logos of the Gospel, most "orthodox" Christianities have a historical Jesus at their center, whether informed by a philosophical-like quest or not. Science does not retreat easily: where such a Jesus is proclaimed, the tradition of rational historical inquiry developed in the past several centuries is sure to follow.

–8–

Voegelin's "On Hegel: A Study in Sorcery"

David Walsh

I still recall opening the envelope in which Eric Voegelin sent me an offprint of his essay, "On Hegel: A Study in Sorcery."[1] It was like being invited into the guild of scholars who viewed one another as equals (even when that was clearly not the case). Heady stuff for a twenty-two-year-old! Naturally I was bowled over by the forceful power of the analysis and regarded his treatment as the definitive guide to Hegel. This remained the case as I proceeded to write a dissertation that was heavily focused on the same subject. Since then I have gradually managed to distance myself from that overwhelming impact to develop my own quite different and often contrary account of Hegel.[2] The journey has not been easy, involving as it did relinquishing the security of Voegelin's reassuring self-confidence. I now see that it is a mistake, even if it is initially inevitable, to presume that even the great scholars always hit the mark. Science, as Voegelin would remind us, advances through the unremitting scrutiny it turns on itself. It is in that spirit that I turn to Voegelin's most notorious characterization of Hegel as a sorcerer, beginning first with the evolution of his understanding of the great Idealist, then to the misgivings that initially strike us about it, followed by a more extended account

1 Eric Voegelin, "On Hegel: A Study in Sorcery" (1971) in *Published Essays 1966-1985*, ed. Ellis Sandoz, *CWEV* Vol. 12, 1990, 213–55. Hereafter cited as Voegelin, "On Hegel." Originally published *Studium Generale*, Vol. XXIV (1971), 335–68. A longer version of the paper was delivered at The First Conference of the International Society for the Study of Time, 1969.

2 This revised understanding is set forth in *The Modern Philosophical Revolution: The Luminosity of Existence* (Cambridge: Cambridge University Press, 2008). See especially Ch. 2, "Hegel's Inauguration of the Language of Existence."

of the principal charges of Hegel's culmination of history and displacement of God, before concluding with some observations on the relationship of Voegelin to Hegel as a whole.

1. Evolution of an Approach

The first thing to note about Voegelin's reading of Hegel is that it occurred later in his scholarly career. There is no analysis in the *History of Political Ideas* largely written in the 'forties. Only Comte, Marx, and Bakunin get an extended treatment there. Nietzsche receives a passing glance and there is the very admiring chapter on Schelling that, in Voegelin's own admission, opened his eyes to the flawed conception of a history of ideas approach. The odd aspect of this famous "turn" away from the notion of a history of ideas is that Voegelin was already on his way toward it before the realization dawned. Most readers are struck by the extent to which *The History of Political Ideas* departs from a conventional narrative of ideas to pursue the motivating sentiments that drive them. Long before Voegelin proclaimed that there are no such things as ideas but only the experiences and symbols from which they are derived, he already exemplified that insight. The Sacrum Imperium was the evocative aspiration that organized the medieval period even though it was never a concretely realized idea. What is significant is that it was contact with German Idealism, specifically Schelling, that brought this insight into full awareness. To the extent that the Idealists were engaged in a common project, that of locating reason within reality rather than outside of it, completing the Kantian self-limitation of reason, it is arguable that this was the most fertile philosophical corpus for Voegelin's own inquiry. The impact that the abbreviated exposure to Schelling had is sufficient evidence of the potential. But for some reason Voegelin did not linger any further in material he thought he had sufficiently grasped to determine its irrelevance. No doubt a big part of the explanation is that his interest was really in the messianic activists of the nineteenth century who drove the modern revolutionary movement. The ideological convulsions that gripped the twentieth century were the main target. In light of that upheaval the Idealist predecessors appeared as an inconsequential prelude. Very far in the past lay Voegelin's insightful reading of Kant that might have provided a bridge into the philosophical richness of the Idealists.[3] For the moment the narrative of history pointed toward the ideological madness that had come to dominate world politics in Voegelin's own time.

That was the lens through which Voegelin later returned to Hegel whom he eventually came to see as the great exemplar of the project the secular messiahs sought to accomplish. The apocalypse of man ran through the murder of God. From Hegel to Nietzsche, as Karl Löwith had conceived a parallel study, would henceforth color the reading of Hegel.[4] In other words, the return to Hegel when it did occur would be within a context that looked forward to the great aberrations of his thought rather than to its significance within his own intellectual setting. The pattern is not unique to Voegelin, as the allusion to Löwith indicates. Hans Urs von Balthasar had reached a similar judgment, as had Henri de Lubac, to cite only two of the best informed contemporary readers.[5] As always Voegelin did not go out on a limb but sought confirmation in the scholarly literature of the day. Certainly there were few authorities who defended the validity of the Hegelian conception or for that matter of any of the Idealists. In that respect we are in a very different situation today when finally something of a consensus, and indeed a highly appreciative consensus, has formed around their interpretation. The study of German Idealism is now one of the liveliest and most consequential fields of investigation, with attenuations that reach as far as analytic language philosophy and Catholic theology. Seen in their own terms, the Idealists emerge as the greatest philosophical explosion in the modern period, an achievement so singular and significant that the very self-understanding of modernity turns upon it.[6] The expansive attention now lavished on the

3 Eric Voegelin, "Ought in Kant's System," (1931) in *Published Essays, 1929-1933*, ed. Thomas Heilke and John von Heyking, *CWEV* Vol. 8, 2003, Ch. 8.

4 Karl Löwith, *From Hegel to Nietzsche*, trans. David Green (New York: Doubleday, 1967; original 1941).

5 Hans Urs von Balthasar, *Die Apokalypse der deutschen Seele*, 3 Vols. (Salzburg: Pustet, 1937-39); Henri de Lubac, *La posterité spirituelle de Joachim de Fiore*, 2 Vols. (Paris: Lethielleux, 1979-82).

6 See Robert Pippin, *Hegel's Idealism: The Satisfaction of Self-Consciousness* (Cambridge: Cambridge University Press, 1989), hereafter cited as Pippin, *Hegel's Idealism*, and Terry Pinkard, *German Philosophy 1760-1860: The Legacy of Ide-*

Idealists is driven in large part by the realization that they possess a unique relevance for the mode in which philosophy must proceed in an age defined by empirical science and the reign of technology. Many of the subsequent philosophical developments draw upon it and are properly seen as a resumption of the impulse that lay within it rather than a rejection of it. Today it would be hard to see Voegelin resisting the scholarly preponderance that has emerged over the decades since he stopped writing. Instead he would be more likely to appreciate the extent of his own convergence with Hegel, an apprehension that was not entirely absent from his later assessments even if they do not arise within his most famous blast against Hegel as a sorcerer.

The assimilation of Hegel to his activist successors is not of course the only handicap under which Voegelin labored. A deeper and closer reading of Hegel was simply not afforded by the direction in which Voegelin's scholarly investigations drew him. When I first met him he was already five to ten millennia back in his historical focus on the Neolithic passage graves. The first three volumes of *Order and History* are devoted to the cosmological world of myth, the Israelite revelation, and the Greek discovery of reason. The subsequent enlargement of the empirical horizon in the *Ecumenic Age* broadens the inquiry but retains only a tangential reference to the modern materials. The theoretical deepening of the final volume does nothing to lessen the summative character of the treatments. Yet even then there is evidence of a reconsideration of Hegel. All we can say is that his account of Hegel remained underway and the first great proclamation in the sorcery essay was not his final word. Yet it was his first word, for Voegelin conceded that he had long avoided Hegel as a result of insufficiently understanding him.[7] Clearly he had

alism (Cambridge: Cambridge University Press, 2002), hereafter cited as Pinkard, *German Philosophy 1760*-1860, and earlier, Charles Taylor, *Hegel* (Cambridge: Cambridge University Press, 1975).

7 "There is a story to my relation to Hegel: For a long time I studiously avoided any serious criticism of Hegel in my published work, because I simply could not understand him. I knew that something was wrong, but I did not know what. . . .The first relief in this frustrating state came through my study of gnosticism and the discovery that by his contemporaries Hegel was considered a gnostic thinker." Voegelin, "Response to Professor Altizer's 'A New History and a New but Ancient God?'" (1975) in *Published Essays 1966-1985*, ed. Ellis Sandoz, *CWEV* Vol. 12, 1990, 296.

bided his time before tackling his most daunting predecessor. Early glimpses of the angle he would take had already emerged in *Science, Politics and Gnosticism*, essays that were themselves deliberately polemical.[8] Significantly none of it appeared in the major intervening volume, *Anamnesis*, assembled with the kind of care that marked the volumes of *Order and History*. It was outside of the settled body of work that Voegelin continued to work in a more exploratory manner on Hegel. Somewhere towards the end of the 'sixties the assessment had crystallized sufficiently to be presented in the essay published in 1971. For better or worse Hegel had become the quintessential modern gnostic. Further reading on the Renaissance magus phenomenon, the Corpus Hermeticum and Jacob Boehme, which were very much at the center of Voegelin's interest at the time, served only to confirm that the characterization of Hegel as a conjuror was on the right track. Notably absent is any reference to current Hegel scholarship, with the exception of the idiosyncratic Kojève, or any clear evidence of a rereading of the Hegelian texts. Reliance on a wider scholarly context had reassured Voegelin he could neglect commentators more closely tied to the Hegelian enterprise. Indeed by this stage Voegelin had even come to disdain and distrust scholars who were too conventionally close to their material. They would never be able to delineate the full apocalyptic proportions of the enterprise they were investigating. Once he had seized on the most dramatic profile of a thinker Voegelin was often loath to revisit and reconsider it. In this regard we recall his treatment of such conventionally acceptable figures as Isaiah and Husserl.[9]

2. Misgivings

It is to Voegelin's credit, however, that this initial characterization of Hegel as the supreme manipulator of the God-man relationship did not remain without qualifications. The need to return to the gnostic apocalypse the great sorcerer had accomplished necessitated a review of it in other perspectives.

8 Eric Voegelin, *Science, Politics and Gnosticism* (1959) in *Modernity Without Restraint*, ed. Manfred Henningsen, *CWEV* Vol. 5, 2000.

9 See the treatment of Isaiah in *Order and History, Volume I: Israel and Revelation* (1956), ed. Maurice P. Hogan, *CWEV* Vol. 14, 2001, esp. 501-42, and Husserl in *Anamnesis: On the Theory of History and Politics* (German edition 1966), ed. David Walsh, *CWEV* Vol. 6, 2002, Ch. 2.

Even the conception of the gnostic apocalypse begins to modulate, as Voegelin gains a greater appreciation of the project on which Hegel had been engaged. We are in the final volume, *In Search of Order*, very close to the admission that Hegel had resumed the challenge that remained since the breakthrough to transcendence that marked the great turning points of history. How was it possible for the symbolization of the transcendent, of Being, to be contained within time? Gnosticism in either its ancient or modern forms, as liberation from the cosmos or absorption within it, could never be regarded as a satisfactory response. In the end Hegel would come to occupy the same position as St. Augustine in recognizing the dead end of any movement that left nothing further to do within time. Just as the Manicheans had reached the perfection that made spiritual growth impossible, an end of history would abolish all that made history meaningful.[10] Kojève had reached that insight in regard to Hegel but he seemed to assume that the same realization never occurred to Hegel.[11] At any rate neither Voegelin nor Kojève gave full weight to the attention that Hegel lavished on history itself, especially in the great lecture courses on history, art, religion and philosophy. No one with that level of empirical fascination could possibly wish to see it concluded in some putative culmination. Instead he would be much more likely to realize that the fulfillment of history within time robs it of all meaning. Talk of the eschatological end of history is of course quite different, as Augustine understood. It is therefore a great mistake to take Hegel's remarks about an end as pointing only to an immanent conclusion. He may have left open that suggestion, but his own wide-ranging historical inquiry works forcefully against it. Far from effecting a speculative consummation, Hegel had immersed himself in the unending diversity of materials.

The only thinker who combines the same theoretical penetration with equivalent empirical mastery is Voegelin himself. It is a rare combination in the history of thought, dominated as it is by thinkers for whom the philosophical challenges themselves take precedence. The type

10 Peter Brown, *Augustine of Hippo* (Berkeley: University of California Press, 1967), Ch. 5.

11 Alexandre Kojève, *Introduction to the Reading of Hegel*, trans. James H. Nichols (New York: Basic, 1969).

inaugurated by Aristotle, for whom exposure to the manifold details is just as important, are far less frequent. Even Voegelin's criticisms of Hegel's occasional smoothing of historical untidiness cannot quite disguise the realization that the same tension was present in his own work. It was acknowledgement of just such a strain that had persuaded Voegelin to abandon the chronological framework he had first imposed on *Order and History*.[12] The irreducible complexity of historical reality could not be contained in a single overarching narrative. But was that not the problem that first surfaces in the Hegelian inauguration of a philosophy of history? The problem of the point of view from which the construction of history is undertaken is first seriously broached there. Augustine had intuited his way toward an eschatological viewpoint but he had not made the theoretical requirement sufficiently clear. It was Hegel and the Idealists who worked explicitly toward it. They had seen that history could not be regarded as a field of phenomena an observer must investigate from the outside. Rather, history consisted of lines of meaning that reach forward to include the investigator as well. The only definitive standpoint from which it can be apprehended is the turning point that transcends it, the beginning or end or intersection of the timeless and time. The irruption of the transcendent is the privileged moment from which history can be viewed as history. That is what Hegel named the advent of the absolute or absolute knowledge. Whatever the infelicities of that term, it is clear that both he and Voegelin regarded this as a possibility that definitively turned on the appearance of Christ. It was the arrival of Christ that opened the condition of the possibility of God and man knowing one another. That was always a possibility from the beginning of history but its recognition takes a long historical unfolding. The assertion that "history is Christ written large" now occurs within a global horizon that is open to multiple breakthroughs to transcendence.[13] Whatever the shortcomings of his elaboration of this insight, it would be hard to deny that

12 Eric Voegelin, *Order and History, Vol. IV: The Ecumenic Age* (1974), ed. Michael Franz, *CWEV* Vol. 17, 2000, "Introduction." Hereafter cited as Voegelin, *Ecumenic Age*.

13 Eric Voegelin, "Immortality: Experience and Symbol," in *Published Essays 1966-1985*, ed. Ellis Sandoz, *CWEV* Vol. 12, 1990, 78.

Hegel had inaugurated the pattern of an "order of history that emerges from the history of order."[14]

It is no wonder that the bluntness of Voegelin's dismissal of Hegel in the sorcerer essay should sit so uneasily. As the sorcerer's apprentice Voegelin must surely have been aware of his dependence on the path that had been opened before him. Indeed there is more than a hint of sorcery in the rhetorical blasts Voegelin throws on his predecessor, especially at points where a measured exposition might well have been more persuasive. It is regrettable that a deeper reading of the Idealists did not begin to dislodge the paradigm of the secular messiah as the defining pattern of the nineteenth century. Even the Idealist for whom Voegelin had expressed the most unqualified admiration, Schelling, did not merit a return visit after the initial treatment. This is all the more striking in view, not only of the impact that the reading of Schelling had on Voegelin's own development, but also in light of the enormous convergence that exists with the later Schelling's massive project of a *Philosophy of Mythology* and a *Philosophy of Revelation*.[15] Continuous allusions back to these illustrious predecessors can never quite dispel that sense that Voegelin might have overlooked something indispensable for his own work. They had attempted a spiritual paradigm that would be adequate to a world dominated by rational science and open to a multiplicity of centers of order while at the same time retaining the full sweep of the classical and Christian tradition. Their attenuated connection with the Promethean strand of the modern impulse is far from defining them, for they are at root Voegelin's collaborators rather than his rivals. This is what explains the peculiar strategy he employs in this most condemnatory treatment.

3. Hegel's End of History

Voegelin announces this strategy early in the essay where he declares that he is going to follow the programmatic statements of Hegel's intentions rather

14 This is the opening sentence of *Order and History, Israel and Revelation*.

15 For a convenient selection see *Schelling's Philosophy of Mythology and Revelation*, trans. and reduced, Victory C. Hayes (Armidale: Australian Association for the Study of Religions, 1995), and also *Historical-Critical Introduction to the Philosophy of Mythology*, trans. Mason Richey and Markus Zisselsberger (Albany: State University of New York Press, 2007).

than the more laborious route of a careful reading of the texts.[16] He wanted to dramatize the audacious character of Hegel's project of self-divinization, an impossibility the actual texts are designed to obscure. The sorcery turns on Hegel's claim to the self-knowledge of God without having to assert that he has become God. If that is indeed Hegel's project then there is no doubt that Voegelin has hit upon a secret that might not readily be discerned in the exoteric texts. But what basis do we have for the assertion other than Voegelin's insistence that the programmatic statements do yield this unambiguous interpretation? When we do read such infamous suggestions as that the love of wisdom will be replaced by its actual possession we might be inclined to suspect, with Voegelin, that something quite radical is underway but we might still hesitate to convict on the basis of what in the end may be a rhetorical flourish.[17] The evidence, even as it is marshalled by an able prosecutor, complete with the dramatic moment of Napoleon parading outside Jena, may give us pause but we cannot quite shake the impression that it remains largely circumstantial. One must have already determined that Hegel is guilty of wicked intentions, but that is precisely what is at issue. Statements that amount to little more than flashes of ambition, even overweening ambition, are hardly enough to justify the charge of sorcery. What is at issue is how such declamations are to be taken. For that the statements themselves are not sufficient evidence. We must probe the actual performance. Even if Voegelin is right that the discursive unfolding is little more than an elaborate second reality to conceal the enormity of the travesty Hegel intends, then it is precisely the exposure of that ambiguity that must be demonstrated. Admittedly that is a more arduous task, yet it cannot be avoided. Voegelin's own justification for avoiding it, viz. that the programmatic assertions are starker than any attempt to achieve them, cannot be sustained. It may well be that the goals clarify what remains obscure in the muddiness of their implementation, but we cannot even be sure of what the goals are before we have gained a clear appreciation of what they are intended to bring about. Ends and means form a unity that must be interpreted as a whole.

It is almost as if Voegelin is departing from his customary hermeneutic of a close reading of the texts. Here we have only a selective reading where

16 Voegelin, "On Hegel," 232.

17 Hegel, *Phenomenology of Spirit*, Preface, par.5.

even the selections lack an adequate basis to judge their meaning. Are thinkers to be condemned for the rhetorical excesses with which they festoon their writings rather than for the contents themselves? Can we even be sure that the claims are excessive if we are not sure how they are to be taken? What in the end can the claim to absolute knowledge mean if we have not weighed the different constructions that can be placed upon it? If there is ambiguity then it must be exposed unambiguously. Ambiguity cannot even be determined apart from the attempt to clarify it. But that means that we begin with a suspension of judgment regarding motivations and intentions. The philosophical construction must reveal the goal behind them rather than the other way around. Statements of purpose must be taken in light of what is accomplished rather than on the first impression with which they may strike us. Results and intentions are a dialectic and while reading a text we are continually in the search of the heart from which it emerges. The shortcoming in Voegelin's account in this essay is that he allowed himself to be captivated by the first brilliant suggestion that Hegel was a sorcerer. That became the key to unlocking the texts and increasing confidence in the diagnosis meant that interpretation became a quest for confirmation. In the end it is a ringing denunciation but it is a far cry from an actual understanding of Hegel. This explains why Voegelin's essay is rarely cited in the Hegel literature and is a poor place to begin if one wants to understand Hegel. That was my experience when I began, for I was struck by the absence of any detailed reading of what Hegel actually said and was prepared to overlook it in my admiration for Voegelin. I was under his spell.

When I persevered in reading Hegel it became apparent that one could only make progress if one began with a more generous spirit. Where the texts are ambiguous it is a better hermeneutic principle to put the best possible construction on them, rather than the worst. If one eventually agreed with Voegelin's harsh judgment, then one would be on firmer interpretive ground and could not simply be accused of a misjudgment of intentions. When this is done one finds it is possible to place an orthodox construction on the claim to absolute knowledge. It does not mean that Hegel has become God but that he has reached the divine viewpoint as the highest on all things. The wisdom he now possesses does not abolish the love of wisdom. It is simply an alternative formulation of the Delphic judgment of the wisdom of Socrates. He knew that he knew nothing and in that was wiser than all others. Absolute knowledge was the measure that he did not possess and in that he possessed it. There is no doubt that Hegel courts the misconstructions Voegelin and others attribute, but there is no necessity to impose them. Talk of absolute knowledge does suggest one has grasped what is unavailable to all others, but it need not. It can just as easily mean one has glimpsed what can be glimpsed by all even if most do not. The absolute is not possessed but is the condition of the possibility of all knowledge. Kant had inaugurated this reflection of knowledge on itself and Hegel had merely carried it a little further. The language of consciousness and Geist could have been a subterfuge to cover the ambiguity of the operation, but it could just as easily have been a consequence of the internal unfolding of the meditation. When Hegel asks about that within which consciousness lives then it can only be known from within. There is neither man nor God but only the poles within which the relationship unfolds. We are remarkably close to Voegelin's own highlighting of the Metaxy as the horizon within which all our thinking occurs. Rather than accusing Hegel of mishandling Aristotle's famous formulation of "thought thinking itself," we are perhaps on safer ground in seeing it as an effort to more precisely delineate its meaning.[18] In Hegel's account thought thinks itself more clearly in light of that which is beyond it. Standing in relation to the absolute is inexorable.

There is no need to accuse Hegel of abolishing the depth beyond consciousness or of absorbing everything within the dynamics of consciousness.[19] None of what he says makes any sense on the basis of that premise. Voegelin admires the extent to which Hegel recognizes the impossibility of human life and reflection sustaining itself on the basis of its own autonomy. Kant had come dangerously close to that suggestion before

18 Eric Voegelin, "Reason: The Classic Experience," in *Published Essays 1966-1985*, ed. Ellis Sandoz, *CWEV* Vol. 12, 1990, 284.

19 "The principle of construction in the *Phänomenologie*, however, is so simple that it will not be unfair to call it a sleight of hand. As it would prove impossible even for the constructive genius of a Hegel to grind the real God and real man through the machinery of dialectics and come out with a man-god, he roundly does not concede the status of reality to either God or man. The *Phänomenologie* admits no reality but consciousness." Voegelin, "On Hegel," 223.

pulling back from it. Hegel and the other successors worked strenuously to avoid the implication of a self-contained reason. The contemporary admirers of Hegel place considerable emphasis on the notion of reason as embedded in its historical unfolding. Even if that is the closest they dare go to acknowledging the full metaphysical achievement of Hegel, it is still a step down a path that can eventually accept the full weight of Hegel's profession of faith. At the same time full disclosure requires us to acknowledge that even Hegel's contemporaries had difficulty in concluding his orthodoxy.[20] Hermeneutical procedure, however, requires us to withhold judgment until all the evidence is in. We should at least consider the possibility that the misunderstanding was present from the beginning. After all, access to the texts was extremely limited. First impressions and subsequent distortions have a way of hanging around. But our responsibility is to give the widest latitude to the possibility that Hegel might be the one who most thoroughly grounds the metaphysics of philosophy and Christianity in the modern era. When objective science has usurped the claim to knowledge, on what can knowledge of what transcends space and time base itself? It can only be on that which provides the condition of possibility of science that can itself never be included with it. Science rests on the absolute that itself has no basis other than the absolute itself. That is the dialectic on which Hegel launches us. It leads inexorably to the recognition that even scientific mastery cannot dispense with that which grounds its own possibility.[21] It is in relation to the absolute that all unfolds. That is the story of history.

This means, contrary to the common misperception to which Voegelin here subscribes, that Hegel does not claim that history has reached its end. As Kojève acknowledged, an end of history would deprive history of all meaning. Why would Hegel have subscribed to such an outcome? This is particularly remarkable given that there was absolutely no necessity for him to do so. Hegel surely understood what was apparent to Augustine, that

20 Schelling was recalled to Berlin in order to "stamp out the dragon's teeth of Hegelianism." See Schelling, *Philosphie der Offenbarung*, 1841/42, ed. Manfred Frank (Frankfurt: Suhrkamp, 1977), "Introduction."

21 I have amplified on this in "Science Is Not Scientific," *Faith and The Marvelous Progress of Science*, ed. Brendan Leahy (Hyde Park, NY: New City Press, 2014: 107–20), now included in Walsh, *The Priority of the Person* (Notre Dame: University of Notre Dame Press, 2020), Ch. 15.

history could only be perceived from its end point but that the end point could never be included within it. The viewpoint that renders history meaningful is strictly eschatological. Whenever Hegel talks about the end of history it should be taken in this sense. There is a meaningful movement to history by which it heads toward the fuller revelation of what is present from the beginning but never fully unfolded within time. Despite the modern emphasis on historical progress toward an immanent fulfillment, it is far more plausible that Hegel understood the dialectical overturning that constitutes its eschatological horizon. Indeed the unfolding discovery of history is that there is nothing in history that accounts for the possibility of history. The blind link in the chain of necessity to which Hegel alludes and Voegelin quotes is, in the process of contemplating history, at the same time already transcending it.[22] There is no necessity to conclude that this signifies a determination to bring history to its conclusion within the system imposed upon it. It may even be that Hegel did not have a system at all. Even his references to an end of history can be seen as an identification of the absolute viewpoint from which alone it can be perceived.[23] Invocation of an end is thus not an apocalyptic pronouncement but a methodological necessity. Without the end history would scarcely even be visible. It is only from the perspective outside of it that history can be perceived. The outcome of history is thus the progressive advance in awareness of what constitutes history as the now that is not yet and can never be fully realized within it. The fact of revelation is its content, as Voegelin remarked, an observation that could equally well have originated with Hegel.[24]

22 Voegelin, "On Hegel," 221.

23 "*Time* is the *concept* itself in its existence (*der da ist*), as it presents itself to consciousness as an empty intuition (*Anschauung*); that is the reason the *Geist* appears of necessity in time, and will appear in time as long as it has not … abolished time." Voegelin, "On Hegel," 227. Viewing history from the perspective of eternity is not the same as evincing a will to abolish it.

24 Voegelin, *The New Science of Politics* (1952), in *Modernity without Restraint: The Political Religions; The New Science of Politics; and Science, Politics and Gnosticism*, ed. Manfred Henningsen, *CWEV* Vol. 5, 2000, 151, a remark he repeated in *Order and History, Volume V: In Search of Order* (1987), ed. Ellis Sandoz, *CWEV* Vol. 18, 2000, 87. Hereafter cited as Voegelin, *In Search of Order*.

It is not surprising therefore that there are virtually no unambiguous pronouncements of the end of history in Hegel, despite its widespread attribution to him. The passages Voegelin quotes are the main proof texts but they do not admit of a univocal interpretation. Instead we must concede that they can equally be rendered in eschatological terms. For this reason we must have recourse to Voegelin's own hermeneutical method which is to find the core of a thinker's perspective and interpret the writings in relation to it. In this case, however, Voegelin rushed to judgment once he concluded that Hegel was at his core a self-divinizer who sought to make all of reality revolve around himself. The Great Man of history had succumbed to the temptation of abolishing the reality that made him great. A more considered examination of Hegel's actual historical practice, especially in the extensive historical courses of lectures on history, philosophy, art, and religion, would make it clear that there is scarcely a whiff of the suggestion of a culmination. It is the movement of history rather than the conclusion at which it arrives that draws his attention. How else could he lavish such attention on the vast field of historical materials, or meditate so persistently on the rich complexity of forms in the history of art, philosophy, or religion? Far from concluding that the later unfoldings had rendered the predecessors obsolete, Hegel could more properly be seen as arguing for the indispensability and irreplaceability of every stage. Just as there is no such thing as progress in the history of art, there is scarcely more validity to the notion within the history of philosophy or religion. Even politics is an historical whole in which the present cannot be understood except in reference to what it has left behind and which is, for that reason, never simply left behind. Hegel is, in other words, stunningly close to Voegelin's own eventual admission of the simultaneity of all of the phases of history that now stand in relation to one another as the only adequate disclosure of their meaning.[25] Voegelin's own abandonment of the

25 In explaining why the new form philosophy of history had to take was "definitely not a story of meaningful events to be arranged on a time line," Voegelin went on to sketch what it is. "In this new form, the analysis had to move backward and forward and sideways, in order to follow empirically the patterns of meaning as they revealed themselves in the self-interpretation of persons and societies in history." *Ecumenic Age*, 106.

chronological framework is tantamount to the admission that he too had been guilty of suggesting that what came before only had the purpose of serving what succeeds it. An immanent end had been built into this conventional narrative. But it is arguable that the insight that overturns it was already present in the Hegelian profession that history was transacted, not in relation to the present, but in light of the absolute. To the extent that Hegel is a philosopher of the absolute he is the ultimate bulwark against the historically relative. Kojève's reduction of the end of history to its absurdity is only the negative transmission of this insight.[26] Its positive presentation that all that we do, and thus all that constitutes history, is undertaken in relation to the eternal, is the insight of Kierkegaard.[27]

4. The Displacement of God

The big question is whether Hegel meant anything substantive by the term "absolute." Did it have the same theological reference as Kierkegaard gave it? Is the absolute God? This is the great charge Voegelin lodges against Hegel. He is accused of invoking the absolute only as thinly veiled disguise for the removal of God. Within the dynamics of consciousness history reduces to its diurnal unfolding and makes no reference to anything beyond it. History is itself the highest framework and the depth has been abolished. It is curious that this is exactly the position evinced by one of the dominant schools of Hegel scholarship today. While rejecting the charge of imposing a culmination on history, they are at pains to demonstrate Hegel's commitment to history as the indispensable medium of philosophical development while adamantly rejecting any intrusion from beyond the horizon of history.[28] History stands on its own bottom in this uncompromisingly secularist view. Where Voegelin complains about Hegel's abolition of any depth beyond the historical dialectic, the historicality of

26 Barry Cooper, *The End of History: An Essay on Modern Hegelianism* (Toronto: University of Toronto Press, 1984).

27 Søren Kierkegaard, *Concluding Unscientific Postscript to Philosophical Fragments*, 2 Vols., trans. Howard V. Hong and Edna H. Hong (Princeton: Princeton University Press, 1992).

28 See Pippin, *Hegel's Idealism,* and Pinkard, *German Philosophy 1760-1860.*

reason school embrace the unrelievedly immanentist horizon it generates. Voegelin bemoans the disappearance of metaphysics while Pippin applauds it. The resulting characterization of Hegel is, however, the same and equally questionable. Not only does it rest on a studied avoidance of Hegel's invocations of the absolute and God, but it makes it impossible to understand what it was that made Hegel's project possible. It may indeed be that Hegel admitted the impossibility of "metaphysics," as Voegelin also asserted, and it may be that history remained the unsurpassable horizon of thought, as Pippin and others insist. But that did not obliterate Hegel's consciousness of the impossibility of reducing everything to the immanence of history. It may be that Hegel did not find the most perspicuous formulations of what he had in mind and thereby left himself open to such misconstructions. He did nevertheless hold firm to the intuitions that guided him as he set philosophy on the path of a movement rather than a stasis. This was what accounted for the often tortured language of the absolute and of consciousness as the unfolding of Geist. The immanent dialectic Voegelin criticizes and Pippin rejects is the very means by which he keeps alive the awareness that history cannot include what makes it possible. It is in the nature of the condition that it cannot enter what it conditions. How then can they be held together if they can neither be united nor divorced? Hegel's answer is that they remain in unending relationship to one another within the dialectic that never permits them to rest in endless identity. If Hegel's project, as both the theological and secularizing critics admit, is the transformation of truth into a movement rather than a possession, it is the dialectic of movement that is its most appropriate characterization. What cannot be included in history is thereby rendered present but always in the mode of what is not present because it sustains the movement itself. Without abolishing God, Hegel acknowledges God in the only way that the transcendent can be acknowledged. That is, as the movement toward transcendence that can never be absorbed within immanence. To say that "the state is the march of God in the world,"[29] is not to say anything about God or the state that would substantively identify them. But it is to intimate the relationship between them which is all that really matters. Neither the state nor God is what it

29 *Philosophy of Right*, a lecture addition to par. 258.

is in isolation, but only in the relationship to one another. Just as history can only be known from the viewpoint of the eschaton and the eschaton cannot be included within history, they can however be apprehended within this realization. The elevation of that realization to self-consciousness is the signal achievement of Hegel and the aspect in which he advances beyond Augustine. It is certainly the case that the latter had reached the same realization, for he wrote the *City of God* in full awareness of the eschatological status of the two cities. Yet he did not raise his awareness to methodological consciousness. It is for this reason it had to be continually lost and recovered over the succeeding centuries. With Hegel's elevation of it to a methodological principle there is at least the possibility of retaining it within our intellectual framework. Even the mischaracterization of Hegel as engaged in the consummation of history that abolishes it has had the merit of rendering his insight less mistakable. We now have at least the possibility of holding the transcendent as transcendent because it is represented not as a resting place but as its continual supersession. This was an acknowledgment of Hegel's contribution that Voegelin later came to make in a far more ungrudging fashion.[30] One suspects there is a similar dynamic at work in the more secularizing admirers of Hegel who find, in his relentless overturning of all finite manifestations of the divine, a means of nevertheless holding onto it. The mystery remains within the dialectic as its inaccessible underpinning.

If it is thus possible to redeem many of Hegel's formulations without prejudicing them and indeed to concede, as Voegelin later does, that they converge with his own, one wonders what it was that prevented this more capacious reading at the beginning. The need to find an ultimate bearer of responsibility for the later modern disaster was surely strong. But Voegelin even in this essay never simply reached an outright condemnation of his great predecessor. Instead it was always generously leavened with admiration for Hegel's achievement of an account of truth that no philosopher could

30 "Hence, the preceding enumeration should not be read as a critique of Hegel but, on the contrary, as an attempt to clarify and stress his achievement. His rediscovery of the experiential source of symbolization, as well as his identification of the fundamental problems in the structure of consciousness is irreversible." Voegelin, *In Search of Order*, 85.

afford to neglect.[31] The accusatory rhetoric of sorcery, Gnosticism, and apocalypse would for most readers eclipse the more muted expressions of appreciation. Yet they were both inescapably present. The challenge of reconciling them was not one to which Voegelin was attracted, intrigued as he was by the discovery of ever new aspects of the Hegelian edifice. We may conclude that Voegelin was no more interested in presenting a balanced account of Hegel than he was of any other thinker. He was interested in the contribution Hegel could make to the problem of sorcery rather than the other way around. The excitement of discovery always captured Voegelin's attention. But this meant that he did not always see the instability embedded in his own assessments. In the case of Hegel it is surely the conception of him as a mystic manqué that seems to give fixity to what is not really a definitive judgment. Voegelin may continually overturn it in his assessment of Hegel as still a mystic, one who gives voice to the in-between status of existence just as it emerges in all the great symbolizations of order back to Plato's coinage of the notion. The problem is, however, that once the manqué has been pronounced it blocks the way to its own overcoming. All that most readers remember of Voegelin's account of modernity is the jeremiad, not the reassessment that would lead modernity into its own fuller realization. The revolt against God is still an affirmation of God.

Voegelin knew this well, but he did not manage to find his way to a satisfactory articulation of the extent to which the modernity that seemed to carry theophanic revolt remained tied to theophany. It is arguable that the treatment of Hegel was the most promising opportunity for reaching that more comprehensive assessment. There is no doubt that Voegelin approaches it repeatedly, especially in his remarks about the equivalences that unite both the acceptance and the rejection of the transcendent. We are tantalizingly close to the admission that the mystic manqué remains a mystic. He still lives in relation to the hidden which, for all the claims of disclosure, is finally never disclosed.[32] The decisive element is thus not the

31 "As a genus of philosophical literature, the *Phänomenologie* is a treatise on *aletheia*, on truth and reality, and a very important one indeed; no philosopher can afford to ignore it." "On Hegel," 222.

32 We recall the derivation of "mystic" from the hidden or the mysteries into which the initiates entered.

distortion that seeks to abolish the tension of existence, but the acknowledgment that it has not been so superseded. Even if Hegel sought to effect the apocalypse of history, it is not the apocalypse but his standing within it as what cannot be surpassed that is of most significance. The end of history bears witness to the eschaton that is beyond history. Voegelin is right that it is the constancy of structure that is most notable.[33] Distortion is premised on what cannot be distorted. The lie can never obliterate the truth, for it depends too intimately upon it. The terminology of first and second reality to which Voegelin returned over and over again seemed to suggest something of his own dissatisfaction with its conceptual power.[34] Each time he came back it seemed as if it was to discover something that had eluded him. Could it be that it was the dialectical character of truth, adduced most penetratingly by Hegel, that was the overlooked aspect? The division into first and second realities has the unfortunate consequence of suggesting that there are competing alternatives. It obscures the extent to which there is only one reality on which the distorting impulse is highly parasitic. None of this is to concede that Hegel is guilty of engaging in a lie or inserting deliberate ambiguity. Indeed I have strongly argued the contrary. It is simply to suggest that even if he was guilty he provides the means of his own remediation. Hegel can always be invoked in the redemption of Hegel.

That is the greatness of his thought that Voegelin intuits strongly. Hegel unleashes the fluidity of thinking that can overcome the fixities of which he might be charged. There may still be considerable debate and disagreement about the heterodoxy of one or another formulation of Hegel. But what cannot be doubted is that orthodoxy is the horizon for that examination. Truth is what makes falsity possible. Hegel thoroughly grasped this and it accounts for the penetrating power of his thought. We cannot think outside of the horizon of truth for we move within its dialectic before we have even begun. At a time when the Kantian revolution seemed to terminate in the irresolvability of the antinomies, Hegel and others grasped the

33 See the long discussion of this in *The Ecumenic Age*, Ch. 5, section 2.

34 A lengthy exploration is contained in "Wisdom and the Magic of the Extreme," *Published Essays 1966-1985*, ed. Ellis Sandoz, *CWEV* Vol. 12, 1990, Ch. 13.

bridge that was tentatively constructed in the Third Critique.[35] Truth is not something at which we have to arrive but the possibility of any arrival at all. We are already one with truth before we ever set out. It is this realization that is at the core of Hegel's philosophical project as he shifted speculation from thinking about being to thinking within being. It is not so much that logic is the apparatus through which we approach reality as that it is the apparatus through which reality discloses itself to us. All of that reversal accounts for the linguistic strangeness of his thought with its emphases on consciousness, spirit, notion, Idea, and concept arriving at their own truth. Such terms do not function as hypostases but as indices, to use Voegelin's own usage, of the boundary within which thinking is carried on. As the internal dimensions of experience, they do not eliminate the substantive realities of God and man but enable their inner relationship to be explored more adequately. Just like the poles of Voegelin's Metaxy which can never be included within it, they are nevertheless real as the indispensable condition of anything being between. The further we go with such reflections the more we realize the convergence of Voegelin and Hegel in their thought worlds. There is even the vulnerability of each to the charge of drawing all into the dynamics of consciousness or experience.

Once the shift has been made from the objectifying account of reality to the prior relationship that makes that possible, from intentionality to luminosity, then the danger of immanentism arises. We may be charged with absorbing all within the dynamics of consciousness. In many respects Hegel may be better placed for a rebuttal of the charge than Voegelin. The latter relies so heavily on the language of experience that it is difficult to defend it in non-experiential terms. Hegel seemed to be aware that no defense was possible except by going through the logic of disclosure itself. That is, that what emerges or appears is itself testament to the wherefrom that cannot emerge or appear. This was a line of reflection that was later fruitfully pursued by Heidegger. The crucial realization, in any case, is that consciousness is always consciousness of something. There may be debate about the reality status of what it intends but there cannot be any doubt that it is not identical with consciousness. This was the vein that Hegel

35 *Critique of the Power of Judgment*, trans. Paul Guyer and Eric Matthews (Cambridge: Cambridge University Press, 2000).

mined so successfully that we must regard his work as indispensable to rebutting all charges of solipsism. He even went as far as an examination of his own exercise in phenomenology. If phenomenology drives beyond the phenomenon, how do we characterize the exercise itself? Is it part of phenomenology or is it more properly regarded as a science of reality? This tension was well reflected in Hegel's two "systems" where the *Phenomenology* was first conceived as a ladder to the *Logic*, and later became an integral part of the *System of Science* within the *Philosophy of Spirit*. Science itself rests on what is not science and yet for that reason must be included within it. The sophistication and depth of the Hegelian analysis is in other words breathtaking, and it must be viewed as regrettable that Voegelin was able to make so little use of it as he painfully made his way toward an almost identical position. They are virtually united in the insistence that consciousness not only knows reality but is also a part of it, for its most pivotal disclosure is not what it intends but what it renders luminous from within. In light of that massive convergence we must be inclined to regard all talk of Hegelian sorcery as largely beside the point. In Voegelin's defense we can only say that he was far from alone in the misreading, for this more positive appreciation of the position of Hegel is only of very recent vintage, apart from the occasional schools of idealism that flourished without themselves being well recognized by the philosophical mainstream.[36]

5. The Impossibility of Dispensing with Hegel

In the end we are inclined to attribute the misreading to the power of metaphor itself. Once the epithet of sorcery had been hurled in Hegel's direction it became difficult to find any alternative account of its fundamental structure. Indeed Voegelin's essay itself partakes of some of the mesmerizing effects of sorcery as a rhetorical device. Even today it is difficult to avoid being swept up in its powerful thrust, as we are launched upon a

36 One thinks, for example, of British Idealism that is carried forth by F. H Bradley, Bernard Bosanquet, as well as R. G. Collingwood and Michael Oakeshott. A parallel Idealist stream continued in America. Neither connected well with the dominant analytic schools or even with the existentialist approaches on the Continent.

condemnation against which there is no defense. Any imputed defense would itself be further confirmation of the conjuring power of the speculator who is prepared to stir up the depths if he cannot storm heaven. Countervailing arguments serve only to solidify the charge. There is in other words something dangerous about invoking sorcery for it has embedded within it something of the fascinating power it seeks to abhor. We ourselves experience something of its irresistible effect for rhetorically this essay evinces considerable impact. In my own case it has taken decades to break free of its overwhelming force. Could it be that, if Hegel is the sorcerer, Voegelin is the sorcerer's apprentice? The suggestion is not as outlandish as it appears for it does seem that in many respects Voegelin is as much the victim of the rhetorical effects he seeks to control. This is evident in the abandonment of his customary scientific coolness, dispensing with the actual texts for an esoteric reading of the motives behind them, and the readiness to rush to judgment on the basis of a rather slim marshalling of evidence. Sorcery is a dangerous game for both the proponent and the opponent. Like metaphor it has its own entrapments built in where the possibility of reversal and overturning is endemic. Perhaps it is better to avoid its incendiary potential altogether and proceed with a more pedestrian if less exciting reading of the texts.

In this regard we may draw a second lesson from the shortcomings of Voegelin's reading. That is, that Hegel can only be properly understood if he is placed in the context of his philosophical predecessors and successors. He is after all engaged in an extended conversation with Kant and a widening collaboration with the other Idealists who sought to enlarge the revolutionary opening Kant had made.[37] No longer concerned about whether we know reality or can ground our moral convictions, now it became apparent that all of our endeavors would have to presuppose as much. There could be no thinking outside of the possibility of thought, just as there could be no morality apart from the admission of

37 Some sense of the remarkable convergence on problems and questions can be seen in the manifesto that is so representative that its authorship remains in dispute. "The Oldest Systematic Programme of German Idealism," Frederick Beiser, ed. and trans., *The Early Political Writings of the German Romantics* (Cambridge: Cambridge University Press, 1996), 3–5.

moral responsibility. We are already within an intelligible reality and a moral universe before we begin. Hegel and the Idealists made explicit what was only implied by Kant's more cautious delineation of the transcendental. There is a horizon of being within which we move. Human beings cannot hold reality at a distance as if they were outside of it, for they are thoroughly embedded within it. Indeed they are the point at which the self-disclosure of reality occurs. The history of philosophy after Hegel is not the story of the collapse of his great systematic ambitions, but the progressive deepening of the actual meaning of the system as a system of life. What Hegel had called his system was never completed but an ever-living invitation to actualize the impulse of thought from which it had always drawn its vitality. The lecture additions every year came to overwhelm the margins of the "system" which, it turns out, was only a syllabus for a viva voce performance.[38] In the hands of Kierkegaard and Nietzsche and, to a lesser extent, Marx, this existential character of philosophy became more abundantly clear. Philosophy became more and more what it had always been, a way of life rather than a speculative result. Contrary to the conventional perception that this was all a reaction against the Hegelian system, we are now more inclined to see it as a continuity and fulfillment. Far from arresting the movement of philosophy and bringing it to a dead end, Hegel had launched it on a new dynamic form that more faithfully reflects the dynamism of life itself. One of the things that makes his formulations both impenetrable and elusive is that he understood that stasis is the death of thought. Only thinking that is continually going beyond itself is true to what it is. To convey that movement through the fixity of words is a considerable challenge, but it is arguable that Hegel presented a tolerable demonstration of it. Voegelin knew this but he did not recognize his own path from the fixity of ideas to the underlying dynamic of experiences and symbolizations as an almost identical transition.

It was only later that he began to acknowledge that his own enlargement of intentionality to the horizon of luminosity contained much of the

38 The famous *Encyclopedia of Philosophical Sciences* which comprised *The Logic*, *The Philosophy of Nature*, and the *Philosophy of Spirit* expanded with the lecture additions that were supplied each year.

Hegelian insight.[39] Then he was prepared to admit his filiation with the sorcerer he had previously excoriated. In light of that later reconsideration we are naturally inclined to view the earlier essay in a different perspective. Once the convergence with Voegelin's own thought becomes apparent we must revisit the essay with the suspicion that something more is at work than univocal condemnation. Could it be that Hegel is Voegelin's double? Or more accurately that Voegelin is Hegel's double? It is surely the latter suggestion that accounts for the peculiar vehemence of the essay as Voegelin seeks to distance himself from the great predecessor to whom he suspects he is so eerily close. A whiff of parricide may even waft the air. But that as Voegelin knew is impossible. Killing the father is tantamount to killing the self once the identity of their projects is apprehended. If Hegel is the true echo of Voegelin's meditative exploration of the materials of history, then he can no more be denounced than Voegelin can renounce his own work. Instead Hegel must be viewed as a collaborator who, even with his flaws, was embarked on the same course and therefore an indispensable resource who could not simply be tossed aside. Voegelin's later more appreciative return to Hegel is an indication of his own growing awareness of the relationship. If it had occurred and included a wider appreciation of Idealist and post-Idealist philosophy it might well have expanded Voegelin's theoretical apparatus as well as prompted a revision of the wider modernity narrative. The thread of continuity goes all the way back to the Parmenidean statement that thinking and being are the same, for the whole of Western philosophy can be read as a meditation upon it. In Voegelin's terms it is the realization that intentionality, the object relationship, is contained within luminosity, the embracing reality relationship. To the extent that we recognize this as the Hegelian core we must conclude that the denunciatory tone

39 Even the title of the second chapter of *In Search of Order*, "Reflective Distance vs. Reflective Identity," bears the mark of Hegel's influence, as Voegelin fully acknowledged. Perhaps the most poignant passage is where he sees the connection between Hegel and Hesiod, both of whom must symbolize the gods who are absent, albeit in divergent fashions. "But how does a Beginning begin if there is no acting Beyond and nothing to be acted upon? Hesiod, it appears, has to cope with the same problem as Hegel, with the problem of telling a story that presupposes the experience of the Beyond without symbolizing it." *In Search of Order*, 90–91.

of the present essay is something of an outlier within the gamut of reflections on his great predecessor. As usual it is the later reconsiderations that reveal the relationship more fully even when they remain in a state of incompleteness.

An earlier version of this essay appeared as "On Hegel: Sorcerers and Apprentices" in *An Apocalypse of Love: Essays in Honor of Cyril O'Regan*, ed. Jennifer Newsome Martin and Anthony C. Sciglitano, Jr. (New York: Herder, 2018), 95–119. I am grateful for permission to re-use and expand on that material in the present iteration.

–9–

Eric Voegelin's "On Classical Studies"

Julianne M. Romanello

Eric Voegelin's essay "On Classical Studies" is, among the late published essays included in Volume 12 of his *Collected Works*, both the shortest piece and the one that has been referenced in Voegelin scholarship on fewer occasions than the other pieces.[1] Nevertheless, it is a pithy work that is attractive for its clarity, its precise comparison of the classic and modern perspectives on science, and its blunt critique of the academy. The essay conveys the essential substance of Voegelin's theory of man, consciousness, and history, and it suggests a specific course of action in the effort to restore order and genuine philosophy to the academy. These features make the article accessible and especially helpful to those who are just starting out with Voegelin. But perhaps these strengths might cause readers to overlook its interesting place within Voegelin's expansive philosophic endeavor.

Unlike other essays in Volume 12, "On Classical Studies" offers little new in the way of a philosophic approach, analysis of some phenomena, or effort to symbolize the structure of existence. In his correspondence, Voegelin recalled the "chore" of developing the "notes" that he later published as "On Classical Studies."[2] Given the seemingly unremarkable circumstances and content of the short essay, I would like to suggest that a crucially significant, yet easy-to-overlook, feature of "On Classical Studies"

1 "On Classical Studies" was first published in *Modern Age*, Vol. XVII (1973), 2–8. References to the essay hereafter, will be to the version published in Voegelin, *Published Essays 1966-1985*, ed. Ellis Sandoz, *CWEV* Vol. 12, 1990. Hereafter cited as Voegelin, "On Classical Studies."

2 Eric Voegelin to Robert Heilman, March 24, 1971, in *Selected Correspondence, 1950-1984*, ed. Thomas Hollweck, *CWEV* Vol. 30, 2007, 699. Hereafter cited as *Selected Correspondence, 1950-1984.*

is that, through it, Voegelin provided a model of the way of life guided by the quest for the truth of existence. Voegelin often considered the profound need that human beings have for a guide along the mysterious and strenuous quest for truth, and he conceived of his own quest as both a following and a leading. As a following, Voegelin's quest was deliberately situated in the experiential and theoretical framework of his own philosophic guides—the most important of whom was Plato.[3] As a leading, Voegelin's quest aimed to expand the experiential and theoretical framework for himself and others, and to adapt the framework to the particular social and historical situation of one's own time. In both its explicit arguments and its status as Voegelin's concrete effort to reveal and to remedy levels of disorder, "On Classical Studies" invites us to consider the role of guidance within the genuinely philosophic life. I suggest that "On Classical Studies" gives readers important insights into Voegelin's response to various threats to the philosophic quest and presents us with an intellectual, ethical, and spiritual guide for engaging reality in its variety of levels in a way that is consistent, balanced, and genuinely erotic in the Platonic sense.

The present study begins with a brief examination of Voegelin's approach to Plato and what he looked for and discovered in the writings of his ancient, yet ever-present guide. The next section looks at the affinities between "On Classical Studies" and Platonic philosophy, especially in the concern to evoke a psychic response by clearly opposing order to disorder. This section also raises the question of how Voegelin's intensifying mystical philosophy of consciousness illuminates the effort of developing "On Classical Studies." In order to clarify that question, I consider the historical and experiential framework surrounding "On Classical Studies" in conjunction with Voegelin's deepening insights into the meaning of Plato's symbols. The study concludes with a consideration of how Voegelin's response to the disorder of the academic institution reveals the strenuous effort to maintain a balanced consciousness.

3 See Voegelin, "Experience and Symbolization in History" (1970) in *Published Essays 1966-1985*, ed. Ellis Sandoz, *CWEV* Vol. 12, 1990, 122, where Voegelin made the often-cited claim that, "The test of truth, to put it pointedly, will be the lack of originality in the propositions." Hereafter cited as Voegelin, "Experience and Symbolization."

Voegelin's Platonic Philosophy

On the occasion of "On Classical Studies" and throughout his life, Voegelin was concerned with the order of the soul and its relation to the meaning and purpose of human life. He sought to understand how the soul's order or disorder manifested itself in the concrete features of history and society and its impact on the practices of science and politics. In his effort to clarify these relations, Voegelin recognized that he would need to look beyond the particular perspective on the soul that dominated the milieu of his day. Therefore, he turned to the ancients and to Plato in particular for guidance and insight into the order of the soul because he thought that what Plato had accomplished in his dialogues was, in most ways, *the* paradigm for the genuinely philosophic life.[4]

In "On Classical Studies," Voegelin looked at the situation of the academy and traced its many symptoms of decline to its refusal to recognize the philosophic guidance that Plato and the ancients had to offer. Due to the academy's ignorance, indifference, or hostility to it, the wisdom of the ancients—which involves the passions as well as the intellect—ceased to be a guiding influence. Voegelin's immediate goal for the essay was that it serve as a clarion call to remember the psychic substance of the ancient wisdom so that it could become the basis for a renewal of science and spirit in the academy. The call to remember was issued in the essay's explicit claims, in its form, and in the example Voegelin himself provided through his persistence in preparing it. All these aspects converge into a powerful challenge to the academy to re-appropriate its critical obligation to pursue the truth of the soul in quest for its ground.

A brief sketch of three important features of Voegelin's complex engagement with Plato will help to demonstrate the Platonic character of Voegelin's activity in "On Classical Studies."[5] First, Voegelin understood

4 See Voegelin, "Wisdom and the Magic of the Extreme: A Meditation" (1983). in *Published Essays 1966-1985*, ed. Ellis Sandoz, *CWEV* Vol. 12, 1990, 373–74. Hereafter cited as Voegelin, "Wisdom and Magic."

5 A more comprehensive study of Voegelin's engagement with Plato is contained in Julianne M. Romanello, "Political Philosophy and the Divine Ground: Eric Voegelin on Plato" (Ph.D. Dissertation,, Baylor University, 2012).

Plato's dialogues to be active responses to the social and spiritual breakdown of his time—especially the destructive influence of the Sophists—that aimed to change the situation in tangible ways. As efforts of restoration, Plato's dialogues intend to analyze and to understand (or "to diagnose") the full contours of disorder and to counter (or "to remedy") it by revealing the absurd conclusions of sophistic arguments and promoting the quest for truth as the genuine moral and theoretical obligation of every human life. In other words, the dialogues are meant to create real order in souls by bringing into high relief the dangerous forces that threaten psychic health. Importantly, Plato's resistance to sophistic disorder and his positive effort to orient souls toward order and truth were conducted through powerful symbols that activated the *pathos*, or the experiential core of the soul. In other words, Plato's symbols could communicate meaning precisely because they arose out of and could evoke universal, though essentially ineffable, experiences of psychic order. Plato, Voegelin thought, sought to guide individuals and the community to the objective and unchanging measure of political and intellectual health.

Second, Voegelin thought Plato's science emerged out of his consciousness of the tensional structure of reality. Plato was aware that reality has multiple layers and facets, spanning infinitely beyond the capacity of human knowledge. Even so, reality is luminous to human psyche because psyche, too, is a participation in reality's transcendent ground. Plato's willingness to follow the guidance of the soul's participatory experiences of the transcending order of the divine ground of being became the basis for his science of order. By contrast, Plato's sophistic contemporaries neglected or rejected altogether the reality of the soul and its orientation toward the transcendent ground, concerning themselves with merely arbitrary goods such as wealth or power. Such a partial view of reality leads to the false opinion that problems in politics and society are fully intelligible and soluble in strictly immanent terms. As that fallacy is taken for science and gains in popularity, the society that accepts it slips further into political, intellectual, and spiritual decline, arriving finally at the point where it becomes necessary to construct fictitious accounts of reality designed to convince reason itself that its suspicion of the fallacy is misplaced. The will to alter reality, rather than to accept its guidance, precludes science, the "search for truth concerning the nature of the various realms of being."[6]

On Voegelin's reading, Plato's acute sensitivity to the transcendent reality of the soul and its experiences of the tension of existence was the foundation of a new science of order—psychic, concrete, and historical—that could clarify misconceptions and supply objectively verifiable solutions to problems of society and politics. Plato endeavored to expand and to analyze those guiding experiences of transcendence, recognizing them as the forces that give order and direction to human intellect and illuminate the objects of scientific inquiry. According to Voegelin, Plato's consciousness of the soul's orientation toward the transcendent ground of being that penetrates and directs human intellect provided an empirically sound basis for evaluating the chaotically fluctuating popular opinions about the structure and purpose of human life. From this crucial insight into the structure of consciousness and its participation in the greater structure of existence, Plato could subject all sorts of common symbols, experiences, concepts, and ideas to analysis, exegesis, and critical inquiry in order further to clarify the various levels of being that are present to human psyche. Moreover, the experiential and reflective insights could reveal the problematic features of socially dominant, yet inadequate, symbols in a compelling and objectively verifiable way.

Finally, for Voegelin, Plato was a mystic, and Voegelin's engagement with Plato was mystical. Platonic philosophy was best understood as a meditative inquiry into nothing short of the entirety of being, an inquiry that would reveal the proper order of human life as the loving submission to the guidance of the divine ground of being that penetrates, illuminates, and forms consciousness. The most profound insights emerging out of this meditative inquiry had the character not of doctrines, propositions, or fixed truths, but rather of luminous mysteries—insights that surpass the capacity of reason and language, but which communicate existential obligations that

6 Eric Voegelin, *The New Science of Politics* (1952), in *Modernity without Restraint: The Political Religions; The New Science of Politics; and Science, Politics and Gnosticism*, ed. Manfred Henningsen, *CWEV* Vol. 5, 2004, 91. Hereafter cited as Voegelin, "*New Science.*" See also, Voegelin, "Experience and Symbolization," 123.

make sense to the searching psyche. In order to examine and to communicate these insights in a manner coherent with the tensional process and structure from which they emerge, the philosopher must struggle to evoke further experiences of reality and must recognize that the essentially ineffable insights cannot be reduced to doctrines, concepts, or ideas. Consequently, any genuinely philosophical endeavor is predicated upon a keen awareness of limitations and the inability to grasp reality finally or comprehensively. To accept in openness—that is, without offence or denial—such limitations, and therefore the perennial need for guidance, is the moral requirement of philosophy.

In sum, Voegelin's engagement with Plato yielded three crucial insights into the genuine philosophical endeavor: first, it responds to concrete disorder with resistance directed to the level of the *pathos*; second, it promotes the order of the soul in tension toward the divine ground of being as the basis for science; and, third, it is a mystical quest that illuminates reality and consciousness only partially, therefore demonstrating philosophy's permanent reliance upon divine guidance and serious concern to guide others toward the transcendent reality that brings moral and intellectual order to human life.

"On Classical Studies" as a Platonic Effort

The specific aims and significance of "On Classical Studies" must be understood in light of these Platonic features. First, the essay diagnoses a particular disorder—namely, the pervasive academic hostility to the life of reason as understood by classical philosophers—and contrasts it with a paradigm of health—*viz.* "the effort of the Greeks to arrive at an understanding of their humanity."[7] In this way, Voegelin followed Plato's example of opposing order to disorder in the hope that the opposition itself will generate the psychic anxiety that attests to the problem and initiates the search for a remedy. In "On Classical Studies," the opposition takes the form of a numbered enumeration of the scientific and existential distinctions between the classics and the moderns. Of crucial importance is the manner of the enumeration, which, in order to generate a serious psychic

7 Voegelin, "On Classical Studies," 258.

response from modern readers, had to be pedantically blunt. Take, for example, the distinction as it pertains to education:

> 7. Classic: Education is the art of *periagoge*, of turning around (Plato). Modern: Education is the art of adjusting people so solidly to the climate of opinion prevalent at the time that they feel no "desire to know." Education is the art of preventing people from acquiring the knowledge that would enable them to articulate the questions of existence. Education is the art of pressuring young people into a state of alienation that will result in either quiet despair or aggressive militancy.[8]

Because the modern insensitivity to questions of humanity had escalated so far, Voegelin must explicitly call attention to his technique and invoke an image of gross evil in order to communicate what is at stake in the opposition:

> Moreover, the conflicts have been formulated in such a manner that the character of the grotesque attaching to the [modern] deformation of humanity through the climate of opinion becomes visible. The grotesque, however, must not be confused with the comic or the humorous. The seriousness of the matter will be best understood, if one visions the concentration camps of totalitarian regimes and the gas chambers of Auschwitz in which the grotesqueness of opinion becomes the murderous reality of action.[9]

8 Voegelin, "On Classical Studies," 260.

9 Ibid. For a discussion of Plato's passionate outcry against the "enlightened moderns (*neos kai sophos*)," see Voegelin's commentary on Plato's *Laws* in *Order and History, Vol. III: Plato and Aristotle* (1966), ed. Dante Germino, *CWEV* Vol. 16, 2000, 244, hereafter cited as *Plato and Aristotle*. Quoting Taylor's translation of Plato, Voegelin writes, "When we see all this evidence treated with contempt . . . and that, as any man with a grain of intelligence will admit, without a single respectable reason, how, I ask, is a man to find gentle language in which to combine reproof with instruction (*Laws* 887)."

Voegelin closely followed Plato's guidance in terms of the appropriate method of generating experiences of anxiety. But in adapting to the exigencies of the modern psyche, Voegelin did not imitate Plato simply, for that would belie the entire substance of Platonic philosophy which consists in the exploration and revelation of the transcendent reality itself, not the method by which it is known. Theoretically and morally, the philosopher is obliged to be a guide as well, which Voegelin did by employing symbols like Auschwitz and by presenting the opposition with unmistakable starkness.[10] As I discuss below, especially at this time in his life, Voegelin preferred the language of philosophic myth to propositional claims, but his approach in "On Classical Studies" followed Plato's example in its recognition that the genuine philosopher must often find himself a reluctant guide—forced to lead in a manner that coincides not with his own insight, but rather with the limited capacity of those who depend on him for the health of their souls.

A second way in which Voegelin's engagement with Plato guides "On Classical Studies" is evident in Voegelin's effort to provide a scientific understanding of the situation of the academy by tracing its concrete features back to configurations of the psyche in response to its experience of the tension of existence. As with Plato before him, Voegelin conceived of elemental, or concrete, disorder as a symptom of the larger problem of a foreshortened understanding or hostile rejection of reality—especially its psychic or transcendent dimensions.[11] Voegelin's brief critical-scientific analysis of the general confusion within and about the academy, especially concerning "the purposes and prospects" of classical studies, begins, therefore, with a survey of the elemental disorder present not only in the particular institutions—universities or colleges that have a basic structure, set of practices, and ethos—that carry out academic purposes, but also in the broader sense of the academy as a social entity that claims to be the bearer and representative of the pursuit of science and

10 On the philosopher's obligations, see, e.g., Voegelin, "Wisdom and Magic," 373.

11 See Voegelin, *New Science*, 105–08, for a brief, clear discussion of the effort to connect the rejection of sciences of ontology and philosophical anthropology to certain religious experiences.

learning.[12] The concrete, observable, and physical indications of disorder in the academy included: the "fragmentation of science through specialization," the "deculturation of Western society," and the fact that its protagonists are "firmly established" in the universities, the reduction of Classical studies to "enclaves in vast institutions of higher learning in which the study of man's nature does not rank high in the concerns of man,"[13] the "hostility" to and "waning institutional support for the life of reason," the "fanatically accelerated destruction of the universities since the Second World War," the international student revolt, the turning of students against professors, and students' resort to "uncritical violence."[14] Beyond these indications of the crisis facing the academy, Voegelin goes on to notice that

> No critical attack on the insanity of the "age" can be more devastating than the plain fact that men who respect their own humanity, and want to cultivate it as they should, must become refugees to the megalithicum, or Siberian shamanism, or Coptic papyri, to the petroglyphs in the caves of the Ile-de-France, or to the symbolisms of African tribes, in order to find a spiritual home and the life of reason.[15]

Any thoughtful observer, Voegelin thought, ought to be repulsed by the absurdity of an academy that derides the classics, deplores the essentially human questions, and refuses even to attempt to persuade ignorant students

12 I think it is helpful to consider what Voegelin writes about representative institutions and human society in *New Science of Politics* in relation to the academy—that society is "as a whole a little world, a cosmion, illuminated with meaning from within by the human beings who continuously create and bear it as the mode and condition of their self-realization," and that the nature of representative institutions in society is to be the form through which political society "gains existence for action in history," develops symbols of self-interpretation, and reveals the various phases of its relation to transcendent truth in history (at 109 and 88). See also, in the same volume, Chapter 1, "Representation and Existence."

13 Voegelin, "On Classical Studies," 256.

14 Ibid., 257.

15 Ibid., 262. Cf. Voegelin, *Autobiographical Reflections* (1989), ed. Ellis Sandoz, *CWEV* Vol. 34, 2006, where Voegelin makes a similar point.

to pursue knowledge but does not hesitate to encourage their violent defense of their opinions. But within the climate of opinion, even the common-sense basis for a response of repulsion was anathema. The life of reason, therefore, stood hardly a chance: that "ineluctable condition of personal and social order" necessary for a correct theoretical and moral response to the academic crisis had been destroyed.[16]

Voegelin explained the breakdown of reason as a manifestation of the uniquely modern disease of the psyche, the *libido dominandi.* The *libido dominandi* that runs rampant in the academy is what prevents scientific inquiry into the nature of man that was the core concern of classical Greek philosophy, and which is the pursuit that justifies the existence of the academic institution. Voegelin explained thus:

> The public interest has shifted from the nature of man to the nature of nature and to the prospects of domination its exploration opened; and the loss of interest even turned to hatred when the nature of man proved to be resistant to the changes dreamed up by intellectuals who want to add the lordship of society and history to the mastery of nature. The alliance of indifference and hatred, both inspired by *libido dominandi*, has created the climate that is not favorable to an institutionalized study of the nature of man, whether in its Greek or any other manifestation.[17]

In other words, the academy's hostility to classical studies is a rejection of the insights into the nature of man discovered by the ancient Greeks—especially the insight into human nature as conditioned by existence in the *metaxy*. The sixth point in Voegelin's list (which is the lengthiest and contains historical commentary) explains the nature of the Greeks' theoretical and moral approach to the tension of existence, and the modern counterposition:

> 6. Classic: The feeling of existential unrest, the desire to know, the feeling of being moved to question, the questioning and

16 Voegelin, "On Classical Studies," 257.
17 Ibid., 256.

> seeking itself, the direction of the questioning toward the ground that moves to be sought, the recognition of the divine ground as the mover, are the experiential complex, the *pathos*, in which the reality of divine-human participation (*metalepsis*) becomes luminous. The exploration of the metaleptic reality, of the Platonic *metaxy*, as well as the articulation of the exploratory action through language symbols, in Plato's case of his myths, are the central concern of the philosopher's efforts. Modern: The modern responses to this central issue change with the "climate of opinion."[18]

The Greeks sought *to understand* man's nature and, to that end, they accepted the terms of the quest, strenuous though they were. Reality reveals itself through the mysterious process that confronts the questioner with increasing apperception of the tension of existence, and the contents of its revelations place firm limits on human freedom and perfectibility. The Greeks, in other words, were able to accept the guidance of transcendent truth, which they recognized as *the* force of order and truth in the human intellect and which "culminated in the Platonic-Aristotelian creation of philosophy as the science of the nature of man."[19] But, in a trajectory that Voegelin traced from Locke, through Hegel, Sartre, and Merleau-Ponty, the experiential core of philosophy has given way to the public interest that favors opinion (*doxa*) over science (*episteme*).[20]

To accept guidance is precisely what the *libido dominandi* most abhors. Faced with the moral and theoretical implications of the Greeks' scientific insight into human limits—not to mention the political ones, which run counter to democracy and its value of public opinion—and with the indelible persistence of the question concerning human nature,

18 Ibid., 259.

19 Ibid., 258.

20 Compare the foregoing remarks with what Voegelin argued in *Order and History, Vol. IV: The Ecumenic Age* (1974), ed. Michael Franz, *CWEV* Vol. 17, 2000, hereafter cited as *The Ecumenic Age*. The parallels between "On Classical Studies" and Chapter 4, "Exodus and Conquest" of *The Ecumenic Age* are too numerous to cite and often the arguments and language in the works are identical.

the intellectuals who dream *to dominate* nature, society, and history must resort to constricting the purview of Classical studies, denying their institutional relevance, and suppressing the perennial questions that animate them. Because the modern *libido dominandi* desires what reason itself recognizes as impossible—to establish a "perfect realm of freedom ... in history," a plain contradiction to the psyche's constituent apperception of the existential threat to its order—it must vigorously deny that "Man exists in erotic tension toward the divine ground of his existence."[21] Instead, abandoning even the remnant of persistent community contained in Protagoras' ancient formulation, the modern *libido dominandi* asserts with respect to man's existence in erotic tension, "He doesn't; for I don't; and I'm the measure of man."[22]

In *The New Science of Politics*, Voegelin made a point of the importance of "a tradition of intellectual culture," reminding readers that, "Science is not the singlehanded achievement of this or that individual scholar; it is a co-operative effort."[23] The *libido dominandi*, therefore, precludes scientific insight not only because it denies the truth of metaleptic reality and its revelations, and thereby disorders the activity and conclusions of the intellect, but also because, in making itself—in all its particularity—the ultimate measure, it destroys the community of the intellect that provides the guidance necessary for effective scientific and theoretical inquiry. Once the intellectual community united in its participation in the divine ground has been destroyed, the modern climate succumbs to and often embraces the "fact" of pluralism, the hegemony of opinion, and, finally, the utter denial of the need or possibility of a scientifically valid account of man whatsoever.[24] Within the prevailing hostility to Classical studies, rightly understood—as the strenuous theoretical and moral quest for truth—lies the danger that reason itself will cease to guide the educational process at all. Arbitrary and dangerous urges threaten to assume the status that rightly belongs to the life of reason and genuine scientific insight, a situation that, left unchecked, would lead to the destruction of the life of the academy.

21 Voegelin, "On Classical Studies," 258.
22 Ibid.
23 Voegelin, *New Science*, 105.
24 See "On Classical Studies," 258.

The similarities between Voegelin's denunciation of the diseased climate of opinion in "On Classical Studies" and Plato's counter to the Sophists are numerous. Like Plato before him, Voegelin wrote with an aim beyond description or discussion: he sought to restore concrete order to a situation of grave disorder.[25] And like Plato, Voegelin wrote from the perspective of one who profoundly suffered both the pragmatic and psychic consequences of the disorder. Voegelin's scientific approach to the nature, extent, and implications of concrete disorder was Platonic in character, endeavoring to understand the elemental in connection to the broad perspective of a science of the soul oriented to the divine ground—to which Voegelin added his further insights into the philosophy of history. His fuller consciousness perceived the heights of health and order possible for the soul, but in so doing, made Voegelin's perception of the psychic depths into which the academic climate had plunged all the more painful.

Finally, as with Plato before him, Voegelin's quest to understand the implications and obligations of metaleptic existence became increasingly subtle and mystical as his psychic attunement to transcendence intensified.[26] This last point is crucial to my claim that the great achievement of "On Classical Studies" is what it teaches, by way of example, concerning the role of guidance in the philosophic life. In some respects, the trajectory of Voegelin's late mysticism ran counter to that of the short essay that concerns itself with pragmatic institutions and concrete manifestations of disorder, and therefore complicates our understanding of Voegelin's intents and purposes in writing the essay. As Voegelin opened himself to the mystical aspects of consciousness's quest for the divine ground—especially in the later years of his career, when "On Classical Studies" was written—he became

25 In what follows, I describe the specific prospects for restoration that Voegelin mentions. Importantly, he does not argue for a reassertion of status or authority by proponents of classical studies. The time for that seems to have passed. But because the nature of man cannot be wholly deformed, the questions previously engaged through studies of classical texts will emerge elsewhere—and that is where Voegelin sees a glimmer of hope for a renewal of the life of reason.

26 See *Plato and Aristotle*, 277–93, esp. 290. On the issue of the various stages of philosophical insight and their relations to each other, see "Wisdom and Magic," 343–48.

acutely aware not only of the grim prospects for a renewed engagement with the wisdom of the ancients (even under "the respectable cover" of the historical sciences), but also of any effort—including his own—to reform an institution so badly damaged as the academy.

In order, therefore, to understand the full significance of "On Classical Studies" as an activity motivated by Voegelin's most profound apperceptions of metaxy existence, we must consider two aspects of Voegelin's late approach to the philosophic obligation to guide others toward existential truth. The first is the historical and experiential framework from within which Voegelin penned "On Classical Studies." Voegelin's correspondence (published in Volume 30 of his *Collected Works*) provides a glimpse into this framework and raises the question whether writing this 9-page essay was not really a feat of considerable existential exertion. And the second is Voegelin's evolving understanding of Plato's late mystical insights into the relationship between existential order and disorder, which continued to guide Voegelin's efforts to diagnose and to heal the modern psyche.[27] Of course, the effort to establish a strict delimitation of either one of these aspects from the other is neither possible nor desirable, for each influences and is influenced by the other in a constantly developing process, and both overlap in terms of history and experience. As events in Voegelin's life provided new perspectives into the conditions of existence, he was able to perceive subtler and deeper layers of meaning in Plato's evocative symbolization of metaxy existence. And as he reflected on the further existential insights evoked by Plato's symbols in light of his own meditative-philosophic effort, Voegelin began to recognize both the expansive gap between himself and his counterparts in the academy as well as the distressingly low capacity of human psyche to tolerate the ordering force of the metaleptic encounter. Voegelin's letters, a few of which specifically address the "On Classical Studies" essay, convey his sense of resignation—based on painful personal experience as well as critical analysis—about the possibilities for restoring order to the academic establishment.

Nevertheless, Voegelin, again like Plato his guide, would continue to

27 See, for example, Letter to Manfred Henningsen, June 20/22, 1969, 605–06, in Voegelin, *Selected Correspondence, 1950-1984,* ed. Thomas Hollweck, *CWEV* Vol. 30, hereafter cited as *Selected Correspondence, 1950-1984.*

engage in nothing less than an urgent battle to guide the souls of the young out of the climate of opinion that sought to deform them. And he did not abandon the institution which—though severely damaged—still had to be the theatre of the battle. Remarkably, when faced with the temptation to make a spiritual leap beyond the academy, Voegelin responded in submission to the theophanic event, even accepting the possibility that improvement in the climate might require the transfer of the philosophic quest from the symbols of the ancient Greek philosophers to those in use in the comparative and historical sciences. "In the cultural history of Western society," Voegelin argued, "the splendid advance of the historical sciences has become the underground of the great *resistance* to the climate of opinion."[28] Classical studies are still important within the academy, and Voegelin maintained that the Greek wisdom had set *the* standard for the exploration of metaleptic reality, but classical studies would no longer hold its position of preeminence as the institutional force of the study of the nature of man. They would, rather, have the diminished position as a one participant among many in a broader, shallower approach to the philosophic quest. Although this might have felt to Voegelin as a surrender of the most disturbing sort, it was a forceful preservation of the balance of consciousness he developed through his experiences with institutional failures and his mystical exploration of the serious play of human existence. To suffer the academy to conduct its resistance on a lower level was Voegelin's act of existential restraint. Let us now turn to the letters relevant to the philosophic effort of "On Classical Studies."

The Historical and Experiential Framework of "On Classical Studies" The Michigan Center Meeting

"On Classical Studies" was published in 1973, but Voegelin developed "the notes"—his characterization of the essay—in the Spring of 1971 for the meeting of the Michigan Center for Coordination of Ancient and Modern Studies.[29] Before the meeting, Voegelin wrote to the director, Professor

28 "On Classical Studies," 262.

29 The essay first appears in *Modern Age*, Vol. XVII (1973), 2–8. See Letter to

Gerald Else, expressing his "greatest pleasure" in accepting an invitation to attend the meeting that he thought would be "fruitful" and "productive," and an "absolutely necessary" scholarly endeavor.[30] In anticipation of the first planning meeting for the conference, he attached a list of topics that he thought would generate rich discussion. These reflected his interests in the political-theological and historical concerns animating works such as *The New Science of Politics* and *Order and History* (as it was initially conceived), namely, the types of empire, their politics and expansion, experiences of alienation, and dogmatic ideology. What is significant is that between the time that he accepted Professor Else's invitation and the time of the formal meeting where he delivered the lecture later published as "On Classical Studies," Voegelin abandoned those original discussion points almost completely.

The planning meeting went well, and afterward Voegelin wrote to his friend Friedrich Engel-Janosi, about the efforts of Professor Else and others, noting optimistically that "the intellectual climate is in fact changing drastically," and "Even in the universities, intelligent people are beginning to stir."[31] In his mind, the political and intellectual situation in America gave reason for hope. "In all corners," he wrote, "people are beginning to comprehend that the era of expansive euphoria … is past." He thought he saw the beginnings of a "revolution," and he was pleased to participate in the meeting with Else and the other classical philologists who "felt the urgent need to make noticeable the weight of their classical knowledge in the treatment of the problems of [their] time." He concluded his reflections with the hopeful prediction that, "in one or two years the undertaking that

Manfred Henningsen, March 24, 1971 and Letter to Robert Heilman, March 28, 1971, in *Selected Correspondence, 1950-1984*, 695–98 and 699–700, respectively.

30 Letter to Gerald F. Else, December 1, 1969, in *Selected Correspondence, 1950-1984*, 27.

31 Letter to Friedrich Engle-Janosi, February 3, 1970, in *Selected Correspondence, 1950-1984,* 645. Just over a month later, Voegelin would write to Professor Stephen Tonsor (also at Michigan), to discuss the crucial institutional problems of the academy including their large size, the inflation of departments, and most importantly, the faculty. Letter to Stephen J. Tonsor, March 16, 1970, 647, in *Selected Correspondence, 1950-1984.*

[Gerald] Else started should bring quite interesting results."[32] As with the original plan of discussion topics, the character of Voegelin's initial response to the opportunity of the Michigan meeting and his aspirations for its restorative prospects are important to consider when attempting to discern the moral and philosophic effort of "On Classical Studies" for the obvious reason that not one of them prevailed upon the final form of the essay.

Obstacles at the Michigan Center and the Hoover Institution

By November of 1970, Voegelin's optimism waned as a number of situations hindered his ability to confront the spiritual turmoil of the academy with full vigor. Not only had both Voegelin and his wife suffered health problems, but several institutions with which Voegelin was associated confronted significant obstacles. The Hoover Institution, which Voegelin had hoped to develop into an international "crystallising center" for a new "science in the Philosophy of Man, Society, and History," faced a severely restricted budget that led, in turn, to frustrated plans, indefinite delays, and Voegelin's admission that "the situation is dark."[33] Revealing his diminished enthusiasm, he wrote,

> My eagerness in this matter, however, is only middling. I think that with every day such an organization here at the Hoover becomes more necessary, considering the general mess in this field in the Universities; but I realize that it would take quite a bit of my time and energy to go in for it with a serious effort.[34]

The financial situation at the Hoover Institution was not an isolated event; the Michigan Center was affected too. Upon learning this, Voegelin wrote to Professor Else, expressing his frustration: "I am quite indignant that the

32 Letter to Engle-Janosi, 645, in *Selected Correspondence, 1950-1984.*

33 Letter to W. Glenn Campbell, January 20, 1969, 585, in *Selected Correspondence, 1950-1984.*

34 Letter to Richard Allen, December 21, 1969, 637–38, in *Selected Correspondence, 1950-1984.*

savings should start exactly where valuable work is done."[35] The letter (written in late November, 1970) is significant because it contains, in brief form, the essential points of the published version of "On Classical Studies," which are a full departure from Voegelin's original plan of discussion topics. As noted earlier, Voegelin had been keen to discuss more concrete manifestations of the intersections between historical, political, and theological forces, but this letter aims directly at the academy: its loss of classical reason amidst a degenerate climate of opinion, its urgent need to consult the ancients in order to help guide it back to health, its ideological closure to the meaning of the student revolt, and its depriving the young of the knowledge to which they are entitled. The letter also shows the initial stirrings of the pathos that, in his lecture at the meeting and in the published essay, culminated into his intensely personal denunciation of the forces that threaten to destroy the philosophic quest and the spiritual recalcitrance of a corrupt academic institution, and his evocative symbolization of the existential toll those forces impose on the genuine lover of wisdom. Voegelin's letter is therefore worth quoting at length:

> What you and your colleagues are doing is an attempt at bringing the resources of philology and classical history to bear on the understanding of contemporary problems. That is indeed the central issue for our time, since the loss of classical rationalism is the primary cause of intellectual disorder. …
>
> Ever since the 18th century, every major philosopher has tried to go back to the classics in order to reintroduce their knowledge into a climate of opinion that has been badly damaged by the degeneration of metaphysics and theology. In our century these attempts have been renewed again and again … with signal success for the restoration of our knowledge in science, and almost equally signal failure to penetrate the brazenness of the ideologies dominant in our universities. Not even the student revolt against a university which deprives them of the knowledge every

35 Letter to Gerald F. Else, November 25, 1970, 685, in *Selected Correspondence, 1950-1984*

> young man has a right to acquire, has made a noticeable dent in the anti-intellectualism of our so-called intellectuals. …
>
> For almost fifty years now, I am plagued by the difficulty that we have no intellectual instruments for the interpretation of contemporary social, especially revolutionary, phenomena. This is more than a personal complaint, for the inability of the professional social scientists to understand what is going on all around them, and under their very noses, is one of the major causes of intellectual and spiritual disorientation in Western society at large. Only the concerted efforts of the kind you have taken upon yourself hold some hope to overcome this miserable situation. …[36]

Voegelin's optimism concerning the institutional structure of the academy had given way to ambivalence. To be sure, Voegelin still recognized the potential of the Michigan Center meeting (and the successes of similar conferences), but the personal impact of the steadily increasing momentum of the centuries-long trajectory of spiritual and theoretical failure tempered Voegelin's hope for that potential to develop into an effective counter to the dominant climate of opinion.

The Munich Institute: Voegelin's Platonic Founding and its Decline

The setbacks at Hoover and Michigan were not particularly extraordinary. Nor do they sufficiently explain Voegelin's increasing ambivalence: he had more grit than that. But, when the resistance Voegelin encountered at Hoover and Michigan are placed in the larger context, they are as "the straw that broke the camel's back," so to speak. For around the same time, Voegelin suffered an enormous and personal blow to his restorative effort: the impending institutional and spiritual collapse of the Geschwister Scholl Institute, or the Institute of Political Science in Munich. The collapse of Munich, which spanned the time of the preparation and publication of

36 Ibid., 685–86.

"On Classical Studies," is the last and most important of the events that constitute the historical and experiential framework for the essay.

Not long after he had expressed his hope for a renewal within the academy (he first wrote to Professor Else in December of 1969), Voegelin returned to Munich to visit the Institute that he had established—and which he guided from 1958 through 1969—in order to be the concrete vehicle through which to counter the "spiritual desolation" that pervaded the German academy. Through the Institute, he had hoped to kindle an effective "revolution of the spirit"—a "precondition for being able to judge the past critically" and for the translation of "the life of the spirit into the life of society."[37] And, under Voegelin's careful guidance, the Institute was largely successful in that endeavor. In 1966, despite a general increase of "the provincialism that was the matrix of Hitlerism," Voegelin was able to write, "It seems, however, that the powers of darkness will have to submit to light—at least as far as the Institute is concerned."[38]

For Voegelin, the endeavor at Munich was his own iteration of Plato's exemplary efforts to counter the disorder of the polis by illuminating the truth of the soul to the young, and the equivalency of the experience became the basis for a new level of existential communion between Voegelin and his ancient guide.[39] Plato, Voegelin argued, had founded the Academy "as the institutional instrument by which the spirit can wedge its way back into the political arena and influence the course of history."[40] With Munich, Voegelin had a unique opportunity to do as Plato had done, advancing the philosophic quest concretely and spiritually. Reflecting later on his role in the Institute, Voegelin recounted:

37 Eric Voegelin, "The German University and the Order of German Society: A Reconsideration of the Nazi Era," 3–4, and 18, in *Published Essays 1966-1985*, ed. Ellis Sandoz, *CWEV* Vol. 12, 1990, hereafter cited as "The German Univeristy.".

38 Letter to Robert Heilman, June 19, 1966, 503, in *Selected Correspondence, 1950-1984*. In this letter and the one that follows (Letter to Gilles Quispel, June 23, 1966, 507, in *Selected Correspondence, 1950-1984*), Voegelin mentions the emergence of troubles at the Institute.

39 See Voegelin's discussion of Plato's *Republic*, in *Plato and Aristotle*, especially 126–47.

40 *Plato and Aristotle*, 279–80.

> I not only had to create the institute's structure and deliver lectures, I also had to train the next generation of political science professionals. I went about this task of education, which was both a great joy and a great labor, on the assumption that one day these young people would continue the work I had begun. The success we enjoyed went well beyond anything we might reasonably have had a right to expect.[41]

Moreover, in language that mirrors his exegesis of Plato's *Republic*, Voegelin went on to describe the Institute's success in providing the young with the intellectual and spiritual guidance they longed for:

> From my experience [in Munich] I know that the young are open, that, in the contemporary intellectual confusion, they both seek and accept help and guidance. As soon as they have understood that hard work is necessary in order to gain the freedom and order of a truly human existence, they are ready to work hard to acquire the intellectual weapons needed in order to resist the pressures of the intellectual mad house in which they have been raised. Success was especially apparent with those with whom I was able to work for a number of years. They were no longer theoretically helpless in the face of aggressive ideological nonsense. I was able to observe that in their contact with students, of whatever ideological or temperamental form, they were intellectually prepared for every confrontation. They neither succumbed to the stupor of ideological excitation, nor were they compelled to utter vapid banalities because they had not learned something better. They

41 Letter to Dr. Hedda Herwig, December 13, 1971, 717, in Voegelin, *Selected Correspondence, 1950-1984*. See also "The German University," 1–35, in which Voegelin explains the problems which made a deliberate intervention to train young scholars necessary. He emphasizes the connection between academic and political disorder and traces both to a disease of the spirit, and decries the dominant scholarly approach that could do nothing to reveal the genuine reasons for the atrocities of the National Socialist regime or to prevent their repetition in the future.

> were able to resist and, in doing so, became helpers themselves.[42]

Little by little, however, what Voegelin had accomplished at the Munich Institute gave way, and, by the Fall of 1970, various "powers of darkness" that had long threatened it could no longer be held at bay. Voegelin's visit in October to Munich left him "very depressed," and in November he wrote that "In the Institute things look rather distressing. … The situation is perhaps best characterized by the fact that in eight days in Munich I didn't talk with anyone about a theoretical problem but only heard information on personal intrigues in the battle for positions, little stories and anecdotes."[43] The letter to Else (cited above) that contained, in basic form, the new trajectory of "On Classical Studies" was written just after Voegelin saw for himself that what remained at Munich was no more than the shell of the vital, Platonic substance Voegelin had implanted there. The smarting of Voegelin's wound might have been assuaged by the strengthening of the psychic bond with Plato, who also suffered similar failures, but its profound impact on Voegelin's attitude toward the academic institution was indelible.

Voegelin's Judgment of the Munich Institute: The Letter to Dr. Herwig

By December of 1971, the situation at Munich had gone from "depressing" to a full-fledged "institutionalized crisis" concerning the Chair of Political Science.[44] A letter to Dr. Hedda Herwig in response to that crisis provides crucial insight into the existential significance of "On Classical Studies"—the essay that treats the capacity of the academy to engage in the most important task of guiding the souls of the young. Written in language that

42 Letter to Dr. Hedda Herwig, December 13, 1971, 719, in *Selected Correspondence, 1950-1984.*

43 Letter to Manfred Henningsen, November 12, 1970, 676, in *Selected Correspondence, 1950-1984.*

44 Letter to Dr. Hedda Herwig, December 13, 1971, 715, in *Selected Correspondence, 1950-1984.*

evokes the motivating experiences of Plato's *Gorgias* and *Republic* (both of which are notable for their Myths of Judgment), the letter to Dr. Herwig reveals the Platonic depth of Voegelin's psychic response to the demise of the Institute that he had intended to be a bulwark of genuine philosophical inquiry amidst pervasive forces of destruction. Without reservation, Voegelin condemned what he witnessed on his trip: "I was incensed at the mindless vandalism that has ruined such a wonderful opportunity."[45] If that were not clear enough, he went on to remark: "It is not sentimental sadness over the loss of a past golden age that overcomes me on the occasion of such a visit, but rage."[46] The crisis evoked Voegelin's rage because it was, on Voegelin's interpretation, deeply personal, being "inextricably bound up with the questions of the intentions [he] had for the institute at its founding and which [he] was able to realize for a number of years."[47] And, more importantly, it was a transgression against one of philosophy's most sacred obligations: to lead the young (as he put it later in "On Classical Studies") to "acquiring the knowledge that would enable them to articulate the questions of existence."[48] The conclusion of his letter to Dr. Herwig captures the Platonic-Socratic sentiments underlying the effort of "On Classical Studies" and its prevailing message with substantial precision. It was written after Voegelin first presented the lecture at the Michigan meeting, but communicates an experience (*viz.* the visit to Munich) prior to that presentation. It is quite possible, therefore, that the activity of preparing "On Classical Studies" not only was motivated by the experience conveyed in the following remarks, but also helped Voegelin to clarify for himself the lines of judgment against the utter debacle at Munich:

45 Ibid., 718.

46 Letter to Dr. Hedda Herwig, December 13, 1971, 720, in *Selected Correspondence, 1950-1984*. In this qualification, Voegelin distinguished himself from men like Cephalus, the character in Plato's *Republic* who "represents the 'older generation' in a time of crisis, the men who still impress by their character and conduct that has been formed in a better age." See *Plato and Aristotle*, 111.

47 Letter to Dr. Hedda Herwig, December 13, 1971, 717, in *Selected Correspondence, 1950-1984*.

48 "On Classical Studies," 260.

> The only thing that can help us today is a spiritual *habitus* that is intellectually secure in itself. But this takes years of education that, from Plato and Aristotle to Jaspers and Bergson, has been understood as the *conversio* (Umkehr), the revolution of consciousness. A knowledge of institutions is important but more important is the experience that forms consciousness upon which institutions are built. That in Germany people are still unwilling to grasp this fundamental relationship, not even after Hitler, is an indication of the historical depths of a pathological state of mind and explains, at least in part, why people succumb, again and again, to the magic of ideological intoxication. The idea that the remnants of philosophical politics and intellectual discipline, which are still present in the institute in the persons of those who were trained by me, should be made ineffective by appointing the wrong person to the professorship, that the students should be deprived of the possibility of receiving the training which the institute once offered them, can induce nothing but rage—the platonic *andreia*. Those who abet this baleful activity, whatever role they play, and at whatever level, should be reminded of Plato's dictum: "To corrupt the spirit of young people is to commit a crime that ranks just behind that of murder itself." In sum, that is my answer to the assistants' call for help.[49]

Voegelin's conclusion is written from the perspective of one who, after having had the joy of serving as a philosophic guide to a group of young students who were healthy enough to resist pressures of a corrupt society, suffered intensely as he watched the reassertion of maniacal forces bent on their destruction. Especially notable here is Voegelin's repetition of the expression of "rage—the platonic *andreia*," and his invocation of Plato's analogy between miseducation and murder, which point back to the importance of Voegelin's understanding of Plato for his self-understanding. These and other symbols illuminate the heightened existential connection Voegelin

49 Letter to Dr. Hedda Herwig, December 13, 1971, 719–20, in *Selected Correspondence, 1950-1984*.

felt to Plato, the substance of which is so important for penetrating the existential importance of "On Classical Studies," and a few comments about Voegelin's understanding of the Platonic symbols he appropriates will illuminate the situation of Voegelin's soul as he developed his essay.

Voegelin's evocation of rage and murder recall the motivating experiences of Plato's *Gorgias*, which, as Voegelin argued about 15 years prior, was written as "a declaration of war against the corrupt society and its content."[50] What is at stake in that dialogue's battle between the philosopher and the sophistic society is the soul of the younger generation, and the sides are distinguished by their relation to what is "for all times the decisive question": "Who he is? (447d).[51] In that question is contained the essence of what Voegelin—in "On Classical Studies"—described as the disturbing question of the divine ground that illuminates metaleptic reality. Several times in his analysis of the *Gorgias*, Voegelin argued that the suppression of that question was akin to murder, and he observed that, despite its comedic moments, "The [*Gorgias*'] undertone of grimness, however, as well as our contemporary experiences, remind us constantly that in a decadent society the ridiculous intellectual is the enemy of the spirit and that he is powerful enough to murder its representatives physically."[52] Voegelin's invocation Plato's expression of outrage in the *Gorgias* provides crucial insight into the psychic depth of the loss of spiritual substance at Munich and, therefore, the conditions under which he wrote "On Classical Studies." Their common experiential bases suggest that Voegelin's judgment of Munich and the academic institution as a whole, would not be far from the judgment Plato leveled against his society millennia ago: "The *Gorgias*," Voegelin argued, "is the death sentence over Athens."[53]

As we saw earlier, Voegelin's letter to Dr. Herwig also draws on the symbolism of Plato's *Republic*, and in it, he establishes himself as following the guidance of Plato and assuming the role to be a saving guide to the young who sought his help. Twice—once at the beginning and here at the conclusion—Voegelin drew the connection between his intervention at

50 *Plato and Aristotle*, 78.
51 Ibid.
52 Ibid., 79.
53 Ibid., 93.

Munich and his efforts to develop the spiritual *habitus* and Socrates' response to the young men who, hoping to be saved from the insatiable *Eros tyrannos* (572d-573b) that threatens their substance, issued a "cry *de profundis*" to their helper.[54] Voegelin's concluding remarks emphasize the *Republic*'s principle that the helper's response to the searchers' plea must reveal the distinction between consciousness, or the soul, and the institutions or elemental forms that determine and are determined by it. In calling attention to this distinction, Voegelin seems to be struggling with the question of whether—without first disentangling the soul from its institutional fetters—a spiritual restoration could hope to be effective at all.

Moreover, by establishing the equivalencies between Socrates of the *Republic* and himself, Voegelin also intimated his own reluctance "to return to the darkness of the Cave and to dispute shadows with the prisoners."[55] What is present in that depth and responsible for the neglect of the soul is the intoxicating magic of psychopathology, or what Plato symbolized as the *Eros tyrannos* (or *libido dominandi*, in "On Classical Studies"), the potential of the soul "to lose itself by closure [to metaleptic reality] and reliance on its own resources."[56] Voegelin ends this section of his analysis of the *Republic* with the chilling observation that,

> Plato was acutely aware of the spirituality of evil and of the fascination emanating from a tyrannical order. The *Eros tyrannos* … has its qualities of luciferic splendor. In this conception of tyranny, as related to the foundation of the perfect polis through a metamorphosis of Eros, we touch perhaps the most intimate danger of the Platonic soul, the danger of straying from the difficult path of the spirit and of falling into the abyss of pride.[57]

If the complex symbolism of Plato's *Republic* illuminates the manifold of Voegelin's deepest psychic response to Munich's collapse, it is appropriate to

54 See Ibid., 134–36, and 180–81, and Plato, *Republic*, Books I, II, and VIII, especially 366a-368c, and 572a-574.

55 Ibid., 170.

56 Ibid., 181.

57 Ibid.

consider that he also faced "the most intimate danger of the Platonic soul." Perhaps, in being confronted with the institutional failure of Munich to guide the young to the reality of the soul and also with the apperception of the *Eros tyrannos* responsible for it, Voegelin felt on some level the temptation Plato had felt: to yield to the intoxicating lure of the abyss, to brush aside the ordering revelations of transcendence, and, therefore, to reject the revealed insight into the philosophic duty to be a guide to others. With the collapse of Munich, Voegelin's resolve to re-enter the Cave and his hope for any effective counter to the climate of opinion were, if Voegelin's existential connection to Plato is instructive, themselves in danger of being swallowed by the depth.

Reconsidering the Restoration of Order within the Academy

Voegelin's myriad efforts within the academic institution to guide others—especially the vulnerable young—to the truth of the soul were met with adversity at each turn. Despite Voegelin's tenaciousness, experience called for a sober reconsideration of the prospects for spiritual and intellectual renewal in the academy and a reevaluation of the exertion of effort to prepare "On Classical Studies" for the Michigan Center meeting.[58] In correspondence from after the Munich trip (but prior to the Michigan meeting) he wrote the following to a colleague:

> Thank you ever so much for this perceptive review which indeed brings out the problem that worries me all the time: Whether anything can be done about the intellectual and spiritual disorientation of the time in an effective manner, or whether one must let the social process run its course, with the hope only of perhaps helping this or that man in his personal troubles. At present, I am rather inclined to believe that nothing really effective can be done, but that the philosophical work must go on, in order to keep alive the possibility of return for those who are willing to turn around. Whether the situation arises in which

58 See *Ecumenic Age*, 281, where Voegelin explored the classic philosophers' recognition of the limits of their efforts and the impending fall of the polis, which would be "superseded by a new type of society."

> such a turning around becomes socially relevant, however, I do not know. And this ignorance means really that I consider it quite possible that such a turning point may arrive any day, as ever more people are fed up with disorientation and are looking for order again. Hence, I am pessimistic with regard to personal effectiveness, but quite optimistic with regard to favorable change. Things simply do not go on in the same way forever.[59]

Voegelin's remarks suggest a lost hope and growing doubt about his role within the dramatic contest over the soul, and the ambivalence expressed here spilled over into his attitude toward participating in the Michigan meeting, which he now counted among the "chores" that made his schedule "a bit strenuous." "For that one," he wrote, "I had to write a ten-page piece on Classical Studies (I revenged myself by giving it a humorous cast)."[60] And, in a dry expression of frustration, he added, "In order not to be bored to death with my active self, I do a little reading on the side."[61]

59 Letter to Thomas Molnar, November 17, 1970, 678, in *Selected Correspondence, 1950-1984*. Compare with Voegelin's comments in *Plato and Aristotle*, at 83: "In the *Theaetetus*, where Plato comes close to characterizing the enemies as beasts, he nevertheless restores community by observing that in private conversation it is possible at least to scratch the thick crust of the vulgarian and to touch in him a spark of his renounced humanity."

60 This remark calls to mind his earlier description of the "grimness" and comedy of Plato's *Gorgias* (*Plato and Aristotle*, 79) as well as the warning, in "On Classical Studies," about mistaking "the grotesque" with "the comic or the humorous." Compare also with Voegelin's 1966 analysis of the academic level of the science of man in *Anamnesis*, where he argued that only the form of satire could properly describe the "peculiar mixture of *libido dominandi*, philosophical illiteracy, and adamant refusal to enter into rational discourse" that pervaded German universities and was becoming a force in American universities as well. But, Voegelin observed, even satire would be ineffective for "it is next to impossible to write satire when a situation has become so grotesque that reality surpasses the flight of a satirist's imagination." Numerous parallels between the *Anamnesis* essay, "Remembrance of Things Past," and "On Classical Studies" are evident. "Remembrance of Things Past," in *Published Essays 1966-1985*, ed. Ellis Sandoz, *CWEV* Vol. 12, 1990, 308.

61 Letter to Robert Heilman, March 28, 1971, 699–700, in *Selected Correspondence, 1950-1984*.

Voegelin's Mystical Philosophy and the Effort of "On Classical Studies"

The effort of "On Classical Studies," which Voegelin undertook in order to support a concrete movement aimed at reorienting the academic community to the life of reason, was now relegated to the status of a distraction from more important pursuits, such as the new theoretical perspective of *The Ecumenic Age*. Voegelin's work on that volume proceeded "very haltingly," which he explained thus, "I have been sitting for several weeks working on the next paragraph of *Ecumenic Age*, on 'Conquest and Exodus'... Unfortunately I am constantly interrupted by diversions like the notes 'On Classical Studies.'"[62] That "paragraph" and the one that follows ("The Pauline Vision of the Resurrected"[63])—chapters 4 and 5, respectively, of *The Ecumenic Age*—contain Voegelin's exploration of the mythical and revelatory dimensions of the soul's existence within the Metaxy. Written at the same time as "On Classical Studies," they reveal the important mystical turn that came to characterize Voegelin's later meditative exploration of the metaleptic reality.

Voegelin's later mystical philosophy illuminated and gave symbolic expression to his most subtle insights into previously-obscured dimensions of human existence, especially the intimate and often indistinguishable commingling of the forces of order and disorder. Voegelin's exploration of that aspect of metaxic structure was not new: he had dwelt on it extensively in *Plato and Aristotle*. But Voegelin's late approach to the metaxic tension would be conducted on a new level as his meditative quest deepened and as his experiential basis was enlarged—by developments such as the founding and collapse of Munich. That experience was

62 Letter to Manfred Henningsen, March 24, 1971, 695, in *Selected Correspondence, 1950-1984*.

63 Voegelin mentioned this chapter specifically in a letter to Henry Regnery, describing its subject as "a rather tough problem that had loomed on [his] horizon for several years." In the same letter, Voegelin offers "On Classical Studies" for publication by *Modern Age*, explaining that he had "gotten it out of" the *Political Science Reviewer*, which was to be the original publication venue. Letter of August 4, 1972, 736, in *Selected Correspondence, 1950-1984*.

formative in all respects: early on, Voegelin lived out the philosophic obligation to expand the community of the spirit by opposing the forces that would deform it. By his receptivity to the revealed obligation, Voegelin became increasingly attuned to its divine ground, his apperceptions of the tensional structure of existence becoming ever more subtle. Moreover, in its many equivalences to Plato's ancient philosophic effort—in terms of its psychic motivation, its orientation, and its eventual collapse—Munich intensified Voegelin's attunement to the heights and depths of the Platonic soul. This psychic participation with Plato, which proceeded through multiple dimensions of order and history in an ineffably complex mythical quest, had a crucial impact on Voegelin's late mysticism for it illuminated new levels of meaning in Plato's symbolic exploration of the psyche's permeation by transcendent forces of order and disorder.

Voegelin's mystical discovery of these new levels of meaning had practical consequences. As the mystic philosopher discerns more facets of the structure of existence, his understanding of the complex configuration of soul in relation to society increases, but the bonds that hold him to his society diminish. For, while order and disorder are perpetually conjoined, the philosopher who is in a continual process of transformation by the theophanic force of order is infinitely distanced from those who are not. In a passage of *Plato and Aristotle* that seems to apply to himself as much as to Plato, Voegelin described the inevitable separation of the mystic philosopher from the community he has tried so earnestly to heal:

> And what has become of the philosopher-kings? Gone is the hope that their numbers could unite in the erotic community of the philoi . . . there is only one "who has knowledge of these things," that is, Plato himself. All he can do is to provide the nomoi that will exert the divine pull on the lesser souls who in this, their lower rank, are all equal. The "one" is withdrawing from the community of men because the community of equals has failed to be his equal; and he is withdrawing toward the divinity, into the neighborhood of the God who pulls the strings. . . . It sounds as if the Stranger, in his transport, had for a moment forgotten that

> even his fellow wanderers are not quite his equals and that one must speak to them with a little caution.[64]

Plato's experience of his own philosophic separation from the polis was a direct result of a mature understanding—"drawn from the cosmic depth in [his] soul"[65]—of the inseparability of order and disorder within the human psyche. Plato's expanding historical, psychic, and symbolic experiences revealed new dimensions of the near-insurmountable limits and entanglements that burden the human psyche and hinder the quest for attunement to the divine paradigm of order. For example, the late symbolization of Plato's *Timaeus* communicated his discovery that

> The resistance to the idea has now become as eternal as the idea itself; and to overcome this resistance in creation is the permanent task of the Nous. In the Parable of the Cave the emphasis was on the ascent of the soul from the Cave to the intellection of the Idea; the emphasis has now shifted to the descent and the imposition of the Idea on formless reality. . . . the descent has now become the crucial problem, and Plato for the first time gives full attention to the force of the soul which carries the Idea from being into Becoming.[66]

Analyzing Plato's further development of these concerns in the *Critias*, Voegelin concluded, "The lust of existence is as ultimately divine as its overcoming through the ascent to the intelligible realm."[67] What previously, in

64 *Plato and Aristotle*, 288. Although Voegelin wrote this passage before the markedly different approach that characterizes his later period, the late insights into time and eternity support the use of earlier formulations in bringing clarity to later ones. On the various "periods" of Voegelin's career, see James M. Rhodes, "On Voegelin: His Collected Works and His Significance," *The Review of Politics*, Vol. 54 (1992): 621–47.

65 Ibid., 290.

66 Ibid., 256.

67 Ibid., 267. Compare also with Voegelin's remarks about how "the tale that saves" is perpetually threatened by "the forces of death," in "Wisdom and Magic," 335–39. Other relevant passages include "The Gospel and Culture,"

the *Republic*, was experienced as a temptation to the philosopher to renounce his duty to those imprisoned in the Cave, was now incorporated into the foundation of Plato's science of soul and society. Plato's mystical apperception of the commingling of order and disorder led to the disturbing revelation that, for the majority of people, "the divine measure cannot be the living order of the soul."[68] Hence, the shift from the optimism of the *Republic* and its "vision of the Agathon" to the more sober symbolization of the *Laws* and its "dogma with obligatory force."[69]

Voegelin went on to argue (again, still in *Plato and Aristotle*) that, faced with the diminished capacity of the human material to accept the ordering force of the spirit, Plato would be tempted to conduct his effort to restore concrete political order to Hellas through "the violent, tyrannical solution" of "unification through tactical means in power politics."[70] Plato did not succumb, and the complex political and historical basis for these remarks are beyond the present scope, but suffice it to say that, even early on, Voegelin saw that Plato's personal mystical encounter with transcendence brought with it certain dangers. From Voegelin's later perspective of heightened sensitivity to Plato's later insights into the commingling of order and disorder—their meaning and implications—Voegelin's existential proximity to the dangers faced by his ancient guide would have increased as well.

Voegelin explored the dangers of mystical ascent in the chapters of *Ecumenic Age* that he was writing at the same time as "On Classical Studies," and, if the above analysis is sound, it is likely that Voegelin also felt the dangerous urge to relent, in so doing, and to reject the tension of existence. Voegelin's repeated experiences of the ineffectiveness of any effort to salvage the institutional vessel, which claimed to be—but in reality was not—the center of the philosophic quest, tempted him to abandon the vessel altogether. His enthusiasm for the Michigan meeting that he had committed to with excitement before was all but gone and, in his ascent to the exploration

in *Published Essays 1966-1985*, ed. Ellis Sandoz, *CWEV* Vol. 12, 1990, 183–88, and "Reason: The Classic Experience," ibid., 278–83.

68 *Plato and Aristotle*, 317.

69 Ibid.

70 *Plato and Aristotle*, 279.

of the peak of the philosophic myth, engagement with the broken academic institution was a bother and a burden.

The existential distance between himself and the institution he once hoped to guide toward flourishing was now a truth that would seem to make the effort of "On Classical Studies" absurd. Again on this point, Voegelin's letter to Dr. Herwig is revealing, for Voegelin's reflection on its purpose and prospects might apply equivalently to "On Classical Studies." Voegelin wrote: "I very much doubt that this letter will meet with any success in moving the issue along in the direction which you would like to see it take. Indeed, in a certain sense, this letter is absurd.... My repeating these wishes here will hardly change that." And, with some resentment, Voegelin clarified that the concrete controversy concerned not merely "the scholarly interest of the two candidates," but extended to "far more important things," about which—in a terse line that borders on closure—Voegelin wrote, "there is nothing new to say."[71] If the letter to Dr. Herwig provides any indication, it is that Voegelin's attitude toward the academy as a whole, the Michigan meeting, and the essay "On Classical Studies" (which also does not say anything new) was beset by the temptation to leave the broken and futile projects to suffer their just fate. By this time, Voegelin was, after all, intensely preoccupied by mystical exploration of the structures of consciousness, the features of noetic Vision, and the Beyond, and to engage in a hopeless struggle for institutional reform at the expense of those productive explorations would appear to be not only absurd, but perhaps even destructive.[72]

The Balance of Consciousness: Following Plato's Guidance on the Obligation to be a Guide

Nevertheless, Voegelin continued to follow the guidance of Plato, who never abandoned his obligation to promote the genuine psychic flourishing

71 Letter to Dr. Hedda Herwig, December 13, 1971, 716, in *Selected Correspondence, 1950-1984.*

72 See, for example, the cited chapters of *The Ecumenic Age*, at 274–339. Also, Voegelin's book *Anamnesis* and his essay, "Wisdom and Magic," dwell on these topics.

of his society and the individuals who sought his guidance, even as his mystical encounter with the transcendent ground reached new levels. Therefore, Voegelin's invocation of the Platonic symbols in his letter is important not only because it illuminates the basic experiential complex of Voegelin's writings, but also because it demonstrates his *deliberate resistance* to the temptation to withdraw. In *Ecumenic Age*, Voegelin revisited the analysis of Plato's dialogues, this time from the perspective of a mystical analysis of his insights concerning the relation between metaleptic reality and historical process. What Voegelin emphasized in his later study of Plato's noetic consciousness was Plato's restraint and "the postulate of balance."[73] Plato, Voegelin observed, was able to hold together the ineluctable mystery of a quest for the truth that, while grounded in the transcendent Beyond, must be conducted within the cosmos that somehow participates in that Beyond and, moreover, is perpetually in danger of being relegated to a state of untruth in relation to the fullness of truth attached to the transcendent Beyond.[74] Or, as Voegelin would later put it in his masterful 1977 essay, "Wisdom and the Magic of the Extreme: A Meditation:"

> Plato's vision, thus, is not a sudden flash of illumination but the late clarity of a truth apprehended only dimly when he was young; the truth of history has grown historically in his existence. … Plato wants this this many-faceted process to be understood as a whole whose past must not be dismissed as irrelevant now that it has culminated in the present of the *Laws*. There is no truth of history other than the truth growing *in* history. This conception of truth as a growth of luminosity in the process of reality imposes respect on the thinker and his present; he must respect his past as much as he respects his present that will be a past for a future present. The philosopher's existence derives its truth from accepting itself as an event of participation, but as no more than such an event, in a process of reality that is becoming luminous; and inversely, the structure of the historical process will not become luminous for its truth unless

73 *Ecumenic Age*, 291, ff.
74 Ibid., 292.

> it becomes luminous at the point of its concrete occurrence in the present of the thinker's consciousness.[75]

As his psychic bond to Plato continued to expand and intensify, Voegelin discerned in Plato's philosophy of the myth the more intimate apperception not only of the comingling of existential order and disorder that drives a rift between the philosopher and his society, but also of the strenuous philosophic obligation to love—and to respect—reality in all its configurations, even those that fall terribly short of the philosopher's paradigmatic response to the metaleptic reality. If one is to maintain the balance of consciousness that is essential to psychic health, the effort to conduct any philosophic restoration must be grounded in the recognition that the historical dimension of the process imposes limits on and generates possibilities for *all* reality's attunement to the divine ground, no matter the level of existential emptiness or fullness.

In Voegelin's later reflections on Plato's *Laws*, he observed two important imbalances of consciousness that occur when older symbols of order are no longer able to illuminate the psyche's experiences of order and disorder. Both responses intend to supply new symbolizations that are more adequate to the historical movements of experiential consciousness, but they lose balance by contracting the metaleptic reality into one or the other of its poles. The first imbalance is the Sophistic form, which overemphasizes the human partner in the participation and leads to a denial of divine reality. In the argument of "On Classical Studies," Voegelin forcefully opposed the more dangerous Sophistic contraction of reality, which leads to the mass social deformations of noetic consciousness—the destruction of the life of reason. In its modern form, the imbalance of the Sophistic type included the deliberate rejection of balance altogether—the *libido dominandi* that made Auschwitz possible. But in the effort and activity of "On Classical Studies," Voegelin resisted the personal temptation to lapse into something similar to the second type of imbalance: the Eleatic form, which overemphasizes the divine One so that all other reality has the status of untruth or nonbeing.[76] As a representative or symbolization of the philosophic quest,

75 "Wisdom and Magic," 343.

76 Ibid., 350–57. Cf. *Ecumenic Age*, 291, ff.

the academic institution (at every level) had suffered a severe loss of reality and became inadequate to Voegelin's scientific and mystical approach to the quest. In light of his existential separation from it, the restorative effort of preparing "On Classical Studies" could easily have been reduced to nothingness as well. But that, of course, did not happen.

When confronted with the "absurd" effort of writing to Dr. Herwig to try to salvage what he could of Munich, Voegelin explained the existential justification of his effort in Plato's terms, writing: "I cannot simply ignore a call for help and moral support in such an important matter."[77] Voegelin's invocation of Plato's symbol is meaningful not only for its experiential insight, but also for its recognition that the elemental or concrete or institutional reality does not become unimportant by its inability to be ordered by the living paradigm of the philosophic soul. That insight governs Voegelin's approach to "On Classical Studies" and to institutional reform of the broken academy as well. In following Plato's guidance in the conduct of his mystical quest, Voegelin discerned the philosophic prohibition against withdrawal and the related obligation to approach the imperfect vessels—whether language symbols or institutional structures—that are often the only vehicles to existential consciousness available to the vast majority of human beings with Platonic *philia. Philia* is Plato's visionary insight into partnership of the whole that—while permeated by the opposed forces of order and disorder, and therefore often seeming to be irreparably split—is one by virtue of its ontological ground. The insight reveals "the order of the soul as the loving quest of truth in response to the divine drawing from the Beyond; the divine-human movement and countermovement of love is the source of man's knowledge concerning his existence in truth."[78] The order of the soul and the order of the cosmos are existentially bound together, and the "Word of truth" that restores order "must not remain a mute event in the soul of the man who was touched by grace, or it will be lost."[79] Although the constant discord between the saving Word saved from death and its nonacceptance by man in society and history can be experienced so

77 Letter to Dr. Hedda Herwig, December 13, 1971, 717, in *Selected Correspondence, 1950-1984.*

78 Voegelin, "Wisdom and Magic," 333.

79 Ibid., 335, ff.

intensely that the reality of the discord rather than the reality of the saving Word will be sensed to be the truth of the "message," the philosopher's love of truth and the reality it grounds obliges him to participate in the messy process, "…following the pull of the golden cord as far as the counterpull of the steely cords will allow."[80] Voegelin's openness to the guidance of Plato's luminous vision of cosmic *philia* generated the existential strength to prevail in his duty—through efforts such as "On Classical Studies"—to provide the philosophic guidance that might awaken others to truth of metaleptic reality. In this way, "On Classical Studies" teaches a powerful lesson concerning the moral requirements of the philosophic life.

Concluding Remarks

Voegelin did not succumb to the temptation to abandon the broken institution. He prepared the lecture for the Michigan meeting and published the essay roughly two years afterward. Not simply the text, but also, and more importantly, the example Voegelin provides through the effort of "On Classical Studies" is his concrete response to the disturbing revelations of the ineluctable admixture of order and disorder within soul and society. To consider the effort of preparing "On Classical Studies" in light of, first, Voegelin's sobering experiences with concrete institutions and, second, his pursuit of a significantly different theoretical perspective on order and history points to a level of ethical and philosophic meaning that extends beyond the theoretical claims of the essay on their own. "On Classical Studies," considered in its totality, provides a paradigm for how the mystic philosopher must continue to engage the society that cannot keep pace with his existential ascent.

Over the course of his life, Voegelin's approach to the restorative effort changed to accommodate the frailty of the human psyche and its need for institutions. Like his guide Plato, Voegelin discovered that he must work to support the institutions in a way that those institutions could handle—like preparing a paper and publishing the essay that encourages specific actions necessary for the turning-around (such as the turn to historical and

80 Ibid., 338. The images of the cords are drawn from Plato's Myth of the Puppet Player, at *Laws* 644–45.

comparative studies and their symbols). Writing a nine-page essay might not seem like a grand effort at restoration, especially for someone as prolific and influential as Voegelin, but considering it in light of Voegelin's later meditative quest reveals its significance. Despite all odds and the personal burden it inflicted, Voegelin continued to engage the academy so as to guide it toward the level of the existential order it could bear. Perhaps, then, the measure of achievement of "On Classical Studies" is the demonstration of the remarkable fortitude of Voegelin's noetic understanding, which tempered his rage at the destruction of souls.

–10–

Voegelin's "Reason: The Classic Experience"

William Petropulos

Eric Voegelin's essay, "Reason: The Classic Experience" was published in 1974.[1] In the following pages I want to focus on the essay's place in Voegelin's philosophizing, the heart of which I take to be the insight that he expressed in 1930 into meditation as a "fundamental form of philosophical thinking."[2] My commentary is divided into two sections. Section I is devoted to some of the essay's most salient points, and the sub-headings (e.g., "The Tensions of Existence" and "Psychopathology" conform to how Voegelin titled the segments of his original essay. In my Section II second, which references Voegelin's *Theory of Governance*[3] (c. 1930), and some later writings that were published in *Anamnesis*[4] (1966), I will relate these points to Voegelin's understanding of philosophical meditation and discuss 1) the act of meditation, and 2) the literary record of a meditation as invitation and guide to the reader to enact his own.

Section I

In volume 12 of *The Collected Works of Eric Voegelin*, the essay "Reason: The Classic Experience" comprises twenty-seven pages: an untitled introduction

1 Eric Voegelin, "Reason: The Classic Experience," in *Published Essays*, 1966-1985, ed. Ellis Sandoz, *CWEV* Vol. 12, 1990, 265–92. Hereafter cited as Reason."

2 Eric Voegelin, The Theory of Governance and Other Miscellaneous Papers, 1921–1938, ed. William Petropulos and Gilbert Weiss, *CWEV* Vol. 32, 226. Hereafter cited as "*CWEV* Vol. 32."

3 Ibid., 224–373.

4 Eric Voegelin, *Anamnesis: On the Theory of History and Politics*, ed. David Walsh, *CWEV* Vol. 6, 2002. Hereafter cited as "*Anamnesis*."

(pp. 265–67), followed by segments #1, "The Tension of Existence" (pp. 267–73); #2, "Psychopathology" (pp. 273–79); #3, "Life and Death" (pp. 279–87); and #4, "Appendix" (pp. 287–91).

From the outset of the essay, Voegelin capitalizes the word "Reason" to emphasize that there is not on the one hand, Divine Reason, and on the other, human reason, but rather one Divine Reason in which human-being participates. While human participation in the mystery of the community of being[5] has always been through Reason, in the life of philosophy Reason becomes luminous to itself. Differentiations in the experience of human participation are what constitute history, with each differentiation marking a "before" and "after" in the life of the spirit. Moreover, each successive differentiation in the experience of participation affects the meaning of earlier symbols. So, for example, if once, the terms "life and death" referred primarily to states of organic being, in the life of philosophy they refer in the first instance to the degree of a person's conscious participation in being. In this way the life of Reason becomes the norm and measure of what it means to be "alive."[6] This does not mean that Reason is the last word in the differentiation of the experience of participation and Voegelin refers to the "pneumatic revelations" in Judaism and Christianity, to mysticism,[7]

5 "God and man, world and society form a primordial community of being. The community…is, and is not a datum of human experience. It is a datum of experience insofar as it is known to man by his participation in the mystery of its being." Eric Voegelin, *Order and History, Volume I: Israel and Revelation*, ed. Maurice P. Hogan, *CWEV* Vol. 14, 2001, 39. Hereafter cited as "*Israel and Revelation*."

6 The philosopher refers to the life and death of the spirit. Consequently, Socrates, to the court that had sentenced him to death, declares: "Now it is time that we were going, I to die and you to live, but which of us has the happier prospect is unknown to anyone but God." Plato, *Apology*, 42a.

7 "In my work on the 'History of Political Ideas' the fundamental methodological question arose: Which categories provide the constants needed for an understanding of the entire period…The position of the mystic is methodologically the most correct because it is systematically general enough to accurately describe the deeper levels of the historical concretizations in the light of their respective relativities. Nor in regard to the political-historical dimension is this choice accidental: historically, the mystical positions emerge with decisive im-

and to tolerance in doctrinal matters, as further acts of differentiation.[8]

1. The Tension of Existence

The term "tension of existence" refers to the perennial human experience of "unrest" that agitates the heart because man is aware that he is a created being and not a self-grounding entity. Such experiences motivate him to ask questions concerning his origin and destiny. Thus the "tension of existence" has a direction. But the direction does not originate in man. Specifically, in the life of the love of wisdom, man feels himself "moved" by some unknown force to ask questions, he is "drawn" into the search. Sometimes he must first overcome an apathy that is rooted in ignorance. This leads to the symbol of the "flight from ignorance" and of "turning around" [Plato's *periagoge* and the Christian *conversio*]:

> "The man who asks questions, and the divine ground about which the questions are asked, will merge in the experience of questioning as a divine-human encounter.... The ground is not a spatially distant thing but a divine presence that becomes manifest in the experience of unrest and the desire to know."[9]

Voegelin adds that Plato and Aristotle did not use the term "*metaxy*" to articulate the Divine-human encounter but symbols that they had inherited from their predecessors, and which denote various concrete modes of

portance at precisely those times when the deeper levels of historical concretization begin to dissolve, such as in the ancient Christian Imperium at the time of Augustine or the mediaeval-Christian empire at the time of Eckhart and Cusanus." Letter of Eric Voegelin to Karl Löwith, December 17, 1944, in *Selected Correspondence 1924-1949*, ed. Jürgen Gebhardt, *CWEV* Vol. 29, 2009, 414–418. Here 416.

8 "Reason," 266.

9 Ibid., 271.

tension—among them *philia, eros, pistis*, and *elpis* [friendship, love, faith, and hope].[10] In Christian terms, human participation in the mystery of the community of being is a form of the *amor Dei.*[11]

2. Psychopathology

When the human being revolts against the *amor Dei* he closes his soul to Reason.[12] Voegelin calls this state of spiritual-intellectual derailment, "psychopathology." Historically such derailments were preceded by attempts to reduce philosophy to propositions. But such reductions destroy philosophy. For philosophy is a way of life: the pursuit of wisdom on the part of those who have adequately responded to the experience of the heart's "unrest." And the language that philosophers use to mark the stages of their cognitive and existential response cannot be minted into propositions or information that can disclose the meaning of such a life to those who do not embark on the same course.

When propositions concerning Reason usurp the life of Reason the dialog of the soul grows silent and statements about a realm of spirit, treated now as an entity in world-immanent reality, become attempts to "master" and "control" spirit. It is Voegelin's view that the loss of the life of Reason characterizes modernity and that in order to overcome this disorientation the "bond between Reason and existential *philia*, between Reason and openness toward the ground," must be made "thematically explicit."[13] What is at stake is life or death. For:

> "Reason is differentiated as a structure in reality from the experiences of faith and trust (*pistis*) in the divinely ordered cosmos, and of the love (*philia, eros*) for the divine source of order; it is differentiated from the *amor Dei* in the Augustinian sense, not from the *amor sui.*"[14]

10 Ibid., 273.
11 Ibid.
12 Ibid., 274.
13 Ibid.
14 Ibid., 273.

3. Life and Death

To express the meaning of existence between life and death Voegelin uses the Greek term "*metaxy*" taken from Plato's *Symposium* and *Philebus.*[15] The philosophers discovered that man is more than mortal. He is an "unfinished being, moving from the imperfection of death in this life to the perfection of life in death" who "experiences himself as tending beyond his human imperfection toward the perfection of the divine ground that moves him."[16] The *metaxy* is "the reality of 'man's converse with the gods'" (*Symposium* 202–03).[17]

The truth that man exists between "death" and "life" can be obscured if one immanentizes the poles of the *metaxy*—the height of eternal spiritual being (Divine Nous) to which the mind aspires, and the depth (Apeiron) out of which entities emerge and into which they must return. In terms of Christian psychology, the denial of life in the In-Between between mortality and immortality leads to the substitution of apeironic lust for the life of the spirit, i.e., the *superbia vitae* (*libido dominandi*) which is the theological definition of original sin. In other words, in the derailment of Reason, Divine creation is ignored or reduced to a "projection" of man who asserts that reality is world-immanent and that his own being is self-grounding.

When modern man rejects the life of Reason he does so in the name of Reason[18] and substitutes an inner-worldly program or process for the world-transcending movement of the spirit. However all such attempts to impose a merely inner-worldly meaning on human life are open to Kant's

15 Ibid., 279. Cf. "Dazwischen" in Hugo Perls, *Lexikon der Platonischen Begriffe* (Bern and Munich: Francke, 1973), 50ff.

16 "Reason," 279.

17 Ibid. In Christian terms: "The human being is a between *(Zwischen)*, a border (*Grenze*) and a passage, an appearance of God in the current of life and an eternal overcoming of life over itself." Therefore, it is not correct to say that the "human being prays." The fact is that human-being "is the prayer of life overcoming itself." The human being does not "seek God," the human "is the living X which seeks God." Max Scheler, *Vom Umsturz der Werte*, ed. Maria Scheler, Vol. 3 of Scheler's *Gesammelte Werke* (Bern: Franke Veralag, 1955), 186–90.

18 "Reason," 277.

objection to the program of Progressivism, which Voegelin summarized in the words: "participation in the meaning of history was no substitute for the meaning of personal existence because it offered no answer to the problem of a man's personal death in time."[19] At the center of the individual engaged in the subversion of Reason is the loss of faith, hope, and the love of being.[20]

To recapitulate: Man exists in the tension between mortality and immortality, between the apeironic depth and the noetic height. The human being lives in the *metaxy* and is not in control of the height or the depth of the community of being in which he participates. Those who reify the height and the depth falsify the nature of human participation by reducing it to world-immanent existence.

4. Appendix

In the appendix Voegelin offers a graphic presentation of human participation in being.

↓ ↑	PERSON →	SOCIETY →	HISTORY →
Divine Nous			
Psyche-Noetic			
Psyche-Passions			
Animal nature			
Vegetative nature			
Inorganic nature			
Apeiron-Depth			

19 Ibid., 282ff.
20 Ibid., 286.

The top horizontal column lists the dimensions of human existence. A *horizontal arrow* running from the person to society and history illustrates the order of foundation: Person, Society, History.

The left, vertical, column depicts the hierarchy of being between Reason and the Apeiron. Two *vertical arrows* run between the Divine Nous and the Apeiron-Depth. The arrow pointing down refers to the order of formation which is from top to bottom; the arrow pointing up refers to the order of foundation which is from bottom to top.

Voegelin notes three principles govern the understanding of this graphic presentation of the various levels and spheres of human participation:

Principle of Completeness:

A philosophy of man must cover the whole field, from top to bottom, right to left, and back again. "No part of the grid can be hypostatized into an autonomous entity, neglecting the context."[21]

Principle of Formation and Foundation:

"The order of formation and foundation must not be inverted or otherwise distorted," for example by transforming one of the orders into a causally determined process working from the top to the bottom or from the bottom to the top. Nor are inversions in the horizontal column permissible which "hypostatize society or history as an absolute, eclipsing personal existence and its meaning."[22]

Principle of Metaxy *Reality*:

Reality is determined by the coordinates of the In-Between. The *metaxy* is the intelligible unit of meaning; Nous and Apeiron are its limiting poles.

Attempts to reduce the luminous–cognitive and existential—experience of participation in being to propositions obscure the reality of the

21 Ibid., 290.
22 Ibid.

In-Between and pave the way for the spiritual derailments that deny the fullness of being.

Finally, the reality of the *metaxy* includes the "genuine eschatological or apocalyptic symbolisms which imaginatively express the experience of a movement within reality toward a Beyond of the *metaxy*, such as the experiences of mortality and immortality."[23]

I take this last sentence concerning the "movement within reality toward a Beyond of the *metaxy*" to be the heart of the matter and therefore the center of philosophizing. To explore this issue, I turn to Part II of this paper and Eric Voegelin's discussion of the act of meditation as a fundamental form of philosophizing.

Section II

In this section I examine the relationship of Voegelin's 1974 explication of Reason to his earlier writings on philosophical meditation. My focus is on the life of Reason and I will forego comments on the problem of the revolt against Reason.[24]

1. The Act of Meditation

What Voegelin referred to in 1974 as the "movement within reality towards the Beyond of the metaxy" was also explored by Voegelin in 1930 in his discussion of the philosophical form of meditation. The discussion took

23 Ibid.

24 We read in 1974 that those engaged in the subversion of Reason are motivated by the loss of faith, hope, and the love of being. The resulting "anxiety" is the wage of this form of life. Voegelin's most comprehensive discussion of this problem is in the essay "In the middle of the note, the citation should read as: "Anxiety and Reason," in *What is History and Other Later Unpublished Writings*, ed. Thomas A. Hollweck and Paul Caringella, *CWEV* Vol. 28, 1990, 52–110. See also Peter J. Opitz's Afterword to the German translation of this essay, "Die Entdeckung der Vernunft. Anmerkungen zu Eric Voegelins 'Anxiety and Reason'" in: Eric Voegelin, "Angst und Vernunft." German translation by Dora Fischer-Barnicol. Edited and with an Afterword by Peter J. Opitz. *Voegeliniana – Occasional Papers* (Munich: 2016), 79–100.

place in the posthumously published *Herrschaftslehre* (*Theory of Governance*),[25] part of Voegelin's study of the theory of the state (*Staatslehre*) in which he pursued the question of the spiritual-intellectual roots of society. Voegelin criticized contemporary forms of *Staatslehre* for neglecting these roots and, instead, for treating the "normative sphere" as a "given" without reflecting on its origin in human experience.[26] To explicate the center of human-being Voegelin turned to "a fundamental form of philosophical thinking that, following the name given to it by Descartes, we will call *meditation*,"[27] and identified one of its origins in the investigations into memory that St. Augustine carries out in Books X and XI of his *Confessions*.

Every meditation has a beginning that gives it its direction. For Augustine the experience of the heart's unrest leads to the search for God. Augustine does not seek a concept of God but "the point in the movement of his soul" at which the soul finds peace. Augustine's meditation is a step-by-step elimination of all that is merely world-immanent: "The mystic's *via negationis*, the rejection of all empirical levels of being, leads at last to the highest level of being, that which all world immanent things are not."[28]

In Book XI, and complementing the mode of meditation explored in Book X which proceeds through the levels of being, Augustine meditates on time and eternity.[29] Both meditative ways lead to the same goal:

> "[T]he meditating person to God and therewith the understanding person to insight into the essence of the human person, who can be characterized by his openness to a transcendent being, by his being a frontier between the world, with its being and becoming, and a super-world [Überwelt]. The person is… the point of intersection between divine eternity and human temporality…."[30]

25 Voegelin,"The Theory of Governance," in *CWEV* Vol. 32, 224–372.

26 Eric Voegelin, *Race and State*, ed. Klaus Vondung, *CWEV* Vol. 2, 1997, 7.

27 Voegelin, "The Theory of Governance," 226.

28 Ibid., 227.

29 Ibid., 231–36.

30 Ibid., 236.

Thus, in 1930, with the exploration of meditation as a fundamental form of philosophy we find important points that Voegelin returned to in "Reason: The Classic Experience."

A. Participation

In 1930 Voegelin followed Augustine's question: what do I love when I love God? Augustine loves the things of the world, not as things of the world, but because they participate in God. Therefore in his discussion of worldly things, he simultaneously sets and negates their desirability, stating finally: "I love not these things when I love my God [*Conf.* X. c. 6]." Yet, because these things participate in God, they are also loved—*in deo*. Voegelin comments: "At the highest point of this negation [Augustine] follows with *et tamen* [and yet]." This reflexive turning back indicates "that, though God is none of this, 'nevertheless' for the soul, He is this as well. ... [A]ll the propositions have been simultaneously asserted and cancelled in order to determine the locus where the fullness of being is to be found [i.e., in God]."[31] In 1974, in a central passage that we have already quoted, Voegelin writes: "Reason is differentiated as a structure in reality from the experiences of faith and trust (*pistis*) in the divinely ordered cosmos, and of the love (*philia, eros*) for the divine source of order; it is differentiated from the *amor Dei* in the Augustinian sense." In both 1930 and 1974 the center of human participation in the mystery of the community of being is "love."

B. Response

Augustine's meditation is the heart's response to God. In the 1974 essay Voegelin writes: The philosopher feels himself "moved" by some unknown force to ask questions, he is "drawn" into the search.[32]

C. Direction

The direction of the meditation is not a path through space and time but a response to love and therefore constituted by love. The meditation's

31 Ibid., 228.
32 "Reason," 269.

movens, *intentio*, and *causa finalis* are three faces of love. The meditative act ascends through the levels of worldly being and the human soul until the human's love of God (*amor Dei*) merges with God's love for His creature (*amor Dei*). So Augustine: "'I have been divided amid times, the order of which I know not; and my thoughts, even the inmost bowels of my soul, are mangled with tumultuous varieties, until I flow together unto Thee, purged and molten in the fire of Thy Love.'"[33] In 1974 Voegelin writes: "The man who asks questions, and the divine ground about which the questions are asked, will merge in the experience of questioning as a divine-human encounter…"[34]

D. *Amor ascendens*

The meditation is a spiritual act. Therefore the "place" where the soul stands before God can only be seen by the one who follows the spiritual movement of the confession, who himself has "enacted the confession to God."[35] Likewise, in 1974 we read: "philosophy in the classic sense is not a body of 'ideas'" about the divine ground "but a man's responsive pursuit of his questioning unrest to the divine source that has aroused it."[36] For this reason the meditation (1930) and the life of Reason (1974) cannot provide information or results to those who do not take the same path.

E. Completeness

"The course of the meditating person in pursuit of his or her goal is not an arbitrary wandering but strictly determined by the structure of being. … The meditation proceeds from the world of the senses and passes through all of its levels upward toward the soul, where it penetrates to the soul's core. From the core of the soul follows the crossing over [Überschritt] to

33 Augustine *Confessions* (XI. C. 29). Quoted in "The Theory of Governance," 234.

34 "Reason," 271.

35 "The Theory of Governance," 227.

36 "Reason," 272.

God."[37] In the Appendix to his 1974 essay Voegelin sketches three principles of "completeness" as the necessary preconditions for adequately exploring the structure of being: The principles of "formation," "foundation," and "*metaxy* reality." The full range of being must be taken into account, from the depth of the Apeiron to the height of Divine Nous. The relationship of foundation, from the base to the apex, and of formation, from the apex to the base, must be observed. Likewise, the foundation of human order, proceeding from the person, to society, and to history must not be reversed. Thus Voegelin's words on the meditation of Augustine in 1930 apply equally to his description of the life of Reason. Only by rigorously adhering to the structure of being can the meditation's *amor ascendens* successfully complete its course: It is this rigorousness "that persuades the meditating person that the course was the correct one and the goal that was found was the one sought."[38]

F. Life and Death

In 1930 we read that the *amor ascendens* is the driving force that leads the soul towards God, the Beyond of reality. As we noted above, in 1974 Voegelin wrote of the "movement within reality toward a Beyond of the *metaxy*," and we called this the "heart of the matter."

Let us look at the "heart of the matter" in more detail. Created being participates in the mystery of being and the Beyond of being. At the level of human-being, with the discovery of Reason, the creature's participation becomes luminous to itself in the *metaxy*: in *philia*, *eros*, *pistis*, *elpis*, and the *amor Dei*. Love is the center of the life of man and of the cosmos because it is the center of God. It is not static, for God's love does not cease with creation, any more than creation, moved by God's love, ceases to develop. And thus, human participation in God's eternal presence can be deepened in individuals, and through individuals, in society, at any point in the life of the spirit:

> "They begin to leave who begin to love.
> Many are leaving unbeknownst,

37 "The Theory of Governance," 228f.

38 Ibid., 228.

For the feet of those leaving are the affections of the heart:
And yet, they are leaving Babylon."[39]

The words "they begin to leave who begin to love"—the *amor ascendens*—describe perfectly the life of the Platonic periagoge and the Christian conversio.[40]

With few exceptions, what we call the *periagoge* or the *conversio* does not refer to a single event in a person's life. For most individuals the symbols refer to a lifetime's effort of trying to overcome the *amor sui* in the response to, and turn toward, the *amor Dei*. But whether it takes place in a dramatically short time or over a lifetime, the soul's ascent toward the Divine Nous means the deepening of the individual's Reason and practice. Borrowing a term from Max Scheler, we may refer to the hierarchically structured and dynamic "world" of acts, goods, and values that a person loves (and which also defines the acts, goods, and values that he rejects) as that person's *ordo amoris*.[41]

A person's *ordo amoris* is never complete, for the "center" of love is self-transcendence in the *amor ascendens*. Therefore:

> "Whichever form the exodus may adopt—that of a real emigration from society or that of a collision within society between

39 Incipit exire qui incipit amare. /Exeunt enim multi latenter,/et exeuntium pedes sunt cordis affectus:/exeunt autem, de Babylonia. Saint Augustine, *Enarrationes in Psalmos*. Quoted in Voegelin, "Eternal Being in Time," in *Anamnesis*, 337.

40 "In the experience of the flowing presence, there occurs a meeting of time with eternity, and of man with God. An experience of this *metaxy*, therefore, can put its accent modally on either the human seeking-and-receiving pole, or on the divine giving-and-commanding pole. When the modal accent is put on the human seeking-and-receiving pole and expressed in a way that the knowledge experienced about the *metaxy* and the order of being becomes dominant, we speak of philosophy. When the modal accent is put on the divine giving-and-commanding pole in such a way that human knowledge of the experience is reduced to a communication of the divine irruption, we speak of revelation." Ibid., 335.

41 Max Scheler, "Ordo Amoris" in *Selected Philosophical Essays*, tr. David R. Lachterman (Evanston: Northwestern University Press, 1973), 98–136.

> representatives of higher- and lower- ranking orders—the dynamism and direction of the process stem from the love for eternal being. The Exodus in the sense of *incipit exire qui incipit amare* is the classical formulation of the substantive principle of a philosophy of history."[42]

A "philosophy of history" reflects the record of the differentiations of the experience of participation in the mystery of the community of being. The reading of this record—both in the literal and metaphorical sense of "reading"—brings me to the second point of this section:

2. The Literary Record of a Meditation as Invitation and Guide to the Reader to Enact His Own Meditation

In a letter to Alfred Schütz in 1943 Voegelin returned to the theme of philosophical meditation and reiterated its characteristics and purpose. The meditation is the gradual overcoming of the content of the world. It proceeds methodically from the corporeal world to the spiritual "in order to reach the point of transcendence in which, put in the Augustinian manner, the soul can turn in an *intentio* toward God." Although the act of meditation is an event in the life of a particular individual, it can be recorded and in its literary form can become the starting point for the reader to begin his own original meditation.[43]

In a broader sense the record of every real attempt to engage the spiritual-intellectual participation of humanity in the mystery of being, in short, all serious religious, philosophical, and literary works, are based either on the author's own meditation, or are derived—at however great a distance—from the meditations of others. In reading such a text, Voegelin writes, one must penetrate to the point "where it is rooted in the [author's] experiences of transcendence." "Only when intellectual history is pursued with its sights set on this methodological goal can it attain its philosophical goal" which is to "understand the historical

42 "Eternal Being in Time," in *Anamnesis*, 337.

43 Eric Voegelin, "Letter to Alfred Schütz Concerning Edmund Husserl," September 17, 1943, 57, in *Anamnesis*, 45–62.

embodiments of spirit as variations on the theme of the experiences of transcendence."[44]

Reading with this intention is a "cathartic exercise"[45] in which the reader confronts his own *ordo amoris* with that of the text and its author. Where the reader finds the text wanting, he draws the categories for his critique from the depth of his own meditation.[46] Where the reader is confronted with a deeper and more comprehensive *ordo amoris*—a greater differentiation in the understanding of the experience of participation—than his own, it is up to him to open himself to being persuaded.[47] *De facto* this is how everyone reads—or fails to read. But then the failure is indeed a failure because one has interrupted the *amor ascendens* and violated the center of life in the *metaxy*.

A final note on Reading: Whether consciously present as one reads, or in the background as a "silent partner," each individual in his confrontation with the reality of human participation in the mystery of being "reads" from the point of transcendence that he has thus far achieved. In the specific case of Eric Voegelin, this point of transcendence was realized in the re-enactment of the literary record of Augustine's meditation which opened his way to understanding Plato's *metaxy*. Thus, in "Reason: The Classic Experience," Voegelin links the Greek philosophers' *philia*, *eros*, *pistis*, and *elpis* to the Christian philosopher's *amor Dei*. And Augustine's meditation is present throughout Voegelin's writings, sometimes, as in the *Theory of Governance*, in the form of quoting longer passages, at other times as short references, and perhaps most subtly, and at the same time prominently, in the words

44 Ibid., 55.
45 Ibid., 61.
46 Voegelin's critique of Husserl in his letter to Schütz, ibid., 45–61, esp. 57ff.
47 As Voegelin remarked to a group in 1967: "Now what does *participation* mean? What it actually means you can experience, of course, only in meditative experience. One would have to go through, reading with care, Plato's *Symposium*, for instance, or the great meditation that ends in the transcendence point, the *anima animi* in Augustine's *Confessions* Book X.": Eric Voegelin, "Conversations with Eric Voegelin at the Thomas More Institute for Adult Education in Montreal, in *The Drama of Humanity and Other Miscellaneous Papers, 1939-1985*, ed. William Petropulos and Gilbert Weiss, *CWEV* Vol. 33, 2004, 243–344. Here, 252.

that preface the five volumes of *Order and History* and which are also a note on reading:

> "In the study of creatures one should not exercise a vain and perishing curiosity, but ascend toward what is immortal and everlasting."[48]

48 "In consideratione creaturarum non est vana et peritura curiositas exercenda; sed gradus ad immortalia et semper manentia faciendus." Augustine, *De Vera Religione*, quoted by Voegelin with his translation in *Israel and Revelation*, 18.

–11–

Voegelin's "Response to Professor Altizer"

Paulette Kidder

In 1975, Prof. Ray L. Hart, then in the sixth of his ten years (1969-1979) as editor of the Journal of the American Academy of Religion, asked Thomas J. J. Altizer to review Voegelin's *The Ecumenic Age*, the fourth volume of *Order and History.* Hart invited Altizer to review Voegelin's book because, as he said, "Voegelin's monumental oeuvre has not received the attention in North America which it richly deserves, especially among scholars of religion(s)."[1] Altizer's own work, in contrast, had received extensive public and scholarly attention, ranging from admiration to hostility. Today counted by critics as being among the outstanding theologians of the twentieth century,[2] Altizer in 1975 was a Professor of Religious Studies at SUNY Stony Brook. He had previously held a position at Emory, which he almost lost after becoming the public face of what was termed the "Death of God" movement.[3] This was a term for a loosely allied group of

1 Eric Voegelin, "Response to Professor Altizer's 'A New History and a New but Ancient God?'" in *Published Essays 1966-1985*, ed. Ellis Sandoz, *CWEV* Vol. 12, 1990, 292. Altizer's review, and Voegelin's response to it, originally appeared in *JAAR* Vol. XLIII (1975). Hereafter cited as Voegelin, "Response to Altizer."

2 John B. Cobb, Jr., "Altizer: The Religious Theologian, Then and Now," in *Resurrecting the Death of God: The Origins, Influence, and Return of Radical Theology*, ed. Daniel J. Peterson and G. Michael Zbaraschuk (Albany: State University of New York Press, 2014), 66: "At some point in the future Thomas Altizer may be recognized as the greatest theologian in the second half of the twentieth century." Hereafter cited as Peterson and Zbaraschuk, *Resurrecting the Death of God.*

3 Daniel J. Peterson, "Introduction: Resurrecting the Death of God," in Peterson and Zbaraschuk, *Resurrecting the Death of God,* 1. Hereafter cited as Peterson, "Introduction."

"radical" theologians that also included William Hamilton, Paul van Buren, and Gabriel Vahanian. In 1965 and 1966, *Time* famously published stories describing the broader movement, including accounts of Altizer's theological views which he had developed in works such as *Mircea Eliade and the Dialectic of the Sacred* (1963), *Radical Theology and the Death of God* (1966), and *The Gospel of Christian Atheism* (1966).[4]

According to *Time*, Altizer saw "the collapse of Christendom and the onset of a secular world without God as necessary preludes to the rediscovery of the sacred."[5] This description captures something of the tensions and paradoxes within the Death of God movement. The thinkers who made up the movement were passionate theologians, not indifferent atheists. They saw Christianity as practiced in the churches as moribund, along with its vision of what God is. God, instead of being encountered as a personal divine presence, was experienced as an absence, within a thoroughly secular American culture. For some thinkers in the movement, the felt absence of God was directly tied to the horrors of the Holocaust.[6]

But in proclaiming the "death of God," the radical theologians of the movement were not advocating for a rejection of the sacred or of the deeper meanings that could be learned from, for example, the life of Jesus. Rather, they were engaged in clearing away the cultural accretions upon a primordial experience of the sacred and promoting a recovery of that experience, no longer characterized as an encounter with "God." In that sense, as Sarah Pinnock writes, "the death of God is also a birth."[7] As Altizer wrote in 1963,

4 *Time*'s second article on the Death of God movement inspired its cover for the April 8, 1966, issue, featuring red letters on a black background ("Is God Dead?"). This cover is considered one of the most iconic of the late 20th century. See https://time.com/isgoddead/, accessed August 10, 2022.

5 "Theology: The God Is Dead Movement," *Time,* October 22, 1965, Vol. 86, 17.

6 For an overview of the movement, see Rosemary Radford Ruether, "The Death of God Revisited: Implications for Today," in Peterson and Zbaraschuk, *Resurrecting the Death of God*, 23–41. Hereafter cited as Reuther, "The Death of God Revisited."

7 Sarah K. Pinnock, "Holocaust, Mysticism, and Liberation after the Death of God: The Significance of Dorothee Soelle," in Peterson and Zbaraschuk, *Resurrecting the Death of God*, 84.

"the moment has arrived to engage in a radical quest for a new mode of religious understanding. The first requirement of such a quest is a forthright confession of the death of the God of Christendom, a full acknowledgement that the era of Christian civilization has come to an end, with the result that all cognitive meaning and all moral values that were once historically associated with the Christian God have collapsed."[8]

Altizer's version of the death of God was steeped in his encounters with visionary thinkers, artists, and interpreters of ancient myths and symbols that included Blake, Jung, Eliade, and Hegel. Rosemary Radford Ruether points out that Altizer's Hegelianism is fundamental to his theology, since "for Altizer there is no God or Son of God who remains in heaven, but rather God creates the world by a total self-alienation into temporal existence...[F]or Altizer the death of God happens with the appearance of the world and temporary existence itself.... Every new moment in temporal existence is a new incarnation of God..."[9] Altizer's Hegelian theology is *kenotic*, so-called because for Altizer, God the Father "empties Himself (Greek, *kenosis*)" into Christ and Christ in turn empties himself into the Holy Spirit.[10] Like Hegel's *Geist*, Altizer's God does not exist separately from the world but in dialectic with it. Those who seek to recover a sense of the sacred in our time must accept the Hegelian insight that the sacred is not to be found in some separate "beyond" or in another world, but that in our time it is to be found through embracing this world in full openness to the sacred meaning embedded in it.[11]

This sketch of Altizer's central themes and concerns is enough to show why Altizer was a logical choice to review *The Ecumenic Age.* Clearly, Altizer

8 Thomas J. J. Altizer, *Mircea Eliade and the Dialectic of the Sacred* (Philadelphia: Westminster Press, 1963), 13.

9 Ruether, "The Death of God Revisited," 26.

10 Peterson, "Introduction," 3.

11 See for example, Altizer, *Mircea Eliade*, 18: "No longer can the Christian believe that his existence here and now is a kind of prologue to his future life in a transcendent Kingdom of God. Nor can he believe that his life in 'this world' derives its meaning and reality from an 'other world' in the Beyond...[This] very collapse...has made possible a new epiphany of Christ: a Christ who has not descended from 'above,' but who is *wholly* and *fully* incarnate in our midst."

and Voegelin potentially had a great deal in common intellectually: a desire to recover engendering experiences of the sacred from underneath the accretions of dogma; a deep appreciation for the sacred dimension of reality that is expressed in myth and symbol; a dedication to very wide-ranging historical scholarship; and a willingness to stake out original, controversial claims with little regard for the safe harbors of either conservatism or liberalism (though Altizer willingly embraced the label of "radicalism"). And indeed, Altizer's review, which was titled, "A New History and a New but Ancient God?" begins with praise for Voegelin: "Certainly one of the major thinkers of our time, and major religious thinkers, is Eric Voegelin."[12] Altizer predicts that Voegelin's *Israel and Revelation* "may someday be perceived as the most important work of Old Testament scholarship ever written in the United States,"[13] written as it was by "one who was at once a Greek scholar of first rank and a philosophical mind equal or superior to any in America today." *Order and History* uniquely showed "the coinherence of noetic understanding and biblical faith as the primary and indispensable ground of Western civilization."[14]

Altizer notes that the long delay between the publication of Volume 3, published in 1959, and Volume 4, published in 1975, was occasioned by a "breakdown of the original project," and that "this breakdown may well signify the end of what we have known as history." Voegelin, he writes, has rejected the "unilinear" timeline that guided the first three volumes, having come to view the symbolism of historiogenesis—a view of history as a unified line of development in one direction—which had informed the earlier volumes, as inadequate. "Historiogenesis," Altizer writes, "is [for Voegelin] an ancient imperial creation, its intention being to sublimate the contingencies of imperial order in time to the timeless serenity of the cosmic order itself."[15] Instead of portraying human development as a linear progression, Voegelin emphasizes certain constants such as "the cosmos of the primary experience, a cosmos that is the whole, *to pan*, of an earth below and a

12 Thomas J. J. Altizer, "A New History and a New But Ancient God? A Review-Essay," *Journal of the American Academy of Religion* XLIII (1975), 757.

13 Ibid., 757.

14 Ibid.

15 Ibid., 758.

heaven above, and a cosmos full of gods."[16] Its ground is "the tension of existence out of non-existence," and the "precarious balance on the edge of emergence from nothing and return to nothing."[17] To describe the loss of this precarious balance during the Ecumenic Age (from the rise of the Persian Empire to the fall of the Roman Empire), Altizer quotes Voegelin at length: "the cosmos dissociates into a dedivinized external world and a world-transcendent God... What cracks is the cosmological style of truth as far as it tends to conceive all reality after the model of In-Between reality; and what dissociates is the cosmos of the primary experience. But neither of these consequences of differentiation affects the core of the primary experience, i.e., the experience of an In-Between reality. On the contrary, it is still with us."[18]

Altizer stresses, then, Voegelin's claim that an existential constant persists throughout historical experience. He wryly comments that "While [the primary experience of an In-Between] may still be with us, it surely is heard or spoken by few. Eric Voegelin is one of those few."[19] If one thinks of Voegelin as one who seeks to combine the study of history with ontology, he is, Altizer suggests, "very lonely."[20] Understood, instead, as a "religious thinker," Voegelin might find himself "not so lonely." Would it be fair, then, to call Voegelin a theologian? According to Altizer, Voegelin rejects theological terms and distinctions in part because he is trying to say something so new. Voegelin's prose style "is clear and obscure at once, and its clarity is indistinguishable from its obscurity."[21] One might take this comment as sarcastic or humorous, but Altizer seems to mean it seriously, his point being that Voegelin's central theme turns out to be, not just history, but the exposure of a central mystery of human existence. Obscure language is to be expected when one is pushing the boundaries of theological thought.

Despite Voegelin's rejection of the label of theologian and the difficulty

16 Ibid., 759.

17 Ibid.

18 Eric Voegelin, *Order and History, Volume IV: The Ecumenic Age,* ed. Michael Franz, *CWEV* Vol. 17, 2000, 127–28. Hereafter cited as Voegelin, *The Ecumenic Age.* Cited in Altizer, "A New History," 759.

19 Altizer, "A New History," 759–60.

20 Ibid., 760.

21 Ibid.

of assimilating his work to extant categories of theology, Altizer finds that "it would be difficult to deny that his primary quest is to unveil the identity of God."[22] Voegelin's God, however, is not "the God of our theological understanding," but rather a process that is "at once cosmic, noetic, and divine."[23] Consciousness is the site of luminosity, an experience of the In-Between, or Metaxy. "The Metaxy, for Voegelin, is the concrete psyche of concrete human beings in their encounters with divine presence."[24] Plato is central to the revelation of this structure as noetic, and Plato's articulation of the Metaxy is "structurally equivalent to the Israelite experience of revelation…The God of Plato and the God of Moses are one God, and this God is both the historical and the ontological ground of our universal humanity..."[25]

Where Christians went wrong during the Ecumenic Age, as Altizer reads Voegelin, was in losing the tension of the In-Between, by first creating a Scripture that became "a doctrinization of the Word," and second by "identifying the transfiguring incarnation with the historical and dogmatic Christ."[26] As Altizer reads Voegelin, "The Incarnate Word is not a man; it is rather the eschatological movement of the Whole, of reality itself."[27] Separating out and hypostatizing the human and divine, we have created an "anthropology" and a "theology" as distinct fields of inquiry that never should have been separated. "The death of God, then, originates in Christianity, and it originates precisely in Christian faith in the transcendent God. So likewise, the modern revolt against God, the modern murder of God, is simply a development of the Christianity against which it is in revolt."[28]

Altizer's reading of Voegelin up to this point has articulated aspects of Voegelin's thought that coincide largely with Altizer's own theology: that the divine is in process and is revealed in human consciousness, especially in key historical theories, myths, and symbols, and that Judeo-Christianity

22 Ibid., 762.
23 Ibid., 760.
24 Ibid.
25 Ibid., 760–61.
26 Ibid., 761.
27 Ibid.
28 Ibid., 762.

has gone astray by reifying into dogma the original experiences of the sacred. In characterizing Voegelin's thought as being about "the death of God," and as being "radical," Altizer portrays Voegelin as a theologian in Altizer's own mold. Yet what Altizer gives with the right hand, he takes away with the left, characterizing Voegelin, along with Paul Ricoeur, as "both radical and reactionary at once and altogether."[29]

In what sense is Voegelin "reactionary," in Altizer's view? The key reason seems to be that Voegelin's attitude toward modernity is largely negative, or more dramatically, that Voegelin undertakes a "violent assault" against modern thought. "Our real time and world are present in these volumes only in a negative form…[and] one will look in vain in these volumes for the positive presence or influence of twentieth-century philosophical thinking, just as he will be aware that the modern revolutions in literature, art, and science are present here only in their all too significant absence."[30] While for Altizer, thinkers such as Nietzsche and many modern artists and writers point the way to a new direction for theology, for Voegelin, the desired new direction is precisely a rediscovery of the underlying meaning of Platonic and Judeo-Christian thought. The "balance" sought by Voegelin "was established for all time in the ancient world."[31]

Altizer's characterization of Voegelin as both radical and reactionary is connected to his critique of Voegelin's comments on Hegel. As mentioned above, Hegel's thought is foundational for Altizer's, and Altizer's summary of Voegelin's "theology" stresses its similarities to Hegel (a theology of the whole unfolding in cosmic process, the tension of the human and divine occurring in historical consciousness, the pivotal importance of the Incarnation). Altizer sees Hegel as the source of much that is fundamental to Voegelin's approach, and yet, surprisingly, "Hegel is the great villain of *The Ecumenic Age*. He looms so large in these pages as to be a virtual Antichrist…"[32] Altizer includes a long quote in which Voegelin characterizes Hegel as engaged in "libidinous revolt" against the structure of reality, taking unto himself "the two natures of God and man…[and considering

29 Ibid., 758.
30 Ibid., 764.
31 Ibid.
32 Ibid., 762.

himself] the new Messiah…While the structure [of reality] remains the same, the revolt results, personally, in the destruction of existential order and, socially, in mass murder."[33] Altizer interprets this passage to mean that "Ideology is self-deification, wherein the subject of consciousness becomes the ground and source of all, and it ultimately issues in the tyranny and mass murder of the twentieth century."[34] Thus for Voegelin, Hegel's brand of "self-deification" opened the door to the mass killings by twentieth-century ideologues and dictators.

Altizer finds Voegelin's critique of Hegel to be wildly exaggerated. To say, for example, as Voegelin does, that Hegel's *Geist* is no more than his ego, is "absurd and grotesque."[35] "May we not with far more justice say that Voegelin's hatred of Hegel is an attempted Oedipal murder of his father?" Like Hegel, Voegelin combines history and ontology, and like Hegel, Voegelin sees that "the transfiguration of reality only realizes a full consciousness of itself when it becomes historically conscious as the Incarnation of God in Man."[36] Like Hegel, Voegelin views Hinduism and Buddhism as undifferentiated forms of thought in comparison with the thought of the foundational thinkers of the West. In all these respects, in Altizer's eyes, Voegelin's rejection of Hegel is unfathomable, given the debt that Voegelin owes to his philosophical progenitor.

If Altizer's two central critiques of Voegelin are that he fails to see anything positive in modernity and that he rejects Hegel even though Voegelin's own thought is profoundly Hegelian, then Altizer might be implying that there are greater resources in modern thought for Voegelin's project than Voegelin himself acknowledges. Altizer does not draw this point out explicitly. Certainly, in Altizer's own work, modern thinkers that Voegelin rejects became a rich source of inspiration. Altizer concludes his review by comparing *The Ecumenic Age* to the earlier volumes of *Order and History*. Altizer finds the earlier analyses of Plato and other Greek and Jewish thinkers to be more powerful than the treatments of later thinkers in the

33 Voegelin, *The Ecumenic* Age, 320–321. Cited in Altizer, "A New History," 762.

34 Ibid., 762.

35 Ibid., 763.

36 Ibid.

fourth volume. And he expresses unease once again over Voegelin's call for a return to "the cosmic world of pre-modernity." Voegelin's rejection of modernity seems to Altizer too high a price to pay in return for a return to "a God who is no longer recognizable as God to us."[37] While Voegelin shares many of the radical views of the Death of God movement, in Altizer's eyes, the two thinkers part ways over whether to look to the ancients or the moderns for a way beyond inherited Christian doctrines to a more genuine contemporary theology.

Voegelin's Response

Voegelin's response to Altizer, published in letter form in the same volume of *JAAR*, thanked Altizer for his "perceptive and brilliant" study of Voegelin's work[38] and for his "sympathetic and generous" review.[39] Voegelin responds to three key issues raised by Altizer: the relationship between Voegelin's language and that of theology, Voegelin's critique of Hegel, and Voegelin's failure to recognize the positive contributions of modern thought.

On the subject of Voegelin's "obscure" language, Voegelin understands Altizer to be saying that to be concerned with "mystery" is incompatible with using standard theological language. "[H]e assumes a conflict between my inquiry into the 'mystery' and the Christianity of the church. He goes even as far as to find implied in my study the belief 'that the primary failure of Christianity is its misidentification, its misreading of Christ.'"[40] Voegelin explains his use of "neutral" language rather than contemporary philosophical and theological terminology as being due to his looking for divine revelation wherever it occurs, whether it be in theology, philosophical reason, poetry, or ancient petroglyphs. Voegelin's terminology is not limited to that of philosophical and theological texts because he sees experiences of the divine expressed in many other genres.

Voegelin "modestly decline[s]" the claim that he is doing something original or even un-Christian when he distinguishes between (religious)

37 Ibid., 764.
38 Voegelin, "Response to Altizer," 292.
39 Ibid., 303.
40 Ibid., 293.

experience and doctrine: "There were always Christian thinkers who recognized the difference between experiences of divine reality and the transformation of the insights engendered by the experience into doctrinal propositions."[41] The Church Fathers, Origen, Augustine, Anselm, and others all discussed this distinction: "It is definitely an intra-Christian tension."[42] The term "divine reality," which Voegelin uses, is not original to Voegelin, he claims, but is a translation of *theotes*, a neologism when it appeared in *Colossians*. Voegelin sees himself as following Anselm's notion of faith seeking understanding, and not only Christian faith. Voegelin cites Aquinas as saying that Christ is the head of the mystical body that embraces all humankind throughout history. "In practice this means that one has to recognize, and make intelligible, the presence of Christ in a Babylonian hymn, or a Taoist speculation, or a Platonic dialogue, just as much as in a Gospel."[43]

For Voegelin, then, to speak of Christianity is to speak of a complex and nuanced tradition, whose foundational thinkers understood well the difference between experience and dogma and who would not have been surprised at Voegelin's efforts to discern the sacred in a wide range of traditions and literary forms. In these senses, Voegelin does not see his work as being in tension with the Christian tradition. But he agrees with Altizer that later Christian leaders and thinkers have "allowed the dogma

41 Ibid., 293–94.

42 Ibid., 294.

43 Ibid. This passage by Voegelin may appear at first to be a defense of the claim that all religious and literary traditions are striving toward an expression or acknowledgement of Christianity as the one true faith. Voegelin is making a different point here: not that all traditions express reality insofar as they agree with Christianity but that Christianity, properly understood, is an expression of the universal human relationship to the divine. The context is that Voegelin is explaining why he does not restrict his language to accepted (presumably Christian) theological terminology. The passage, taken in context, makes sense as an expression of what Glenn Hughes calls "mystical ecumenism" rather than "Christian triumphalism." For a full discussion of this argument, see Glenn Hughes, "The Mystery of Divine Presence and 'Christianity,'" paper presented at the American Political Science Association Annual Meeting, Boston, 2002. Accessible at: https://sites01.lsu.edu/faculty/voegelin/wp-content/uploads/sites/80/2015/09/Hughes1.pdf.

to separate in the public consciousness of Western civilization from the experience of 'the mystery' on which its truth depends."[44] Dogma is formulated for good reason (to preserve important insights), but a "nominalist and fideist conception of Christianity" that began in the late Middle Ages gave rise to the "cultural disaster" that now sees doctrines as mere opinions. Returning to a genuine appreciation for mystery will require "as many centuries of effort as have gone into the destruction of intellectual and spiritual culture."[45]

Regarding the second issue that Voegelin chooses to respond to, his view of Hegel, Voegelin quotes the more colorful remarks of Altizer on this subject, compliments Altizer's "sensitivity for the central problems of my study," and then turns to "a few emendations."[46] Voegelin writes that he has not "attacked" Hegel, but rather simply submitted his work to analysis as he has done with other thinkers. Voegelin suggests that the difference in the resulting analysis is due to a "difference of spiritual stature" between Hegel and the others. He compares Altizer's "outburst" to the response of Marxists who had accused Voegelin of falsifying Marx's texts when he quoted them verbatim.[47]

Voegelin recounts the story of his relation to Hegel, whom he started out not being able to understand. He admired Hegel for his command of historical scholarship and his intellect but could not follow Hegel's philosophical reasoning. It was Voegelin's introduction to Gnosticism and the discovery that Hegel was seen by his contemporaries as a gnostic that provided a breakthrough.[48] Understanding Hegel's relationship to Neoplatonism provided another key, for it illuminated Hegel's triadic dialectic and his use of the encyclopedic literary form. Lastly, Hegel's comment that the *Phenomenology* was a work of "magic" was illuminating to Voegelin. Through making this series of scholarly connections, Voegelin came to see Hegel as part of a long tradition of hermeticism. He now connects Hegel's thought to Marsilio Ficino's comment that "the Divine

44 Ibid., 295.
45 Ibid.
46 Ibid.
47 Ibid., 295–96.
48 Ibid., 296.

Mind 'may glow into our mind and we may contemplate the order of all things as they exist in God.'"[49] Eliade's work on alchemy provided a further clue. Today, "alchemist magic is primarily to be found among the ideologists who infest the social sciences with their efforts to transform man, society, and history."[50] This broader historical perspective on Hegel has an "obvious implication," that the problems of modernity have their roots in older traditions that rely on esoteric knowledge and magical operations to control and change reality.

Hegel went wrong in his project, Voegelin writes, precisely when he confused the relationship of Being and Thought, a misconstruction "which he needs for his misconstruction of 'Christianity,' which he needs for his misconstruction of history, which he needs if he wants to place himself at the climax of history as the fully revealed and revealing Logos who completes the revelation that was left incomplete by the Logos who was Christ."[51] Voegelin agrees with Hegel's project of locating the divine in the human mind, to the extent that it is best to return to an experience of divine reality in the "heart" of human beings, as opposed to believing in a God who is reified in doctrines rather than known through experience. Hegel, he writes, was attempting, at his best, to reinstate the Metaxy in our understanding of the divine. However, Hegel faltered when he did away with the limitations upon consciousness, turning mystery into "mastery of real knowledge concerning the Whole that comprehends both God and man. Philosophy, the loving search of the divine *sophon*, has come to its end in the absolute knowledge of Hegel's system."[52] In affirming the existence of absolute knowledge and doing away with the limitations on human understanding of the divine, Hegel plays "magical con games."[53] Characterizing Hegel in these terms is not, Voegelin writes, attacking Hegel, but rather providing ways to understand "the contemporary disorder."[54]

The last issue that Voegelin takes up is the question of whether he has neglected twentieth-century contributions to the problems he is studying.

49 Ibid., 297.
50 Ibid., 298.
51 Ibid., 299.
52 Ibid., 300.
53 Ibid., 302.
54 Ibid.

Voegelin points out that he has made extensive use of the "magnificent" work of contemporary historians. It is the historians who have exposed the "ideological systems of the eighteenth and nineteenth centuries…as pitifully inadequate and obsolete interpretations of reality…"[55] The advances made by historians have not yet undermined the ideologies that dominate the social sciences, but Voegelin predicts that they will do so eventually. These advances include the exploration of Gnosticism and similar movements, scholarship that illuminates early Judeo-Christian life, and new knowledge concerning prehistoric peoples as well as early societies of India, China, Africa, and the Americas.[56]

Voegelin's response to Altizer follows the tone of Altizer's review—respectful and even complimentary while at the same expressing fundamental criticisms, and sometimes employing strong rhetoric as a tactic (although in this instance, Voegelin's cutting rhetoric is milder or at least more veiled than Altizer's). Counterbalancing the compliments he pays his reviewer, Voegelin implies that in his defense of Hegel, Altizer is like the Marxist ideologues who deny the accuracy of direct quotes from Marx that cast their master in a bad light. In calling Hegel a con artist and a magician, he implies that Altizer has been gulled by Hegel's tricks. He implies that Altizer has failed to appreciate the nuance and complexity of the foundational Christian texts that Altizer claims have been superseded by cutting-edge theologians.

Perhaps surprisingly, Voegelin does not directly dispute two of Altizer's central themes: that Voegelin's thought is consonant with that of the "death of God" movement, and that Hegel is the unacknowledged "father" of

55 Ibid.

56 In response to the claim that he did not make use of modern authors, Voegelin could here have mentioned his studies of modern literature, which certainly informed his thinking in general but perhaps not the argument of *The Ecumenic Age.* Charles Embry notes that Voegelin was quite familiar with the works of Shakespeare, Cervantes, Stefan George, Mallarmé, Valéry, T. S. Eliot, James, Proust, Mann, and others. Voegelin drew from the novelists Robert Musil and Heimito von Doderer the symbol of a "second reality," which became important to his critique of modernity. Charles Embry, "Introduction," *Voegelinian Readings of Modern Literature* (Columbia and London: University of Missouri Press, 2011), 2.

much that is foundational to Voegelin's own thought. Let us consider each of these themes.

Does Voegelin believe that "God is dead" in the sense that Altizer means it? I have outlined above several ways that Voegelin and Altizer share a similar approach to theological questions. Voegelin agrees with Altizer that Christian leaders have allowed dogma to take the place of the experience of the divine within the human heart, and in that sense, it seems fair to call Voegelin an ally of the "death of God" movement. But Voegelin would not use the language that "God is dead" without numerous qualifiers. If by "God," one means an all-powerful existing entity, Voegelin might agree that God is dead, or rather he might say that to imagine God as an entity is to misperceive what God is. But this has been known within Judeo-Christianity for millennia, though it is regularly forgotten. The discoverers of the pneumatic differentiation that occurred in Israel "called Israel to the belief in the One who is neither a supremely powerful specimen of the type of beings called 'gods,' nor anything at all contained in the cosmos of beings."[57] As Eugene Webb points out, Aquinas also asked whether God was an entity and answered, "no."[58] So if God is dead in the sense that we may no longer imagine God as a powerful being in heaven, Voegelin could say that God in this sense has been dying throughout Judeo-Christian history.

However, if by "God," one means the pull of transcendence, then God is not dead at all. "However we may conceive of the divine existence, we must live *for* or *toward* the divine principle—or, in Voegelin's terms, the divine pole of our experience of existential tension—if we are to live in accord with the inherent structure and dynamism of our existence as conscious persons."[59] The fact that "God" can be understood in this latter way, and that Voegelin sees this understanding of God woven throughout history, accounts for his apparent indifference to the death of God movement.

57 Eugene Webb, "Eric Voegelin at the End of an Era: Differentiations of Consciousness and the Search for the Universal," in *International and Interdisciplinary Perspectives on Eric Voegelin*, ed. Stephen A. McKnight and Geoffrey L. Price (Columbia and London: University of Missouri Press, 1997), 172.

58 Ibid., 173.

59 Ibid., 176.

Deeply understood, the Judeo-Christian tradition already knows that the hypostatized God is dead, but that God as the divine pull in human experience is eternally "alive."

This line of thought also accounts for why Voegelin does not deny that Hegel is his intellectual "father," even though he declines to back down from his objections to Hegel's hermeticism, alchemy, and gnosticism. Hegel is indeed an important thinker who makes a fundamental contribution. As Voegelin points out in the reply to Altizer, Hegel by locating the divine within human experience was attempting to restore the Metaxy to a central place in philosophical and theological thought. In this, Hegel restored a conception of God that genuinely accounted for the human experience of the pull of the divine—rightly undermining the idea that God was a separate spiritual being in an imagined far-away place. One may respect Hegel for this while still objecting to his taking the additional step of claiming absolute knowledge of, and a kind of identity with, the divine.

Voegelin habitually criticizes Hegel far more often, and more memorably, than he praises him, and the reply to Altizer is no exception. Perhaps Voegelin expresses his disagreement with Hegel so vehemently because it is easy to mistake the difference between his thought and that of Hegel; the difference can be missed easily by those who are not attuned to it. Voegelin implies that Altizer has not grasped the difference, and if Voegelin is correct about this, then Altizer, in adopting Hegelian methods, runs the risk of losing, as Hegel and other moderns did, the sense of utter reverence and awe toward the divine that Voegelin saw in ancient thinkers. [60]

It is not my task here to judge whether Voegelin was right in his implied criticisms of Altizer—certainly they could be taken as caveats or guideposts rather than outright criticisms. Altizer himself seems to have been in no hurry to reject Voegelin's caveats, expressing finally not a dismissal of

60 In adopting Hegelian methods, Altizer might participate, in Voegelin's eyes, in the "murder" of God rather than simply in the recognition of God's "death." For a discussion of Voegelin's account of modernity as the "murder" of God, see Michael Franz, "Brothers under the Skin: Voegelin on the Common Experiential Wellsprings of Spiritual Order and Disorder," in *The Politics of the Soul: Eric Voegelin on Religious Experience*, ed. Glenn Hughes (Lanham: Rowman and Littlefield Publishers, Inc., 1999), 149–50.

Voegelin's "reactionary" views but a troubled sense of questioning that Voegelin inspired in him. As Altizer concludes, "Only a thinker of first rank could force us to ask such questions."[61]

61 Altizer, "A New History," 764. It is interesting to note that Altizer wrote another essay on Voegelin in 1993. See Thomas J. J. Altizer, "The Theological Conflict Between Strauss and Voegelin," in *Faith and Political Philosophy: The Correspondence between Leo Strauss and Eric Voegelin, 1934-1964*, ed. and trans. Peter Emberley and Barry Cooper (University Park: The Pennsylvania State University Press, 1993), 267–77. The article takes up many of the same themes as Altizer's review of *The Ecumenic Age*. Here, Altizer memorably refers to Voegelin as a "demonologist," who "surpasses his historical predecessors by finding demons everywhere in our world." (272) As he did in 1975, Altizer characterizes Voegelin as an isolated thinker, delving once more into Voegelin's complicated relationship to Hegel, and exploring Voegelin's Christology as expressed in *In Search of Order* (1987). In a comparison between Voegelin and Strauss, Altizer asks, "[Is] it possible that the far lonelier path of Voegelin is a consequence of a deeper turn of mind?" and concludes, "Only time will tell." (277)

–12–

Voegelin's "Remembrance of Things Past"

Paul Kidder

The essays collected in Eric Voegelin's book, *Anamnesis*, published in German in 1966, are drawn from periods ranging from the 1930s through 1960s, and thus form a "recollection" of the historical studies and theoretical insights whereby he deepened and transformed his convictions regarding the forces of order in human governance and history. Because Voegelin believed some of his key insights to have occurred in the context of his longstanding dialogue with the social philosopher, Alfred Schütz, Part One of the book's German edition reproduced letters to Schütz and reflective essays on the issues at stake in that dialogue. Preparing an English translation of *Anamnesis* in the late 1970's, Gerhart Niemeyer, convinced that what English-speaking readers wanted was a straightforward statement of Voegelin's theory of consciousness, sought to cut specialized historical studies from the book, as well as material in Part One that seemed overly focused on debates particular to the German scene.[1] From that section Niemeyer succeeded in eliminating, most significantly, a long letter to Schütz in which Voegelin critiqued Edmund Husserl's essay, *The Crisis of European Sciences and Transcendental Phenomenology*.[2] To fill the resulting gap at the beginning of the book, in 1977 Voegelin provided

1 Gerhart Niemeyer, "Editor's Preface," in Eric Voegelin, *Anamnesis*, trans. and ed. Gerhart Niemeyer (Notre Dame, IN: University of Notre Dame Press, 1978), xxi-xxii.

2 Edmund Husserl, *The Crisis of European Sciences and Transcendental Phenomenology*, trans. David Carr (Evanston, IL: Northwestern University Press, 1970). Hereafter cited as Husserl, *Crisis*.

Niemeyer with a new first chapter—"Remembrance of Things Past"—a brief autobiographical statement that describes the course of the author's intellectual development and explains some of the issues in the material excised from the English-language edition of the book. When David Walsh restored the original form of *Anamnesis* for the *Collected Works* edition in English, "Remembrance of Things Past" was moved to Volume 12 as a stand-alone essay.[3]

Voegelin's titling of the essay with the Shakespearian phrase that had been used for the first English translation of Marcel Proust's series of novels, *À la recherche du temps perdu*, appropriately reflects the expanse of Voegelin's recollections across many decades, yet Voegelin's essay contrasts starkly with Proust's work in its exceptional brevity and economy of expression. It is this compression in Voegelin's telling of his tale, I would like to suggest, that gives "Remembrance" a continuing value. While in an obvious sense the essay is superseded by the restored materials in *Anamnesis* and the much more complete *Autobiographical Reflections* that were prepared through the efforts of Ellis Sandoz,[4] the limited scope of this short essay forces Voegelin to select the most decisive elements among the vast range of experiences and ideas from which he could draw, and because he chooses to concentrate on early influences, we are given a sense of those authors and interlocutors who decisively shaped the interpretive horizon within which his many subsequent studies were conducted.

It is through this lens, then—viewing the author as making strategic priority decisions in fashioning a narrative of his formation—that I want to frame my account of the essay's central themes. Voegelin's strategy differs somewhat in the three sections into which the essay is divided, each of which is oriented to a particular temporal perspective. The first section evokes the

3 *Anamnesis: On the Theory of History and Politics* (original German edition 1966), ed. David Walsh, *CWEV* Vol. 6, 2002. Hereafter cited as Voegelin, *Anamnesis*. Eric Voegelin, "Remembrance of Things Past," (1977) in *Published Essays 1966-1985*, ed. Ellis Sandoz, *CWEV* Vol. 12, 1990, 304–14. Hereafter all references to this essay will be to this version, cited as Voegelin, "Remembrance."

4 Eric Voegelin, *Autobiographical Reflections* (1973), *Revised Edition*, ed. Ellis Sandoz, *CWEV* Vol. 34. Hereafter cited as Voegelin, *Autobiographical Reflections*.

perspective of 1943, at which point he could look back on his training in the 1920s, his early studies in America, his flight from the Nazi regime, and his settling in Baton Rouge. Voegelin here assesses the influences and motivations through which, by that time, he had moved away from the more mainstream European philosophical orientation of his fellow refugee, Schütz. A second section describes the interpretive perspective that his orientation gave him regarding both academic and political developments from the 1950s into the 1970s—a perspective that is, in good measure, a polemical one. The third section returns to the specific debate with Schütz regarding Husserl, Voegelin recapitulating his critique in the letter of 1943, but from the vantage point, now, of 1977, when he could look back on the whole of the correspondence that ended with Schütz's death in 1959.

My commentary will consider these sections individually, taking the liberty of providing each with a thematic title.

Section One: Sources and Horizons

In describing the intellectual avenues by which he developed his theoretical orientation up to 1943, Voegelin distinguishes thinkers and movements that he came to oppose and those he embraced, providing a list that he has whittled down to a handful of decisive figures on either side of the equation.

It seems to be an early intuition of Voegelin's that political science requires the broadest possible approach to the study of human society. But because many of the methodological practices in the German-speaking milieu of the early twentieth century aimed at a rigorously "scientific" discipline on the model of the natural sciences, their orientations made little use of pre-modern or non-Western thought and their subject matter tended to be reduced to objects and forces that were conducive to objectivistic empirical investigation and rational control. So, for example, Marburg Neo-Kantianism, following the empirically restricted transcendentalism of Kant's first critique, opposed the interpretation of humanity via philosophical anthropology or traditional self-interpretation, seeking, instead, to derive through transcendental reasoning the universal categories by which human life could be rationally understood and organized. But as this scientistic form of Kantianism had difficulty rationally legitimizing the subjective world of moral convictions, the southwest German school of Neo-Kantian value theory undertook to complement the approach by positing human values as objects that could be examined to determine their cross-cultural validity. Viennese logical positivism (which eventually migrated to England through the influence of Wittgenstein) restricted the scope of human sciences further by pursuing the hypothesis that the structures of logic and/or language severely limit what one can legitimately postulate about the structure of the world and society.[5]

These philosophical movements were well established in Austrian and German universities throughout the 1920s as Voegelin was making his way academically. While none of them could be simply avoided, some he was made to imbibe deeply. Among the figures included on Voegelin's list is Max Weber, whose meticulous approach to the study of patterns of human social functioning is echoed every time Voegelin voices the demand that political science be empirical, yet whose fact-value distinction seemed to Voegelin to stitch together Marburg Neo-Kantianism and southwestern German value theory without addressing the narrowness of either.[6] Hans Kelsen's legal positivism Voegelin needed to master thoroughly, as Kelsen oversaw his (as well as Schütz's) doctoral thesis, and while one can observe Voegelin engaging Kelsen at later points in his career, the two were generally critical of one another. Voegelin could never join forces with a methodological approach that would attach law to politics purely by means of the logical relations among legal structures.[7] To remove from the discussion the

5 Voegelin, "Remembrance," 304. Sebastian Luft and Fabien Capellières, "Neo-Kantianism in Germany and France," in *The History of Continental Philosophy*, Vol. 3, ed. Alan D. Schrift (Chicago: University of Chicago Press, 2010), 47–85.

6 Voegelin, *Autobiographical Reflections*, 39–41. Eric Voegelin, *The New Science of Politics* (1952), in *Modernity without Restraint: The Political Religions; The New Science of Politics; and Science, Politics and Gnosticism*, ed. Manfred Henningsen, *CWEV* Vol. 5, 2000, 102–05. Hereafter this volume will be cited as Voegelin, *Modernity without Restraint.*

7 See Eric Voegelin, "The Pure Theory of Law and of State" (1924), in *Published Essays 1922-1928*, trans. M. J. Hanak, ed. Thomas W. Heilke and John von Heyking, *CWEV* Vol. 7, 49–99. See also Barry Cooper, *Beginning the Quest: Law and Politics in the Early Work of Eric Voegelin* (Columbia: MO: University of Missouri Press, 2009), 75ff.

founding human purposes of political community Voegelin considered far too abstract to capture the most important issues at stake.[8]

Voegelin had studied Edmund Husserl's phenomenology extensively as well, granting, in both his early studies and his dialogue with Schütz, that Husserl had gone further than other theorists who took the epistemological approach to the human sciences, his phenomenology recovering dimensions of human subjectivity that had been banished from the human sciences by the positivists.[9] And yet, because Voegelin's objections to the sciences of his day ran deeply into the very methodological questions that ground the epistemological approach, Voegelin, in "Remembrance," must place Husserl on the side of those in the restrictive horizon rather than an expansive one.

There were, then ("of course," he says), Marx and Freud.[10] He does not elaborate on them here, but we are familiar from many other works with how Voegelin interprets them as restrictive. The systems of each are outgrowths of positivist immanentism and millennialism, Marx construing society as a product of material production whose ultimate meaning is revealed through violent revolution, and Freud finding the full realization of humanity in the act of taking the divine, conceived as a psychological projection, back into the human.[11]

As we turn to the account of authors who helped expand Voegelin's intellectual horizon, we see that his short list contains fifteen names, many of which belong to the fields of language and literature, and nearly half of which are tied, in one way or another, to the Stefan George Circle of the early twentieth century. Voegelin locates George's importance in his "restoration of the German language" after a degradation that occurred, he

8 Voegelin, *Autobiographical Reflections*, 48–51.

9 Voegelin, *Anamnesis*, 45–46, 61.

10 Voegelin, "Remembrance," 304.

11 See, for example, Eric Voegelin, *Science, Politics, and Gnosticism* (1959), in Voegelin, *Modernity without Restraint*, 261–75. Voegelin, *Autobiographical Reflections*, 76–77. Eric Voegelin, "The Meditative Origin of the Philosophical Knowledge of Order," in *The Drama of Humanity and Other Miscellaneous Papers 1939-1985,* ed. William Petropulos and Gilbert Weiss, *CWEV* Vol. 33, 394. Hereafter this volume will be cited as Voegelin, *The Drama of Humanity*.

tells us in *Autobiographical Reflections*, "during the imperial period of Germany after 1870."[12] But this is something of an understatement, for the significance of the George Circle (for both German culture and for Voegelin personally) is broad and deep. George did indeed seek a revitalized German poetic communication that was meant to form the spiritual core of his selective community of artists and scholars, and he was, at certain points, an advocate for Germanic locutions over dully latinized ones,[13] but his approach to language was also, from the beginning, cosmopolitan. He identified with the best of linguistic artistry in many languages, and especially English, Italian, and French, reproducing in his own circle what he had experienced in Paris among devotees of the symbolist, Stéphane Mallarmé, and inculcating among his disciples a strong reverence for Dante and Shakespeare.[14] This same multi-lingual literary appetite is reflected in Voegelin's inclusion, on his own list of positive influences, of Marcel Proust, Paul Valéry, and James Joyce.[15]

The George Circle's members formed a passionate and rigorous society of learning outside of the university system and, to a good extent, in competition with it, as the university was to them, it seems, more a museum of culture than its creative core. The circle's fraternal members were united by ideals of "governance and service," but equally by a personal loyalty to a demanding charismatic poet-leader, fealty to whom was an absolute requirement. Voegelin gave an account of these ideals in an unpublished manuscript of the early 1930's, "The Theory of Governance," in which he explicates Friedrich Wolters' presentation of the circle's vision in his 1923 book, *Herrschaft und Dienst*.[16] To gauge the impact of George-influenced political ideas on Voegelin one need merely notice how classically Voegelinian are the terms in which he describes Wolters' account:

12 Voegelin, "Remembrance," 306. Voegelin, *Autobiographical Reflections*, 45. Cf. "Autobiographical Statement at Age Eighty-Two" (1984), in Voegelin, *The Drama of Humanity*, 434.

13 Robert E. Norton, *Secret Germany: Stefan George and His Circle* (Ithaca, NY: Cornell University Press, 2002), Ch. 12. Hereafter cited as Norton, *Secret Germany*.

14 Norton, *Secret Germany*, Ch. 4.

15 Voegelin, "Remembrance," 306.

16 Friedrich Wolters, *Herrschaft und Dienst* (Berlin: Georg Bondi, 1923).

> The fundamental state of the human being, from which the powers of governance emanate, is the human being's openness to divinity.... The analysis faithfully follows the structure of the dialectical theme of the constitution of existence that begins with the self-given-ness [*die Selbstgebung*] of the human being as a being open to transcendence and then, in objectifying terminology, differentiates the sphere of transcendent divinity from that of immanent existence.[17]

Literary studies by authors in the George Circle focused on the power of symbols, both their richness in classical myth and their appropriation in German romanticism and other literatures. The first of the two critics that Voegelin explicitly names, Friedrich Gundolf, made a spirited defense of the function of symbol in illuminating the inter-involvement of self and world, as opposed to what he called allegory (which he viewed as a more detached manipulation of narrative objects) and lyric (the expression of undifferentiated immediacy).[18] Max Kommerell's early work advocated the idea of the "poet as leader," taking inspiration from German "classic" literature (particularly Goethe) as well as Nietzsche's replacement of Christian asceticism with an organic will to power spiritualized through art. Kommerell was a master of close readings, interpreting works always within an understanding of the cultural significance of literature as a whole.[19] His

17 Eric Voegelin, "The Theory of Governance" (c. 1930-32), in *The Theory of Governance and Other Miscellaneous Papers, 1921-1938,* ed. William Petropulos and Gilbert Weiss, *CWEV* Vol. 32, 224–372, at 340. Hereafter cited as Voegelin, "Theory of Governance."

18 René Wellek, "The Literary Criticism of Friedrich Gundolf," *Contemporary Literature,* Vol. 9 (Summer 1968) 394–405, at 401.

19 René Wellek, "Max Kommerell as Critic of Literature," in Beda Allemann and Erwin Koppen, eds., *Teilnahme und Spiegelung: Festschrift für Horst Rüdiger* (Berlin: Walter de Gruyter, 1975), 485–98. Max Kommerell, *Der Dichter als Führer in der Deutschen Klassik: Klopstock, Herder, Goethe, Schiller, Jean-Paul, Hölderlin* (Berlin: Georg Bondi, 1928). See also Thomas Hollweck, "Der Dichter als Führer? Dichtung und Repräsentanz in Voegelins frühren Arbeiten," Eric-Voegelin Archiv, Ludwig-Maximilians-Universität, Occasional Papers, 2009. On Gundolf and Kommerell, see also Voegelin, *Autobiographical Reflections,* 44–45.

influence can be felt in Voegelin's claim that in literary interpretation one must "exhaust" one's source, and that literature's creative expression participates crucially in the articulation of meaningful symbolizations of reality.[20]

Equally vital to members of the George Circle was the interpretation of ancient texts—the literary classics of drama and verse, but equally the dialogues of Plato, with members of the circle producing many studies and translations of them.[21] New worlds of Platonic scholarship had been opened up by Friedrich Schleiermacher's elevation of the dramatic dimension in Plato's works and by Ulrich von Wilamowitz-Moellendorff's unification, in classical studies, of philology, history, and archeology.[22] But scholars in the George Circle wanted to deepen the political interpretation of Plato, seeing in Socrates' establishment of an informal community of wisdom-seekers, and then Plato's formal version of the same in the Academy, paradigms for their own community's dedication to the transformation of society through the power of their creative vision and personal fraternity (including the kind of intense but spiritualized homophilia celebrated in the *Symposium*).[23] Long on enthusiasm and short on philological minutiae, the George Circle

20 On Voegelin's principles of literary criticism, see Charles R. Embry, *The Philosopher and the Storyteller: Eric Voegelin and Twentieth-Century Literature* (Columbia, MO: University of Missouri Press, 2008), 16–21; and Eugene Webb, "Eric Voegelin and Literary Theory," in *Politics, Order and History: Essays on the Work of Eric Voegelin*, ed. Glenn Hughes, Stephen A. McKnight, And Geoffrey L. Price, (Sheffield: Sheffield Academic Press, 2001), 502–15. Hereafter this volume will be cited as Hughes, et. al., *Politics, Order and History*.

21 Stefan Rebenich, "'May a Ray from Hellas Shine upon Us': Plato in the George-Circle," in *Brill's Companion to the Classics, Fascist Italy and Nazi Germany*, ed. Helen Roche and Kyriakos N. Demetriou (Leiden: Brill, 2017), 178–204. Hereafter cited as Rebenich, "Plato in the George-Circle."

22 Julia A. Lamm, "Schleiermacher as Plato Scholar," *The Journal of Religion*, Vol. 80 (April 2000) 206–39. Ulrich von Wilamowitz-Moellendorff, *Platon*, 2 Vols. (Berlin: Weidmannsche Buchhandlung, 1920). E.N. Tigerstedt, *Interpreting Plato* (Uppsala: Almqvist & Wiksell, 1977), 40–44, 50–51.

23 William Petropulos, "Stefan George und Eric Voegelin," Eric-Voegelin Archiv, Ludwig-Maximilians-Universität, Occasional Papers, 2005, 24–29. Hereafter cited as Petropulos, "George und Voegelin." Kurt Hildebrandt, "Einleitung," in *Platons Gastmahl*, trans. and ed. Kurt Hildebrandt (Leipzig: Felix Meiner, 1912), 1–42. Rebenich, "Plato in the George-Circle," 188–89.

studies of Plato seek to bring him and his mentor, Socrates, to life, seeing in their cultural vision a heroism parallel to (though also in vigorous competition with) the kind that is found in Nietzsche's figure of Zarathustra.[24]

Two of the Plato interpreters that Voegelin names, Edgar Salin and Kurt Hildebrandt, are largely unrecognized in the annals of classical scholarship (Salin being best known as an economist and Hildebrandt trained in medicine), but Voegelin cites them over Wilamowitz or his famous academic successor in Berlin, Werner Jaeger, a fact that has to do, no doubt, with the intensity with which the George disciples, even more than the academics mandarins, believed in Plato as a potentially transformative political voice.[25] Salin's Plato book interprets the *Republic* and *Laws* as initiating a long tradition of utopian political visions.[26] Hildebrandt saw in Platonic community the kind of elite that emerges out of its own merits, establishing its power, as Nietzsche envisioned, on its internal spiritual authority. This Platonic-Nietzschean ideal, in the case of Hildebrandt, eventually warped into Nazi ideology, with Hitler usurping, in Hildebrandt's devotions, both Plato and George, as the latter departed to spend his last days in Switzerland, where Salin, the Jew, also fled, assuming an appointment at the University of Basel.[27]

The third Platonist mentioned by Voegelin, Paul Friedländer, presents a more complicated case and probably the most important, for he sought a synthesis of all the scholarly forces at work in his time. A protégé of Wilamowitz, he was equally inspired by the tremendous power and relevance of Plato that came through in the George Circle interpretations. Friedländer's readings show great attention to the literary and mythological dimensions of the *Dialogues*, while yet making a concerted effort to follow the lines of philosophical reasoning.[28] Voegelin emulated Friedländer's ability

24 The competition is the major theme in Kurt Hildebrandt's *Nietzsches Wettkampf mit Sokrates und Plato* (Dresden: Sibyllen-Verlag, 1922).

25 On the preference for the George Circle scholars over Wilamowitz and Jaeger, see Petropulos, "George und Voegelin," 28. .

26 Edgar Salin, *Platon und die griechische Utopie* (Munich and Leipzig: Verlag Duncker & Humbolt, 1921).

27 Mauro Bonazzi, "Towards Nazism: On the Invention of Plato's Political Philosophy," *Comparative and Continental Philosophy* Vol. 12 (2020), 182–96.

28 Paul Friedländer, *Plato*, Vol. 1: *An Introduction*, trans. Hans Myerhoff (New York: Pantheon Books, 1958). Rebenich, "Plato in the George-Circle 194–96.

to draw on the full range of scholarly approaches available in Platonic studies, appropriating a passion for the contemporary applicability of Plato's thinking while digging deeply into its emergence out of the intellectual and social forces of ancient Athens.

From here Voegelin goes on to mention figures associated with his study of Medieval thought. It was remarkable to him, and rather absurd, that German philosophers (and most notably Hegel) had developed a narrative of continuity between the ancient Greeks and modern Germans while leaping over the Middle Ages with seven-league boots, and this despite the fact that German scholars, having been shaped by centuries-old Christian traditions, brought implicit Christian assumptions to their interpretations of the ancients. Voegelin had the advantage of coming to Medieval studies at a time when Catholic scholars were reviving the interpretation of primary sources in their intellectual tradition. The figures that Voegelin notes, Antonin-Gilbert Sertillanges and Étienne Gilson,[29] were part of a generation in France that brought the kind of rigor and insight to the study of Augustine and Aquinas that the German-language scholars had made mandatory in the study of the ancients. Voegelin's many treatments of Christianity interpret their subject from more perspectives that of the systematic Thomism of these authors, but it is clear that the philosophical sophistication of their work set a standard for his treatment of perennial dilemmas in the intersection of faith and philosophy.

Next on Voegelin's list is a reference to the importance of the existentialism of Karl Jaspers, and through Jaspers, Søren Kierkegaard. Voegelin's connection to Jaspers' conception of an "axial" spiritual turning point in history is frequently noted,[30] but Jaspers' thought is recognizable, I would suggest, whenever Voegelin uses the terms "human existence" or "existential," which he never explicitly intends in a Sartrean or Heideggerian sense, but always in the sense of Jaspers' *Existenz*: an ontological situatedness in the world that is equally a transcendence to that world and its unknown ontological horizon. Jaspers writes:

29 Voegelin, "Remembrance," 306.

30 See, for example, Peter Brickey LeQuire, "The Axial Age Debate as Political Discourse: Karl Jaspers and Eric Voegelin," *Clio*, Vol. 43 (2014) 295–16.

> When I face this being as transcendence, I am seeking the ultimate ground in a singular fashion....If I try to advance to the source of being, I drop into the unfathomable.... Yet this abyss, a void for the intellect, can fill up for Existence. I am transcending where this depth has opened and the search as such has become a finding in temporal existence; for a man's possible Existenz may turn his transcending of temporal existence into a *unity of presence and search*—a presence which is nothing but the search that has not been detached from what he is seeking.[31]

To understand symbolization of this mysteriously encompassing transcendence as a living source of meaning, Jaspers argues, we must first see symbols as inseparably caught up in this existential unity of presence and search. We must think of the symbol, in the first place, as a "cipher," a means of decrypting highly individualized experiences of transcendent meaning, and must realize that what we normally call "symbols"—the categorizable formal expressions of that meaning—are abstractions that are a step removed from their founding experiences, such that they can obscure as much as they illuminate, the more so when they are organized by modern scholars into systems of thought as if they were mere concepts.[32] Jaspers is seeking in symbolization, we could say, an equivalence of existential experiences.

As for Kierkegaard, while Voegelin did not hesitate to acknowledge the Danish philosopher's influence, and though he reported the extensive reading of his works, he has remarkably little to say about Kierkegaard in explicit terms. But Brickey LeQuire, Eugen Nagy, and other scholars have identified many affinities between the two thinkers.[33] Special circumstances in the

31 Karl Jaspers, *Philosophy*, Vol. 3, trans. E. B. Ashton (Chicago and London: University of Chicago Press, 1971), 4. Hereafter cited as Jaspers, *Philosophy*, Vol. 3.

32 Jaspers, *Philosophy*, Vol. 3, 113–23.

33 Peter Brickey LeQuire. "Eric Voegelin: Politics, History, and the Anxiety of Existence," in *Kierkegaard's Influence on Social-Political Thought*, ed. Jon Stewart (Burlington, VT: Ashgate, 2011), 209–30. Hereafter cited as LeQuire, "Politics, History, and Anxiety." Eugen L. Nagy, "Noesis and Faith: Eric Voegelin and Søren Kierkegaard," in *Eric Voegelin and the Continental Tradi-*

case of Kierkegaard inevitably complicate such efforts. The study of his work tends to divide along two broad paths. A standard scholarly approach immerses one in the context of Danish philosophical and theological controversies of the 1840s and '50s, demands mastery of the dialectical nuances among Kierkegaard's cast of fictional authors, and follows the trajectory of his pietist Lutheran stance on Christian faith and practice. But an approach that seeks the adaptable philosophical insights from across his works will take less interest in the controversies of Copenhagen and will often simply appropriate the ideas, omitting attribution so as to avoid the accusation of misrepresentation.

Were we to see Voegelin as among this latter class of Kierkegaard enthusiasts we would look for family resemblances, seeking them among the hermeneutical assumptions that Voegelin brings to a variety of inquiries. On this score, surely, reflections on the nature of anxiety would figure prominently, by which I mean the existential state of "sympathetic antipathy" toward the transcendental ground of our being.[34] Added to this, and elaborating on it, is the conception of self that we find in Kierkegaard's *Sickness Unto Death*, defined as the active relation of the psycho-physical subject to its ultimately divine source, a relating that determines, for Kierkegaard, the meaning of "spirit."[35] A weakness of spirit (such as results from living by the illusion that one is the ground of one's own existence) leads to forms of despair that may manifest themselves openly or may remain latent until the day that one realizes not only that one is in despair, but that one was always thus.[36] It is this Kierkegaardian configuration of meanings that one may recognize in Voegelin's use of the term, "spirit," and not the Hegelian or Nietzschean meanings of that term. It is in the weakness

tion: Explorations in Modern Political Thought, ed. Lee Trepanier and Steven F. McGuire (Columbia, MO: University of Missouri Press, 2011), 85–107.

34 Søren Kierkegaard, *The Concept of Anxiety*, trans. and ed. Reidar Thomte (Princeton, NJ: Princeton University Press, 1980), 42. Glenn Hughes, *Transcendence and History* (Columbia, MO: University of Missouri Press, 2003), 91–92. LeQuire, "Politics, History, and Anxiety," 217–19.

35 Søren Kierkegaard, *The Sickness unto Death*, trans. and ed. Howard V. Hong and Edna H. Hong (Princeton, NJ: Princeton University Press, 1980), 13–14.

36 Ibid., 14–17, 26–28.

or collapse of spirit, in this same Kierkegaardian sense, that Voegelin sees a decisive source of the political excesses of *libido dominandi*. One thinks of the description, in *The Sickness unto Death*, of a man who is in despair because he wanted to be Caesar but failed in that goal. The source of his despair, the author argues, lies not in his political failure but in the poverty of spirit that required political power before he could feel that he *was* something.[37]

In Voegelin's meditations on time and eternity one also hears many echoes of Kierkegaard—the notion that the eternal is always present in existence yet must be experienced and understood through the mode of temporality.[38] Kierkegaard was polemical against Hegel for his impossible claim to have discovered a logical system of existence, with the implication that this system somehow rises above history so as to interpret its meaning.[39] Such polemics are echoed in Voegelin's own condemnations of Hegel.[40] Kierkegaard was frustrated that Hegelian theologians were replacing faith with reason and were collapsing the absoluteness of transcendence into an absolute that unfolds within world history. In Voegelinian terms, we might say, Kierkegaard was resisting an immanentization of the eschaton.

Kierkegaard's views on these matters are not discovered in isolation but in dialogue with traditions that he shared with Voegelin, including preoccupations with Plato and with Christian thinkers such as Augustine. But there are also parallels in their hermeneutic approaches to such thinkers. Regarding Plato, they both emphasize the literary dimension of the *Dialogues* that allows Socrates to emerge as a uniquely normative person in history. Regarding Christianity, for all of Voegelin's immersion in Thomist sources, he resists the incursion of philosophical proofs into the realm of faith, insisting on the definitive role of uncertainty, as had Kierkegaard against the Catholics and Danish Hegelians. While there is no conclusive

37 Ibid., 19.

38 Ibid., 13. Søren Kierkegaard, *Either/Or, Part II* trans. and ed. Howard V. Hong and Edna H. Hong (Princeton, NJ: Princeton University Press, 1987), 139.

39 Søren Kierkegaard, *Concluding Unscientific Postscript to Philosophical Fragments*, Vol. I, trans. and ed. Howard V. Hong and Edna H. Hong (Princeton, NJ: Princeton University Press, 1992), 118–25.

40 For example, in Eric Voegelin, "On Hegel: A Study in Sorcery" (1971), in *Published Essays 1966-1985*, ed. Ellis Sandoz, *CWEV* Vol. 12, 1990.

way to determine which of these parallels and affinities reflect Kierkegaard's direct effect on Voegelin and which derive from shared influences on both, still the sheer number of connections easily explains Kierkegaard's presence on Voegelin's short list of early inspirations.

Finally, Oswald Spengler is named at the end of the list, with an indication of his dependence on the work of the prodigious scholar of the ancient world, Eduard Meyer. A key contribution of these historians—both of them prominent in the 1920s—is their rejection of the linear idea of progress in history and their promotion, instead, of models that trace the rise and fall of civilizations in history. Spengler is by far the more famous of these two, but that is by virtue of his sensational claim, in *The Decline of the West*, that the Euro-American culture of modernity represented not the pinnacle of human achievement but a decadent phase of a great civilization.[41] Spengler's audacious pronouncements made him, for many readers, a kind of prophetic witness to the sins of the twentieth century; but Meyer, with whom Voegelin studied in Berlin in 1922-23, was the patient scholar who had discerned the pattern of phases in his careful and sensitive studies of the ancient world.[42] It is Meyer's meticulous scholarship that Voegelin emulated, though he did not hesitate, on many an occasion, to offer his own prophetic pronouncements on the state of the West.

Section Two: Decline and Its Resistance

The second section of "Remembrance of Things Past" attempts, in the briefest of terms, to characterize the historical and intellectual environment

41 Oswald Spengler, *The Decline of the West: Volume One: Form and Actuality*, trans. Charles Francis Atkinson (New York: Alfred A. Knopf, 1961), Ch. 1. Eric Voegelin, "Cycle Theory and Disintegration" (c. 1946) in Voegelin, *The Drama of Humanity*, 41–52. See also Stephen A. McKnight, "*Order and History* as a Response to the Theoretical and Methodological Problems Confronting Historians in the Twentieth Century," in Hughes, et. al., *Politics, Order and History*, 259–81.

42 Voegelin, *Autobiographical Reflections*, 42–43. Alexander Demandt, "Eduard Meyer und Oswald Spengler: Lässt Sich Geschichte Voraussagen?" in *Eduard Meyer: Leben und Leistung eines Universalhistorikers*, ed. William M. Calder III and Alexander Demandt (Leiden: E. J. Brill, 1990), 159–81.

over the decades-long period in which Voegelin continued to develop the new approach to philosophy, history, and politics that is formulated in the pages of *Anamnesis*. Here he sees three dynamics at work: a continuing story of barbarous political folly in the course of the twentieth century, a failure of mainstream academics to address that folly adequately, and the recognition of a promising undercurrent of scholars working in an expansive horizon who seek the roots of the conflicts of the day.

The age through which Voegelin had lived he describes as one of political mass movements that produced the slaughter of the world wars and the unbridled hegemonic conflicts that followed them. So little meaning is there behind these movements that Voegelin describes the history as "a tale told by an idiot," "a febrile impotence that cancers out in bloody dreams of greatness" among "mentally diseased ruling cliques."[43]

Voegelin judges the university environment in the decades after World War II to be incapable of meeting the challenge of the century's atrocities, as the intellectuals seemed to be preoccupied with relitigating the ideological debates of the Weimar period that Voegelin had endured long ago. But in the post-war era they had been diluted by their latter-day disputants' lack of skill in languages and knowledge of world cultures, compared with the standards by which Voegelin and his fellow students had been measured. With the swelling of academia after World War II, with universities fragmenting into siloed specializations, with the content of liberal arts education being randomized across increasing numbers of competing fields, and with the influx of faculty so quickly rushed into the classroom that Voegelin derides them as "functional illiterates," the debates seem to him to be caricatures of the versions he had known in his early days, with no promise of bearing any better fruit.[44]

But the third point he makes strikes a note of hopefulness, for the tolerance of modern universities does have the benefit of creating a place where one can work in opposition to reigning intellectual trends. In this environment Voegelin sees scholars making great strides in their skill in understanding cultures of the past and present.[45] And we must remember that

43 Voegelin, "Remembrance," 307–08.
44 Ibid., 308.
45 Ibid., 308–09.

this period from the 1950s to 1970s was the richest period of Voegelin's own career, the period in which he produced the works most definitive of his reputation. For this reason he was known to temper his condemnations of the state of learning in America. The nation had welcomed him when the Fascists and Soviets would not, and he was able to pursue his studies with a certain degree of support and a relative lack of disturbances. Voegelin appreciated the way democratic institutions in America, as well as American traditions of common sense, can function as a hedge against extremist ideologies even as he railed against the dominance of those ideologies among many intellectuals.

A further point of optimism is to be found in Voegelin's conviction that the symbols of reality, when studied with an openness to their depth, can serve as resistance to the power of ideologies. For reality inherently militates against second realities. Experience militates against the distortion of experience. The act of unrestricted thinking has always functioned as a force against unthinking powers of domination.

Section Three: Seeking Philosophical Openness

But the challenge of thinking with an open horizon presents many obstacles, and here Voegelin returns, in the essay's third section, to the particular breakthroughs that moved him out of the restrictive horizons of his early studies, most particularly the phenomenological horizon that he had once shared with Alfred Schütz. Let us consider some philosophical background to that horizon.

The tale of the growth of the modern European sciences is one of continuity and discontinuity. The modern sciences maintain a degree of continuity with the ambitions of the ancient philosophers who sought to uncover the intelligibility of the world and human life, looking behind the vagaries of immediate experience to the permanent principles that make things to behave as they do. In Husserlian terms, the goal is to determine the transcendental conditions for empirical reality. It is what philosophy had always sought through mathematics and logic, but equally through ethics and politics. The discontinuity that modernity had brought to the task, however, resulted from a perceived failure of the traditional philosophical methods of dialectic and metaphysics, with early moderns like

Bacon and Descartes calling for a shift in the paradigm of rationality to that of the burgeoning natural sciences, as well as to their values of instrumentality and technological progress. In the heady early days of the Enlightenment, there was a hope that the health and prosperity resulting from this shift would eliminate the scarcity at the heart of all hegemony and war, ushering in a humanism such as had never been seen.[46]

By the 1920s this Enlightenment project was perceived by some of Europe's most captivating intellectuals to be in crisis. When Husserl used that word, "crisis," in the title of his last major formulation of his philosophical method, one could say that it was really a three-fold crisis that he had on his hands. There was, first, a crisis of epistemological justification in scientific methodology; second, a disintegration of the traditional unity of the human sciences, reflected especially in the rise of positivism; and third, a pragmatic crisis of world war and the breakdown of social order. The first crisis Husserl had been addressing throughout his career; the second becomes a particular focus in his "Vienna Lecture" of 1935 and *Crisis* essay;[47] the third remains curiously unaddressed, even as it was impinging on the philosopher from all sides.

Regarding the first dimension of the crisis, the Enlightenment's initial claims to unparalleled, or even apodictic, certainty in the conclusions of empirical science had been dealt an early blow by David Hume's charge that experience does not present to us the causality that science claims to discern there, nor does logic provide that causal certainty, since the only logic that is certain deduces its particular conclusions from general principles, whereas empirical science moves in the reverse direction. Kant's solution to this dilemma was to assert that categories such as causality are contributed to experience by consciousness (they are "transcendental" in this sense), deriving their certainty from the unchanging categories of a transcendental logic.[48] With the proviso that the claims of science must be

46 See, for example, Francis Bacon, *The New Organon*, ed. Fulton H. Anderson (New York: Macmillan, 1960), 117–19.

47 Husserl, "The Vienna Lecture," published as Appendix A in Husserl, *Crisis*, 269–99.

48 Immanuel Kant, *Critique of Pure Reason*, trans. Norman Kemp Smith (New York: Macmillan, 1978), 102–75.

limited to appearances, science can thus be certain, because its discoveries will always be grounded in the *a priori* categories through which appearances must necessarily appear. While this Kantian solution limits the legitimacy of metaphysical application of the transcendental categories to supersensible things in themselves (which application he calls "pure reason"),[49] he defends a legitimacy to moral reasoning that makes sense of our transcendental category of freedom and the aesthetic reason that draws conclusions from the free play of our cognitive faculties. By this solution, argued across several major works, Kant granted a pre-eminence to natural science while re-establishing a new kind of continuity with the larger range of subjects in philosophy's traditional purview.

For Husserl, the methodological crisis prompted by Hume, though partially resolved by Kant, must be undertaken at a deeper level, i.e., in the very formulation of the epistemological problematic. In that formulation, modern thinkers, whether rationalist, empiricist, or Kantian, begin with a model of confrontation between subject and object, a model that is neither empirically nor transcendentally derived but functions, rather, as a mere assumption. The model is, moreover, fallaciously abstracted, ignoring that subjects and objects are both situated within being, that subjectivity is always already involved with the world, and that all objectivity is established (or "constituted") in the consciousness of subjects. Though Kant realized this last point, his confrontationalist assumptions prevented him from exploring its full implications. Better, then, to put the whole confrontation thesis (the "natural attitude") out of play, exploring, through description, the behaviors of all entities that reveal, through their patterns of constancy and change, the unchanging eidetic grounds of their intelligibility.[50] This is the task of phenomenology as an ongoing, collaborative, interdisciplinary project that has been pursued by dedicated Husserlians, now, for more than a century. The self, as the foundation for the phenomenological project, emerges, in that project, not only as an empirically existing agent, but as a

49 Ibid., 297ff.

50 Husserl, *Crisis,* Section 38. Edmund Husserl, *Ideas Pertaining to a Pure Phenomenology and to a Phenomenological Philosophy, First Book*, trans. F. Kersten (The Hague: Martinus Nijhoff, 1983), 51–53, 56–57. Voegelin, "Theory of Governance," 238.

transcendental ground, the unitary "I" in which *eide*, with all of their universality, come to light, such that phenomenology, through its bracketing of preconceived ideas about subjects and objects, and through its constant clarification of the transcendental ego, achieves what Descartes and other philosophers unsuccessfully sought: the indubitable starting point for all knowledge.[51]

Early in his career Voegelin saw himself as practicing this method. His 1922 dissertation in sociology under Hans Kelsen and Othmar Spann, "Interaction and Spiritual Community," drew on Husserl to help identify a concept of spiritual community that would be more formal and stable than any concept that social psychology alone could produce.[52] In "The Theory of Governance" Husserl's method is used as a model for the practice of philosophical meditation, wherein all of one's personal experiences function as relevant data, while the process of reflection, the free play of variations and comparisons, draws one toward the eidetic elements within that experience, leaving behind what is merely psychological and idiosyncratic.[53] In both of these early works Voegelin was attempting, like Schütz, to adapt a philosophy that is centered on the reflecting individual to the broader study of society and community.

The second dimension of the crisis that Husserl has in mind in his *Crisis* essay is the fragmentation of what the Greeks had meant by the word, "science" (*episteme*). Its comprehensive meaning, which included not only the study of nature, but metaphysics, ethics, and poetics, could still be heard, to some degree, in the German *"Wissenschaft,"* but as the paradigm of natural science became pre-eminent among the Neo-Kantians and utterly dominant in the writings of the positivists, the culturally foundational fields of ethics, history, law, governance, and the arts were losing their academic legitimacy. The narrowed type of science that was beginning to claim exclusive legitimacy was not the kind that could sustain philosophy's traditional cultural

51 Husserl, *Crisis*, Section 50. Edmund Husserl, *Cartesian Meditations* (The Hague: Martinus Nijhoff, 1960), 25–26.

52 Voegelin, "Interaction and Spiritual Community," in *The Theory of Governance and Other Miscellaneous Papers, 1921-1938*, ed. William Petropulos and Gilbert Weiss, *CWEV* Vol. 32, 19–140, see esp. 37–50.

53 Voegelin, "Theory of Governance," 246–55.

role and was, indeed, turning human activity into a mere object of empirical investigation. Meanwhile, there were others who were taking phenomenology into broader fields of study. Schütz's phenomenological study of social life appeared in 1932. Jaspers and Heidegger had taken phenomenological sensibilities into their existential examinations of human being in time and history. Husserl now wanted to be more overt in his recognition of history and the historical development of the "life world." His "Vienna Lecture" (which Voegelin attended) envisions a humanistic study of the spiritual life of Europe that would recover from positivism a full recognition of the overriding importance of specifically human meaning in history. But both this lecture and the *Crisis* largely remain, in regard to this goal, attempts to lay the ground for a larger project of research and unification to be undertaken by others, Husserl making limited efforts of his own at historical scholarship.

The third dimension of the crisis, the pragmatic one, is less observed than felt by the reader of Husserl. It is that the most cherished Enlightenment dreams—of peace through technology-fueled prosperity, of the rationalization of systems of political order, and of the maturation of humankind through the growth of moral autonomy—were blasted to pieces on the battlefields of World War I, where the technological advances of the age produced a degree of slaughter unimaginable in previous times. As a generation of European youth was decimated and society's established bases of wealth and honor collapsed, the old language of rational progress that one hears in Husserl could seem embarrassingly naïve. As the philosopher was writing, moreover, Germany was installing Hitler as "Führer und Reichskanzler." Though Husserl was finally turning his attention to the question of reason in history, history seemed to be moving rapidly in another direction.

Given that Voegelin grew up during times of world war and post-war chaos, and that he was trained in sociology, law, and political theory, it is unsurprising that this third crisis was the one at the top of his list of concerns. That, and other developments in his thinking, most likely doomed his appreciation of Husserl's new launch of phenomenology well before he heard the Vienna lecture or read a word of the *Crisis*. Voegelin had already moved beyond his early affinity with the epistemological debates of the German philosophers, affected, as he was, by the very different cultural concerns of his colleagues in America;[54] he was already convinced that the ordering force in political community was centered in symbolism rather than instrumental reason; and he had come to believe that the human sciences must address the whole of history, throughout the whole of the world, and must do so from the outset rather than working toward that global scope from the confines of European epistemology by a series of methodical baby steps. Voegelin was already an existential thinker of the type against whom Husserl was trying to reassert his universalist transcendentalism, and Voegelin had turned all of his inquiries toward what he was coming to see as the definitive historical constant in history: the human orientation to the divine. Indeed, the question of the nature of reason had become, for him, a theme within the history of divine-human encounter, a symbol illuminative of the ancient Greek philosophers' particular way of exploring the mind's relation to the transcendent beginning and beyond. This Greek understanding had been fruitfully appropriated and transformed throughout the Middle Ages, but had been narrowed, immanentized, and instrumentalized by the founding thinkers of modernity.

With such convictions in the background, Voegelin's response to the *Crisis* in his 1943 letter to Schütz, despite a few moments of ebullient praise, forms a rather thorough rejection of the Husserlian project. Husserl's stereotypically modern view of reason, as something born in Athens and perfected in the German university, Voegelin now calls "a Victorian image of history," negligent of Hellenism, Christianity, and the Middle Ages, engaged with a fraction of the concerns that the Greek conception of reason encompassed, and wedded to a heroic narrative of reason's long struggle to achieve the author's own perfected method. Such patterns of interpretation, which had come to disturb Voegelin deeply, he now saw vividly at work in Husserl's project. Its proclamation of a new apodictic foundation for all future knowledge struck him as the same sort of messianic hubris that formed the heart of modern authoritarian ambitions and ideological mass movements. Returning to the question of philosophical meditation that he had explored through Husserl in "The Theory of Governance," Voegelin now finds Husserl narrow on the subject—missing, in his identification with Descartes, the way the latter's thinking

54 See Voegelin, *Autobiographical Reflections*, 56–61.

undertakes an interaction with God, recalling thereby, in its structure, many medieval meditations.[55]

In a letter of reply to Voegelin, Schütz complains that his friend is blaming Husserl for addressing Husserl's problems rather than Voegelin's. Voegelin seems to Schütz to have lost interest in the questions of critical philosophy, claiming that they are not fundamental; yet certainly it is at least a matter of debate whether the question of knowledge is a fundamental philosophical question.[56] Michael Barber, whose careful review of the Voegelin-Schütz correspondence takes a position sympathetic to Schütz, describes Voegelin's shift away from phenomenology in a telling way. He characterizes Voegelin as providing a "metaphysical critique of modern political theory" that "led him to emphasize sub-rational, metaphysical factors and to suspect epistemological/methodological approaches, like phenomenology, that proceed independently of them."[57] And Barber offers this objection:

> But this enmity toward epistemology, which guarantees a kind of radicality to Voegelin's thought, constitutes part of its shortcoming since it allows Voegelin to be less than self-reflective about his own epistemological suppositions and to fall into an unwitting dogmatism....[58]

55 Voegelin, *Anamnesis*, 58–61.

56 Gerhard Wagner and Gilbert Weiss, eds., *A Friendship That Lasted a Lifetime: The Correspondence between Alfred Schütz and Eric Voegelin*, trans, William Petropulos (Columbia, MO: University of Missouri Press, 2011), 50–51. Hereafter cited as Wagner and Weiss, *A Friendship*. See also Gilbert Weiss, "Political Reality and the Life-World: The Correspondence Between Eric Voegelin and Alfred Schütz, 1938-1959," in Hughes, et. al., *Politics, Order and History*, 125–42; and Eugene Webb, *Eric Voegelin: Philosopher of History* (Seattle, WA: University of Washington Press, 1981), 31–35.

57 Michael D. Barber, "Endorsement and Eidos: Phenomenology and the Schütz/Voegelin Correspondence," in *Phenomenology 2005: Selected Essays from North America, Part 1*, ed. Lester Embree and Thomas Nenon (Bucharest: Zeta Books, 2007), 37–66, at 37. Hereafter cited as Barber, "Endorsement and Eidos."

58 Barber, "Endorsement and Eidos," 52.

The charge is stated here more aggressively than Schütz's own response, but it gets at the heart of the disagreement. If Voegelin is rejecting critical philosophy, where is to be found the critical element in his own interpretations of history?

Schütz had a tendency to see Voegelin as doing eidetic thinking in spite of himself, examining particular historical cases of experience and symbolization to discover encompassing complexes such as "Gnosticism," a category that Voegelin expands, one could say, by something like a phenomenological process of free variation and pattern-recognition across many religious as well as secular traditions.[59] But Voegelin remained unmoved by his friend's ongoing defense of phenomenology or any characterization of his own work by that term. In a letter of 1957, late in their correspondence, Voegelin is suggesting that Husserl should be studied as a Gnostic,[60] and in "Remembrance of Things Past," he is still looking back on his reactions to the *Crisis* in 1943 as a decisive life event: "Something had to be done. I had to get out of that 'apodictic horizon' as fast as possible."[61]

It can be difficult to recognize, within the debate with Schütz, Voegelin's hermeneutical conviction that the critical function of inquiry is interior to the concrete process of inquiry itself. Discovering one's immersion in the world, in history, in a fabric of discourses woven over centuries reveals inherent tendencies and directionalities that form the path towards truth that has always been at work in those sources. The critical component is often to be found simply through an openness to what is being said, realizing that the authors of one's sources are more intelligent and insightful than we are. From this hermeneutical stance, the very idea of being somehow apart from that fabric of discourse, of stepping outside, or suspending, or bracketing one's immersion in the great body of meaning that envelops us, distorts the hermeneutic situation and exaggerates one's competence to judge. The very idea of using a "method" is, in Voegelin's view, prone to such errors, replacing, as it does, the ceaseless immersion in one's sources with an abstract, ahistorical verification algorithm. Better to fathom the

59 Ibid., 55–59.

60 Wagner and Weiss, *A Friendship*, 191.

61 Voegelin, "Remembrance," 311.

fullest range possible of one's involvement in the world and in history, seeking the contours of that involvement even in the formative symbols shaping one's psyche in early life.[62]

The phrase, "remembrance of things past," is ambiguous, for it can refer to one's own personal past or the larger past of human history. But in a scholar such as Voegelin these two meanings merge into one, for in such a case the life of the scholar is one dedicated to that larger and greater remembrance and recovery of meaning. The remembrance is undertaken for a purpose: to counter the folly of forgetting by which the disasters of human history are repeated over and over, fueled again and again by the same blind and unfettered zeal. Service to this countervailing purpose requires powers, not only of research, but of recognition and understanding—the kind of anamnesis of which Plato spoke, wherein the intelligibility at the heart of things comes to the mind with such clarity that it is as if it were something that one knew but had simply forgotten. The movement of this inquiry is meditative, listening for the ways in which the past speaks within one's soul. It is a double movement, of self and of human community, pursued along a single path of endeavor, bearing the hope of healing for humanity's future, a future born out of the permanent light of the past.

62 See Eric Voegelin, "Anamnesis," in Voegelin, *Anamnesis*, 84–98.

–13–
Voegelin's "Wisdom and the Magic of the Extreme: A Meditation"

Michael Franz

Voegelin's meditation, "Wisdom and the Magic of the Extreme" is among the author's greatest and most important writings.[1] These are two distinct judgments, based on different grounds. "Greatness" is an over-used term that I don't resort to lightly, but it is merited in this case on the basis of the piece's many illuminations and insights, which are developed and interwoven with remarkable patience and precision over the course of 60 printed pages. Only a handful of other writings approach this document's effectiveness in conveying Voegelin's philosophizing at the height of its development late in his life. Second, the *importance* of "Wisdom and Magic" stems principally from the light it sheds on Voegelin's fully evolved thinking on problems he had worked on for many decades, most notably, the complex of problems related to *disordered spirituality* as a phenomenon in human consciousness, politics, and history.

My emphasis on the meditation's account of disordered or "deformed" spirituality as the preeminent source of its importance might not seem obvious to some readers who have already worked through it carefully, so I hasten to make a clarifying concession even as I explain my emphasis. "Wisdom and Magic" sheds light on many problems or mysteries other than

1 "Wisdom and the Magic of the Extreme: A Meditation," reprinted in *Published Essays 1966-1985*, ed. Ellis Sandoz, *CWEV* Vol. 12, 1990. Hereafter cited as "Wisdom and Magic." Initially delivered as a lecture at the Eranos Conference in 1977 in Ascona, Switzerland, and published in *Eranos Yearbook*, Vol. 46 (1977, 341–409), the text reprinted in *CWEV* follows the publication in *Southern Review*, n.s., Vol. 17 (1983), 235–87.

ones associated with disordered spirituality, and indeed, the meditation delves deeply into "wisdom" as well as "magic" (though it is worth noting that the word "wisdom" does not appear in the first 29 pages of the writing). However, Voegelin completed several other writings that help us see what "wisdom" (broadly conceived) meant to him in the final decade of his work, whereas this meditation is simply unrivaled as an explication of his ultimate understanding of the personal and political disorders he sought to diagnose and resist over the entire span of his career. To expand upon this contrast, if "Wisdom and Magic" had not been left to us, we could limp along well enough toward understanding what Voegelin regarded as "wisdom" in the final years of his work with the aid of other publications and lecture manuscripts left in his papers,[2] but if we did not have access to "Wisdom and Magic," we would be gravely hobbled in any attempt to understand how Voegelin's later work in the theory of consciousness calls us to reassess the disorders treated more famously—but less discerningly—in *The New Science of Politics*. For this particular task, "Wisdom and Magic" is singular and indispensable, and, accordingly, I shall emphasize this aspect of its teaching in this commentary.[3]

2 These would include the essays analyzed in the present volume, along with *In Search of Order* and addresses such as "The Drama of Humanity," "Structures of Consciousness," "The Beyond and Its Parousia" and "The Beginning and the Beyond: A Meditation on Truth."

3 While acknowledging the costs entailed in my decision to emphasize Voegelin's "diagnostic" work in "Wisdom and Magic," I should add that the meditation's treatments of "orders" and "disorders" of the spirit are intertwined throughout the document, and that valuable points of connection must be cut if this commentary is to achieve anything valuable without becoming absurdly lengthy. "Wisdom and Magic" is by far the longest of the essays included in Vol. 12 of *CWEV* while also being among the most dense and intricate, and concessions to this are unavoidable. Yet, they remain costly: Voegelin's "diagnoses" of "spiritual disorders" among important thinkers such as Hegel, Marx, and Nietzsche can seem remarkably audacious or arrogant to readers when first encountered, though this reaction should be soothed by Voegelin's conscientious identification of spiritual *disorders* by way of careful and explicit contradistinction from healthy *orders* of the soul. Regarding such healthy, ordered, and "balanced" consciousness, readers would do well to carefully consider the meditation's treatment of Shakespeare, Baudelaire, and—above all—Plato.

As we shall see, Voegelin's intricate treatment of disordered spirituality is not only different in "Wisdom and Magic" from treatments in some famous earlier writings—employing significantly altered analytical underpinnings—but also at odds with them in several important respects (though it supplements them in other ways that bolster their continuing value). Indeed, this writing is the "last word" regarding Voegelin's life-long struggle against the complex of personal and political disorders treated under headings including "gnosticism,"[4] "political religion," "pneumopathology," "ideology," "egophanic revolt," and "metastatic faith." More pointedly, this is to say that a much more-widely read text such as *The New Science of Politics* is definitely not Voegelin's last word on this complex of problems, though it is often treated as though it were, especially by those who have neglected to work through the very challenging "Wisdom and the Magic of the Extreme."

4 Voegelin's use of the term "gnosticism" is problematic for multiple reasons. Sometimes he uses the word as a proper noun referring to the beliefs of the historical Gnostics, whereas at other times he uses the term as an adjectival designation for modern patterns of thought and symbolization that have no evident connection with the Gnostic sects, or even associates the word with figures long preceding them, such as the prophet Isaiah and his "metastatic faith." In my publications addressing works in which Voegelin employs the term, I've tried to simply dispense with it in favor of "pneumopathological consciousness," but of course this is impossible when quoting from Voegelin. Eugene Webb proposed, as a way out of this problem, capitalizing the name of the ancient Gnostic movement while using the term *gnosticism* for "all movements based on claims of gnosis of any sort." This enhances clarity in some instances but not in others, as I have written and as Webb has acknowledged. However, as no preferable solution has been offered, I will follow Webb's usage whenever possible in the pages that follow when the term must be used, though some inconsistency is inevitable when quoting Voegelin, who was inconsistent in his use of "Gnosticism" versus "gnosticism." On this problem, see my *Eric Voegelin and the Politics of Spiritual Revolt: The Roots of Modern Ideology*, Louisiana State University Press, 1992, 18–20 (hereafter cited as *Voegelin and the Politics of Spiritual Revolt*); Eugene Webb, *Eric Voegelin: Philosopher of History*, (Seattle: University of Washington Press, 1981), 200–02 (hereafter cited as Webb, *Eric Voegelin: Philosopher of History),* and Webb, "Review of Michael Franz, *Eric Voegelin and the Politics of Spiritual Revolt*," in *Voegelin Research News*, Vol. 3, February 1997.

Those who strive to do justice to this study by working through it rigorously will find plenty of "work" involved. Although elegantly written, Voegelin did not structure it to make things easy for readers, and those who become frustrated along the way might conclude understandably that he barely structured it at all. I will comment on the text's unusual flow in a detailed footnote below, but the most important observation to make initially is that the document is explicitly characterized as a *meditation*, which is something importantly different than a straightforward "analysis" set forth in a series of declarative propositions. "Wisdom and Magic" is written in a way that invites readers to join in a process of reflective contemplation. This means more than one thing. It means contemplating a set of problems and realities reflectively, returning repeatedly to the problems and realities from different perspectives that Voegelin "rolls out" in a meditative narrative that seems to "roll along" in a way this is quite unusual in scholarly writing.[5]

5 This becomes apparent from the unusual structure of "Wisdom and Magic"—or, more precisely, its seeming lack of structure if it is simply picked up and read from start to finish. After an opening that runs for only a page (in the *CWEV* pagination), a section "I" sets the problem to be meditated upon in 10 pages by introducing some key concepts and sources. Section "II" is the "meditation proper," running for fully 45 pages, followed by a Section "III" that is barely longer than two pages and is obviously a sort of afterword, as it begins with the sentence, "What has come to its end is a *meditation*, a philosopher's effort to explore the structures of existential consciousness" (371; emphasis in original). Within Section II (326–71), the text I've described as "rolling" bears no headings or punctuating structural markings. Rather, there are just eight points where the reader encounters double line breaks or "returns" (333, 339, 345, 348, 352, 355, 357, 365). A few of these are separate passages where the meditation takes a notable turn, but just as many are situated between paragraphs and sections that aren't clearly distinct, leaving readers to wonder whether they have encountered a structural marker when coming to these breaks, or simply been invited by Voegelin—the lead meditator—to take a deep breath. Questions regarding the author's intention behind the double line breaks are not answered clearly by the detailed "Synopsis" provided by Voegelin at the very end of the chapter in the *CWEV* edition. The "Synopsis" identifies 13 separate themes or sections within Section "II," yet the double line breaks divide this Section into only 9 portions. My analysis of whether the double line breaks conform to Voegelin's listing of separate themes yields six negative results, five positive ones, and one that is stubbornly

The process of reflective contemplation to which Voegelin invites his readers also means *self*-reflective contemplation, which is something quite different than being a spectator watching a writer describe phenomena in the manner of a subject discussing objects.

The unusual nature of the document as a meditation also bears implications for one who offers a "commentary" on it, as I am here. Because "Wisdom and Magic" is—as noted above—"something other than a straightforward 'analysis' set forth in a series of declarative propositions," I risk doing a disservice to Voegelin as well as my readers if I lapse into setting forth declarative propositions about this meditation that seem to "settle issues" in a way that obviates the need of readers to engage the meditation directly. To phrase this a bit differently, doing justice to this document as a reader means, ultimately, reading the meditation meditatively. Obviously, that task falls to each serious reader individually, and that's no less the case because someone has offered a commentary on the document. Consequently, my task is unusual, in keeping with the unusual nature and purpose of "Wisdom and Magic." My intention here is not to "explain" the meditation, but rather to offer some contextual and analytical guidance that might assist readers in undertaking their own meditative encounter with the document. My objective here is to help with the initial "spade work" that may enable others to dig more deeply into the meditative interior of "Wisdom and Magic." Stated more fully, I hope to highlight some of the writing's most novel and distinctive aspects by comparison to Voegelin's other writings (particularly regarding disorders of the spirit), offer

opaque. A check of the 1983 version of "Wisdom and Magic" from *Southern Review* (which Voegelin might well have proofread, whereas that would have been impossible for the *CWEV* version) shows two additional line breaks that were not replicated in the *Collected Works* version. The first of these is on p. 242 in *Southern Review*, and would appear prior to the first new paragraph on 323; the second is on p. 259 in *Southern Review*, and would appear prior to the first new paragraph on 342. Both of these do indeed conform to new entries in Voegelin's "Synopsis," but that still leaves roughly half of the line breaks unexplained. The upshot is that "Meditation" isn't just an arresting word in the subtitle of "Wisdom and Magic." It also serves as a disclosure to readers that they should check their habits and preconceptions at the door—before entering what will likely be a quite unfamiliar mode of philosophical participation.

some pointers toward crucial passages that can illuminate the meditation as a whole, address some assertions that can prompt dismissive reactions if they aren't "unpacked" and explained more carefully than Voegelin did himself, and offer an assessment of his achievement in this, the last major writing finished by his own hand.

Origins of the Meditation

Although a close reading of the meditation can leave no doubt of the importance of "Wisdom and the Magic of the Extreme," it remains somewhat surprising that the document was written at all when considered in relation to the timing of the work. According to Ellis Sandoz's note at the outset of the version in Vol. 12 of *CWEV*, it first took form as a lecture presented at the Eranos Conference in 1977 in Ascona, Switzerland. The very substantial effort required to write the meditation was thus undertaken in the aftermath of the publication of *The Ecumenic Age* (Vol. IV of Voegelin's magnum opus, *Order and History*), a book that appeared only after a 17-year hiatus since the publication of Volumes II and III. The extraordinary lapse in the publication of *Order and History* was widely and energetically addressed in the many reviews that were published upon the appearance of *The Ecumenic Age*, as was the "break" with the original theoretical program of the series that Voegelin announced and explained in the book's lengthy "Introduction," which concludes with mention of a "…next and last volume, entitled *In Search of Order*," … [which] "will study the contemporary problems that have motivated the search for order in history."[6] In light of the controversy in the extensive secondary literature regarding Voegelin's "break" from the original program for *Order and History* as well as the new theoretical directions pursued in *The Ecumenic Age*, it would have been entirely reasonable to assume that he would pour all of his energies into the completion of *In Search of Order* at this stage in life in his late 70s.

6 *Order and History, Vol. IV, The Ecumenic Age*, (1974) ed. Michael Franz, *CWEV* Vol. 17, 2000, 107, hereafter cited as Voegelin, *The Ecumenic Age*. Voegelin's reasons for the so-called "break" with his program for *Order and History* which he "abandoned" because its conception proved "untenable" are examined at length in my "Editor's Introduction" to the *CWEV* edition, pp. 1–28, along with a critical account of some of the more important (and heated) reviews that were published after 1974.

However, Voegelin clearly devoted a great deal of thought, energy, and time to "Wisdom and Magic," as evinced by the sheer length of the writing, its complexity and theoretical scope, and its originality by comparison to earlier works addressing related problems (especially on the "Magic" side as opposed to the "Wisdom" aspect). Moreover, Voegelin worked with it repeatedly in public presentations. Sandoz indicates that after the Eranos lecture in 1977 it was also "given as the thirty-eighth of the Edward Douglass White Lectures on Citizenship at Louisiana State University" during April of 1980.[7] Additionally, I found preparation notes (in the Voegelin archive at The Hoover Institution) indicating that Voegelin also turned to it for a lecture at Princeton in October of 1979 as well as in Minnesota in February of 1980. These notes look like more than mere memory aids for consultation at the lectern; rather, they show Voegelin "re-meditating" the meditation by altering the expression and emphasis of its major themes. Evidence indicates that he was every bit as intent upon publication of the document as he was on using it as the basis for presentations, as he was already working with Lewis P. Simpson, editor of *The Southern Review*, to publish it in the USA even before the *Eranos Yearbook* finally appeared in print. Voegelin also wrote that he intended to include it in "...a volume of essays I plan as soon as the Vol. V is properly under way."[8]

Having established that this work was important to Voegelin even when he had other, very pressing writing obligations to tend to, we might well inquire into *why* this undertaking seemed worthy of such an investment. For starters, the invitation to speak at and participate in the Eranos conference was no small honor even for a scholar of Voegelin's caliber, especially as these remarkable seminars often involved thinkers whose areas of research and methodological versatility were comparable to his (for example, Martin Buber, Joseph Campbell, Mircea Eliade, Carl Gustav Jung, Karl Löwith, Gilles Quispel, Gershom Scholem and Paul Tillich).[9] Second, the topic chosen for the 1977 conference, "The Sense of Imperfection," connected easily to problems of great importance to Voegelin. His

7 "Wisdom and Magic," 315.

8 Letter to Lewis P. Simpson dated 6 July, 1980.

9 For a broader account, see *The Eranos Movement: A Story of Hermeneutics*, edited by Tilo Schabert. Wuerzburg: Koenigshausen & Neumann, 2016. In a

meditation hews closely to it at the outset, and circles back to it repeatedly, though other participants at the conference not versed in Voegelin's thought could be excused for losing the thread of continuity at multiple points.[10] As I have written elsewhere regarding Voegelin's fully mature understanding of spiritual and political disorder, the sources of disturbance that are deepest, most perennial and widespread are revolts against the fundamental experiences of imperfection, uncertainty, and mortality, which are "fundamental" on grounds of being aspects of the human condition that are not particular to time, place, or personal circumstances.[11] I'll return to this important point below, but suffice it to say that the Eranos conference's topic of "The Sense of Imperfection" was pitched straight into Voegelin's "wheelhouse," to borrow a term from baseball, and he responded with a commensurately zestful swing.

Third, the topic as well as the ethos of Eranos conferences and their multi-disciplinary rosters all lent themselves to the literary and expository form of a meditation, which Voegelin was very keen to explore in the last decade of his life and work.[12] I shall return to the text's nature as a meditation

letter to Eugene Webb dated 11 September 1977, Voegelin reflected that: "The Eranos meeting, at which I delivered a lecture on 'Wisdom and the Magic of the Extreme,' was highly interesting, because I participated in it for the first time. The ten participants, and their wives, live together in houses of the foundation and have their meals together. It is a fairly close knit fraternity, though the composition changes in part every year.... The dominant temper seems to be historical; and I am not sure that my philosophical attempt pleased everybody." *Selected Correspondence 1950-1984*, ed. Thomas Hollweck, *CWEV* Vol. 30, 2007, 826.

10 Indeed, the published text seems utterly implausible as a lecture that could be followed comprehendingly in real time by anyone, however prepared even by very extensive reading in Voegelin's earlier work. His notes for the presentations in Minnesota and at Princeton help indicate the portions that he might actually have emphasized when presenting the meditation verbally.

11 See my "Brothers under the Skin: Voegelin on Spiritual Order and Disorder," in *The Politics of the Soul: Voegelin and Religious Experience*, ed. Glenn R. Hughes, Rowman and Littlefield, 1999, 139–61, 143 ff.

12 The best account of Voegelin's understanding of a meditation as a form of philosophical expression currently available is Barry Cooper, *Consciousness and Politics: From Analysis to Meditation in the Late Work of Eric Voegelin*, St. Augustine's Press, 2018, 329–41.

below, but it is interesting that the Voegelin papers at the Hoover Institution include a handwritten, untitled version of lecture notes (clearly for "Wisdom and Magic") with opening entries reading, "(2) Literary Form – Anamnetic Meditation" following "(1) Eranos Occasion" under the heading, "Introduction." I can't say whether this set of notes was for Voegelin's lecture at the conference in Ascona or for a later presentation that simply acknowledged its initial delivery there, but this makes little difference. What seems significant is the adjective "Anamnetic" attached here to the noun "Meditation," and this significance is at least two-fold. On one hand, the meditation recollects the historical (or perennial) attractiveness of "the magic of the extreme"[13] stretching back millennia by means of an analysis of consciousness, juxtaposing the allure of disordered activism to the balanced—but spiritually trying—mode of consciousness subsumed under the word, "wisdom." Additionally, the meditative form affords Voegelin an opportunity to recollect and resume his lifelong search for order by way of *personal resistance* to surrounding disorders, which was a highly distinctive characteristic of his philosophizing and political thinking stretching back to the 1930s. I choose the word "resume" here because problems of spiritual disorder were not central to *The Ecumenic Age*, though that book bears passages indicating that Voegelin had altered his understanding in important ways since his most famous analysis in *The New Science of Politics*, published a quarter-century earlier. I choose the words "recollect" and "personal" here because the diagnostic standpoint of the "Wisdom and Magic" is also quite different from that of *The New Science*, being less concerned with explaining the *historical progression* of disorder into modernity than with exploring the *human possibility* of disorder within consciousness *per se*,[14] drawing not only on historical

13 The term, "*die Magie des Extrems*," is quoted from Nietzsche, *The Will to Power*, aphorism 749. Voegelin does not accuse Nietzsche of creating or asserting the fascinating and seemingly magical potential of "the extreme" for transforming reality, but rather credits him for his "psychological acumen" in discerning the perennial power of the extreme to fascinate—even as he succumbs to that power. "Wisdom and Magic," 324–25.

14 The nature of this shift and some of its conceptual expressions have either gone unnoticed or been misunderstood by many of Voegelin's readers, including some accomplished commentators. Manfred Henningsen shows a precise awareness of the shift when observing that Voegelin's "...intellectual interest

documents but also on Voegelin's own empathetic reflections and personally valued sources such as the Sonnets of Shakespeare, the poetry of T. S. Elliot, Karl Kraus and Baudelaire, and the dialogues of Plato. With this noted, I hasten to ward off any possible misunderstanding of my point here: this writing is definitely not the nostalgic musing of an old man, but rather a quite distinctive and very effective mode of philosophizing by a thinker who was evidently still at the peak of his powers.

Opening Salvo...In a Meditation?

The text of "Wisdom and Magic of the Extreme" begins in a way that isn't particularly meditative in appearance, looking much more like an opening salvo in a combative context:

> The topic chosen for this Conference is the Sense of Imperfection.
>
> The choice is as judicious as it is provocative in a time when all of us are threatened in our humanity, if not in our physical existence, by the massive social force of activist dreamers who want

in Gnosticism as the speculative signature of the modern West began to fade... " after the 1950s. He also rightly observes that Voegelin did not "change his mind with regard to recognizing a fundamental equivalence in the ancient and modern gnostic experiences." Consequently, as we shall see below, Voegelin never quite chose to "...drop the Gnosis thesis altogether...," though Henningsen concludes that Voegelin "...had simply lost interest in the genealogy of the deformation of modern consciousness." My only objection to this very valuable formulation is that I don't read Voegelin as having "lost interest" in the "genealogy" of modern disordered consciousness. The shift can be phrased more accurately by observing that he *rejected* the approach from the 1930s through the 1950s that later manifestations were A) *descended from* earlier ones, in favor of understanding them as B) essentially independent upwellings of a pattern of spiritual revolt that are fundamentally equivalent as revolts against timeless sources of tension in human existence. Henningsen, "Introduction" to *Modernity without Restraint: The Political Religions, The New Science of Politics, and Science, Politics, and Gnosticism*, *CWEV* Vol. 5, 2000, 15–16.

> to liberate us from our imperfections by locking us up in the perfect prison of their phantasy. Even in our so-called free societies not a day passes that we are not seriously molested, in encounters with persons, or the mass media, or a supposedly philosophical and scientific literature, by somebody's Utopian imagination.[15]

With its references to threat, force, and prison, the passage sets a tone that seems reminiscent of some of the more sharply adversarial (and widely quoted) sections of *The New Science of Politics* and *Science, Politics and Gnosticism*. The sentences that follow after a paragraph break seem to reinforce this initial impression:

> No more than these two sentences are needed to introduce the issue of activist imagination and symbolization, of their violence and destructive effects, as the subject matter of the present lectures. The intellectual and linguistic corruption of the age, implacably intruding its atrocity into everybody's life, is a matter of common knowledge[16]

15 "Wisdom and Magic," 315. This is not the only passage in Voegelin's writings that could strike some readers as excessively alarmist or hyperbolic. When I first chaired a roundtable panel of the Eric Voegelin Society on "Voegelin's Impact on Political Science" at a meeting of the American Political Science Association on September 5, 1987, a panelist who shall remain un-named opened his remarks with a sarcastic reading of the following passage from Voegelin's review of Hannah Arendt's *The Origins of Totalitarianism*: "The putrefaction of Western civilization, as it were, has released a cadaveric poison spreading its infection through the body of humanity. What no religious founder, no philosopher, no imperial conqueror of the past has achieved—to create a community of mankind by creating a common concern for all men—has now been realized through the community of suffering under the earth-wide expansion of Western foulness." A significant number of those present tittered or laughed in response, at which time I recall Ellis Sandoz replying from the audience (in his calm but still booming voice) with something quite close to: "That foulness referenced by Voegelin was the stench emitted by the death camps of the Holocaust." That brought an end to any tittering at the panel session, and was the most memorable moment I've witnessed during more than 30 annual meetings of the Society.

16 Ibid.

Eric Voegelin was not a man known to shrink from a fight, as was clear from the earliest years of his career in Austria, when he fought back against racists, authoritarians, fascists, and communists, doing so in print, and well before he had achieved security in his academic career, not to mention his physical safety.

Readers encountering this opening during the third decade of the 21st century might understandably regard it as curiously overheated. However, they would do well to remember that totalitarianism, the Cold War, and the so-called Age of Ideology were still running at full tilt in 1977, with "the sense of imperfection" under repeated assault from would-be world purifiers of multiple sorts, be they intellectuals, political insurgents, programmatic autocrats, or military dictators. This is hardly the occasion to recount all of the events of the time, but it is worth recalling that the time span from when Voegelin likely began the project to when it was first published includes the North Vietnamese takeover of Saigon, the Khmer Rouge genocide in Cambodia, the installation of Cuban-backed Marxist governments in Mozambique and Angola, the Soviet invasion of Afghanistan, the Sandinista seizure of power in El Salvador, and the Islamist revolution in Iran. No less important contextually is the fact that ideologues of various stripes occupied prominent positions in public discourse and especially in universities, where the Marxists among them were not wizened beneficiaries of a tenured afterlife (as they have been for decades since then), but rather esteemed "authorities" in multiple disciplines in the late 1970s. Although we shall see that Voegelin traced the deepest sources of utopian activism not to the circumstances of particular time periods but rather to an inability to bear up under perennial tensions that inhere in the human condition broadly conceived, that does not mean that utopian activism doesn't wax and wane from time to time. It was definitely waxing in the mid- and late-1970s, and the sharpness of Voegelin's act of resistance should be seen in light of that reality.[17]

17 My examples are intended to offer context for understanding the opening section of the meditation, but they shouldn't be mistaken as implying that Voegelin's point is now dated. As I write this in 2022, Afghanistan has been re-taken by the Taliban, which is resuming its project of "purification;" Africa is now tormented by the likes of Boko Haram, Al-Shabab, and the Lord's Re-

Regardless of how readers may regard the striking opening of the document today, Voegelin himself draws attention immediately to an important flaw in the passage by noting that, "...the two sentences, reflecting in everyday language on a familiar situation, not only introduce the activist corruption as the object to be explored analytically; they also present, by their very formulation, an instance of the corruption itself." The particular problem lies in Voegelin's felt need to use "...the term *Utopian* in its activist meaning..." in the two sentences "...if they were to achieve their purpose of establishing a preliminary consensus about the topic without lengthy explanations...."[18] By contrast to the "activist meaning" of Utopia as a symbolism, he recalls the original meaning created by Thomas More to illustrate what a society might be like if not marred by the *superbia vitae* (or pride of life), noting that More "knows what he has omitted and is conscious of his truncated image of reality as a Nowhere." In the "activist meaning," a "Utopia still means the model of a perfect society that cannot be realized because an important sector of reality has been omitted from its construction, but *its author and addicts have suspended their consciousness* that it is unrealizable because of the omission."[19]

Before returning momentarily to these remarks on Thomas More, we should observe that Voegelin's wording here is tellingly indicative of several important aspects of his account of spiritual revolt and activism in "Wisdom and Magic." First, it bears emphasizing that the locus of the problem is identified as *consciousness* (specifically, consciousness in the "in-between" tension of existence strung between lived imperfection and the imaginary possibility of perfection), rather than in the practical or historical or literary realms. Second, both the authors who create activist utopias in the first place and those who are subsequently "addicted" to them are implicated, and in both categories, it is a "suspension of consciousness" that is at issue, rather than ignorance or brainwashing; the problem is not cognitive or

sistance Army, and Daniel Ortega now rules as tyrant in Nicaragua in ways closely resembling those of Anastasio Somoza Debayle, whom Ortega and his Sandinista comrades were struggling to overthrow in the late 1970s. As older forms of messianism based on claims of secret knowledge abate, others arise, as in the case of QAnon. Adding other current examples would be all too easy.

18 "Wisdom and Magic," 315–16, emphasis in original.

19 Ibid., 316, emphasis added.

psychological, but rather personal and spiritual. Third, Voegelin's wording suggests that the problem at issue involves an important element of volition or will, which is to say, the authors and addicts are aware to some extent that the desired utopia is unrealizable, but choose to suspend their consciousness of that fact, which again shows that the phenomenon is at root personal and spiritual.

These aspects of "Wisdom and Magic" can be illustrated by considering how Voegelin addresses Thomas More (whom he wisely considers at the outset of the meditation) and Karl Marx, who is noted as "a model case" and an "astute connoisseur of his own dream story."[20] Viewing More in historical retrospect, having witnessed multiple modern disasters that ensued from attempts to actualize "utopias," we can observe with some justification that he was playing with fire when elaborating what Voegelin terms his "… dream of a supposedly perfect society by eliminating from its structure an important sector of reality…."[21] What More omitted was "…the *superbia vitae*"… "the pride of life in the sense of John 2 : 16" … "but he knows what he has omitted and is conscious of his truncated image of reality as a Nowhere."[22] Playing with fire is not the same as actually setting fire to something, which is what an activist dreamer does when acting on the dream, and consequently Voegelin goes on to observe that,

> In its contemporary usage by activist thinkers and nonthinkers, the meaning of the symbol has been transformed in a peculiar manner. A Utopia still means the model of a perfect society that cannot be realized because an important sector of reality has been omitted from its construction, but its author and addicts have suspended their consciousness that it is unrealizable because of the omission.[23]

This formulation is very helpful because it shows how "utopian thinking" or "utopian dreaming" is understandable in the context of an analysis of

20 Ibid., 319 and 318 for the two quotations, respectively.
21 Ibid., 316.
22 Ibid.
23 Ibid.

consciousness—specifically, consciousness in the tension of existence in the *metaxy*.

On one hand, Thomas More is aware of the fact that the human being is strung between an imperfect existence and a perfect one that can be imagined by subtracting human sin, and he effectively highlights the sin of pride and its consequences in "real life" by means of his imagination. The activist dreamer is likewise aware of the imperfection of existence, and shares the capability of imagining a perfected one. However, an activist dreamer such as Marx seeks to excise imperfections by violent means after altering his consciousness in a way that More did not, specifically, by suspending his consciousness that what he seeks to excise is a feature of human life that is natural and, consequently, immutable. In the specifics of Marx's case, he suspends his consciousness of the natural and immutable human characteristics of selfishness and acquisitiveness. To say that he "suspends his consciousness," is to employ an active verb, and rightly so, as Marx's utopia is not the result of an "oversight" or a "mistake." Rather, Marx sets out to theoretically *work his way around* the immutable characteristic of acquisitiveness by contriving a "materialist conception of history" in which selfishness and greed can be attributed to mutable phases in the history of human production rather than immutable attributes of human nature. He then issues a call for violent revolution that will usher in a property-less and hence classless society.

We know of the horrors that resulted from others answering Marx's call, so those need not be detailed for the moment. We also know that Marx himself never physically killed anyone in the course of his career as a "revolutionary," so we may say that he was also playing with fire, but in a different sense than Thomas More. He was an *activist* dreamer, which is to say (picking up on Voegelin's phrasing) that he "authored" a dream and then called for its actualization, with the result that gun-toting "addicts" of Marx's prospect of a perfected world free from scarcity, inequality, political struggle or stultifying labor put the torch to "real life" and killed millions while trying to actualize Marx's dream—which was a dream arising precisely from the tension of existence in the *metaxy* in which real life is imperfect but perfection can nevertheless be imagined. Understood in this light, Marx is not innocent simply because he never shot anybody. He is guilty, but to be precise, he is guilty on grounds of peddling addictive utopian dreams, peddling them with all the brilliance at his disposal and peddling them with calls for violence to achieve their actualization.[24] His guilt is of a different sort than that of communist functionaries who built party membership and engaged in various sorts of organizational activities, just as their guilt is different from those who did indeed shoot people. Marxists are not all of one piece, and they cannot all be "diagnosed" in a uniform manner, as one's emphasis when speaking of "activist dreamers" should fall on the noun in some cases but the adjective in others. However, their varying sorts of guilt (and the varied spiritual disorders underlying them) can all be understood in the context of the *metaxy*, as I believe this account demonstrates. To be clear, Voegelin was very explicit and precise on this last point, as the passage from which I've been working here is followed immediately in "Wisdom and Magic" by a cautionary observation that is among the most important of the many he wrote on political, ideological, or "religious" extremism over seven decades of work:

> I am speaking cautiously of a suspension of consciousness, because it frequently is difficult, if not impossible, to determine in the case of an individual activist whether the suspension is an act of intellectual fraud or of persuasive self-deception, whether it is a case of plain illiteracy or of the more sophisticated illiteracy imposed by an educational system, whether it is caused by a degree of spiritual and intellectual insensitivity that comes under the head of stupidity, or whether it is due to various combinations of these and other factors such as the desire to attract public attention and make a career.[25]

24 Marx's peddling of addictive utopian dreams—after suspending his consciousness of the natural and permanent attributes of human beings that would prevent the actualization of his dreams—explains why Voegelin was justified in identifying him as a "swindler" in a 1958 lecture in Munich that resulted in a "shocked reaction." On the reaction, see Henningsen's "Introduction" to *Modernity without Restraint,* 3; for Voegelin's identification of Marx as a swindler, see *Science, Politics, and Gnosticism*, in *Modernity without Restraint, CWEV* Vol. 5, 264–65.

25 "Wisdom and Magic," 316.

This passage's importance is at least twofold. First, it bespeaks a more nuanced appreciation of the variety of factors and motivations underlying instances of spiritual revolt and activism than was indicated in almost all Voegelin's earlier accounts of ideological or "Gnostic" movements. Second, in its focus on "the case of an individual activist," it displays a methodological advance (or at minimum a refinement) in recognizing that neither "movements" nor "ideologies" are the proper units of analysis once the work of diagnosing instances of spiritual revolt is founded on a theory of consciousness rather than a history of ideas approach.

The quoted rundown of the multiplicity of possible factors and motivations underlying perfectionist activism is certainly not exhaustive, and though Voegelin could easily have lengthened it,[26] the implication is clear: he was moving away from the sweeping "diagnoses" seen in earlier works, which not only spanned widespread movements involving widely dissimilar individuals, but even entire eras. For example, in *The New Science of Politics*, Voegelin saw fit to entitle one of his chapters, "Gnosticism: The Nature of Modernity" and, in a famous passage toward the end of the book, wrote of

> ...a civilizational cycle of world-historic proportions. There emerge the contours of a giant cycle, transcending the cycles of the single civilizations. The acme of this cycle would be marked by the appearance of Christ; the pre-Christian high civilizations would form its ascending branch; modern Gnostic civilization would form its descending branch.[27]

26 It is not difficult to compile long lists of differing motivations for activist individuals in extremist movements, but doing so is important in the interest of scientific accuracy when addressing such movements in a "diagnostic" manner. For examples as well as a rationale, see my "Spiritual Disorder and Terrorism: On Barry Cooper's *New Political Religions*," in *Hunting and Weaving: Empiricism and Political Philosophy*, Thomas Heilke and John von Heyking, eds., St. Augustine's Press, 2013, 91–114, esp. 104–07.

27 Voegelin, *The New Science of Politics: An Introduction* (1952), in *Modernity without Restraint: The Political Religions; The New Science of Politics; and Science, Politics and Gnosticism*, ed. Manfred Henningsen, *CWEV* Vol. 5, 2000, 221. Hereafter cited as Voegelin, *NSP*.

This passage, with its reference to something as broad as a "Gnostic civilization," is starkly different from Voegelin's careful meditative exploration of the psycho-spiritual attractiveness of "the magic of the extreme," which is almost always considered as an attractiveness to individual "activist dreamers" in the meditation as published in 1983. However, seasoned readers of Voegelin's *oeuvre* learn to be careful not to over-estimate the shifts and turns displayed across his writings; later works often seem to depart more from earlier ones than turns out to be the case on fuller examination.[28] With that caveat noted, "Wisdom and Magic" addresses spiritual disorder in a manner that is indisputably different than that of *The New Science*; there is nothing in the pages of the meditation to support the notion of something like a "Gnostic civilization."

Understanding "Wisdom and Magic" in Light of *The Ecumenic Age*

Still, it is very important to be measured when assessing the degree to which "Wisdom and Magic" breaks from earlier works like *The New Science* and *Science, Politics and Gnosticism*, neither dispensing with earlier treatments that retain merit nor ignoring the advances in "Wisdom and Magic" that should be fully appreciated despite the meditation's more challenging form and method. Arriving at such a measured assessment can be aided significantly by considering the shifts in Voegelin's thinking set forth in the most important work published in the interim separating these works, namely, *The Ecumenic Age*, published in 1974 as Vol. IV of *Order and History.*

28 Unfortunately, not all Voegelin's readers can be characterized accurately as fully "seasoned readers." *The New Science* is a challenging book, but the challenges that it poses pale by comparison to the additional challenges of working through *Anamnesis* and the theory of consciousness developed there, not to mention the rigors required to absorb the altered philosophy of history set out in *The Ecumenic Age*. As I shall argue more fully here, these tasks stand as prerequisites for appreciating fully the meditative exploration set out in "Wisdom and Magic," but it is evident that not all of those who see fit to write about Voegelin's views have taken up these tasks. Although I'm alluding to something bordering on laziness here, that is not quite what I have in mind, as anyone who has achieved a deep appreciation of *The New Science* is hardly lazy. But neither can they be said to have completed the work that Voegelin set out for his readers—by a long shot.

Judging from a review of the secondary literature on *The Ecumenic Age* (and characterizations of Voegelin's work that continue to appear), the importance of this book for understanding his evolving analysis of spiritual disorder and revolt remains under-appreciated among scholars. Early reviews of the book were overwhelmingly devoted to accounts of a methodological "break" announced by Voegelin from his initial plan for *Order and History* and especially to expressions of surprise, disappointment, and even anger regarding the book's treatment of Christianity. These issues effectively overshadowed shifts from the writing on "Gnosticism" in *The New Science*, but the shifts are present nonetheless in *The Ecumenic Age*, and they point in the direction to be seen in "Wisdom and Magic."

Voegelin's analysis in *The New Science* had been, at once, specific, wide-ranging, vehement, and exhortatory. In 1974, readers who opened *The Ecumenic Age* in search of a similarly stirring account of the development of gnosis as the symbolic form of modern national states (as suggested by the program announced in *Israel and Revelation*), were to find something quite different. These differences surely displeased some readers, especially those who heard a sort of pro-Christian, anti-modern rallying cry in Voegelin's earlier writings on gnosticism. In *The Ecumenic Age*, Voegelin no longer seemed inclined to identify gnosticism and modernity, or to limit it to any particular period in time, or to associate it with historical occurrences that could even keep it circumscribed within the West. The range of thinkers and activists associated with gnosticism was expanded, but expanded in an unanticipated and perhaps unwelcome manner to include Christian figures and influences.[29] Whereas *The New Science* spoke of an immediate crisis in which the forces of civilization are arrayed against identifiable enemies arising from a specific historical process and marked by a pronounced "otherness," *The Ecumenic Age* deprived would-be anti-gnostic combatants of their marching orders by stripping the conflict of much of its particularity in terms of time and place, and by making it much harder to distinguish friend from foe.

29 To quote but one example: "Considering the history of Gnosticism, with the great bulk of its manifestations belonging to, or deriving from, the Christian orbit, I am inclined to recognize in the epiphany of Christ the great catalyst that made eschatological consciousness an historical force both in forming and deforming humanity." *The Ecumenic Age*, 65–66.

Voegelin's immersion in the theory of consciousness is the single most fruitful line of explanation for the alteration of his analysis of spiritual disorder between the years 1952-1957 (which saw publication of *The New Science* and the first three volumes of *Order and History*) and 1974-1977 (which included publication of *The Ecumenic Age* and presentation of "Wisdom and Magic" at the Eranos Conference). We shall see that Voegelin's analysis was also altered in response to his encounter with new historical source materials between 1957 and 1974, but the task of understanding the evolution of his thinking that led to "Wisdom and Magic" is best begun with consideration of his immersion in problems in the theory of consciousness. This resulted in the development of a largely original theory that was expressed most extensively in the German edition of *Anamnesis* and which radicalized Voegelin's break with the history of ideas approach that characterized his writings prior to 1950, which was still present to a reduced degree in *The New Science* and the first three volumes of *Order and History*. It is difficult to summarize the change in Voegelin's diagnosis of spiritual disorder and gnosticism across these years without losing some important nuances, but I believe the following formulation is not misleading: the change involved *a shift from viewing instances of gnostic thought and action as connected events in literary history to viewing them as independent but essentially equivalent events in consciousness.*[30]

Before the shift, Voegelin wrote as if later instances of gnostic thought resulted from influences from earlier writings. When considered in this way, it made sense to trace the gnosticism of one such as, say, Marx, back to the ancient Gnostics by noting the intervening figures who served as transmitters;

30 Two caveats should be noted here. First, I describe the change that became apparent in *The Ecumenic Age* as a shift because one can find passages in writings prior to the book (including passages in *The New Science of Politics*) in which Voegelin seems to lean toward treating gnosticism as an event in consciousness. It would be an overstatement to suggest that the change is a simple, before-and-after affair, with *The Ecumenic Age* lying between the before and the after. Second, the proposition that independently arising gnostic phenomena such as, say, Joachitic millennialism and Marxian speculation on the imminent rise of communism are "essentially equivalent" is controversial and extremely complicated. I have pursued the issue at considerable length in *Eric Voegelin and the Politics of Spiritual Revolt.*

Marx was an admirer of Thomas Münzer, who was in turn a follower of Joachim of Flora, who was in turn acquainted with ancient Gnostic writings. Or, to use another example, the Puritan sectarians noted by Voegelin as exemplars of gnosticism may be said to have acquired gnostic or quasi-gnostic patterns of thought from sects such as the Ortliebians, Paracletes, and Adamites, who may have been inspired by the Albigensians, who may have been influenced by the writings of Scotus Erigena, whose views were affected by the still-earlier writings of Pseudo-Dionysius.[31] Following this approach to gnosticism, it would make sense to speak of a gnostic "stream" in history that may swell at certain times while receding at others, or to refer to certain periods (such as the Renaissance or the mid-19th century) as periods marked by a "growth" of gnosticism. However, if one follows the approach to gnosticism that first became fully apparent in *The Ecumenic Age*, such notions no longer make sense.

While continuing this account of the development of "Wisdom and Magic" by reference to *The Ecumenic Age* and Voegelin's late work more generally, we should pause to make two observations. The first is that the term "Gnosticism" is entirely absent from "Wisdom and Magic," and the word "Gnostic" appears only three times, with each usage seemingly pointing to the "historical Gnostics" rather than to spiritual disorder in a general, conceptual manner. Second, Voegelin's account of spiritual disorder in the meditation is largely dissociated from particular historical periods or chains of literary influence and is established instead on an analysis of human consciousness that is more perennial in nature than historical in the sense of being developmental or sequential.

The importance of these dimensions of "Wisdom and Magic" can hardly be overstated, and the principal reason is that these attributes remain underappreciated even among scholars who are conversant with Voegelin's work. This is evinced by the continuing appearance of writings arguing for the continuing theoretical viability of the concept of gnosticism within Voegelin's work on disordered spirituality.[32] Why this continues to be the

31 On these connections see Eugene Webb, *Eric Voegelin: Philosopher of History*, 199–204.

32 Such writings are not all of one piece. Some acknowledge important shifts in Voegelin's thought but argue that these can still be appreciated while retaining

case in secondary expositions on Voegelin's thought is a matter for speculation, but plausible hypotheses include the much greater difficulty of the account in "Wisdom and Magic" than the one in *The New Science*, which results from the much greater difficulty of work in the philosophy of consciousness than the history of ideas. Additionally, the account in *The New Science* is much more suitable for polemical purposes by the Christian conservatives who remain very prominent among Voegelin's admirers in North America, whereas the account in *Wisdom and Magic* ultimately encourages

gnosticism as his central diagnostic concept, e.g., James L. Wiser, "From Cultural Analysis to Philosophical Anthropology: An Examination of Voegelin's Concept of Gnosticism," *The Review of Politics*, Vol. 42, no. 1, 1980, 92–104. By contrast, in a 2021 publication Voegelin was characterized as though "Gnosticism" could accurately reflect his lifelong analysis of spiritual disorder in retrospect, namely, Paul Gottfried's "Remembering Eric Voegelin: Anti-Gnostic Warrior" in *Chronicles*. His assessment utilizes none of Voegelin's late writings and mischaracterizes his fully evolved thinking in passages such as this: "As far as his own theological position was discernible, he was a Neoplatonist with strong mystical proclivities, who hated modern totalitarians. His widely expressed distaste for Gnostics may have hidden Voegelin's own attraction to Gnostic ideas, for example, his stress on an inward awareness of spiritual truth and his lack of interest in conventional religious ritual. Most Gnostics came out of a Neoplatonic tradition of thought, but moved from there into a heretical form of Christianity. Still, according to Voegelin, they had fallen into disastrous error. They allowed themselves to become derailed and went from their exploration of being into projects of cosmic transformation. From there it was only one more step to the dangerous revolutionary religions of the modern world, in which Gnostic elements were still allegedly present." I believe Voegelin would bristle at the suggestion that he held a "theological position" (and that Jürgen Gebhardt, Gregor Sebba, Ellis Sandoz, and Peter Opitz were among his "disciples"), but more to the point, one wonders what it means to suggest that the historical Gnostics engaged in "projects of cosmic transformation," or what was involved in the "only one more step" that led to the activism of atheistic modern ideologies. Casting the most philosophically insightful and historically sweeping analysis of the perennial phenomenon of spiritual revolt as the work of an "Anti-Gnostic Warrior" is particularly lamentable, but mischaracterizations are virtually inevitable among those who limit themselves to what Voegelin wrote in the 1950s. See https://www.chroniclesmagazine.org/remembering-eric-voegelin—anti-gnostic-warrior a measure of understanding and even empathy for those who cannot manage the great difficulty of maintaining "the balance of consciousness," as we shall see. An additional hypothesis is that many admirers of Voegelin during his life (as well as some of his students and their students in turn) were very disappointed in *The Ecumenic Age* and either would not—or could not—embrace its philosophical underpinnings, which are prerequisites for appreciating the important advancements in analysis of spiritual disorder embodied in "Wisdom and Magic."

Be that as it may, having shown how Voegelin's analysis of "Gnosticism" or "gnosticism"[33] was altered by his studies in the theory of consciousness, it should also be noted that changes were dictated by the historical materials that he encountered between 1957 and 1974. In the *Introduction* to *The Ecumenic Age*, Voegelin notes that as his

> ...knowledge of materials increased, the original list of five types of order and symbolization turned out to be regrettably limited; and when the empirical basis on which the study had to rest was broadened so as to conform to the state of the historical sciences, the manuscript swelled to a size that easily would have filled six more volumes in print. That situation was awkward enough. What ultimately broke the project, however, was the impossibility of aligning the empirical types in any time sequence at all that would permit the structures actually found to emerge from a history conceived as a "course."...[T]he conception was untenable because it had not taken proper account of

33 Readers who skipped over footnote 4 above to concentrate on the main text of this commentary would do well to circle back to it for my initial explanation of the thorny problem of capitalization of this word. This is an interpretive and even theoretical problem rather than a mere stylistic matter. I acknowledge that shifting between renderings of the term can be confusing or even irritating, but is nevertheless necessary for distinguishing between Gnosticism and what we know about the historical Gnostics, on one hand, and the use of this term to characterize a much broader pattern of spiritual disorder on the other. In this latter usage, "gnosticism" can have almost nothing to do with the Gnostics and may even be a pan-historical problem for humanity as cast by Voegelin within the tension of existence in the metaxy.

> the important lines of meaning in history that did not run along lines of time.[34]

Once Voegelin had taken proper account of the lines of meaning that did not run along lines of time, he rejected the conception of history as a *course* in favor of the view that history "is not a stream of human beings and their actions in time, but the process of man's participation in a flux of divine presence that has eschatological direction."[35] These dramatic shifts in Voegelin's conception of history as a whole carried similarly dramatic implications for conceiving the history of "Gnosticism" in the sense in which he had used that term in *The New Science*. If it no longer made sense to speak of a course when conceiving of history as a whole, it could no longer make sense to conceive of the history of gnosticism as a "course" or a "stream" or an "unbroken continuum of movements"[36] leading from the ancient writings through a series of medieval sectarian transmitters to the "modern gnostics" of the ideological movements. Moreover, if history was "definitely not a story of meaningful events to be arranged on a time line," but rather a "movement through a web of meaning with a plurality of nodal points" requiring an analysis that "had to move backward and forward and sideways,"[37] then it could hardly make sense to focus on blocks of time as the meaningful units in history.

Additionally, if blocks of time were not meaningful units, they could not be adequately described by reference to any single element, however prominent. Thus, from the perspective on history that informs *The Ecumenic Age*, it could no longer make sense to speak—as Voegelin had in *The New Science of Politics*—of Gnosticism as "the nature of modernity." Indeed, once Voegelin began viewing instances of gnostic thought and activity through the lens of his philosophy of consciousness, he found that even when the instances were separated by many centuries and by widely varying civilizational circumstances, they exhibited remarkable parallels as aggressive

34 Voegelin, *The Ecumenic Age*, 46.

35 Ibid., 50.

36 See Voegelin, *Order and History, Vol. I: Israel and Revelation* (1956), ed. Maurice P. Hogan, *CWEV* Vol. 14, 508.

37 *The Ecumenic Age*, 106.

reactions to a human condition which does not—in its essentials—vary over time. Consequently, the Eric Voegelin who could, in 1952, admonish readers to "recognize the essence of modernity as the growth of Gnosticism" could later, after finding that modern ideologues were exemplars of a disordered consciousness also observed in the ancient world, ask the question in 1974: "What exactly was modern about modernity…?"[38] Thus we can see that Voegelin's studies in the theory of consciousness and his transformed conception of the structure of history combined to produce a significant alteration of his analysis of "gnosticism." By comparison to the analysis of *The New Science of Politics*, his treatment in *The Ecumenic Age* is vastly more intricate and sophisticated, and the treatment in "Wisdom and Magic" is more sophisticated still. Indeed, just as Voegelin concluded in 1974 that, "…the project of *Order and History* as originally conceived had to be abandoned,"[39] he also chose to essentially abandon usage of the term "Gnosticism" when first presenting "Wisdom and Magic" in 1977—along with some of the fundamental presuppositions underlying the usage of that term in 1952's *New Science of Politics.*

Conceptualizing Spiritual Revolt in "Wisdom and Magic"

As noted above, across the 60 pages of *Wisdom and Magic* in the *Collected Works* edition, the term "Gnostic" appears only three times—and the term "Gnosticism" is entirely absent. The first appearance of "Gnostic" on p. 338 in a reference to "Gnostic thinkers" is a reference to the *historical* Gnostics in the era shortly following the appearance of Christ; this is made clear by Voegelin's connection of the term to a "…myth of a fall in the realm of divinity" that attributed "…the creation of the world…to an evil demiurge, to a devil." To sharpen my point here, we can simply observe that Voegelin uses the word "Gnostic" as a specific noun rather than a

38 Ibid., 52; see also p. 118, where Voegelin poses the question, "…what is modern about the modern mind, one may ask, if Hegel, Comte, or Marx, in order to create an image of history that will support their ideological imperialism, still use the same techniques for distorting the reality of history as their Sumerian predecessors?"

39 Ibid., 106.

categorical adjective, as he often did in *The New Science* to refer to a whole slew of outbursts both ancient and modern. The third usage of "Gnostic" on p. 366 is also indisputably a reference to the historical Gnostics, as the time frame is identified as falling "...as early as the second century A.D., under the pressure of the Marcionite and Gnostic movements." Only the second usage of "Gnostic," on p. 339, could be characterized with any plausibility as a reference to modernity or modern persons. At that point in the text, the term does not stand on its own, but is utilized in a reference to "the Gnostic-satanistic movements" that probably points back to the first reference (on the preceding page) and its mention of the historical Gnostics, with the term "satanistic" picking up on Voegelin's noting of their references to "...an evil demiurge, to a devil." This third, rather indeterminate usage of "Gnostic" is murky in part because it arises in the midst of a remarkably long sentence (including four semicolons as well as a grammatical "em dash") that identifies all sorts of misconceptions, doctrines, and ideologies that have "...piled up such mountains of incidental debate on the problems of vision and noesis that incisive reflections on the form Plato has given to it have become rare among modern thinkers." I will cite the entire sentence in a footnote to let readers judge for themselves without overburdening the main text here.[40] To state the upshot simply, the textual evidence weighs

40 "The medieval misconception of classic philosophy as an enterprise to find the truth of reality by 'natural reason'; the doctrinaire distinction between 'natural reason' and 'supernatural revelation' as the sources of truth; the consequent development of the distinction into the two truth enterprises of 'theology' on the one side, and of 'metaphysics,' 'ontology,' and 'critical' philosophy on the other side; the hardening of these doctrinal issues into the popular opposition of 'religion' and 'science'; the doctrinal subconflicts among 'theologies' since the sixteenth century and among their successor doctrines, the 'ideologies,' since the eighteenth century—all this doctrinal abundance and conflict, further aggravated and complicated by the growth of, and interaction with, the Gnostic-satanistic movements, has piled such mountains of incidental debate on the problems of vision and noesis that incisive reflections on the form Plato has given to it have become rare among modern thinkers." Voegelin, "Wisdom and Magic," 339. I believe any fair reading of this sentence yields the finding that Voegelin is no longer using "Gnostic" here as a categorical adjective under which all the many misbegotten ideologies and movements of modernity can be subsumed, as he did in *The New Science*. The fact

overwhelmingly against those who maintain that "Gnostic" or "Gnosticism" remained Voegelin's core diagnostic concept for designating spiritual disorder in the most fully developed phase of his thought. Issues of word choice aren't sufficient by themselves to demonstrate the broader point that Voegelin's analysis of disordered spirituality in "Wisdom and Magic" departs in important ways from the analysis of *The New Science*, but they are indicative of an important change that can be demonstrated with supplementary observations.

Whereas the term "Gnosticism" is conspicuous by its absence from "Wisdom and Magic" in the way it was employed in *The New Science* (as a general concept for the perennial phenomenon of spiritual revolt or "pneumopathology"), the meditation bristles with references to "*activist dreamer*" as the diagnostic term Voegelin had chosen instead by 1977. In just the first 13 pages of the meditation, well before "Gnostic" appears at all, Voegelin employs either the singular or plural version of "activist dreamer" 6 times, "activist" 28 times, and "dreamer" in 15 instances. Hopefully simple arithmetic will suffice to establish with finality the point that Voegelin effectively abandoned the concept of Gnosticism while still working at the peak of his powers, which he came very close to doing at a 1978 conference devoted to "Gnosticism and Modernity."[41] That may be too much to hope

that he notes "ideologies" apart from "the Gnostic-satanistic movements" is probably enough to prove the point all by itself, given that in *The New Science* Voegelin wrote of ideologies as exceptionally important manifestations of "Gnosticism." If that point isn't regarded as conclusive, one might ask whether the author of this sentence still believed that "Gnosticism" was "The Nature of Modernity"—or rather believed merely that certain movements which could be likened in their doctrines to the historical Gnostics by way of analogy were among the many tributaries into what we call "modernity."

41 I use the term "abandoned" advisedly, echoing the verb chosen by Voegelin in *The Ecumenic Age* when announcing his "break" from the original program for *Order and History*. That break did not sit well with admirers of Voegelin's earlier writings who chose to stay seated rather than follow him on his philosophical quest, as I have written elsewhere. See my "Gnosticism and Spiritual Disorder in The Ecumenic Age," *The Political Science Reviewer* (Vol. 27, 1998), 17–43, and "Editor's Introduction" to Voegelin, *The Ecumenic Age*, 18–23. Yet the forcefulness of his word choice left no doubt about the options provided to his readers, and it might have been better if Voegelin had been equally

for realistically, as the arresting term "Gnosticism" has kept Voegelin's admirers and even serious scholars arrested for 70 years. However, it may help to inquire into *why* Voegelin emphasized "activist dreamer" in "Wisdom and Magic," and to show what he emphasizes as the key characteristics of the human beings he designated by use of this term.

To explore this carefully even at the risk of being wearisome for a bit, we can begin with the simple observation that not all dreamers are activists, nor are all activists "dreamers" in the senses in which Voegelin uses the term. Moreover, it is possible for "activist dreamers" to be distinct from activists or dreamers, and not just terminologically but also in psycho-spiritual terms. So, for example, most of what we know about the historical Gnostics suggests that they were dreamers but not activists. They turned their backs on the physical world, so to speak, rather than seeking to transform it (and this is a key reason why the name of their sect is so problematic when used in relation to modern ideologists). Continuing, we know from thousands of examples that a high percentage of rank-and-file activists in movements bent on pragmatic world transformation are not dreamers (nor much troubled with thinking, an observation made famous by Hannah Arendt under the heading of "the banality of evil"). We know this is true regarding a high percentage of rank-and-file extremist activists of all sorts, including Nazis, Marxists, and terrorists of all stripes, ranging from old-style secular ones to members of so-called "new" terror organizations engaged in causes that are purportedly religious, regardless of the religion in question.[42] The activist

forceful regarding the concept of Gnosticism, employing a term like "abandoned" rather than simply noting at a conference in 1978 (devoted to "Gnosticism and Modernity" at Vanderbilt University) that he would "...probably not use that term now if he were starting over again...." Quoted in Webb, *Eric Voegelin: Philosopher of History*, 200.

42 An exceptionally careful, balanced, and inclusive treatment of the range of motivations to be found at the level of the individual in violent extremist organizations is provided by Jessica Stern's *Terror in the Name of God: Why Religious Militants Kill* (Ecco / HarperCollins), 2003. For a more extended account of why it is methodologically problematic to use diagnostic terms like "pneumopathology" or "gnosticism" in connection with organizations or sects, see my "Caution and Clarity in Thinking About ISIS and Apocalyptic Activism," VoegelinView.com, January 21, 2018: https://voegelinview.com/caution-clarity-thinking-isis-apocalyptic-activism/

dreamers who are treated so frequently and searchingly in "Wisdom and Magic" are neither world-denying escapists (who are benign in pragmatic terms) nor gun-toting order-followers (who are hardly benign but aren't self-directed world transformers). As for specific individuals who are discussed as examples of activist dreamers in "Wisdom and Magic," the three who are addressed repeatedly are Hegel, Marx, and Nietzsche, but it is clear that the "set" is much more inclusive than just "thinkers" such as these three. Although their influence shouldn't be minimized, their influence as three individuals doesn't add up to a situation in which "...all of us are threatened in our humanity, if not in our physical existence, by the massive social force of activist dreamers who want to liberate us from our imperfections by locking us up in the perfect prison of their phantasy."[43] Many followers of different types are required to add up to a "massive social force," and though a high percentage of activists don't think or dream vividly enough to fit Voegelin's description of "activist dreamers," there remain plenty of activists (hundreds of thousands), who really do set out to purify and perfect the world according to a dream they've consciously adopted of building a propertyless society or a thousand-year Reich or a post-apocalyptic paradise free from infidels and apostates. Hegel, Marx, and Nietzsche are utilized in "Wisdom and Magic" because they were thoughtful enough to understand and express the revolt against imperfection they were engaged in—and candid or arrogant enough to disclose it. The precise nature of this revolt and the motivations underlying it offer the key to understanding who and what Voegelin had in mind when writing of "activist dreamers."

"Revolt" is a dramatic word, of course, more so than "reform," but less broadly dramatic than "revolution," because revolts can be either personal or political, whereas revolutions are always widespread events that seek to overturn a public state of affairs, whether it be political, social, or economic. As it is analyzed in "Wisdom and Magic," the revolt with which Voegelin is concerned is not at first a public event but rather a personal reaction at the level of the individual soul among those who cannot bear the tension of existence in the *metaxy*. As he notes early in the meditation, "The dreamers do not want to reform this or that situation considered to be imperfect and capable of improvement; their drive is a radical revolt against the real agony

43 "Wisdom and Magic," 315.

of man's existence in the tension of imperfection and perfection."[44] The precision of this sentence is impressive, conveying the difference between a spiritual revolt and a commonsense effort at reform, but it also conveys something close to a paradox that can be overlooked if read too quickly: the "dreamers" are by definition not engaged in a realistic endeavor, but the state of affairs they revolt against is real, and indeed a "real agony." This empathetic insight—which differs significantly from the combative approach expressed frequently in *The New Science*—isn't merely dropped into the text in passing, but is spelled out in detail (twice) before Voegelin places it back in the context of a revolt against reality (twice) in the following passage:

> There is enough "darkness" in reality to provide the grievances from which a revolt can start. The life of man is really burdened with the well-known miseries enumerated by Hesiod. We remember his list of hunger, hard work, disease, early death, and the fear of the injustices to be suffered by the weaker man at the hands of the more powerful—not to mention the problem of Pandora. Still, as long as our existence is undeformed by phantasies, these miseries are not experienced as senseless. We understand them as the lot of man, mysterious it is true, but as the lot he has to cope with in the organization and conduct of his life, in the fight for survival, the protection of his dependents, and the resistance to injustice, and in his spiritual and intellectual response to the mystery of existence. The burden of existence loses its sense, and becomes absurd, only when a dreamer believes himself to possess the power of transfiguring imperfect existence into a lasting state of perfection.[45]

These "miseries" are real, but the dream of transfiguring imperfect existence into a lasting state of perfection is an ages-old pathology of the spirit and a revolt against reality. Naturally, even a dreamer can't hope to transfigure existence by himself, so action is required to enlist others in the effort, which is the point at which a dreamer becomes an activist dreamer.

44 Ibid., 317.
45 Ibid., 318.

The action taken is typically the initiation of a project to identify in writing a key cause of the most miserable imperfections, along with construction of a reasonably plausible project for turning the key in a way that can eradicate them. Voegelin writes of these aspects of a revolt as the writing of a "dream story" that can enlist others in actions to erect a "dream world."[46] As examples of such dream stories or "second realities" he notes progressivism, positivism, behaviorism, Marxism, and Fascism, and notes that it wouldn't have mattered if "…the example chosen [for detailed examination] had not been the construction of Marx but that of Comte, Hegel or Freud."[47] Enlistment efforts of this type by an activist dreamer will succeed or fail based on whether or not the effort to "…eclipse our image of reality by a counterimage…will furnish a plausible basis for the action he calls for. In order to serve this purpose it must fulfill two conditions: it must cover the structure of reality with sufficient comprehensiveness to appear, by the standard prevailing at the time, debatable as a true image; and it must be analytically obscure enough not to reveal its character of a dream image at the first glance."[48]

In a move that shows how far Voegelin had shifted in his method and emphasis from his *History of Political Ideas* to the consciousness-focused "Wisdom and Magic," he side-steps the task of "disproving" counterimage dream stories, based on the awareness that their contents are—however plausible and alluring—bad faith effluents of a spiritual revolt, which is where our attention should be targeted:

> If we were to accept the activist's counterimage as the "theory" it claims to be, as a theory to be verified or falsified on the positivistic level, we would play the activist's game, even if our examination of the details should turn out to be devastatingly negative.…Nevertheless, they are of symptomatic importance only and must not analytically obscure the intended analytical obscurity of the activist dreamer. Only if we disengage the dream story from the complicated counterimage can we bring

46 Ibid., 320–21.
47 Ibid.
48 Ibid., 318–19.

> the truly theoretical issue of reality and imaginative dreaming into focus.[49]

Voegelin elects to concentrate on the psycho-spiritual phenomenon of activist dreaming at the level of consciousness, side-stepping the particular claims in the "second reality" dream story, but never losing sight of what is at stake in the first reality. As he expressed this, ending with a crucial observation, Voegelin wrote:

> ...[E]ven if we reject this claim as nonsense, the dreamer who raises it with social effectiveness is still very much a part of the reality in which we live—as all too many who could not believe that totalitarian activists would inflict their murderous nonsense on real human beings had to discover to their grief. In the activist's claim, there is more at issue than the cognitional value

49 Ibid., 319–20. Some readers might well be alarmed when seeing Voegelin elect here to bypass rather than falsify the details of the writings he decries as spiritually disordered dream stories, and might regard my phrase "side-step" as a euphemism for a "dodge." I was concerned on this ground when first reading the meditation many years ago, but now think Voegelin was correct that the "truly theoretical issue" is understanding and conceptualizing the consciousness underlying an ideology, and that disproving an ideology's particulars is of secondary importance. The case of Marx and Marxist revolutions and regimes is illuminating in this regard. Neither countless volumes filled with scholarly refutations nor an innumerable sequence of broken promises and evident horrors could deflate the seductiveness of Marx's dream story for successive generations of new recruits, lending credibility to the assessment that neither the "theory" nor the "praxis" were the sources of Marxism's seductive powers in the first place. As for whether Voegelin was engaged in a "dodge" in the passage quoted here, consider the words that appear in the text at the point I added an ellipsis to shorten the quote: "The counter-image, it is true, may prove at odds with reality at numerous points; moreover, the activist may be discovered to indulge in gross falsifications of fact in order to protect the truth of his dream; and the phenomena of this class must certainly not be neglected in specialized studies of such counterimages. Even more, they usually are the phenomena that will bring the peculiar deformation of the activist's account to the observer's attention—at least they did so in the cases I have studied myself."

> of the dream; behind the claim that is untenable in rational discourse, there rises the will to identify dream and reality. We are faced with the ultimately murderous unwillingness to distinguish between dream and reality.[50]

What I have pointed to as the "crucial observation" that concludes this passage is a clause that can appear quite odd and possibly even incoherent on its face. For starters, "unwillingness" in relation to almost anything seems like a passive state, and it looks odd when set alongside a term like "murderous." Additionally, "dreamers" are hardly the most fearsome type that we encounter in everyday life. However, recalling that the "dream" issues from a revolt at the level of the spirit against a reality that is experienced as intolerably flawed, we can accurately re-phrase what Voegelin is pointing to as "a will to identify dream and reality," which in turn entails—in the most extreme cases—a will to burn down the real world in a futile attempt to erect a dream world on the smoldering wreckage left behind.

Not all cases are this extreme, but Voegelin continues from this point by recounting historical cases showing that the phenomenon in question, namely, "...a disturbance in the spiritual and intellectual order of the dreamer's existence," is an ages-old one, including eras prior to the historical Gnostics, and essentially unrelated to any particular age at all—because its taproot extends down to the fundamental and perennial reality of tensional existence in the *metaxy*. Voegelin notes that "...the Greek thinkers diagnosed it as a disease of the psyche...," indicating that "...Heraclitus and Aeschylus, and above all Plato, speak of the *nosos* or *nosema* of the psyche... ." He goes on to indicate that "The Stoics, especially Chrysippus, were intrigued by the phenomenon, and Cicero, summarizing the findings of the preceding centuries...calls it the *morbus animi*, the disease of the mind, and characterizes its nature as an *aspernatio rationis*, as a rejection of reason."[51]

50 Ibid., 321–22.

51 Ibid., 322. Voegelin also notes parallel diagnostic concepts such as "Second Reality" from Robert Musil and Heimito von Doderer, as well as Doderer's "refusal to apperceive reality," which he likens to Cicero's *aspernatio rationis*. Ibid., 323.

Following this historical catalogue of diagnoses, Voegelin returns to what he had characterized as "the ultimately murderous unwillingness to distinguish between dream and reality" with a formulation couched in more active language that is also much more striking and controversial: "When [the activist] acts, he expects such action to form the first reality into conformity with the Second Reality of his dream. The activist dreamer must know the trick action, as distinguished from ordinary action, that will have the extraordinary result of transfiguring the nature of things. *He must imagine himself to be a magician*."[52] This may be the most controversial sentence in the entire meditation, surprising those readers already versed in Voegelin's writings while eliciting dismissiveness or even derision among those new to his work, but who are familiar with works by Hegel, Marx, Nietzsche, and other figures noted in the course of "Wisdom and Magic."

Magic in "Wisdom and Magic"

For both groups noted above, the source of possible consternation is—of course—Voegelin's assertion that the set of individuals Voegelin had in mind when writing of "activist dreamers" imagined themselves to be magicians. For starters, I'll simply mention the reason why readers already steeped in Voegelin's writings might have been surprised by this when the meditation was first published in 1983, circling back to offer a likely explanation after addressing the even more important matter of why new readers should think twice before dismissing Voegelin's assertion.

For those who had been following Voegelin's work closely up to 1983, the question elicited by the sentence might be as simple as, "why just magic?" We know that, by 1971 at the latest, Voegelin had become interested in the role of "wisdom traditions" other than Gnosticism that flowed from earlier eras into modernity and possibly affected its course and character. Among the reasons for Voegelin's interest was that it became increasingly clear—due to archaeological finds made known after publication of *The New Science*—that the historical Gnostics were inclined much more toward rejection of the world rather than transformation of it. Given that the "gnosticism" that Voegelin had associated with "The Nature of Modernity" in *The New Science*

52 Ibid., 324. Emphasis added.

was radically, hubristically immanentist, there was an increasingly obvious problem of "fit" between the Gnostics and analyses subsumed by Voegelin in the category I am referencing as "gnosticism."[53] According to Stephen A. McKnight (a historian who is by far the Voegelin scholar most knowledgeable about this problem and the traditions connected with it) Voegelin took serious interest in the influence of Marsilio Ficino and other Renaissance Neoplatonists. Additionally, he writes that Voegelin delved into specialized scholarly monographs on the *prisca theologica*, a "...compendium of a wide array of esoteric religious and pseudoscientific traditions, including Orphism, Zoroastrianism, Hermeticism, Cabala, alchemy, and magic."[54] Eugene Webb adds apocalypticism, theurgy, and scientism" to this list,[55] and I don't doubt that we could lengthen this list with a little more digging. However, the list is already more than long enough to show the pertinence of the question, regarding the 1983 publication, "why just magic?"

Because we can't turn to Voegelin himself for an answer, there's no avoiding some measure of speculation when addressing the question. Those who are averse to speculation (or who read the word "speculation" as a euphemism for "guesswork") could scour the works of influential modern thinkers for traces of the nine "wisdom traditions" just identified, and then argue for the salience of the residues from the wisdom traditions in shaping the contours of the influential theories and ideologies. This would be more admirable than "guesswork," but not necessarily more fruitful, as only a moment of reflection is needed to conclude that this undertaking would land us back in a "history of ideas" approach that Voegelin himself rejected explicitly. As an alternative, I'd prefer to offer a simple but possibly compelling guess. Sometimes simplicity is a virtue, and if the reader will pardon a combination of clichés, here's a way to employ Occam's razor to cut the

53 For an especially valuable treatment of this problem—which is actually more like a thicket of problems—see Eugene Webb, "Voegelin's 'Gnosticism' Reconsidered," *The Political Science Reviewer*, Vol. 34, 2005, 48–76, esp. 50–61. Hereafter cited as Webb, "Voegelin's 'Gnosticism' Reconsidered."

54 Stephen A. McKnight, "Gnosticism and Modernity: Voegelin's Reconsiderations Twenty Years After *The New Science of Politics*," *The Political Science Reviewer*, Vol. 34, 2005, 122–42, esp. 128–29.

55 Webb, "Voegelin's 'Gnosticism' Reconsidered," 49.

Gordian Knot: Voegelin came to realize sometime in the late 1970s that it was pointless backsliding to accumulate spiritual or literary traditions as "tributaries" flowing into modernity that could supplement Gnosticism as influences explaining problematic aspects of modernity, for this reason: *To the degree that* any *of these traditions sought special knowledge or powers that could permanently transform human existence, they were reactions to the same trying aspects of the metaxy.* This seeking of special transformative powers or knowledge would—of course—make them somewhat akin to important strands that we associate with modernity. And yet, they should not be considered as "causes" of these strands in modernity, but rather as parallel instances of escapist efforts in relation to the same fundamental source, namely, the tension of human existence between imperfection and perfection. This is the view counseled by "Wisdom and Magic," though not the view of *The New Science*.

A few clarifications should be offered before we address the question of why only "magic" appears in "Wisdom and Magic," with these other wisdom traditions going unmentioned. When referring to "parallel instances of escapist efforts," I don't mean to suggest that there is no intersection or overlapping of what McKnight calls, "a wide array of esoteric religious and pseudoscientific traditions." We know that many individuals have inquired into a multiplicity of these wisdom traditions in ancient, medieval, and modern eras, and also across the time periods that have been conventionally named with those labels, with individuals looking "sideways" for insight from other traditions or "backwards" to earlier sources.[56] I don't intend the word "parallel" as it is used in geometry, but rather as a suggestive term, one for which the word "analogous" might be a synonym, in the sense that there is a common or shared motivation at work, one that seeks insight into the underlying workings of reality (whether sacred or "natural") as well as practical understanding of how reality can be altered or redirected. Those who are seeking esoteric knowledge or practical leverage to alter reality in preferred ways share an initial motivation (dissatisfaction with reality as they

56 Many of these are curious dabblers who pose no threat to anyone; others are intent upon acquiring knowledge conferring powers they would readily employ if possible, and still others are dangerous because they will resort to ordinary force out of frustration when esoteric projects fizzle.

find it) as well as an ongoing objective (to rework reality by drawing on divine, secret or hitherto unused powers). I think it likely that Voegelin settled upon a single, overarching term that could point accurately to these shared motivations and objectives (i.e., experiences) without stirring up all the distracting esoterica (i.e., symbols) by which the experiences engendering the various "wisdom traditions" are expressed. And I believe that term is "magic."

As we work toward a concluding set of problems, I should note that the foregoing observations seem to solve an important question about "Wisdom and Magic," but the solution can't be definitive or final, and it raises an important question even as it answers another. Voegelin's repeated use of the term or concept of "magic" helps us understand where his thinking stood in this last writing to issue from his pen—which effectively abandons "Gnosticism" and makes no effort to patch it up by recourse to Hermeticism, alchemy, etc.—but it would probably be a mistake to regard his focus on magic as a "last stand" in his lifelong effort to conceptualize spiritual disorder. Where Voegelin "stood" in 1983 when *Southern Review* published his approved version of "Wisdom and Magic" offers little assurance that he would have "stood still" if he had been able to continue sustained work past that time, and the compelling consideration that deprives us of assurance is that Voegelin never "stood still" for long in his evolving conceptualization from the 1920s onward. This was partly a function of his tireless search for new insights from new source materials or ones he reconsidered after shifts and developments in his approaches and methods. It was also a function—especially in the last two decades of his work—of Voegelin's deepening wariness about how particular terms and concepts can "ossify," losing their initial usefulness as language symbols for illuminating experiences and turning into focal points in their own right, ones that effectively cloak the experiences they were intended to reveal. In a commentary that argues against exalting *The New Science* or "Gnosticism" as though they were "the last word" in from Voegelin on problems of spiritual disorder, I don't want to make the same mistake with the term, "magic." It too might have receded or even been discarded if Voegelin had been able to continue writing.

And yet, of course he wasn't able to continue writing, so "magic" is indeed the last word as a matter of biographical and written fact, even if not in the broader and looser sense of "the last word" that we use in everyday speech. He employs the term repeatedly in the meditation, and at crucial points, and in ways that could easily lead even readers of the highest caliber to scoff at it rather than understand what he means to convey with it. An important example is the section running from p. 323 over to 324, where he specifies the point of departure for activist dreamer from philosophers, writing that it is,

> ...possible to identify the point of divergence as the activist's faith in his power to transfigure the structure of reality. When he acts, he expects such action to form the first reality into conformity with the Second Reality of his dream. The activist dreamer must know the trick action, as distinguished from ordinary action, that will have the extraordinary result of transfiguring the nature of things. He must imagine himself to be a magician.

I noted the last sentence in this quotation earlier, but now we are better prepared to examine it more seriously and critically. Voegelin is here suggesting straightforwardly that activist dreamers *per se* imagine themselves to be magicians, and he employs the term "activist dreamers" quite inclusively in the meditation but also directly when addressing Hegel and Nietzsche and above all Marx. So, we should ask directly: Why should we believe that Marx imagined himself to be a magician, and what did Voegelin mean when suggesting this with a word as strong as "must"?

Noting in advance that imaging something is not quite the same as "really believing" it, those of us who have studied Marx's works and correspondence carefully can attest that they contain nothing supporting the notion that he really believed himself to be a "magician" in the way that almost anyone uses that word. He thought of himself as the founder of "scientific socialism," which resulted from historical analysis of the progression of economic modes of production leading up to capitalism, and particularly, insight into the key "drivers" that both explain that progression and permit extrapolation to understanding of the modes of production and their resulting societies in the future, namely, socialism and communism. Marx spent almost all of his life in his study, and later in the reading rooms of the British Museum, and at first blush, it seems jarringly implausible to see him characterized as a man who imagines himself to be a magician. The very concise and direct speech delivered at his graveside by Engels depicts Marx in this way, as a self-styled "scientist," and yet it also shows that his self-understanding can't be encapsulated so easily, judging from how he was regarded by those who knew him best:

> Just as Darwin discovered the law of development or organic nature, so Marx discovered the law of development of human history.... But that is not all. Marx also discovered the special law of motion governing the present-day capitalist mode of production, and the bourgeois society that this mode of production has created.... Such was the man of science. But this was not even half the man.... For Marx was before all else a revolutionist. His real mission in life was to contribute, in one way or another, to the overthrow of capitalist society and of the state institutions which it had brought into being, to contribute to the liberation of the modern proletariat, which he was the first to make conscious of its own position and its needs, conscious of the conditions of its emancipation. Fighting was his element.[57]

My use of ellipses makes it apparent that I patched this quotation together, but the entire speech from 1883 at Highgate Cemetery in London consists of just 717 words, and can be read in two minutes to check the fairness of my abbreviation of it. Marx the "revolutionist" was not just a thinker but also a fighter looking for a fight. By making the modern proletariat "conscious of its own position and its needs, conscious of the conditions of its emancipation," and by advocating violent revolution, he believed he could intervene in the process of history and accelerate the advent of its culmination. This culmination was both envisioned and depicted in writing as a never-ending state of affairs marked by the "emancipation" of human beings

57 Friedrich Engels, "Speech at the Graveside of Karl Marx," in *The Marx-Engels Reader*, Second Edition, ed. Robert Tucker (New York & London: W. W. Norton & Co. 1978), 681–82.

from scarcity, involuntary toil, domination by others, and even political activity itself, once national states "withered away" for lack of any problems to address or any interests to advance on behalf of any privileged class. The emancipation to be enjoyed eternally by the "new men" of the communist future sounds a lot like emancipation from "...the well-known miseries enumerated by Hesiod" that Voegelin recounted and expanded upon in "Wisdom and Magic."

But the issue remains unsettled, as it isn't yet clear that we can reasonably side with Voegelin in his assertion that a man like Marx "...must imagine himself to be a magician." Here the distinction between what someone "imagines" and what someone "really believes" can be quite helpful. If we frame the question as, "Did Marx really believe he was a magician?" it seems initially that the answer should be negative, out of respect for Voegelin's own empirical principles and his attentiveness to the self-understanding of those whose consciousness he sought to understand and conceptualize. Marx "really believed" he was a scientific socialist rather than a magician. However, Marx also "really believed" his scientific socialism could permit human beings to make a violent incision into "history" to cut out the conditioning factors that produced the "well known miseries" that have mistakenly been attributed to divine creation or "nature," and that humans could quite literally re-make themselves thereby, utilizing nothing beyond their own efforts as instructed by Marx. Keeping this in mind, if we return to Voegelin's striking assertion that "he must imagine himself to be a magician" but consider this to be what a logician would call a "contingent proposition" (or an "IF ... THEN" statement), it yields the following formulation: IF Marx "really believes" he can effectively teach human beings how to emancipate themselves from God, nature, and the manifold miseries experienced across the ages, remaking themselves in the process as they wish, THEN he must imagine himself to be a magician. That, I submit, is a true statement.

Personal Disorder and Social Contagion

I readily acknowledge that the assertion that a man like Karl Marx "must imagine himself to be a magician" will look like baseless nonsense to most first-time readers of "Wisdom and Magic," but I hope to have shown that

that's a mistaken impression. I also grant that my verb "teach," in the clause, "effectively teach human beings" in the contingent proposition above will be objected to by any well-versed Marxist, as it smacks of "idealism" rather than "materialism." And yet, as we noted above, Marx never shot anybody—he was a writer and speaker. To the degree Engels was correct when assessing Marx as a world historical figure on the level of Darwin, it would be merited solely by his "teaching." To quote Engels again, "Fighting was his element. And he fought with a passion, a tenacity and a success such as few could rival." If there is any truth in this heroic-sounding praise, it would boil down to any fighting Marx engaged in not with deeds, but with words.

Were they "magic words," in any meaningful sense? The short answer is yes, and the sheer number of otherwise moral and sane individuals who have been "entranced" by Marx's writings offers encouragement that an affirmative response is on the right track. Breaking briefly from the example of Marx, we can observe that—although the very notion of magic words can seem outlandish when first encountered—Voegelin shows in "Wisdom and Magic" that understanding of the potentially "magic" power of words is not a novelty of his creation, but rather an awareness that extends back to the ancient world. However, this understanding is not merely an awareness to be dusted off from antiquity; on the contrary, his account rings true to our contemporary experience, and only commonsense reflection—rather than anything esoteric or exotic—is needed to gain awareness of the reality to which he directs our attention. Finally, looking ahead to the concluding observation in this commentary, Voegelin's illumination in "Wisdom and Magic" of the potentially disordering power of magic words offers a solution to a potentially thorny problem that arises from his thorough shift in the meditation to analyzing spiritual disorder by way of the theory of consciousness. We can describe the problem in advance, and do so easily enough. Voegelin's analysis of pneumopathology (or activist dreaming, or Second Reality consciousness, etc.) in "Wisdom and Magic" is overwhelmingly focused on the individual as the proper unit of analysis, with personal revolt against the tension of imperfection-perfection identified as the phenomenon under analysis. However, we know from history as well as recent experience that disorders of the mind and spirit can "spread" in ways that make them menacing at the broader levels of society and politics. Voegelin's insightful treatment of "magic words" can help us to understand these phenomena simultaneously and in relation to one another, doing so without losing focus on the personal dimension by resorting to imprecise coinages such as "Gnostic civilization."

Taking up these tasks in order, Voegelin's treatment of "magic words" in the meditation is relatively brief, and he indicates that he only seeks to "evoke" what he calls "the millennial knowledge of intoxication by the magic of the Word." Although he continues by implying a need for brevity when writing that, "An evocation it has to remain," he suggests that "at least it can be given by some reminders of its time range, selected to intimate the analytical meaning of magic, as well as the relation between the phenomena of word intoxication and drug addiction."[58] As for the "time range" and cross-cultural expansiveness of what Voegelin is addressing, it is worth noting that the "evocation" follows a section drawing on Shakespeare that closes with an allusion to the work of Bronisław Malinowski and his work on "the magic enterprises of the Trobriand islanders."[59] When providing reminders of the "time range," Voegelin turns to the *Encomium of Helen* by Gorgias of Leontini. According to Voegelin,

> ...[H]e stresses in his analysis the power of language as the source of disorder, the power of the *logos* as a cosmic force that can be used by man for good or evil purposes in accordance with the order (*kosmos*) or disorder (*akosmia*) of his psyche. Speech (*logos*) is for Gorgias a great and powerful master (*dynastes megas*); it operates with magic force (*goeteia*, *mageia*) on man; the spell of divinely inspired language (*entheoi epoidai*) can swerve the soul when it is weakened by passion or lack of knowledge, toward opinion (*doxa*) in conflict with the truth; the power of the *logos* over the soul can be compared to that of a drug (*pharmakon*) over the body; as the drug can heal or kill, harmful persuasion can drug and bewitch the soul.... Speech is the powerful thing, the *dynastes megas*, that can form or deform the order of man and his actions, while in their turn the

58 "Wisdom and Magic," 330.

59 Ibid., 328–30. Shakespeare is referred to on 328 as, "...the master of dream and reality, of their tension, and of the language of their conflicts...."

> movements of the psyche can move language toward truth or untruth.[60]

Without taking any illegitimate liberties with this passage, we can extract some especially pertinent clauses to suggest that the "inspired" (and inspiring) language of Marx or Nietzsche can "swerve the soul" of a person that is "weakened by passion or lack of knowledge" toward "opinion in conflict with the truth." Anyone who has encountered undergraduate students who have become enraptured after dabbling with Marx or Nietzsche can corroborate this sketch, including its wonderfully appropriate characterization of the effect their writings can have, which is to "swerve the soul" of those who have become enraptured.[61]

I have used the term "entranced" when describing the condition, and Voegelin follows Gorgias when using the phrase, "drug and bewitch the soul." These words are intelligibly close to what one would expect as the effects of "magic words," if one is open to the possibility that such words exist. Regarding the vulnerability of an individual soul to be "swerved" or "bewitched," Voegelin seems correct in pinpointing "when it is weakened by passion or lack of knowledge." There are many passions, of course, so we can't know precisely which ones Voegelin had in mind, but sticking with the example of a young student "entranced" by Marx or Nietzsche, such passions might be identified—first with regard to Nietzsche—as a radical assertion of independence or rebelliousness against authority, whether that authority be parental, social or religious. In instances of young people becoming entranced by reading Marx, a passionate anger over injustices or against inequalities might lead to susceptibility, as might a lack of knowledge regarding the virtual ubiquity of injustice and inequality. Continuing along this line, those of us who work with fervent but immature students in university settings often find that the "trance" of the "entranced" is often

60 Ibid., 330–31. All references to Greek words appear as in the *CWEV* original.

61 In the interest of inclusiveness, we should note that Hegel's writings can also have this effect, though usually only with graduate students. As an aside, Voegelin was ambivalent to a degree regarding both Marx and Nietzsche, recognizing their powers of intellect and crediting them for certain important insights. See my monograph, *Voegelin's Analysis of Marx*, Occasional Papers, Eric Voegelin Archiv, University of Munich, August, 2000.

broken (like a fever) by experience, enhanced knowledge, and the seasoning of time informed by them. For example, outrage against one's nation tends to soften as one learns of the injustices and inequalities that plague all other nations in all other time periods. However, for the passionate soul lacking in knowledge, we expect too much if we expect that "the well-known miseries enumerated by Hesiod" be accepted as "the lot of man, mysterious it is true but as the lot he has to cope with in the organization and conduct of his life." If the miseries are real and if the causes underlying them are mysterious (as Voegelin explicitly acknowledges in both cases), then some measure of rebelliousness among those with moral and spiritual sensitivity is actually to be expected. Or so it seems to me. Voegelin is not quite wrong when he writes, "No list, however long, of real sufferings, perhaps accompanied by a list of realistic proposals for their alleviation, will radiate by itself a promise of transfiguration."[62] This sentence is almost certainly a reference to *Manifesto of the Communist Party* by Marx and Engels,[63] and I believe it comes up just short of error by dint of the choice of the words, "promise of transfiguration." Voegelin is correct, no *transfigured* state of affairs is *promised* by any list of real sufferings accompanied by a list of realistic proposals for their alleviation, but the possibility of a *meaningfully reformed* state of affairs certainly seems *possible* by extension from such lists, and enticing enough to prove "entrancing" to those with an abundance of passion but a paucity of knowledge.

We know that acquisition of knowledge and the sobering process of maturation are usually the "cures" for activist dreamers who become "disenchanted," awakening from their dreams. But we also know that time alone offers no assurance of maturation among human beings, and that human resistance to cognitive dissonance is a very powerful barrier. Aristotle's *spoudaios* or "mature person" is hardly the norm but rather an exemplar against which "the many" are to be measured. Moreover, though we know that enhancements of knowledge can temper outrage and rebelliousness, we also know that they do not "explain" mysteries, much less resolve the problems cloaked

62 "Wisdom and Magic," 318, and for the foregoing quotation as well.

63 I write "almost certainly" not because Voegelin points to the *Manifesto*, but rather because it is essentially unique among writings by either Marx or Engels—singly or as co-authors—in its inclusion of "realistic proposals."

in mystery. The result of this is that a steady stream of human beings will indeed "experience as senseless" the miseries and injustices of human life, rebelling against the reality that many other human beings—usually *most* others—can accept as "the lot of man," regardless of whether they are reflective enough to perceive the mysteriousness of this "lot" or whether they just slog through it with sober determination, day after day.

Voegelin's analysis of spiritual revolt against reality in "Wisdom and Magic" focuses on the interior lives of individuals, for the very good reason that he understood that "movements" are populated by activists with varied motives, as we have seen. His attention is focused particularly on those activists who are also "dreamers," rather than those individuals who gravitate to movements with mixed motives that include—along with attraction to the "phantasies" cast before them by the dreamers—more mundane grievances or desires for revenge against those depicted as responsible for the miseries they are no longer prepared to endure. We know empirically that the rank-and-file members of many movements are better described as "activists" than "activist dreamers," and we know a lot about how activist dreamers manage to build entire movements in pursuit of their phantasies of a transformed world. This is accomplished by of a combination of means, including, first of all, "magic words." All movements need an animating narrative that resonates with the experience of genuine miseries among potential recruits, identifies comprehensibly the causes and agents of the miseries, and proposes a plausible plan of attack on the causes and agents that could result in a transformed reality. This is a very tall order for an activist dreamer, which explains why—historically—many more activist dreams fall flat than swell into movements of pragmatic consequence. Additionally, some measure of charisma on the part of the dreamer or those who annunciate the dream will be required for success, along with enemies who are arguably wicked and loathsome enough to be demonized in the movement's animating narrative. A last key factor ("last" only for purposes of this analysis, which cannot be exhaustive) is a relatively widespread disturbance of those components of everyday life that usually provide orientation and the capacity for coping with the demands imposed by a persistently imperfect reality. These supportive components might be classified as social, political, economic, cultural, or religious, and in some historically extreme instances, many of the components grouped under these headings may be disturbed at once. Recognizing this, Voegelin digresses momentarily in "Wisdom and Magic" when recounting identifications of activist dreaming as a spiritual disease by thinkers from antiquity (such as Heraclitus, Aeschylus, Plato, Chrysippus, and Cicero) to observe that,

> After the conquest of Alexander, then, in the period of the Hellenistic and Roman empires, the disease appears to have *spread* widely over the new ecumene, induced by the destruction of the older political cultures which had sheltered man's existence, just as it is today an ever wider-spreading social phenomenon, induced by the destruction of traditional cultures through the industrial revolution and the growth of the global ecumene.[64]

The historical accuracy of these observations seems beyond doubt, but the process Voegelin points to with the word "spread" is very much worth exploring. Different diseases spread differently, and though Voegelin was surely always aware of this, "Wisdom and Magic" will lead a careful reader to think about the transmission as well as outbreaks of pneumopathology differently than a reader who stopped reading after *The New Science*. The disease (or *nosos* or *nosema*) of the psyche surely did "spread" during the period of the Hellenistic and Roman empires, but that does not mean that the affliction was anything close to universal, or that these eras can be designated accurately as "diseased ages," or ages defined by the spread of the disease. Human reason, which we can think of as the immune system of the soul, was not swept away wholesale by the "spread" to which Voegelin refers, even though it remains true that "outbreaks" of symptoms such as messianism and apocalypticism became more frequent, and also more magnetic for a larger percentage of populations than in earlier eras.[65] Reason

64 "Wisdom and Magic," 322. Emphasis added.

65 I have suggested some ways in which we can think about the "spread" of pneumopathology in terms of transmission and regarding instances of "outbreaks," but it may also be helpful to indicate ways that we should *avoid* thinking about spiritual disorder at the two extremes of a continuum. It is almost never simply idiosyncratic or "siloed," at one extreme, nor does it afflict everyone in a particular environment at the other extreme. The following examples are unpleasant, but they serve their purpose. At the former extreme, we would be

and common sense prevailed more often than it failed, just as it does in our time (when only a tiny percentage of populations turn to terrorism in so-called "breeding grounds"), or during the period beginning in the mid-19th Century that some refer to as "The Age of Ideology."

The magic of the extreme can be irresistible for extremists, but extremists are designated as such because of their relative rarity. Ideology—at least when understood as Voegelin understood it—is indeed a disease of the mind, but its manifestation as a full-blown disease is relatively rare in the years since 1848, and from the perspective of "Wisdom and Magic," it is unacceptably imprecise to refer to "modern gnostic civilization," as Voegelin did in *The New Science.*[66] Undoubtedly there was something like an "outbreak" of the pattern of consciousness that Voegelin formerly referred to as gnosticism during the period that is conventionally designated as "modern," but it is unacceptably imprecise to speak of Gnosticism as "the nature of modernity," as Vogelin also did in *The New Science.*[67] From the perspective

mistaken in thinking about pneumopathology as being akin to a "birth defect," or at least those birth defects with no evident causation from transmission or inherited predisposition. For example, multiple individuals are born with idiopathic scoliosis (which comprises about 80% of cases of scoliosis), but these individuals don't contract it from one another, and though it can run in families, often it does not; its causes are essentially unknown, and hence it is not simply "genetic" nor is it at all "transmissible." At the other extreme, pneumopathology isn't a disorder that descends upon an entire population regardless of how chaotic or disorienting an era may be due to political or economic upheaval. In this sense, it is not simply "environmental," as in the example of the environment in the Dubrovka Theater in Moscow in October of 2002, which was filled with toxic gas by Russian special forces in order to neutralize Chechen terrorists who had occupied the theater and held the audience hostage. The gas killed almost all of the terrorists and audience members, and permanently harmed almost all of the few survivors. The human immune system has no resistance to the vaporized derivative of fentanyl that was the active ingredient in the gas, but human reason—which I have likened to the immune system of the soul to pneumopathology—is strong enough in most people to ward off diseases of the mind. More work remains to be done in conceptualizing spiritual disorders, but we know that the phenomenon we are diagnosing resides between these two extremes.

66 Voegelin, *The New Science*, 222.

67 Ibid., 175.

of "Wisdom and Magic," if it is meaningful at all to designate a time period as "modernity," it cannot be meaningful to speak of its nature as "Gnostic," because the disordered manifestations of consciousness that Voegelin formerly subsumed under that heading are understood to predate 1500 CE by at least two millennia, and probably much longer.[68] For this reason, we can work backwards through the last sentence to conclude that is it probably *not meaningful* to designate a time period as "modernity," as Voegelin had already implied by 1974 when asking, "what is modern about the modern mind?" and, "what is modern about modernity?" in *The Ecumenic Age*.

As we have seen, Voegelin's work in the philosophy of consciousness altered his understanding and conceptualization of pneumopathology in important ways, and the findings—as published in "Wisdom and Magic"—seem to hold implications for the future that differ from the outlook suggested in *The New Science*. Stated concisely, *The New Science* seems to foresee a pitched battle in the form of a "world wide" reaction against an expanding, driving gnosticism, whereas the analysis in "Wisdom and Magic" makes it seem more likely that the future will—like the past—be marked by inconclusive skirmishing along many fronts.[69] I have phrased this last sentence at least half metaphorically to avoid drawing conclusions that are more conclusive than the wording of the two texts can properly permit. In *The New Science*, Voegelin opts against making specific predictions regarding the timing of a coming struggle, alluding at some points to a clash that will consist of "spiritual and intellectual resistance," but at several other points, writing of a coming "explosion" that is more suggestive of outright combat, also observing that "...the date is less distant than one would assume...."[70] "Wisdom and Magic" seems to take the time dimension almost out of play, at least in relative terms, suggesting that "modernity" is better understood as a conventionally designated time period when spiritual

68 I write, "...probably much longer" here because only the diagnostic terminology begins to appear around the time of Heraclitus; the symptoms are surely much older, as the tension of imperfection-perfection and of the metaxy are essentially timeless—even though the tension is heightened as the world is "de-divinized" and understanding of the human condition within reality is increasingly differentiated.

69 Voegelin, *NSP*, 221.

70 Ibid., 223.

disorders happen to be waxing than as a "civilization" that will need to be broken physically as well as intellectually and spiritually.

Although I'm confident that this contrast is valid in relation to an important difference between the two writings, I don't wish to overplay it to an extent that underplays the fact that Voegelin continued to believe, in the late 1970s, that a high-stakes clash was underway between activist dreamers and defenders of wisdom. The opening sentences of "Wisdom and Magic" can leave no doubt that he did indeed believe such a clash was underway. However, the meditation that follows makes it clear that such a clash *has always* been underway, both in public realms and even in the souls of individuals. This was an important finding that flowed from advances in Voegelin's application of the philosophy of consciousness to the study of history. However, the finding does not make the acute phase of the clash in the 20th century seem any less like a monstrously destructive crisis. When the dreams of activists seeking to banish imperfections from human life were inflamed by new technological possibilities as well as scientistic hubris, the political and military dimensions of the ages-old clash really did result in nightmarish realities. *The New Science* is surely not wrong about any of this, but still, the analysis of "Wisdom and Magic" lays to rest any possibility that "wisdom" could someday exert a power to overcome—once and for all—the allure of activist dreams of an "extreme" beyond our human existence in imperfection.[71]

All eras are beset by individuals who revolt against the mysterious but permanent imperfections of existence, as we learn from evidence Voegelin provides stretching back almost as far as we have written records existing to record such revolts.[72] It remains true that some times and places will be

71 Neither *The New Science* nor "Wisdom and Magic" include sustained considerations of potentially workable "therapies" for the spiritual diseases addressed in them, and Voegelin never undertook a full account in any single writing. However, a reasonably full inventory of the difficulties can be pieced together from his many publications. See my chapter, "The Search for Therapeutic Wisdom" in *Eric Voegelin and the Politics of Spiritual Revolt*, 107–22.

72 At least back to Heraclitus, 2,500+ years ago, and Isaiah and his metastatic faith, going back roughly another 200 years, and perhaps to the Egyptian author of "Dispute of a Man, Contemplating Suicide, with His Soul," another millennium earlier.

more badly afflicted than others, either because of broadly disorienting events (such as globalization or the collapse of empires) or due to the presence of particularly spellbinding activist dreamers whose "magic words" can entrance other dreamers in pragmatically consequential numbers. Because worldly imperfections and their mysteriousness are permanent, we cannot take refuge in the hope that revolts against them will cease altogether—as opposed to merely waning during some eras. However, broadening and sharpening our understanding of the spiritual wellsprings of such revolts is a philosophical achievement of a very high order, one that recommends "Wisdom and Magic" to any reader prepared to undertake the repeated reflective encounters required to do justice to the meditation.

–14–

Voegelin's "Quod Deus Dicitur"

Thomas Heilke with Paul Caringella

"Quod Deus Dicitur"[1] was Eric Voegelin's last essay, the effort to write it consuming the final two weeks of his life at the beginning of 1985. While clearly unfinished, it was published as the lead essay in the issue of the Journal of the American Academy of Religion (JAAR) that marked the 75th anniversary of the Academy's founding in 1919. "Quod Deus Dicitur," taken from the *Summa Theologica* of Thomas Aquinas, was Voegelin's chosen title.

The essay form was an important medium of scholarly exchange and knowledge sharing for Voegelin, who published nearly ninety essays as book chapters and journal articles in the course of his sixty-three-year-long academic career.[2] An essay is an "attempt" (French: "*essayer*"), a literary genre first named and made famous by the work of Michel de Montaigne, who published a large collection of short, sometimes fragmentary writings under the title *Essays* (*Essais*) in 1580. An essay, as Montaigne first formed it, is "an imperfect and partial

1 Eric Voegelin, "Quod Deus Dicitur," (1985) in *Published Essays 1966-1985*, ed. Ellis Sandoz, *CWEV* Vol. 12, 1990, 376–94. Hereafter cited as Voegelin, "QDD."

2 This count includes the thirteen chapters of *Anamnesis*, most of which were first published elsewhere, but not his dozens of book reviews and other occasional writings, nor his many unpublished but essentially completed essays. (For a selection of Voegelin's book reviews, see Eric Voegelin, *Selected Book Reviews*, ed. Jodi Cockerill and Barry Cooper, *CWEV* Vol. 13, 2001.) His unpublished writings include *History of Political Ideas*, published as Volumes 19-26 of *The Collected Works*, along with various other essays collected and published in volumes 27, 28, 32, and 33 of *The Collected Works.*

composition."[3] We therefore need not treat the unfinished nature of Voegelin's final effort as an indictment of its importance, its interpretability, or its closing place in that corpus of his writings published with his explicit intent and consent.

The Genesis of "Quod Deus Dicitur"

Ray L. Hart, who put together the long introductory note[4] for the 1985 publication of the essay, was at that time the President of the American Academy of Religion and had previously been the editor of the JAAR for many years. He admired the work that Voegelin had done in the first four volumes of *Order and History*, and he seemed particularly grateful for the response to Thomas J. J. Altizer's review of *The Ecumenic Age* that Voegelin had published in the Journal nearly a decade earlier.[5] As the 75th anniversary of the Academy approached, Hart invited Voegelin to be one of the keynote speakers at the celebration in Chicago in December, 1984, and Voegelin accepted. Paul Caringella believes Voegelin saw the occasion as an opportunity to present an account of his late work, especially of his thought as it was developing in the writing of the final (and also unfinished) volume of *Order and History.*[6]

In late 1983, however, Voegelin arrived home seriously ill from a trip to the Holy Land and Rome accompanied by his wife, Lissy, and Paul. Hospitalized at Stanford almost immediately upon his return, he knew, with Lissy, that his overall condition, which was determined primarily by congestive heart failure, would only become progressively worse, and that he did not have much time left to devote to his work. He nevertheless accepted the invitation from Ray Hart, but it was only as the deadline approached that he began to plan his lecture.

3 Barry Cooper, *The End of History: An Essay on Modern Hegelianism* (Toronto: University of Toronto Press, 1983), 3.
4 Voegelin, "QDD," at 376–77.
5 See Eric Voegelin, "Response to Professor Altizer's 'A New History and a New but Ancient God?" (1975) in *Published Essays 1966-1985*, ed. Ellis Sandoz, *CWEV* Vol. 12, 1990, 292–303.
6 Eric Voegelin, *Order and History, Volume V: In Search of Order* (1987), ed. Ellis Sandoz, *CWEV* Vol. 18, 2000. Hereafter cited as *In Search of Order*.

Voegelin had gotten as far with *In Search of Order* as his health would permit. As Lissy wrote in the Foreword in 1987: "In late 1983 his health began to fail and the strenuous concentration required for writing became more and more difficult. By that time he had already sent a good part of the manuscript to the Louisiana State University Press, always hoping that someday he would be able to write again."[7] Three letters—one to David Walsh on December 13, 1983, and two to Jürgen Gebhardt on April 10 and August 22, 1984[8]—show Eric relentlessly continuing to work out his thinking. The August letter speaks of approaching the gospels through "the analysis of experience ...without bringing in the later theological exegesis" and concludes with a comment that a "first drafting of the problem will emerge in a lecture that I have to give in December on the occasion of the 75th anniversary of the Academy of Religion in Chicago. The title: 'Quod Deus Dicitur.'" Voegelin clearly hoped he would be able to travel to Chicago.

A handwritten outline dated October 6, 1984, that Voegelin had Paul type up laid out his plan for the lecture. He seemed to understand that it was now or never if he wanted to shape a presentation for the December conference.

October 6, 1984 – For December AAR (Chicago)
Component Factors

1. Series of Contingent Events
2. Necessity of Reality
3. Tension of Contingency-Necessity
4. Nomination of the Necessary Pole as "God"
5. Reappearance in Leibniz (post-Cartesian, pre-Kantian)
6. Conception of the Tension as a Syllogism
7. Kant: Syllogism is Faulty
8. Nomination of the Necessary Pole as "Divine" (Anaximander)

7 Lissy Voegelin, "Foreword," in *In Search of Order*, 13.

8 In Eric Voegelin, *Selected Correspondence, 1950-1984*, ed. Thomas Hollweck, *CWEV* Vol. 30, 2007, 872–75. Hereafter cited as Voegelin, *Selected Correspondence, 1950-1984.*

9. Reason for the Nomination as "Divine": Attributes of Polytheistic Gods (Immortal, Eternal, Indestructible)
10. Immortality of the Gods – Beyond of the Gods (Hesiod)
11. Reason of Immortality – Context of Meaning (positive & negative) Beyond the Range Intended by Man
12. Syllogism: Denial of the Existence of Gods – Counter-Assertion of Their Existence
13. The Gods, the God, the Divine (personal and impersonal)
14. Monosis – the One God – one Supreme God (Egypt...Bhagavad-Gita)
15. The One Divine above the Polytheistic Gods – the One Divine above the One Supreme God – the One Divine above the One God
16. "Ontological Proof" (Anselm – Thomas – Kant – Hegel)
17. Pleroma:
    a) Christian
    b) Cosmological Supreme God
    c) Hellenic "Beyond"

This outline was followed by a briefer one, dated October 20th, that simply listed the dichotomies found near the beginning of what became the published unfinished essay.[9]

Soon afterward, however, Voegelin's condition worsened. His doctor, Walter M. Bortz II, a nationally recognized gerontologist, made it clear that Eric's long-term prospects were not good. There is no record of him doing any work on the lecture during November. Near the end of the month he was hospitalized again with the expectation that he might die during his stay. While still in hospital in early December, he planned his funeral and memorial service with Lissy and the Dean of the Stanford Memorial Church, Robert Hamerton-Kelly. The scripture texts that Eric selected for the service were: John 12:24 ("Unless a grain of wheat falls into the earth and dies, it remains alone; but if it dies, it bears much fruit.") and 1 John 2:15–17 ("Do not love the world or anything in the world. If anyone loves the world, love for the Father is not in them. For everything in the world—the lust of the flesh, the lust of the eyes, and the pride of life—comes not

9 Voegelin, "QDD," 378.

from the Father but from the world. The world and its desires pass away, but whoever does the will of God lives forever."). To Lissy's puzzled "Why that?" regarding the part about the lusts, Eric answered simply, "For repentance."[10]

On one critical occasion in the hospital when Paul was alone with him, Eric was overcome by a kind of seizure, an extreme respiratory episode, but as Paul called a nurse, Eric emerged from it to remark to him: "dying is a strange affair; you think it's really happening right now at this minute and then it does not." Lissy reported similar incidents. One night, much closer to his death, at home in his own bed, she saw Eric's eyes seeming to turn inward and scolded him affectionately: "*du alter Gauner*" [you old scoundrel] "you are watching yourself die … but you will not be able to tell anybody about it!" Eric nodded and smiled in his knowing manner, as if to say to her (or did he really say it?): "But *I* will know." He remained a keen observer of the human condition to the very end.

Having been granted a temporary reprieve, Eric was able to return home in mid-December to spend what were expected to be his last weeks in familiar and cherished surroundings. Ray Hart had already been informed that there was no possible way Eric could make the trip to Chicago, much less deliver a plenary lecture there. Hart replied, "Please, if you have the strength to write anything on your subject, send it to me and it will certainly be published in the *Proceedings* in the *JAAR* in 1985." But all that existed as the new year arrived was the outline of October 6th and the much shorter one of October 20. It seemed probable that nothing substantial would be written. Paul typed two short farewell letters for Eric at Christmastime to Brendan Purcell and to Jürgen Gebhardt. On Christmas Day, Eric wrote two lines to Brendan: "I am rather ill, probably not to last too long, but nobody knows how long. All good wishes for the New Year to you."

10 Voegelin gave two full pages to this passage in 1 John in his study, "Nietzsche and Pascal" (1996). He was struck especially by Pascal's Latin translation, which, by three-fold repetition, emphasizes the power of *libido*: *libido sentiendi, libido sciendi, libido dominandi*. Eric Voegelin, *History of Political Ideas, Volume VII: The New Order and Last Orientation*, ed. Jürgen Gebhardt and Thomas A Hollweck, *CWEV* Vol. 25, 1999, 272–73.

Serious scholarly work is not driven solely by high academic and intellectual motivations. The impetus to "get down to it" may sometimes arise from more basic inclinations. With the assistance of his devoted nurse helper, Ms. Hiawatha Moore, Eric had been able before Christmas to begin to ascend the few steps from his bedroom and his study through the living room to the kitchen where he could have a light lunch each noontime with Lissy. On January 2, the eve of Eric's 84th birthday, Ellis Sandoz called from Baton Rouge to offer his "Happy Birthday" wishes. Eric and Lissy were sitting at the little kitchen table, the wall telephone just by Lissy's ear. She told Ellis that Eric had been feeling well enough to get up each day now for their lunch and said that he was grateful to Ellis for his call, but that he was too weak (especially his voice) to actually talk to him on the phone. "But," Ellis asked, "is he able to write anything down or talk into a tape-recorder or dictate something to Paul?" Lissy replied, "Don't think we haven't said that to him! But he just sits there like a dead cow!" adding immediately, "And I am not talking behind his back. You should see the face that he is making at me right at this minute!"

That afternoon when Paul arrived for his daily visit, Eric said to him, "let's try to do something." He had out the two outlines already mentioned. He and Paul settled upon an arrangement in which he would dictate to Paul as many paragraphs as he could. Paul would take home what he had written down and bring back typed pages the next day. Soon they expedited matters by Paul going to a typewriter in the guest room to type up the pages at once to bring to Eric in his study where he would sit puffing the cigar that marked his satisfaction at having gotten some work done. This process was repeated each day, almost always including the ceremonial cigar. He would dictate his revisions, then some new paragraphs. Paul would type these up, and so on … each day. In this way, "Quod Deus Dicitur" came into being.

From the following few notes of their final conversations on January 15 and 16, Paul put together the "texts" that, with his introductory comments in brackets, were published below the essay's unfinished ending.[11] These final jottings that Paul supplied from Voegelin's conversations can also guide the reader to the further meditations that Voegelin foresaw as

11 Voegelin, "QDD," 392–94.

the completion of his essay. Such guidance may be especially helpful in those cases where these references are treated elsewhere in Voegelin's writings.

Handwritten Notes — January 15th [On a single page]
Plotinus
Prayer
& Perfume of "Comprehending"
à "emanation" Metaphor
"Dream" of Chora in Plato
Anaximander — Aristotelian
& "Materialists:
Hesiod – "Matter"
Goethe – "Prayer" p. 142
Zaehner on Atman/Brahman – Personal/Imperial
& Colossians – "Pleroma" & Theotes
& Thomas 13:11 – 3 'Gods'

Last Handwritten Notes — January 16th
Anax – "Divine"
& 2 Dreams of Plato – and Chora
(of Presence) & Prayers for Both
Plotinus – Perfume
& Goethe
——————————————- # of section
& then Christian – a Few Words in Conclusion.

In Paul's recollection, it must have been later in the evening of Wednesday, January 16, or possibly the evening of the 17th that, as Lissy told him later, Eric asked her to call the doctor to request some new medicine, perhaps a strong sedating drug. The after-hours doctor on call was hesitant to make the prescription and to have it delivered and in the end decided that he could not fulfill the request. Eric must have been in considerable discomfort to have asked for this relief. Paul visited him briefly on the afternoon of the 17th and again the 18th, reporting in his letter of Wednesday the 23rd to Gregor Sebba that Eric had still been making corrections to the typescript on the 18th. Paul recognized these minor changes—all to the final section[12]—as Eric's last dictations, and made the alterations for him in the full typescript that he mailed to Gregor Sebba on the 23rd for him and Hart to use for publication.[13]

On the morning of January 19th, while it was still dark, Lissy, sitting by Eric's bed, felt it was safe to call their devoted friend and nurse-helper, Hiawatha Moore, to come keep vigil so that Lissy could rest a while in her own bed. Having expected Lissy's call, Hiawatha arrived without delay. While Lissy rested in her room nearby, Hiawatha thought to read to Eric from the Psalms out of the little softcover copy of the King James version of the New Testament and Psalms that Eric kept nearby. Hiawatha said that she "heard a voice telling me to read." So she opened to the Psalms, and Paul imagines she began with the familiar Psalm 23, "The Lord is my Shepherd." Lissy reported that she heard a soft voice reading and wondered what was being read. Continuing on to Psalm 25, Hiawatha came to the end of a page at verse 16. She reported that as she turned the page and began to read the next verse, "The troubles of my heart are enlarged: O bring Thou me out of my distresses," Eric sighed his last breath, falling silent shortly after sunrise on Saturday, January 19, 1985.[14]

12 Voegelin, "QDD," 390–92.

13 The only change of significance seems to Paul to be right at the beginning of that final "new" section (390)—In its fourth line Eric changed the word "points" to "meanings": "… the meanings that have remained compact in Plato's work." He changed "in" to "on" — "more than one volume on Hellenic philosophy." He inserted "to be" into the phrase "is *to be* a prayer" (391) and a "the" before "gods and goddesses." At the end of the middle paragraph he inserted "as the Invocation of Aristophanes shows" and changed "experientially are dying" to "are experientially dying." At the bottom of the page he replaced "transition" with "change," and finally, "spatial-temporal" became "spatio-temporal."

14 Until the day she died in 1996, Lissy Voegelin carried in her purse a small slip of paper on which she had written "Psalm 25" and the number "17" along with the text of that verse, followed by the drawing of a small heart and a cross. Lissy had copied out for herself the words that Eric heard as he died. For Hiawatha Moore's account of Voegelin's final hours, see Barry Cooper and Jodi Bruhn, eds., *Voegelin Recollected: Conversations on a Life* (Columbia: University of Missouri Press, 2008), 12–13.

Paul's recounting of Voegelin's final hours may remind the reader of the anecdote concerning Plato's last hours to which Voegelin appended an interpretation and then employed to conclude Part I of the third volume of *Order and History*:

> Plato died at the age of eighty-one. On the evening of his death, he had a Thracian girl play the flute to him. The girl could not find the beat of the nomos. With a movement of his finger, Plato indicated to her the Measure.[15]

The measure of the cosmos, the rhythm of its nomos, was delivered to Voegelin in the metric of a Hebrew psalm, read to him by a care-giving family friend.

The Philology of Quod Deus Dicitur

By this account, "QDD" was the product of two weeks' intense work, supported neither by intermittent searches in the library nor by references to books on Voegelin's shelves, but simply by his long life of scholarship itself. He was working only with the outline of October 6 and what he retained in memory. The effort that brought "QDD" into being before Ms. Moore read that final psalm may have been, as Lissy remarked to Paul, a kind of suicide: Eric knew it would more rapidly deplete his little remaining energy. But then, as Paul reflects, he would die in the midst of the search, engaged in what he believed was his life-long calling. Having recounted the story of its genesis and its incompletion, we observe three additional philological aspects of this text.

First, Voegelin inserted pieces of previously written and even published texts into "QDD" as he developed it over the first two weeks of January with Paul as his amanuensis. Paul has reported that "When the dictation reached Anselm's prayer, Voegelin provisionally inserted pertinent pages

15 Eric Voegelin, *Order and History, Vol. III: Plato and Aristotle* (1966), ed. Dante Germino, *CWEV* Vol. 16, 2000, 268. The anecdote, of philologically dubious provenance, can be reviewed in Alice Swift Riginos, *Platonica: The Anecdotes Concerning the Life and Writings of Plato* (Leiden: E. J. Brill, 1976), 194.

from an earlier manuscript, with minor adjustments. He similarly adapted at the beginning of Sec. 5 a paragraph from his "Response to Professor Altizer." . . . His discussion of Hesiod's *Theogony* and Plato's *Timaeus* in the last pages and in the planned conclusion is based on [his] full analytical treatment in the last thirty-odd pages of the unfinished fifth ... volume of his *Order and History*."[16] Ellis Sandoz has likewise pointed out that "QDD" shows close connections to or even direct borrowing from other of Voegelin's late works, including "Wisdom and the Magic of the Extreme,"[17] and the Aquinas Lecture at Marquette University in 1975, "The Beginning and the Beyond: A Meditation on Truth," of which the unfinished manuscript for publication dates from approximately 1977.[18] These links and borrowings direct us to the larger program of study that Voegelin was conducting during the last decade or more of his life, of which this final essay is clearly a part.

Second, the October outline was not strictly followed. There is nothing in the outline of the God-denying existential foolishness that takes up several pages of "QDD," and the section concerning Anselm and the ontological "proof" occurs early, while other preceding sections in the outline do not appear at all in what Voegelin completed. We do, indeed, have a fragment, but one that points to added work Voegelin did elsewhere and to themes and problems that others may presume to take up further.

Third, while several of Voegelin's studies in his last decade of work may constitute a thematic grouping, as judged by his own borrowings and

16 "QDD," 377n1. The passage from "Response to Professor Altizer" can be found in *Published Essays, 1966-1985*, 300–01; compare with "QDD," 383.

17 Voegelin, "Wisdom and the Magic of the Extreme," first published in 1983, and delivered as a lecture on two occasions before that (1977 and 1980), can be found in *Published Essays, 1966-1985*, ed. Ellis Sandoz, *CWEV* Vol. 12, 1990, 315–75.

18 Voegelin intended the lecture for eventual publication, making mention of preparation for publication a task yet to be completed in several letters dating from before the lecture (1974) through to 1983. See Letters 446, 449, 465, 472, 483, 485, and 524 in Voegelin, *Selected Correspondence, 1950-1984*. It now appears in Eric Voegelin, *What is History? And Other Late Unpublished Writings*, ed. Thomas A. Hollweck and Paul Caringella, *CWEV* Vol. 28, 1990, 173–232. Hereafter cited as Voegelin, *What Is History?*

cross-references among them, they also continued themes that he first engaged in the 1930s. This continuity should not be overstated, but neither should it be ignored. A single thread of meaning may run through the entire works of a particular scholar, while others may entertain multiple scholarly interests, abandoning any particular one at some point along the way. Voegelin exercised both options. After publishing two volumes on the European race idea in 1938 that he considered among his better scholarly efforts, he published a related article in 1940, never to pick the topic up again. In 1948, after completing roughly 2000 typescript pages of a study that was originally contracted as a 250-page introductory text,[19] he abandoned *The History of Political Ideas* as a project, turning instead to *Order and History*. Some of what he had written for *History of Political Ideas* found its way into the latter work under extensive revision, but a large portion of the 2000 pages did not appear publicly in his lifetime.[20]

19 See Eric Voegelin, Letter to Laura Barrett, dated December 7, 1948, in *Selected Correspondence, 1924-1949,* ed. Jürgen Gebhardt, and trans. William Petropulos, *CWEV* Vol. 29, 2009, 584. Hereafter cited as Voegelin, *Selected Correspondence, 1924-1949.*

20 For Voegelin's account of this project and its abandonment, see his "Autobiographical Statement at Age Eighty-Two," (1984) in *The Drama of Humanity and Other Miscellaneous Papers, 1939-1985*, ed. William Petropulos and Gilbert Weiss, *CWEV* Vol. 33, 2004, 441–42. Hereafter cited as Voegelin, "Autobiographical Statement." Some sections of *History of Ideas* were published under the editorship of John Hallowell as *From Enlightenment to Revolution* in (Durham, N.C.: Duke University Press, 1975) with Voegelin's approval. In his introduction to this collection, Professor Hallowell provides a useful account of Voegelin's move from *History of Political Ideas* to *Order and History*. Thirty-five years after the event, Voegelin described the decision to abandon *History of Political Ideas* in this way: "Because Schelling was an intelligent philosopher, and when I studied the philosophy of the myth, I understood that ideas are nonsense: There are no ideas as such, and there is no history of ideas; but there is a history of experiences that can express themselves in various forms, as myths of various types, as philosophical development, theological development, and so on. One has got to get back to the analysis of experience. So I cashiered that history of ideas, which was practically finished in four or five volumes, and started reworking it from the standpoint of the problem of the experiences. That is how *Order and History* started." (Voegelin, "Autobiographical Statement," 442).

Manfred Henningsen observes that Voegelin would habitually drop topics that he had explored to his satisfaction on a first pass. For example, having published *On the Form of the American Mind* in 1928, he "never revisited American political themes in a major way." Similarly, having traced the gnostic origins of modernity in *The New Science of Politics*, he "simply lost interest in the genealogy of the deformation of modern consciousness" and approached the problem in other ways.[21] The thread of one question, however, appeared with some clarity for the first time in 1938, in *The Political Religions*,[22] and can be traced through to "QDD." It was the question of God, posed in an unusual manner.

The Political Science of "QDD"

The question of God will have its own fractures and disjunctions in Voegelin's work,[23] but the overall treatment of the problem exhibits a consistency that links "QDD" to *Political Religions* and much in between. Discontinuities—changes in language, emphasis, or points of contact—can be explained in part by Voegelin's continuing efforts more accurately to describe and analyze the historical and psychic events in and through which

21 Manfred Henningsen, "Editor's Introduction," to *Modernity Without Restraint*, *CWEV* Vol. 5, 2000, 13, 16. Hereafter cited as Voegelin, *Modernity Without Restraint.* See also the remarks of David Walsh on Voegelin's habits in this regard and his unique departure from them in publishing *Anamnesis* in his "Editor's Introduction" to Eric Voegelin, *Anamnesis: On the Theory of History and Politics,* ed. David Walsh and trans. M. J. Hanak, *CWEV* Vol. 6, 2002, 1–4. Hereafter cited as Voegelin, *Anamnesis.*

22 Eric Voegelin, *The Political Religions*, in Voegelin, *Modernity Without Restraint*, 23–73. Hereafter cited as Voegelin, *Political Religions.* See also Henningsen's, "Editor's Introduction," especially 5–7. Henningsen is less interested in the links between this early book and the search Voegelin explores in "QDD" and other late writings, but he notes that Voegelin leaves traces that would later become more fully developed. Jürgen Gebhardt, in contrast, draws the connections from the earlier to the later works much more firmly. See his "Editor's Introduction" in Voegelin, *Selected Correspondence, 1924-1949*, 32–36.

23 Barry Cooper, *Consciousness and Politics: From Analysis to Meditation in the Late Work of Eric Voegelin* (South Bend: St. Augustine's Press, 2018), 328. Hereafter cited as Cooper, *Consciousness.*

the question of God has been raised. At other times, the apparent breaks seem to be a matter of the varying contexts in which the question has appeared.[24] In both cases, the writing of "QDD" was not simply a final articulation of a life-long search: a personal search would not have required Voegelin to force himself to dictate "QDD." Instead, he was also reporting the findings of his search. In this important sense, the essay may, in fact, serve as a final bookend to his life's work. To see it in that light, however, requires us to reflect on its close connection to political life, a link that is not entirely obvious.

Reading "QDD" as a political scientist can give one the feeling of falling into a chasm. The feeling is created by the wide gap between practical political considerations on the one hand, and, on the other, the highly abstract, at times mystical, meditative material we encounter in this essay and others of Voegelin's late writings. "QDD" and late related essays are thereby given a decidedly unpolitical cast, appearing to be irrelevant to everyday political concerns of any sort. *Political Religions* relieves this impression. This short book begins with an obviously political question—how to understand the nature and meaning of collectivist political movements—and it raises the question of God as integral to this understanding. Identifying National Socialism in 1938—and alongside Marxism—as the most important and politically successful of the political collectivist movements, Voegelin argues that a moral, literary, or political opposition to this movement is insufficient: it would not be "conducted radically enough, because the *radix*, the root in religiousness, is missing."[25] Political collectivism is misunderstood if it is seen solely as a "political and moral phenomenon," because it contains "religious elements,"[26] and the collectivist movements of the time exhibit a substantive, evil, or Satanic force. What we call God emerges from a sense that there are forces in human society that oppose these Satanic powers. This double awareness leads one to question the Augustinian understanding of evil as an absence or privation:[27]

24 Barry Cooper, *Paleolithic Politics: The Human Community in Early Art* (Notre Dame: University of Notre Dame Press), 50–60.

25 Voegelin, *Political Religions*, 24.

26 Ibid., 23.

27 See Stanley Hauerwas, "Seeing Darkness, Hearing Silence: Augustine's Ac-

> When considering National Socialism from a religious standpoint, one should be able to proceed on the assumption that there is evil in the world and, moreover, that evil is not only a deficient mode of being, a negative element, but also a real substance and force that is effective in the world. Resistance against a satanic substance that is not only morally but also religiously evil can only be derived from an equally strong, religiously good force. One cannot fight a satanic force with morality and humanity alone.[28]

This substantive and active presence of good that seems more than that which we can find in ourselves is, Voegelin suggests, what we perhaps call God. The "ris[ing] up against evil" that all people of good will should embrace in the face of National Socialism and similar collectivist movements requires a "recovery [that] can only be achieved through religious renewal, be it within the framework of the historical churches, be it outside this framework."[29]

As a scientist seeking to understand the characteristics and dynamics of the social and political world of human beings, Voegelin saw his task as necessarily examining the terms his fellow participants in the political realm used to articulate their activity and their reality experienced, to "express the precise meaning" of those terms as faithfully as possible to the sources as he read or otherwise observed them, and to fairly represent the various positions of the participants in the various disputes he was subjecting to scholarly scrutiny.[30] As a participant in the same world in which these movements arose, however, he could not simply assume an "objective" stance. By dint of his participation as a human being among other human beings, he would also be called upon to resist the evil he observed. The world is not an object

count of Evil," in Stanley Hauerwas, *Working with Words: On Learning to Speak Christian* (Eugene, OR: Cascade Books, 2011), 8–32.

28 Voegelin, *Political Religions*, 24 (translation slightly altered).

29 Ibid.

30 Eric Voegelin, Letter to Leopold von Wiese, dated June 24, 1930, in *Selected Correspondence, 1924-1949, 73-74.* For a vivid description of this form of scholarship and its relationship to political realities, see Gebhardt, "Editor's Introduction," in Voegelin, *Selected Correspondence, 1924-1949,* 16-38.

to be viewed objectively from "outside" and subjected to empirical examination in a subject-object mode. We also live in it. This fact does not make it "the task of the political scientist" to "advance moralizing opinions,"[31] but it does mean that the very activity of political analysis, when well conducted, will reveal the shortcomings of the political participants and dynamics under observation. And, if the category fits, it will reveal their satanic qualities. That is what Voegelin saw himself as doing.[32]

This duality of scholarship and participation would be explicitly brought to view in Voegelin's later meditative studies. These begin with assuming a "detached stance,"[33] providing an impartial analysis of the historical *events* in human consciousness that are traced in the writings, artifacts, architectural constructions, and other forms of symbolization that people have left behind concerning these events. But what do these events *mean*; what is the "this" in which all human beings participate and that their symbolizations of reality experienced are attempting to articulate or recall? This interpretive question can only be answered by re-invoking the events themselves in one's own consciousness and recognizing their full plenitude. Until the late modern era, that recognition has included in most such meditations references and symbolizations of a divine presence that is understood as being "beyond" the intra-mundane material existence of the world or cosmos and all material objects and processes within it.

To make this claim was in 1938, and is now, to contradict the prevailing intellectual climate in which a majority of social scientists and other scholars interested in social and political phenomena dismiss out of hand the question of the transcendent givenness under which immanent political reality finds its place.[34] Their dismissal, Voegelin proposed, rests in part on a misunderstanding of that which we call God. The modern tendency to strictly divide the spheres of "religion" from the sphere of politics[35] has

31 Cooper, *Consciousness*, 66.

32 See Voegelin's "Introduction" to *Political Religions*. Voegelin re-emphasized this question of substantive evil in his revised, expanded introduction to the second edition of *Political Religions* in 1939 (See 19–23).

33 Gebhardt, "Editor's Introduction," *Selected Correspondence, 1924-1949,* 17.

34 Voegelin, *Political Religions*, 24.

35 "When one speaks of religion, one thinks of the institution of the Church, and when one speaks of politics, one thinks of the state." Ibid., 27.

resulted in a circumstance in which "the concept of the state is . . . limited to secular-human organizational relationships that do not have any relation to the sphere of the religious."[36] This situation is problematic for an understanding of the modern state and the political movements that inhabit it, because the plurality of powers present in the domestic and international political spheres suggest that above their manifold there must be a source of "legitimation and order" that unifies them. In premodern conceptions, this unifying source was always a "divine principle of unity that is part of the power structure."[37] When fully differentiated in an historical development that encompassed centuries and even millennia, this divine principle would become the "world-transcendent God" in an "order of creation" that also included the mundane political powers and forces in their entirety. This Divine reality is simply ignored in modern formulations by an assertion that state supremacy is ultimate and that this ultimacy is demonstrated in our immanent experience of said ultimacy. Voegelin's conclusion contains the seeds of several thematic threads that continued in his work of the next forty-five years:

> The multitude of powers that mutually hinder one another give rise to the notion of an all-encompassing unity—unless, of course, we refuse to take this intellectual step, decide to remain fixed at this point, and believe that the world is inhabited by demonic powers of equal primacy and that the question regarding unity is pointless. The assertion of primacy swerves from the path of ordered thought: It disregards the rules for examining experiences reasonably, it refuses rational discourse, and the spirit that adopts this assertion will change from being a discussion partner to an adherent of another order, the origins of which we need to study.[38]

At this earliest juncture, Voegelin is working to develop a language that can adequately articulate and analyze the complex of expressed or recounted

36 Ibid., 28.
37 Ibid.
38 Ibid., 29.

experiences, events, and symbolizations that he is examining. The symbols of "seeking" and "finding"[39] will remain a part of his analytical and meditative vocabulary to the end, as will his effort to identify and engage with apt discussion partners concerning this complex across the millennia. This is not simply a trite observation one could make of any competent scholar examining a phenomenon: saying what something is is often difficult conceptual work, and it's nice to have friends who help. Rather, Voegelin is already aware here that the "something" of which he wishes to give account is not merely an object or material process in reality that must be properly identified and categorized within a series of such phenomena. It therefore requires not only a requisite degree of scientific precision, but also an appropriate conceptualization as to the nature of the reality experienced (is it a phenomenon or something else?) and how the experience in question must therefore be approached to be properly understood.[40] Others who have currently or in the distant past engaged in this activity with sufficient technical philosophical prowess to understand this distinction and unpack its meaning are uncommon and therefore valuable interlocutors for one's own efforts.

Voegelin is concerned in *Political Religions* to trace the immanentization (he uses neither this term nor a German equivalent) of the experience of the divine that rules over the kingdoms of this world as it transforms into the mundane, immanent supremacy of the modern state. This closed, "innerworldly" political form makes claims to ultimacy that echo the previously authoritative claims in the Christian tradition of the political community

39 Ibid., 33.

40 For this reason, Voegelin criticized the "construction of empirical types" of civilizational courses as "especially reprehensible." Such constructions neglected entirely the civilizational form as a particular mode of participation in the order of being, because it ignored the transcendent pole of human existence, which is identifiable not merely by noting the existence, say, of temples, pyramids, emperor-worship, or the presence of a priestly class in various civilizations, but by asking what they *mean* as a "manifestation of the constants of human nature in their range of compactness and differentiation." Eric Voegelin, *Order and History, Volume I: Israel and Revelation* (1956), ed. Maurice P. Hogan, *CWEV* Vol. 14, 2001, 102. Hereafter cited as Voegelin, *Israel and Revelation*.

that is founded by and preserved under a cosmos-transcending God.[41] Voegelin shows that this new form of political organization interprets itself with the use of immanent symbols that it extracts from earlier symbolizations of the transcendent that can be traced to usages at least as old as second millennium B.C. civilization. For this reason, "religious" questions are embedded throughout the self-symbolization of the modern state, so that the question of God likewise remains alive throughout.[42]

> The political community is always integrated in the overall context of human experience and the world and God, irrespective of whether the political sphere occupies a subordinate level in the divine order of the hierarchy of being or it is itself deified. The language of politics is always interspersed with the ecstasies of religiosity and, thus, becomes a symbol in the concise sense by letting experience concerned with the contents of the world be permeated with transcendental-divine experiences.[43]

The question of what we call God is central to political order, because it is in and under an answer to that ultimate question—regardless the specific orientations to it—that each and every political regime assumes its authority.[44] The "sacred symbols used to link the political aspects of human life with the divine"[45] are open to exploration and analysis, which includes the structure of existence that they reveal, alongside the ways in which political authority may also obscure their original intention, meaning, and underlying experiences.[46]

41 Voegelin, *Political Religions*, 59.

42 See especially Ibid., 64–70.

43 Voegelin, *Political Religions*, 70 (slightly altered translation). See also Gebhardt's conclusion to his "Editor's Introduction," *Selected Correspondence, 1924-1949*, 33–34. Voegelin added that "Elements of the symbolic expressive forms" that he had "worked out on the basis of the Mediterranean and European examples" could be "found in all high cultures [*Hochkulteren*]" (translation altered).

44 Voegelin, *Political Religions*, 32.

45 Ibid., 42 (cf. 59).

46 Ibid., 59.

The Question and Argument Presumed in "QDD"

"QDD" begins with a statement of the question of what we call God, followed by brief characterizations of several problems the question raises. The question of God may be named in several ways, and the diversity of naming identifies a part of the existential and philosophical problem to which it is a questioning response. It concerns "Divine reality[47];" "the enigma of existence";[48] "the meaning of existence," most especially in regard to the human search for such meaning[49]; or simply, what it is that we mean when we say "God." Yet further namings are available. The beginning of the question lies not in some particular material phenomenon, but in accounts of a search for the meaning or form or structure of the Divine reality experienced. Where, therefore, to begin? Such expressions existed millennia before philosophical inquiry gave them that particular form in the culture of Hellas and its civilizational heirs that has been passed down to us, but those early expressions are only helpful if such historical beginnings can in some way illuminate the problem for us.[50]

Instead of beginning there, Voegelin looks to the work of Thomas Aquinas as a first window into treating these problems of intention and meaning before turning to philosophers across the three-thousand-year span of philosophical inquiry to provide further clarity concerning the problems that the question of God has evoked. Aquinas appears late in the millennia-long quest for God. Voegelin's choice therefore reminds us that the question of what we mean when we say "God" has a history and also a discernible structure within that history, that together these structures and history raise a particular, perennial set of philosophical questions, and that the history is not a linear, progressive one. The outline that

47 Eric Voegelin, "The Beginning and the Beyond," (1977) in *What is History*? 173. Hereafter cited as Voegelin, "Beginning and Beyond."

48 Eric Voegelin, "The Gospel & Culture," in *Published Essays 1966-1985*, ed. Ellis Sandoz, *CWEV* Vol. 12, 1990, 174. Hereafter cited as Voegelin, "Gospel and Culture."

49 Ibid., 175–77.

50 For similarly illuminating beginnings in political philosophy, see Leo Strauss, *What is Political Philosophy?* (Chicago: University of Chicago Press, 1959), 10.

Voegelin wrote up in October, 1984, indicated a broad historical plan of the search for the Divine, but it did not portray an historical "development" or "progression."

Both of these aspects of the question of what we call God are clearly explicated in a "middle" work in Voegelin's corpus, *Israel and Revelation*, published as the first volume of *Order and History* eighteen years after *Political Religions*. There Voegelin lays out a philosophical anthropology that accounts for those initiating events and basic structures in the human experience of existence in which originate the symbolizations of the order in which human beings find themselves. The experience of existence, he argues, is filled with uncertainty. By the very nature of human "participation in the mystery" of the "primordial community of being"—"God and man, world and society"—this uncertainty cannot be resolved into a definitive conclusion about the nature of that existence. Participating in something that is greater than ourselves and of which we can therefore never know conclusively its meaning, purpose, or conclusion is "disturbing" precisely because of that irresolvable and inescapable uncertainty.[51] Even the quest for the divine, which animates important points in the intellectual history of the West from its beginnings, is not the summative "meaning" of history in the sense that we can know such a meaning with absolute assurance. To "know" this meaning by faith, or even to note the historical importance of this quest to intellectual or political history alike is not to declare one's perceived meaning to be indisputably so. Doing so creates an "illusory eidos" of history "by treating a symbol of faith as if it were a proposition concerning an object of immanent experience."[52] While the many representatives of this quest left behind them a plethora of descriptions of the experience and a great many analyses of its content and meaning, those traces are just that—carefully crafted and articulated traces and markers, yet not immanent certainties in themselves nor in that to which they point. At the same time, the "it" in which we participate and the activity of participation itself are accessible to human investigation, articulation, and tentative understanding. Thus, "the concern of man about the meaning of his existence in the field of being does not remain pent up in the tortures of anxiety, but can

51 Voegelin, *Israel and Revelation*, 39.

52 Eric Voegelin, *The New Science of Politics* (1952) in *Modernity Without Restraint*, 185–86.

vent itself in the creation of symbols purporting to render intelligible the relations and tension between the distinguishable terms of the field."[53] Such "venting" is of no small consequence for stable social and political order since, to repeat, it is in the question of God that we find a basis for such order.

The creation of symbols that make the order of existence intelligible can proceed in a methodical way, achieving insight into the human predicament of existing "in uncertainty of [the] meaning" of existence itself, while experiencing it as "an adventure of decision on the edge of freedom and necessity."[54] Interestingly and helpfully, the process of symbolization seems historically to have "typical features" that can be discerned, catalogued, and further queried for precision and insight.[55] In the eighteen years between *Political Religions* and *Israel and Revelation* Voegelin had therefore developed an analytical and descriptive vocabulary that would more precisely articulate the beginning points in human experience that lead humans to the root questions concerning their own existence and the nature of the divine presence in that existence and in the "it" in which they all participate.[56] In *Political Religions* Voegelin describes the originating experience as one in which human beings experience their existence as "creaturely, and therefore questionable," so that "somewhere in our innermost self, at the navel of our soul, at the place where our soul is linked to the cosmos, this question [of our coming into being and what it means] keeps tugging at us."[57] In *Israel and Revelation*, Voegelin argues that this underlying anxiety is translated into the discernment of a structural order—the four poles of the quaternarian order of existence. In the earlier *Political Religions*, Voegelin remains at the level of the inward "states of existence," an ultimately inadequate reference to an experience that is notably difficult adequately to comprehend, conceptualize, or describe, but that is more than "innermost emotions." Voegelin looks to "religious people," who speak of this experience in various

53 Voegelin, *Israel and Revelation*, 41.

54 Ibid., 40.

55 Ibid., 41.

56 Voegelin attributed this symbolization of the "it" to Karl Kraus, in whose work he first encountered it. Cf. Eric Voegelin, "The Meditative Origin of the Philosophical Knowledge of Order," (1981) in *The Drama of Humanity*, 392–3; 398–9; 428. Hereafter cited as Voegelin, "The Meditative Origin."

57 Voegelin, *Political Religions*, 30 (translation slightly altered).

ways to unpack the question. These people speak of "primal emotions when they want to describe the level at the bottom of our soul that is deeper than other feelings and that reverberates through our existence from this depth;" or of "the infinitude of this feeling when they mean that it is not oriented toward specific objects but is a directionless, agitated surge deep within us at the bottom of our soul;" or of "a feeling of simple dependency when they want to describe the experience of being bound to a supra personal, all-powerful something;" and so on.[58]

Voegelin seems here to be describing the psychological manifestations of what he would later call a "primary experience of the cosmos," a term with which he referred to what human beings intuit, feel, understand, or "know" concerning the "it" reality in which they find themselves prior to making any differentiations in philosophical or spiritual reflections that in broad or granular ways unpack the cosmos into its constituent parts.[59] The expression assumes the veracity of an empirical observation: human beings perceive a certain order that has historically displayed a constancy of structure—"man-world-God-society"—[60] that is only differentiated and perhaps even dissolved when an experience of transcendence disrupts it, which only occurs relatively recently in human experience.[61]

In the variety of religious expressions Voegelin listed in *Political Religions*, we also observe "an inexhaustible supply of experiences as well as rationalizations and systematizations of such experiences."[62] Those who have

58 Voegelin, *Political Religions*, 31.

59 Eric Voegelin, "What is History?" (1963) in *What is History?*, 21.

60 "This cosmos of primary experience is neither the external world of objects encountered by man when he has become a subject of cognition, nor is it the world that has been created by a world-transcendent God. It rather is the cosmos of an earth below and heaven above; of celestial bodies and their movements, of seasonal changes, of fertility rhythms in plant and animal life, of human life, birth, and death; and above all, as Thales still knew, it is a cosmos full of gods. . . . This togetherness and one-in-anotherness is the primary experience that must be called cosmic in the pregnant sense." Eric Voegelin, "Anxiety and Reason," (1968) in *What is History?*, 58–59.

61 Voegelin, "Anxiety and Reason," 53, 56, 57. Voegelin also pointed out that the human search for order has included certain constants that occur within or outside a primary experience of the cosmos. Ibid., 56.

62 Voegelin, *Political Religions*, 31.

the experiences imagine "an order of being in which the levels of being are classified in a hierarchy, and in response to the question as to the reason of being they form an order of creation."[63] Voegelin uses the language of seeking and finding, of Being [*Sein*] and Beyond [*Jenseits*], even of "human beings [*Menschen*] and community [*Gemeinschaft*]" and "Nature [*Natur*] and God,"[64] but the sum of these terms does not yet coalesce into the structural precision concerning the primary experience of the cosmos that is given in *Israel and Revelation* and later writings. In those works, Voegelin arrived at a level of articulation of these symbols and empirical evidence concerning them such that he could assert with confidence that God / man / world / society are consistently the four major points of reference regarding the reality in which human beings have historically found themselves to be participating. These four are universally the beginning points for cosmological symbolization (and therefore political, "religious," social, and concerning the natural, physical world all at once) and, when the mode of philosophical inquiry comes into being, for philosophical analysis of their constituent pieces.[65] The wide array of human responses to the mystery of existence that Voegelin lists in *Political Religions* gives way in *Israel and Revelation* to the structure of existence that is revealed in an historical account of these experiences and the historical responses to them and symbolizations of them. These events in history—in human consciousness—are not material objects or processes, but they *are* events open not merely to description and listing, but also to analysis and categorization.[66]

63 Ibid., 32.

64 Ibid., 33.

65 Voegelin, "Anxiety and Reason," 53–58.

66 Voegelin's use of "religion" is itself a problem here. What he seemed to mean in *Political Religions* is now made clearer: "religious" people are those who remain in touch with a primary experience of the cosmos that allows them to answer in better form what we mean when we say "God." Voegelin knew well enough that "religion" is not a concept of the social sciences, but a category, an assemblage of beliefs, practices, and codes of conduct. Included in those beliefs and practices was what he would come to understand as a "primary experience of the cosmos." In *Anamnesis*, Voegelin would describe this experience in a way that showed how we still come to a notion of God in the same way he describes with less refinement in *Political Religions*: "[T]he existence of God is not deduced; instead it is in the experience of the finiteness of the human

The question of order as indicated in *Political Religions* and in the "Introduction" to *Israel and Revelation* manifests itself within the contexts of specific cultural and institutional constructions we call civilizations. These constructions may endure for long periods, as did Egyptian and Chinese civilizations, or for shorter periods, as did the wide-flung, loose community of Greek poleis. Every civilization is "the form in which a society participates, in its historically unique way, in the supracivilizational, universal drama of approximation to the right order of existence through increasingly differentiated attunement with the order of being."[67]

The civilizational form is both communal and personal. It is communal because its symbolization of order and its ordering principles are given in specific institutions, customs, and linguistic expression that are shared amongst its participants. Even when—as commonly occurs—these forms are disputed amongst civilizational participants, that conflict, too, is a kind of sharing insofar as each dispute can only be intelligible within a larger shared context of meaning.[68] It is personal insofar as each participating member of a society so formed must share in them if that person is to participate in the civilization at all. It is also personal in that specific members of a society originate the symbolization of order and, in their articulations in linguistic or artistic form, make these symbols available for common use and the establishment of common understanding. Crises occur when new symbolizations arise that require either a new orientation to the participating reality that has been (re)articulated, or a rejection of such interpretive challenges to the symbolized order that prevails in a society.[69]

A civilization develops and persists over time. Voegelin's descriptive phrase, "increasingly differentiated attunement with the order of being,"

being that the infinite becomes a given. God cannot be called into doubt, for God is implicated in the experience of doubt and imperfection. In the limit situation of finiteness is given, together with this-sidedness, the beyond of the limit." Voegelin, *Anamnesis*, 59. (Thomas Hollweck, the editor of *Selected Correspondence, 1950-1984*, points us to this description in his note on page 444.)

67 Voegelin, *Israel and Revelation*, 102.

68 A version of this argument may be found in Alasdair MacIntyre, *Whose Justice, Which Rationality?* Notre Dame: University of Notre Dame Press, 1988.

69 See *Political Religions*, 34–41; *Israel and Revelation*, 122–55.

implies that the knowledge of the order we perceive is attainable by human effort, and that such attainment is likely not a single-point event, but a development of insight over time. As *Political Religions* already made clear and as Voegelin repeated on many occasions, such insight may also be lost if it is not preserved in those institutions, customs, and linguistic expressions of the civilization in which they find their home. The experience of order within the It-reality in which human beings participate is not a possession for all time, but must be preserved and renewed. The activity of renewal itself has considerable breadth and depth, ranging from the multiple annual ceremonies and rituals of cosmological societies to the annual consumption cycle of modern consumer culture.[70] This possibility implies that some qualities of the order are therefore accessible to human investigation (and intervention),[71] and that such efforts at knowledge may impose changes in the way this order of being is experienced, understood, and inhabited. The effort and its results are themselves events in the order of being. Accordingly, Voegelin was fond of pointing out that even at the level of intellectual inquiry there existed a "fundamentally paradoxical structure of thought that is peculiar to the participatory relation between the process of thought and the reality in which it proceeds."[72]

A complex of problems arises from this dynamic. How, for example, is the exploration of participatory reality made relevant or accessible or its results made persuasive to the inhabitants of a society? How will the order of existence newly discovered be represented, and by whom? To raise the question of God is itself such an event, as is the formulation of what might pass for an answer, so that one aspect of community renewal and reminder is the ongoing statement and restatement of the question concerning God. That restatement and answers to it, as Voegelin had already argued in

70 For a description of the consumption cycle in American culture as a "contemporary version of ancient cosmological religiosity" (p. xiii), see Dell deChant, *Sacred Santa: Religious Dimensions of Consumer Culture* (Cleveland: The Pilgrim Press, 2002). On the rituals attendant on cosmological cycles in antiquity, see, among others, Henri Frankfort et al., *Before Philosophy: The Intellectual Adventure of Ancient Man* (Baltimore: Penguin Books, 1949).

71 Frankfort et al., *Before Philosophy*, 29–36.

72 "QDD," 378.

Political Religions, has a substantive effect on the character of personal and communal existence.[73] It is for this reason that the effectiveness aspect of the question permeates Voegelin's work from 1938 onward: having a direct, abiding, and ineluctable impact on the character of a society, the question of God can be "a matter of life and death,"[74] because the effort civilizationally "to link the political aspects of human life with the divine"[75] is a sociopolitical necessity and constant.

The question of God, therefore, occurs on several levels at once. It is asked by spiritually sensitive people who may achieve the status of the mediating and articulating thinker, poet, or prophet within the community that bears the symbols thrown up in the process of the articulation and differentiation of the question. After all, if no one "believes in" or can make sense of the question of God, efforts to articulate it will achieve nothing and disappear into the sands of history without effect.[76] The life of the spirit, however it may be conceived and however it may be manifested, requires institutions for its preservation among human beings so that, as "a concrete community in pragmatic history,"[77] they may have access to that life. The four completed volumes of *Order and History* can be read in their entirety as an elaboration of this theme. Voegelin described them as a working out of the problem of human experiences that underlie the symbols that scholars may erroneously identify as independently developed ideas, and the fifth volume as a study of the constants that underlie human experience throughout the history of humankind.[78]

73 See also "Gospel and Culture," 172–75; *Israel and Revelation*, 145–50.

74 Voegelin, *Political Religions*, 29, 41.

75 Ibid., 42.

76 "The spirit lives in the world as an ordering force in the souls of human beings. And the human *anima naturalis* has an amplitude of characterological variety that breaks the ordering spirit in a broad spectrum of phenomena. Plato and Aristotle, in the construction of their paradigms of the best polis, which must accommodate the variety of characters, have made this fundamental problem of social order explicit. The prophets, philosophers, and saints, who can translate the order of the spirit into the practice of conduct without institutional support and pressure, are rare." (Voegelin, *Israel and Revelation*, 427).

77 Ibid., 428.

78 Voegelin, "Autobiographical Statement," 442.

The Community of "QDD"

When Voegelin chooses to begin "QDD" with the inquiry of Thomas Aquinas, the choice itself highlights several interrelated aspects of that search that is a constant thread in his work from 1938 onward. First, as we have already pointed out, to say that the problem has a history or even that "the event of the quest is an historical process" is not to say that it therefore develops over time in a strictly linear, cumulative, or otherwise "progressive" fashion. Indeed, Voegelin referred to many modern episodes in this quest as "derailments," "deformations," or events of forgetting. Instead, the question of God, or the quest for clarity into the "something experienced as real before the inquiry into the structure of its reality has begun" presents a paradox with which philosophers since at least Plato, and poetical thinkers as early as Hesiod have wrestled.[79] The qualities of this "primary event" are such that the paradox is inescapable, and its exploration does not equate to the progress one observes in the cumulative accretion of practical and theoretical knowledge in some natural or applied sciences. And even in these sciences, as Werner Heisenberg noted, the observer and the observed interact, if not to the same degree as in the search for God, nevertheless in such a way that the observed cannot be isolated entirely from the act of observation.[80] In the history of the quest we may find figures at widely dispersed times recreating the same event of a primary experience and its accompanying elaboration of the search for "the structure of reality" over which God or a divinity supervenes. Aquinas "had attained a certain degree of clarity" about the paradoxic structures of this quest. Speaking at the AAAR conference to an audience of specialists in the study of religion, it would therefore seem reasonable for Voegelin to bring to hand the work of a towering figure in the pantheon of theological thinkers in the West, especially one who had directly engaged with philosophical perspicacity this problem of what we call God.

79 "QDD," 376.

80 The so-called "observer effect" occurs—generally for commonsensical reasons—in many realms of natural science, but it occurs particularly ineluctably in quantum mechanics. See: Werner Heisenberg, *Physics and Philosophy: The Revolution in Modern Science* (New York: Start Publishing, LLC, 1999), 137.

Second, Thomas' "demonstrations" [*probari*] for the existence of God or for that which we call God may appear at first blush to be an exercise in natural theology. Kant's response to any attempt to demonstrate the "existence" of a cosmos-transcending Deity on the basis Aquinas used in the *Summa* is well-known,[81] and Voegelin accepted Kant's critique as correct and final: there is no philosophical "proof" for the existence of God possible that moves from material causality to an entity or being beyond that chain. Voegelin also held, however, that Kant's critique missed the point of St. Thomas's exercise.[82] Kant "works with the natural science concept of causation and correctly states that the causal chain cannot be extended beyond the immanent realm into the transcendent." Thomas, however, works "with a completely different *causa*, or *aitia*, that has nothing to do with physics."[83] Kant offers a welcome and valid caution regarding "the excesses of speculation," but Thomas is not offering a proof that is intended (inadmissibly) to extend "the natural science chain of causation" from the material universe into the transcendent. Kant "failed to take note of the fact that the proof of God has nothing to do with the chain of causality in world-immanent time (and therefore cannot be said to extend it into the world-transcendent)."[84] But what does this puzzling fact mean, and why would a philosopher of the stature of Immanuel Kant have missed it?

The question that arises out of a primary experience of the cosmos concerns not the origin of all things in the causal chain described by physics, but the nature of the divine beings who are experienced to be a part of the cosmos. A primary experience of the cosmos, however, is no longer visible to the form of reason that Kant subjects to scrutiny in his First Critique.[85] "For the primary

81 Immanuel Kant, *The Critique of Pure Reason*. Norman Kemp Smith, trans. (New York: St. Martin's Press, 1969), 495–531.

82 Voegelin includes Aristotle in this response to Kant's critique, but examining that inclusion would take us too far afield within the confines of the present discussion.

83 Eric Voegelin, Letter to George Jaffé, dated April 1, 1961, in *Selected Correspondence, 1950-1984*, 435–6.

84 Voegelin, Letter to George Jaffé, 437.

85 To be sure, a primary experience of the cosmos will contain—at least implicitly—the form of reason Kant explores in his first Critique, but that is by far not the only manifestation of human reason and rationality. In the first in-

experience of the cosmos, cosmogony is the adequate expression to 'explain' it as it is experienced, the tale of immediate creation, or of creation mediated through levels of being."[86] Thus, "the proof of the first mover (*prima causa*) … is not an extrapolation of the causal series that takes place in world-immanent time, into the sphere of transcendence, but the demonstration of the cosmos's divine mover in the here and now." We look not to the natural sciences, but to human beings for the legitimacy of this approach: "The most likely model of order, for which a mover is to be sought, is the human being in whose experiences of transcendence God has come into view."[87] For Thomas, a parallel to the concerns about "the experienced tension between contingency and necessity" that appears in his "demonstrations" is "the structure in reality which is at issue in the question of divinity." The five "demonstrations" for the existence of God that make up Question 2, Article 3 in Part I of the Summa reflect "five well-known experiences of [a] contingent reality" in which questing human beings experience that tension and the question it evokes.[88] Voegelin

stance, one may be reminded that Kant produced two further Critiques of two other instantiations of reason (practical reason and judgment). We find that in Aristotle, for whom the primary experience of the cosmos was still very much a part of his own experience, reason experienced as "the cognitively luminous center of order in existence" has several dimensions and multiple entry-points into the human condition that are outside of the confines of Kant's First Critique. See, for example, Eric Voegelin, "Reason: The Classic Experience," (1974) in *Published Essays: 1966-1985*, at 267–73.

86 Voegelin, Letter to George Jaffé, 438.

87 Ibid., 439; see also Mark Lilla, *The Stillborn God* (New York: Alfred A. Knopf, 2007), 20–21 for a commonsensical account of this primary experience that would lead to an experience of divinity within the cosmos and subsequent mythical accounts of that experience that we might call "anthropomorphic." For the multiple technical philosophical problems involved, Voegelin's letter to Jaffé in its entirety provides a synoptic overview.

88 It is helpful to note, as Peter Kreeft does, that all five of the "ways" in which the existence of God is demonstrated in the *Summa* are versions of the "cosmological argument," such that all five share the same three premises, which generate two hypotheses concerning the empirical data (in a primary experience of the cosmos). In an "illustrative" and "not exhaustive list," Kreeft catalogues twenty-four other arguments for God's existence distinct from the five demonstrations in the *Summa*. See Peter Kreeft, *A Summa of the Summa* (San Francisco: Ignatius Press, 1990), 60–70.

takes his readers through a careful analysis of the five demonstrations as expressions of the primary experience of the cosmos, the shortcomings in Thomas's philosophical understanding as expressed in the five demonstrations, the reasons for these shortcomings, and several later or earlier philosophical episodes (Descartes, Leibniz, Hegel, and Plato all become interlocutors in this expedition) in which these shortcomings are either overcome or clarified. The search that Thomas conducts is not for a "thing," but for "the partner in a questing search that moves within a reality formed by participatory language" of which we, too, are a part, not as observers, but as participants. That partner, however, is peculiarly silent, because, as Thomas's formulations concerning "that which we call God" all recognize, "[t]here is no divinity other than the necessity in tension with the contingency experienced in the noetic question."[89] The five "demonstrations" in Pt 1, Qu. 2., A3 of the *Summa* do not function as traditional proofs in logic, nor as traditional demonstrations in philosophical argument, nor as either verification or falsification of a natural-scientific hypothesis. They express a persistent, genuine human experience,[90] and none of these exclusions are grounds to abandon the demonstrations as such expressions.

Third, the *form* of Thomas's search and the attendant delivery of the results in his *Summa Theologica* add a dimension to this quest that Voegelin touches only lightly. Thomas identifies the audience of the *Summa*, the "we" of the "*dicitur*," in his "Prologue": it comprises "beginners" in Christian theology. The purpose of the *Summa* is "to treat of the things which belong to the Christian religion in such a way as befits the instruction" of such initiates. The disputational form of the work, for example, aids oral memorization, since it is highly unlikely that most, if any, such students will be able to afford their own copy. The careful ordering of the parts of the *Summa* and the prevention of "frequent repetition" that would induce "weariness and confusion in minds of the readers" are further pedagogical features of the work. The five demonstrations are, then, intended for a

89 "QDD," 379. Along these lines, Wolfgang Leidhold examines the originating experience of God as one of "*abwesende Präsenz*" (absent presence). See Wolfgang Leidhold, *Gottes Gegenwart: Zur Logik der religiösen Erfahrung* (Darmstadt: Wissenschaftliche Buchgesellschaft, 2011), 28–35 and *passim*.

90 Voegelin, "Beginning and Beyond," 173–7.

community of believers who are acquiring initial proficiency in Christian "sacred doctrine" by studying a work that is constructed with purposeful pedagogical intent.[91] Each of the five demonstrations concludes with a similar, but not identical phrase:

"et hoc omnes intelligunt Deum"	"and this everyone understands to be God"
"quam omnes Deum nominant"	"to which everyone gives the name of God"
"quod omnes dicunt Deum"	"this all [people] speak of as God"
"et hoc dicimus Deum"	"and this we call God"
"et hoc dicimus Deum"	"and this [being] we call God"

The "little coda" of repetition at the end of each demonstration offers in each case a corporate affirmation—called forth in the "everyone" or "we" in each instance—of what the demonstration makes manifest. The liturgical form that the coda supplies to this brief section of the *Summa* will be apparent to anyone familiar with some version of a traditional Christian liturgy, as the intended readers would have been. In these particular paragraphs, the readers affirm corporately the same search that Voegelin would, 700 years later, identify as appearing many times in history and explicate in detail.[92]

91 Thomas Aquinas, *Summa Theologica*, "Prologue," in Anton C. Pegis, ed., *Basic Writings of Saint Thomas Aquinas, Volume One* (New York: Random House, 1945), 3.

92 It might also help to recall that in Aquinas's day, as up to the 19th century, the readers would likely have read aloud

If what Kant argued in 1781 and what Voegelin argued Thomas already knew in 1273 to be true about Kant's argument is the case, then what we have here is not so much a philosophical argument concerning the existence of God as a quasi-liturgical, theological—more than philosophical—recollection of a primary experience of the cosmos. This intention best makes sense of the intended audience and the semi-repetitive coda of the five demonstrations, and of the placement of this argument in the *Summa* near the beginning in relation to its insufficiency for a full appreciation of Christian theological claims that follow.[93] It is not by accident that the question occurs nearly at the beginning of the *Summa*. After an introduction concerning the scope and arrangement of his *Compendium of Theology*, which appears to have been intended as a kind of handbook or summary of the *Summa*, Thomas also placed this question as the first matter to be treated in that unfinished work. The single paragraph concerning the existence of

93 Stanley Hauerwas argues that George Hendry saw in the semi-repetitive coda itself "an indication that Aquinas understood the 'proofs' were not proofs" (Stanley Hauerwas, *Performing the Faith: Bonhoeffer and the Practice of Nonviolence*, 112). Hauerwas is citing George Henry, *Theology of Nature* (Philadelphia: Westminster, 1980), 14. Following David Burrell, Hauerwas, in turn, argues that "the 'natural theology' reading of Aquinas was persuasive to many only because they forgot his account of why charity is the form of the virtues," and that "what Aquinas says about the virtues cannot be abstracted from his understanding of our knowledge of God" (112n5). That knowledge, Hauerwas contends, is such that "if you could 'prove' the existence of God, if you had evidence that something like a god must exist, then you would have evidence that the God that Jews and Christians worship does not exist." Aquinas' "understanding of the status of our knowledge of God" was exhibited in these demonstrations and elsewhere to the end that "natural theology" is not "a necessary first step to sustain theology based on revelation" (112). In other words, Aquinas moves the reader past an insufficient natural theology to the need for revelation to teach Christians what they need to know about God (cf. Kreeft, *Summa of the Summa*, 62). Voegelin, in contrast, would have sought to affirm the common, divinely-oriented humanity to be found in Thomas' demonstrations and in similar articulations of the primary experience of the cosmos found in the entire course of human history. He was largely disinterested in the reality of the historical basis for Christian faith, being not in the least interested in the so-called "Historical Jesus" and rejecting the historical reality of the resurrection (see Heilke, "Voegelin's 'The Gospel and Culture,'" infra).

God likewise ends with a version of the coda: "*et hoc dicimus Deum.*" On this interpretation, then, the demonstrations of Part 1, Question 2 of the *Summa* offer not a philosophical "proof" of God's existence,[94] but perhaps a "public" meditation of the kind Voegelin identified around this question in other philosophical writings.[95] They offer a communal expression and affirmation of a primary experience of the cosmos that precedes any further serious work of philosophy or practical theology of the kind Thomas envisioned.

This community keeps that primary experience alive, as Voegelin argued needs to happen in civilizations generally. The community is not constituted by the pursuit of this particular question *per se*, but the question and a particular (Christian) answer to it undergirds the inquiring, worshipping, and quotidian, mundane activities of this particular community, just as Voegelin argued it supported the practical activities of any human community. This specific and circumscribed activity of a natural-theological affirmation of the divine reality is not the self-intended major role of either the *Summa* or the *Compendium*, but it is an ancillary and useful, perhaps even necessary one. Communities of theologians or monastics, too, must renew ever again that primary experience of the cosmos that reminds them of that which we call God, in the same way that all participants in a political society must be similarly reminded from time to time. It was Voegelin's last act to point the readers of JAAR—and us—there.

94 Strictly speaking, the God who transcends the space and time of the cosmos (or universe) does not "exist"—coming into being and passing out of being in the manner of all existing things—but simply, as in the Latin *esse*, "is." But that is a further question for another occasion.

95 See Voegelin, "The Meditative Origin," 384–95, esp. 394–5.

Contributor Biographies

Paul Caringella is Visiting Fellow at the Hoover Institution War, Revolution and Peace at Stanford University, and was Eric Voegelin's personal assistant during the last six years of Voegelin's life. He served as one of four members of the Editorial Board that directed publication of *The Collected Works of Eric Voegelin*, and was editor along with Thomas A. Hollweck of Volume 28, *What Is History? and Other Late Unpublished Writings*.

Barry Cooper, Professor of Political Science at the University of Calgary, has published more than 35 books, several addressing the work of Eric Voegelin, as well as roughly 200 articles. Among his recent books are *Paleolithic Politics: The Human Community in Early Art*, and *Consciousness and Politics: From Analysis to Meditation in the Late Work of Eric Voegelin*. He has received numerous research grants including a Konrad Adenauer Award and a Killam Research Fellowship, and has been a Fellow of the Royal Society of Canada since 1993.

Charles R. Embry, Professor Emeritus of Political Science at Texas A & M University—Commerce has edited or co-edited several books in addition to his *The Philosopher and the Storyteller: Eric Voegelin and Twentieth-Century Literature*. Most recently, he is co-editor with Glenn Hughes of *The Timelessness of Proust: Reflections on "In Search of Lost Time"* and *The Eric Voegelin Reader: Politics, History, Consciousness*.

Michael Franz is Professor of Political Science at Loyola University Maryland. In addition to other writings, he is the author of *Eric Voegelin and the Politics of Spiritual Revolt: The Roots of Modern Ideology*, and editor of *The Ecumenic Age*, Vol. IV of Voegelin's *Order and History*, Vol. 17 in *The Collected Works of Eric Voegelin*. His research and teaching focus on political theory and the philosophy of history, with special emphasis on political violence and terrorism engendered by disordered spirituality and ideological consciousness.

Thomas W. Heilke is Professor of Political Science at the University of British Columbia, Okanagan, having held a variety of administrative posts there and at the University of Kansas. He is author, co-author, editor, or co-editor of more than 50 publications, including *Voegelin on the Idea of Race; Nietzsche's Tragic Regime: Culture, Aesthetics, and Political Education;* and *Eric Voegelin: In Quest of Reality*. His current research focusses on the role of religion in world politics, political pluralism, and political theology.

Glenn Hughes is Professor Emeritus of Philosophy at St. Mary's University in San Antonio, Texas. Among other writings, he is the author of *Transcendence and History: The Search for Ultimacy from Ancient Societies to Postmodernity*, and *From Dickinson to Dylan: Visions of Transcendence in Modernist Literature*, both published by the University of Missouri Press. His numerous awards include a Fulbright Scholar Research Grant.

Paul Kidder is Professor Emeritus of Philosophy at Seattle University. Receiving his Philosophy Ph.D. from Boston College in 1987, he has written and taught on metaphysics, the history of philosophy, Continental philosophy, social and political philosophy, philosophy of art and architecture, and ethics, with an emphasis on ethics in urban affairs and international development. He is the author of *Gadamer for Architects* and *Minoru Yamasaki and the Fragility of Architecture*.

Paulette Kidder is Professor of Philosophy at Seattle University, and has held a variety of administrative posts at that same University. Her research and teaching focus on ethics, the history of philosophy, philosophy of film and literature, feminism, and hermeneutics.

Steven McGuire is the Paul & Karen Levy Fellow in Campus Freedom at the American Council of Trustees and Alumni, where he writes about free speech and academic freedom in American Higher Education. He is the co-editor of *Eric Voegelin and the Continental Tradition*, *Subjectivity: Ancient and Modern*, and *Nature: Ancient and Modern*. His writing has also appeared in the *Inside Higher Ed*, *The Public Discourse*, *Church Life Journal*, *Modern Age*, *Perspectives on Political Science*, *The Political Science Reviewer*, and many popular news outlets.

William Petropulos was Research Fellow at the former Eric Voegelin Archive at the Geschwister Scholl Insitute for Political Science at the Ludwig-Maximilians-Universität in Munich. His publications include *Stefan George und Eric Voegelin*; *Beyond Max Weber's Value Free Science: A Study of Helmuth Plessner and Eric Voegelin*; "Max Scheler and Eric Voegelin on the Eternal in Man," and "Die Rassenidee im Rahmen der Politischen Wissenschaft." With Gilbert Weiss he edited Vols. 32 and 33 of *The Collected Works of Eric Voegelin: Miscellaneous Papers* I (1921-1938) and II (1939-1935).

Julianne Romanello is an independent scholar based in Tulsa, Oklahoma. Her academic research treats of the political philosophies of Eric Voegelin, Plato, and Kierkegaard and has been published in *VoegelinView*, *Expositions*, and *The European Conservative*.

Henrik Syse is Research Professor at the Peace Research Institute Oslo (PRIO), Professor of Peace and Conflict Studies at Oslo New University College, author and editor of many books and articles spanning the fields of philosophy, politics, business, religion, war, and ethics. He also teaches regularly at the Norwegian Defense University College, the University of Oslo, and several other institutions of higher learning, and is Chief Editor (with James Cook) of the *Journal of Military Ethics*. He served a full six-year term as a member of the Norwegian Nobel Committee, which awards the Nobel Peace Prize, serving as its Vice Chair 2017-2020.

David Walsh is Professor of Politics at The Catholic University of America, with teaching and research interests in the field of political theory broadly conceived. His many publications include eight books: *The Mysticism of Innerworldly Fulfillment: A Study of Jacob Boehme; After Ideology: Recovering the Spiritual Foundations of Freedom*; *The Growth of the Liberal Soul*; *The Third Millennium: Reflections on Faith and Reason*; *Guarded By Mystery:*

Meaning in a Postmodern Age; *The Luminosity of Existence; Politics of the Person as the Politics of Being*; and *The Priority of the Person*. His current book project is "The Invisible Source of Authority: God in a Secular Age."